MAR 0 1 2011 *mv*

D0473078

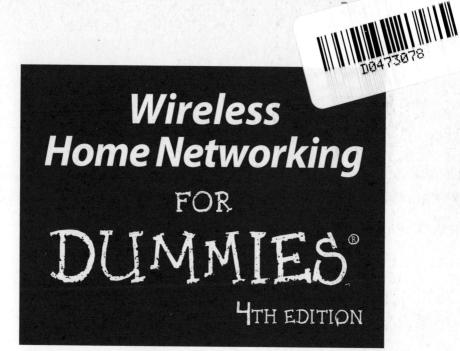

# *Wireless Home Networking*
## FOR
# DUMMIES®
### 4TH EDITION

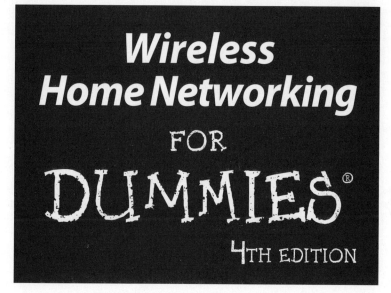

# Wireless Home Networking

## FOR DUMMIES®

### 4TH EDITION

## by Danny Briere and Pat Hurley

3 1336 08538 5962

WILEY

Wiley Publishing, Inc.

**Wireless Home Networking For Dummies®, 4th Edition**

Published by
**Wiley Publishing, Inc.**
111 River Street
Hoboken, NJ 07030-5774
www.wiley.com

Copyright © 2011 by Wiley Publishing, Inc., Indianapolis, Indiana

Published by Wiley Publishing, Inc., Indianapolis, Indiana

Published simultaneously in Canada

No part of this publication may be reproduced, stored in a retrieval system or transmitted in any form or by any means, electronic, mechanical, photocopying, recording, scanning or otherwise, except as permitted under Sections 107 or 108 of the 1976 United States Copyright Act, without either the prior written permission of the Publisher, or authorization through payment of the appropriate per-copy fee to the Copyright Clearance Center, 222 Rosewood Drive, Danvers, MA 01923, (978) 750-8400, fax (978) 646-8600. Requests to the Publisher for permission should be addressed to the Permissions Department, John Wiley & Sons, Inc., 111 River Street, Hoboken, NJ 07030, (201) 748-6011, fax (201) 748-6008, or online at http://www.wiley.com/go/permissions.

**Trademarks:** Wiley, the Wiley Publishing logo, For Dummies, the Dummies Man logo, A Reference for the Rest of Us!, The Dummies Way, Dummies Daily, The Fun and Easy Way, Dummies.com, Making Everything Easier, and related trade dress are trademarks or registered trademarks of John Wiley & Sons, Inc. and/or its affiliates in the United States and other countries, and may not be used without written permission. All other trademarks are the property of their respective owners. Wiley Publishing, Inc., is not associated with any product or vendor mentioned in this book.

LIMIT OF LIABILITY/DISCLAIMER OF WARRANTY: THE PUBLISHER AND THE AUTHOR MAKE NO REPRESENTATIONS OR WARRANTIES WITH RESPECT TO THE ACCURACY OR COMPLETENESS OF THE CONTENTS OF THIS WORK AND SPECIFICALLY DISCLAIM ALL WARRANTIES, INCLUDING WITHOUT LIMITATION WARRANTIES OF FITNESS FOR A PARTICULAR PURPOSE. NO WARRANTY MAY BE CREATED OR EXTENDED BY SALES OR PROMOTIONAL MATERIALS. THE ADVICE AND STRATEGIES CONTAINED HEREIN MAY NOT BE SUITABLE FOR EVERY SITUATION. THIS WORK IS SOLD WITH THE UNDERSTANDING THAT THE PUBLISHER IS NOT ENGAGED IN RENDERING LEGAL, ACCOUNTING, OR OTHER PROFESSIONAL SERVICES. IF PROFESSIONAL ASSISTANCE IS REQUIRED, THE SERVICES OF A COMPETENT PROFESSIONAL PERSON SHOULD BE SOUGHT. NEITHER THE PUBLISHER NOR THE AUTHOR SHALL BE LIABLE FOR DAMAGES ARISING HEREFROM. THE FACT THAT AN ORGANIZATION OR WEBSITE IS REFERRED TO IN THIS WORK AS A CITATION AND/OR A POTENTIAL SOURCE OF FURTHER INFORMATION DOES NOT MEAN THAT THE AUTHOR OR THE PUBLISHER ENDORSES THE INFORMATION THE ORGANIZATION OR WEBSITE MAY PROVIDE OR RECOMMENDATIONS IT MAY MAKE. FURTHER, READERS SHOULD BE AWARE THAT INTERNET WEBSITES LISTED IN THIS WORK MAY HAVE CHANGED OR DISAPPEARED BETWEEN WHEN THIS WORK WAS WRITTEN AND WHEN IT IS READ.

For general information on our other products and services, please contact our Customer Care Department within the U.S. at 877-762-2974, outside the U.S. at 317-572-3993, or fax 317-572-4002.

For technical support, please visit www.wiley.com/techsupport.

Wiley also publishes its books in a variety of electronic formats. Some content that appears in print may not be available in electronic books.

Library of Congress Control Number: 2010938828

ISBN: 978-0-470-87725-8

Manufactured in the United States of America

10 9 8 7 6 5 4 3 2 1

WILEY

# About the Authors

**Danny Briere** founded TeleChoice, Inc., a telecommunications consulting company, in 1985 and now serves as CEO of the company. Widely known throughout the telecommunications and networking industry, Danny has written more than 1,000 articles about telecommunications topics and has authored or edited eight books, including *Smart Homes For Dummies,* 3rd Edition; *HDTV For Dummies,* 2nd Edition; *Windows XP Media Center Edition 2004 PC For Dummies; Wireless Network Hacks & Mods For Dummies;* and *Home Theater For Dummies,* 2nd Edition (all published by Wiley). He is frequently quoted by leading publications on telecommunications and technology topics and can often be seen on major TV networks providing analysis on the latest communications news and breakthroughs. Danny lives in Mansfield Center, Connecticut, with his wife and four children.

**Pat Hurley** is director of research with TeleChoice, Inc., specializing in emerging telecommunications technologies, including all the latest access and home technologies: wireless LANs, DSL, cable modems, satellite services, and home networking services. Pat frequently consults with the leading telecommunications carriers, equipment vendors, consumer goods manufacturers, and other players in the telecommunications and consumer electronics industries. Pat is the co-author of *Smart Homes For Dummies,* 3rd Edition; *HDTV For Dummies,* 2nd Edition; *Windows XP Media Center Edition 2004 PC For Dummies; Wireless Network Hacks & Mods For Dummies;* and *Home Theater For Dummies,* 2nd Edition (all published by Wiley). He lives in San Diego, California, with his wife, beautiful daughter, and two smelly and unruly dogs.

# Authors' Acknowledgments

Danny wants to thank his wife, Holly, and kids, for their infinite patience while he constantly tested new wireless technologies in the house, especially since it usually meant taking something that was (finally) working and replacing it with something that was newer but didn't work at all. At least it looked good! Pat, as always, thanks his wife, Christine, for providing her impeccable judgment when he asks, "Can I write this wisecrack and not offend half the people in the world?" and for her ability to restrain her desire to knock him over the head with a big frying pan when deadlines and late-night writing intrude on their domestic tranquility. He also wants to thank his daughter Annabel, who let him borrow her DSi, Wii, and other gizmos to play with on the network, and for generally being the best first grader ever.

Now that we're on our fourth edition, we have a large and historically significant (to us, at least) list of people to thank, including: Bill Bullock, at Witopia; Melody Chalaban and Jonathan Bettino at Belkin; Shira Frantzich from Sterling PR (for NETGEAR); David Henry at NETGEAR; Karl Stetson at Edelman (for the Wi-Fi Alliance); Mindy Whittington and Ana Corea at Red Consultancy (for Eye-Fi); Doug Hagan and Mehrshad Mansouri, formerly of NETGEAR; Dana Brzozkiewicz, at Lages & Associates, for ZyXEL; Trisha King, at NetPR, for SMC Networks; Fred Bargetzi, at Crestron; Shawn Gusz, at G-NET Canada (still waiting to try Auroras in our cars!); Karen Sohl, at Linksys; Keith Smith, at Siemon; Darek Connole and Michael Scott, at D-Link; Jeff Singer, at Crestron; Amy K Schiska-Lombard, at Sprint; Brad Shewmake, at Kyocera Wireless; James Cortese, at A&R Partners, for Roku; Bryan McLeod, at Intrigue Technologies (now part of Logitech); Stu Elefant, at Wireless Security Corporation (now part of McAfee); Craig Slawson, at CorAccess (good luck, too!); and others who helped get the content correct for our readers.

Our team at Wiley was awesome as always: Amy Fandrei, our "suit" on the corporate side of the house and our project editor Kim Darosett, who deserves a medal, a raise, and perhaps sainthood for putting up with us as we tried to write to deadlines and keep our day jobs at the same time. We'd also like to thank our technical editor, Dan DiNicolo, for helping us look smart. Finally, we always have to thank Melody Layne, who's moved on to a different and exciting job at Wiley, but who has always been our champion at Wiley.

## Publisher's Acknowledgments

We're proud of this book; please send us your comments at http://dummies.custhelp.com. For other comments, please contact our Customer Care Department within the U.S. at 877-762-2974, outside the U.S. at 317-572-3993, or fax 317-572-4002.

Some of the people who helped bring this book to market include the following:

### Acquisitions and Editorial

**Project Editor:** Kim Darosett

**Acquisitions Editor:** Amy Fandrei

**Copy Editor:** Virginia Sanders

**Technical Editor:** Dan DiNicolo

**Editorial Manager:** Leah Cameron

**Editorial Assistant:** Amanda Graham

**Sr. Editorial Assistant:** Cherie Case

**Cartoons:** Rich Tennant
(www.the5thwave.com)

### Composition Services

**Project Coordinator:** Kristie Rees

**Layout and Graphics:** Christin Swinford, Laura Westhuis

**Proofreader:** Sossity R. Smith

**Indexer:** Ty Koontz

---

### Publishing and Editorial for Technology Dummies

**Richard Swadley,** Vice President and Executive Group Publisher

**Andy Cummings,** Vice President and Publisher

**Mary Bednarek,** Executive Acquisitions Director

**Mary C. Corder,** Editorial Director

### Publishing for Consumer Dummies

**Diane Graves Steele,** Vice President and Publisher

### Composition Services

**Debbie Stailey,** Director of Composition Services

# Contents at a Glance

# Table of Contents

# Introduction

**W**elcome to *Wireless Home Networking For Dummies,* 4th Edition. Wireless networking for personal computers isn't a new idea; it has been around since the late 1990s. Two big developments have made wireless go from an expensive niche for geeks to something that just about everyone is familiar with and has used: first the development of industry-wide standards (that ensured that wireless equipment would work regardless of who made it) and then the incorporation of wireless networking capabilities into all sorts of consumer electronics devices (PCs and laptops, netbook computers, smart phones, printers, cameras, even TVs). Now . . . well, wireless is everywhere.

One of the most appealing things about the current crop of wireless networking equipment is the ease with which you can set up a home network, although its reasonable price may be its *most* attractive aspect. In some cases, setting up a wireless home network is almost as simple as opening the box and plugging in the equipment; however, you can avoid many "gotchas" by doing a little reading beforehand. That's where this book comes in handy.

## About This Book

If you're thinking about purchasing a wireless computer network and installing it in your home — or if you have an installed network and want to make sure it's operating correctly or want to expand it — this is the book for you. Even if you've already purchased the equipment for a wireless network, this book will help you install and configure the network. What's more, this book will help you get the most out of your investment after it's up and running.

With *Wireless Home Networking For Dummies,* 4th Edition, in hand, you have all the information you need to know about the following topics (and more):

- Planning your wireless home network
- Evaluating and selecting wireless networking equipment for installation in your home
- Installing and configuring wireless networking equipment in your home
- Sharing an Internet connection over your wireless network

   ✔ Sharing files, printers, and other peripherals over your wireless network

   ✔ Playing computer games over your wireless network

   ✔ Connecting your audiovisual gear to your wireless network

   ✔ Securing your wireless network against prying eyes

   ✔ Finding and connecting to wireless hot spots away from home

   ✔ Creating your own on-the-go wireless networks with 3G wireless

   ✔ Discovering devices that you can connect to your wireless home network

# System Requirements

Virtually any personal computer can be added to a wireless home network, although some computers are easier to add than others. This book focuses on building a wireless network that connects PCs running the Windows operating system (Windows XP, Vista, and Windows 7) or Mac OS X. You *can* operate a wireless network with Windows 98, Me, or 2000 or with Mac OS 9, but these systems are less and less able to handle the rapidly increasing requirements of applications and the Internet. As a result, we focus mostly on the most recent operating systems — the ones that have been launched within the past five years or so. Wireless networking is also popular among Linux users, but we don't cover Linux in this book.

Because wireless networking is a relatively new phenomenon, the newest versions of Windows and the Mac OS do the best job of helping you quickly and painlessly set up a wireless network. However, because the primary reason for networking your home computers is to make it possible for all the computers (and peripherals) in your house to communicate, *Wireless Home Networking For Dummies,* 4th Edition, gives you information about connecting computers that run the latest versions of Windows and the most widely used version of the Mac OS. We also tell you how to connect computers that run some of the older versions of these two operating systems.

# How This Book Is Organized

*Wireless Home Networking For Dummies,* 4th Edition, is organized into 20 chapters that are grouped into five parts. The chapters are presented in a logical order — flowing from planning to installing to using your wireless home network — but feel free to use the book as a reference and read the chapters in any order you want.

# Part I: Wireless Networking Fundamentals

Part I is a primer on networking and wireless networking. In case you've never used a networked computer — much less attempted to install a network — this part of the book provides background information and technogeek lingo that you need to feel comfortable. Chapter 1 presents general networking concepts; Chapter 2 discusses the most popular wireless networking technology and familiarizes you with wireless networking terminology; and Chapter 3 introduces you to several popular complementary and alternative technologies to wireless networking, like Bluetooth and technologies that help you extend the reach of your wired home network.

# Part II: Making Plans

Part II helps you plan for installing your wireless home network. Chapter 4 helps you decide what to connect to the network and where to install wireless networking equipment in your home, and Chapter 5 provides guidance on making buying decisions.

# Part III: Installing a Wireless Network

Part III discusses how to install a wireless network in your home and get the network up and running. Whether your have Apple Macintosh computers running the Mac OS (see Chapter 8) or PCs running a Windows operating system (see Chapters 6 and 7), this part of the book explains how to install and configure your wireless networking equipment. In addition, Part III includes a chapter that explains how to secure your wireless home network (see Chapter 9). Too many people don't secure their wireless network, and we want to make sure you're not one of them!

# Part IV: Using Your Wireless Network

After you get your wireless home network installed and running, you'll certainly want to use it. Part IV starts by showing you the basics of putting your wireless network to good use: sharing files, folders, printers, and other peripherals (see Chapter 10). We discuss everything you want to know about playing multiuser computer games wirelessly (see Chapter 11), connecting your audiovisual equipment (see Chapter 12), using broadband mobile services (3G) to connect when you're away from home (see Chapter 13), and doing other cool things over a wireless network (see Chapter 14).

Bluetooth-enabled devices are becoming more prevalent these days, so you don't want to miss Chapter 15. For that matter, don't miss Chapter 16, where we describe how to use wireless networking to connect to the Internet through wireless *hot spots* (wireless networks you can connect to for free or a small cost when you're on the road) in coffee shops, hotels, airports, and other public places. How cool is that?

## Part V: The Part of Tens

Part V provides three top-ten lists that we think you'll find interesting — ten frequently asked questions about wireless home networking (Chapter 17); ten troubleshooting tips for improving your wireless home network's performance (Chapter 18); ten devices to connect to your wireless home network — sometime in the future (Chapter 19). Finally, we tell you where to go for even *more* information in Chapter 20, where we list our top ten (well, more than ten) places to find out more about the world of wireless.

# Icons Used in This Book

All of us these days are hyperbusy people, with no time to waste. To help you find the especially useful nuggets of information in this book, we've marked the information with little icons in the margin.

As you can probably guess, the Tip icon calls your attention to information that saves you time or maybe even money. If your time is really crunched, you may try just skimming through the book and reading the tips.

This icon is your clue that you should take special note of the advice you find there — or that the paragraph reinforces information provided elsewhere in the book. Bottom line: You will accomplish the task more effectively if you remember this information.

Face it, computers and wireless networks are high-tech toys, er *tools,* that make use of some complicated technology. For the most part, however, you don't need to know how it all works. The Technical Stuff icon identifies the paragraphs you can skip if you're in a hurry or just don't care to know.

The little bomb in the margin should alert you to pay close attention and tread softly. You don't want to waste time or money fixing a problem that you could have avoided in the first place.

# Where to Go from Here

Where you should go next in this book depends on where you are in the process of planning, buying, installing, configuring, or using your wireless home network. If networking in general and wireless networking in particular are new to you, we recommend that you start at the beginning, with Part I. When you feel comfortable with networking terminology or get bored with the lingo, move on to the chapters in Part II about planning your network and selecting equipment. If you already have your equipment in hand, head to Part III to get it installed — and secured (unless you *like* the idea of your neighbor or even a hacker being able to access your network).

If you were thinking of skipping Part I, please make sure that you're up to speed on the latest and greatest version of Wi-Fi wireless networking. — 802.11n — which will dramatically affect your planning. If you aren't up to speed on this new standard, we recommend that you at least take a quick view of Chapter 2 first.

The wireless industry is changing fast. We provide regular updates for this book at www.digitaldummies.com.

Happy wireless networking!

# Part I
# Wireless Networking Fundamentals

The 5th Wave                    By Rich Tennant

"Frankly, the idea of an entirely wireless future
scares me to death."

# In this part . . .

If you've never used a networked computer or you're installing a network in your home for the first time, this part of the book provides all the background info and down-and-dirty basics that will have you in the swing of things in no time. Here you can find general networking concepts, the most popular wireless networking technology, wireless networking terminology, and the latest alternatives in wireless networking. We also delve into cool new options for complementing your wireless network with peripherals networking and home control and home automation standards. Now that's whole-home networking the wireless way!

# Chapter 1

# Introducing Wireless Home Networking

- - - - - - - - - - - - - - - - - - - - - - - - - - - - - - - - - - - - -

- - - - - - - - - - - - - - - - - - - - - - - - - - - - - - - - - - - - -

*W*elcome to the wireless age! Nope, we're not talking about your grandfather's radio — we're talking about almost everything under the sun. What's not going wireless? Wanna say your refrigerator? Wrong — it is. How about your stereo? Yup, that too. Watches, key chains, baby video monitors, high-end projectors — even your thermostat is going wireless and digital. It's not just about computers any more. Your entire world is going wireless, and in buying this book, you're determined not to get left behind. Kudos to you!

A driving force behind the growing popularity of wireless networking is its reasonable cost: You can save money by not running network wiring all over your house, by sharing peripherals (such as printers and scanners), and by using your wireless network to drive other applications around your home, such as your home entertainment center. This book makes it easier for you to spend your money wisely by helping you decide what you need to buy and then helping you choose between the vast array of products on the market. Wireless networks are not only less expensive than more traditional wired networks but also much easier to install (no drilling and no pulling wires through the wall!). An important goal of this book is to give you "the skinny" on how to install a wireless network in your home.

Whether you have 1 computer or 20 (like Danny), you have several good reasons to want a personal computer network. The plummeting cost of wireless technologies, combined with their fast-paced technical development, has meant that more and more manufacturers are getting on the home networking bandwagon and including wireless networking in all sorts of products.

That means that more applications around your house will try to ride your wireless backbone — by talking among themselves and to the Internet. So, wireless is here to stay and is critical for any future-proofed home.

# Nothing but Net (work): Why You Need One

Wireless home networking isn't just about linking computers to the Internet. Although that task is important — nay, critical — in today's network-focused environment, it's not the whole enchilada. Of the many benefits of having wireless in the home, most have one thing in common: sharing. When you connect the computers in your house through a network, you can share files, printers, scanners, and high-speed Internet connections between them. In addition, you can play multiuser games over your network, access public wireless networks while you're away from home, check wireless security cameras, connect your mobile phone to your wireless network, or even enjoy your MP3s from your home stereo system while you're at work — really!

Reading *Wireless Home Networking For Dummies,* 4th Edition, helps you understand how to create a whole-home wireless network to reach all the nooks and crannies of your house. Of course, the primary reason that people have wanted to put wireless networks in their homes has been to "unwire" their PCs, especially laptops (which, these days, come with wireless standard), to enable more freedom of access in the home. But just about every major consumer goods manufacturer is hard at work wirelessly enabling its devices so that they too can talk to other devices in the home — you can find home theater receivers, Blu-ray disc players, gaming consoles, music players, and even flat-panel TVs with wireless capabilities built right in.

## File sharing

As you probably know, computer *files* are created whenever you use a computer. If you use a word processing program, such as Microsoft Word, to write a document, Word saves the document on your computer's hard drive as an electronic file. Similarly, if you balance your checkbook by using Quicken from Intuit, this software saves your financial data on the computer's drive in an electronic file.

A computer network lets you share those electronic files between two or more computers. For example, you can create a Word document on your computer, and your spouse, roommate, child, sibling, or whoever can pull up the same document on his or her computer over the network. With the right programs, you can even view the same documents at the same time! And that's not even getting into online services like Dropbox (www.dropbox.com) that let you store your shared files on a computer *in the cloud* (in other words, on the Internet) so you can access these files whenever and wherever you have an Internet connection.

But here's where we get into semantics: What's a computer? Your car has more computing and networking capability than the early moon rockets. Your stereo is increasingly looking like a computer with a black matte finish. Even your refrigerator and microwave are getting onboard computing capabilities. What's more is that all these devices have files and information that need to be shared.

The old way of moving files between computers and computing devices involved copying the files to a floppy disk (or, nowadays, a USB *thumb drive*) and then carrying the disk to the other computer. Computer geeks call this method of copying and transferring files the *sneakernet* approach. In contrast, copying files between computers is easy to do over a home network and with no need for floppy disks (or sneakers).

What's interesting is that more computers and devices are getting used to talking to one another over networks in an automated fashion. A common application is *synchronization,* where two devices talk to one another and make the appropriate updates to each other's stored information so that they're current with one another. For example, Microsoft's Zune portable media player (www.zune.net) is in many ways similar to Apple's iPod, with one big exception: Zune's wireless capabilities. Whenever you put your Zune in its charger base, it connects to your wireless network and automatically syncs new content (music, audiobooks, podcasts, and videos) from your PC. This means you always have that new content at your fingertips — literally — without having to lift a finger.

## Printer and peripheral sharing

Businesses with computer networks have discovered a major benefit: sharing printers. Companies invest in high-speed, high-capacity printers that are shared by many employees. Sometimes an entire department shares a single printer, or perhaps a cluster of printers is located in an area set aside for printers, copy machines, and fax machines.

Just like in a business network, all the computers on your home network can share the printers on your network. The cost-benefit of shared printers in a home network is certainly not as dramatic as in a business, but the opportunity to save money by sharing printers is clearly one of the real benefits of setting up a home network. Figure 1-1 depicts a network through which three personal computers can share the same printer.

Other peripherals, such as extra hard drive storage for backing up your computers or for all those MP3s that someone in the household might be downloading, also are great to share. Anything connected to your PCs or that has a network port (we talk about these in great detail throughout the book) can be shared anywhere on your wireless network.

**Figure 1-1:**
Share and
share alike:
Share one
printer via
your home
network.

## *Internet connection sharing*

Another driving reason behind many homeowners' interest in wireless home networking is a desire to share an Internet connection. Let's face it: The Internet is a critical part of day-to-day living — from kids doing their home-work to you managing your bank account — so it's only natural that more than one person in the household wants to get online at the same time. And, with the proliferation of *broadband Internet connections* — cable, digital sub-scriber line (DSL), fiber optics, and satellite modems — the demand at home has only soared.

### *Modem types*

Your wireless network helps you distribute information throughout the home. It's independent of the method you use to access your outside-of-home networks, like the Internet. Whether you use a dial-up connection or broadband, you can create a wireless home network. Here's a rundown of the different types of modems:

✔ **Dial-up modem:** This device connects to the Internet by dialing an Internet service provider (ISP), such as America Online (AOL) or EarthLink, over a standard phone line.

Fewer and fewer wireless networking equipment manufacturers support a dial-up connection on their equipment, because the majority of homes (and the *vast majority* of networked homes) use broadband these days. We mention dial-up here only for completeness; not because we recom-mend that you use it.

✔ **Cable modem:** This type of modem connects to the Internet through the same cable as cable TV. Cable modems connect to the Internet at much higher speeds than dial-up modems and can be left connected to the Internet all day, every day.

✔ **DSL modem:** Digital subscriber line modems use your phone line, but they permit the phone to be free for other purposes — voice calls and faxes, for example — even while the DSL modem is in use. DSL modems also connect to the Internet at much higher speeds than dial-up modems and can be left connected 24/7.

✔ **Broadband wireless modem:** The same wireless airwaves that are great for around-the-house communications are great for connecting to the Internet as well. Although the frequency may be different and the bandwidth much less, broadband wireless modems give you connectivity to your home's wireless network, in a similar fashion as DSL and cable modems.

✔ **Satellite modem:** Satellite modems tie into your satellite dish and give you two-way communications even if you're in the middle of the woods. Although they're typically not as fast as cable modems and DSL links, they're better than dial-up and available just about anywhere in the continental United States.

✔ **Fiber-optic modem:** We're in the midst of the fiber-fed revolution as the telephone and cable companies push to outdo each other by installing extremely high-capacity lines in homes to allow all sorts of cool applications. (The biggest example of this in the U.S. is Verizon's FiOS system — www.verizon.com — which connects tens of millions of homes to the Internet by using fiber-optic connections.) Until now, the broadband access link has been the limiting bottleneck when wireless networks communicate with the Internet. With fiber optics, you could see broadband access capacity equal to that of your wireless network.

## Network (very!) basics

When configuring your PCs on a network, you can buy equipment that lets you connect multiple computers to an Internet modem using radio waves with no wires (our focus here, obviously); through special network cables; or even through regular phone lines, the coaxial wiring (cable TV wires), or the power lines in your house. No matter what the physical connection is among your networked devices, the most popular language (or *protocol*) used in connecting computers to a broadband modem is a network technology known as Ethernet.

*Ethernet* is an industry standard protocol used in virtually every corporation and institution; consequently, Ethernet equipment is plentiful and inexpensive. The most common form of Ethernet networking uses special cables known as *Category 5e/6 UTP* (or unshielded twisted pair). These networks are named after their speed — most are 100 Mbps (much faster than alternative networks that run over powerlines or phone lines) and are called 100BaseT.

You also find 1000BaseT (gigabit Ethernet) networks, which run at 1 *gigabit* per second. Figure 1-2 illustrates a network that enables three personal computers to connect to the Internet through a DSL or cable modem. (This network model works the same for a satellite or fiber-optic connection.)

See Chapter 4 for more information about planning and budgeting for your network and Chapter 5 for help in selecting your wireless networking equipment.

**Figure 1-2:** Internet for all: Set up a network that enables many PCs to connect to the Internet through a DSL or cable modem.

# Phone calling for free

With some new wireless phone capabilities, you can get rid of the static of your cordless phone and move digital over your wireless home network, thus saving money on calls by using less-expensive, Internet-based phone calling options (Voice over IP, or VoIP). What started as a hobbyist error-prone service has grown into a full-fledged worldwide phenomenon. Phone calling over the Internet is now ready for prime time:

- ✔ **Free and for-fee services are available.** Services such as Vonage (www.vonage.com) and Skype (www.skype.com) allow you to use your regular phones to call over the Internet for free or for a low monthly cost.

- ✔ **Add-ons to popular software programs are available.** Internet calling and even videoconferencing have been added to instant messaging programs such as AOL Instant Messenger (AIM) so that you can talk to the people you used to only IM.

✔ **New devices make it simple.** New devices, such as the Olympia DualPhone (`http://dualphone.net`), ease access to these Internet calling services — so you don't have to don a headset every time you want to make a phone call.

The best part is that VoIP services are all moving toward wireless too. Throw away that old cordless phone and replace it with a new wireless handset or a neat Wi-Fi phone that you can take on the road to make free calls from any Wi-Fi network you have access to.

The convergence of wireless and Voice over IP is one of the major mega-trends going on in the telecommunications and Internet markets today — you can bet that you want it in your home too!

## Home arcades and wireless to go

If you aren't convinced yet that a wireless home network is for you, we have four more points that may change your mind. Check them out:

✔ **Multiuser games over the network:** If you're into video games, multi-player card games, or role-playing games, you may find multiuser games over the network or even over the Internet fascinating. Chapter 11 discusses how to use your wireless network to play multiuser games.

✔ **Audio anywhere in the household:** Why spend money on CDs and keep them stacked next to your stereo? Load them on your PC and make them wirelessly available to your stereo, your car, your MP3 player that you take jogging, and lots more. Check out Chapter 12 for more info on how to use your wireless network to send audio and video signals around the house.

✔ **Home wireless cam accessibility:** You can check out your house from anywhere in the house — or the world — with new wireless cameras that hop on your home network and broadcast images privately or publicly over the Internet. Want to see whether your kids are tearing apart the house while you're working in your office downstairs? Just call up your wireless networked camera and check them out. (In our generation, we always said, "Mom has eyes in the back of her head"; our kids probably think that Mom is omniscient!)

✔ **Wireless on the go:** This concept is great if you have a portable computer. Many airports, hotels, malls, and coffee shops have installed public wireless networks that enable you to connect to the Internet (for a small fee, of course) via hot spots. See Chapter 16 for more about using wireless networking when you're away from home.

# Wired versus Wireless

Ethernet is the most-often-used method of connecting personal computers to form a network because it's fast and its equipment is relatively inexpensive. In addition, Ethernet can be transmitted over several types of network cable or sent through the air by using wireless networking equipment. Most new computers have an Ethernet connection built in, ready for you to plug in a network cable. The most popular wireless networking equipment transmits a form of Ethernet by using radio waves rather than Category 5e/6 cables.

## Installing wired home networks

Even though we're talking mostly about wireless networks and how great they are, we would be misleading you if we told you that wireless is the only way to go. Wireless and wired homes each have advantages.

Wired homes are:

- **Faster:** Wired lines can reach speeds of 1000 Mbps, whereas wireless homes tend to be in the 20 Mbps to 300 Mbps range. Both wireless and wired technologies are getting faster and faster, but for as far as our crystal balls can see, wired will always be ahead.

- **More reliable:** Wireless signals are prone to interference and fluctuations and degrade quickly over short distances; wired connections typically are more stable and reliable all over your home.

- **More secure:** You don't have to worry about your signals traveling through the air and being intercepted by snoopers, as you do with unsecured wireless systems.

- **Economical over the long term:** The incremental cost of adding CAT-5e/6 voice and data cabling and RG-6 coaxial cabling into your house — over a 30-year mortgage — will be almost nothing each month. That is, as long as you're building or remodeling your home — when your walls aren't open, getting network cables inside of them is a lot more difficult and expensive.

- **Salable:** More and more home buyers are not only looking for well-wired homes but also discounting homes without the infrastructure. As good as wireless is, it isn't affixed to the house and is carried with you when you leave. Most new homes have structured wiring in the walls.

 If you're building a new home or renovating an old one, we absolutely recommend that you consider running the latest wiring in the walls to each of your rooms. That doesn't mean that you won't have a wireless network in your home — you will. It just will be different than if you were wholly reliant on wireless for your networking.

If you choose to use network cable, it should ideally be installed in the walls, just like electrical and phone wiring. Network jacks (outlets) are installed in the walls in rooms where you would expect to use a computer. Connecting your computer to a wired network is as easy as plugging a phone into a phone jack — after the wiring is in place, that is.

Without question, the most economical time to install network cable in a home is during the home's initial construction. In upscale neighborhoods, especially in communities near high-tech businesses, builders often wire new homes with network cable as a matter of course. In most cases, however, the installation of network cable in a new home is an option or upgrade that's installed only if the new owner orders it and pays a premium. Installing a structured wiring solution for a home can cost at least $2,000–$3,000, and that's for starters.

Although the installation of network cable in an existing home certainly is possible, it's much more difficult and expensive than installing cable during construction. If you hire an electrician to run the cable, you can easily spend thousands of dollars to do what would have cost a few hundred dollars during your home's construction. If you're comfortable drilling holes in your walls and working in attics and crawl spaces, you can install the cabling your-self for the cost of the cable and outlets.

The reality is that no home will ever be purely wireless or wireline (wired). Each approach has benefits and costs, and they coexist in any house. If you're building a new house, most experts tell you to spend the extra money on a structured wiring solution because it adds value to your house and you can better manage all the wiring in your home. We agree. But no wiring solution can be everywhere you want it to be. Thus, wireless is a great complement to your home, which is why we advocate a whole-home wireless network for your entire home to use.

## *Installing wireless home networks*

If you're networking an existing home or are renting your home, wireless has fabulous benefits:

- ✔ **Portable:** You can take your computing device anywhere in the house and be on the network. Even if you have a huge house, you can intercon-nect wireless access points to have a whole-home wireless network.

- ✔ **Flexible:** You're not limited to where a jack is on the wall; you can net-work anywhere.

- ✔ **Cost effective:** You can start wireless networking for under a hundred dollars. Your wiring contractor can't do much with that!

- ✔ **Clean:** You don't have to tear down walls or trip over wires when they come out from underneath the carpeting.

What's more, there's really no difference in how you use your networked computer, whether it's connected to the network by a cable or by a wireless networking device. Whether you're sharing files, a printer, your entertainment system, or the Internet over the network, the procedures are the same on a wireless network as on a wired network. In fact, you can mix wired and wireless network equipment on the same network with no change in how you use a computer on the network — your computers don't care whether they're talking over a wire or over a wireless system.

Now for the fine print. We would be remiss if we weren't candid and didn't mention any potential drawbacks to wireless networks compared with wired networks. The possible drawbacks fall into four categories:

 ✔ **Data speed:** Wireless networking equipment transmits data at slower speeds than wired networking equipment. Wired networks are already networking at gigabit speeds, although the fastest current wireless networking standards (in theoretical situations) top out at 300 Mbps. (The real-world top speed you can expect will probably be under 100 Mbps.) But, for almost all the uses we can think of now, this rate is plenty fast. Your Internet connection probably doesn't exceed 20 Mbps (though lucky folks who have fiber-optic lines running to their homes may exceed this rate by a big margin!), so your wireless connection should be more than fast enough.

 ✔ **Radio signal range:** Wireless signals fade when you move away from the source. Some homes, especially older homes, may be built from materials that tend to block the radio signals used by wireless networking equipment, which causes even faster signal degradation. If your home has plaster walls that contain a wire mesh, the wireless networking equipment's radio signal may not reach all points in your home. Most modern construction, however, uses drywall materials that reduce the radio signal only slightly. As a result, most homeowners can reach all points in their home with one centralized wireless *access point* (also called a *base station*) and one wireless device in or attached to each personal computer.

If you need better coverage, you can just add another access point — we show you how in Chapter 18 — or you can upgrade an older wireless network to a newer technology, such as 802.11n, which provides farther coverage within your home.

 ✔ **Radio signal interference:** The most common type of wireless networking technology uses a radio frequency that's also used by other home devices, such as microwave ovens and portable telephones. Consequently, some wireless home network users experience network problems (the network slows down or the signal is dropped) caused by radio signal interference.

✓ **Security:** The radio signal from a wireless network doesn't stop at the outside wall of your home. A neighbor or even a total stranger could access your network from an adjoining property or from the street unless you implement some type of security technology to prevent unauthorized access. You can safeguard yourself with security technology that comes standard with the most popular wireless home networking technology. However, it's not bulletproof, and it certainly doesn't work if you don't turn it on. For more information on wireless security, go to Chapter 9.

Wireless networks compare favorably with wired networks for most homeowners who didn't have network wiring installed when their houses were built or remodeled. As we mention earlier in this chapter, even if you do have network wires in your walls, you probably want wireless just to provide the untethered access it brings to laptops and handheld computers.

# Choosing a Wireless Standard

The good news about wireless networks is that they come in multiple flavors, each with its own advantages and disadvantages. The bad news is that trying to decide which version to get when buying a system can get confusing. The even better news is that the dropping prices of wireless systems and fast-paced development are creating dual- and tri-mode systems on the market that can speak many different wireless languages.

## Introducing the 802.11s: a, b, g, and n

You may run into gear using one of two older standards: 802.11 a and b. For the most part, manufacturers aren't making gear using these systems anymore (at least not for the home — some industrial and commercial network gear still on the market use these systems), but you will still hear about these systems as you explore wireless networking:

✓ **802.11a:** Wireless networks that use the Institute for Electrical and Electronics Engineers (IEEE) 802.11a standard use the 5 GHz radio frequency band. Equipment of this type is among the fastest wireless networking equipment widely available to consumers.

✓ **802.11b:** Wireless home networks that use the 802.11b standard use the 2.4 GHz radio band. This standard is the most popular in terms of number of installed networks and number of users.

Following are the two major wireless systems that have pretty much replaced 802.11b and 802.11a:

- ✔ **802.11g:** The outgoing default version of the 802.11 wireless family, 802.11g was the primary form of wireless networking from 2003 until 2009. In many ways, 802.11g offered the best of both worlds — backward compatibility with the older 802.11b networks we just mentioned (they too operate over the 2.4 GHz radio frequency band) and the speed of the older 802.11a networks also discussed in that section. And the cost of 802.11g has dropped precipitously, so it's now less expensive than the older and slower 802.11b. (You can buy an 802.11g network adapter for less than $20 and a home router for less than $40.)

- ✔ **802.11n:** In late 2009, the IEEE finalized and ratified a newer and faster system called 802.11n. The 802.11n system (like 802.11g before it) is backward compatible, which means that older 802.11b and 802.11g systems can work just fine on an 802.11n network. 802.11n systems can also support the 5 GHz frequencies (though not all do; more on this in Chapter 3), and may therefore be backward compatible with 802.11a as well. A lot of new technology in 802.11n extends the range of the network and increases the speed as well — 802.11n can be as much as *five times* faster than 802.11g or 802.11a networks. Draft versions of 802.11n gear have been on sale since 2007; now that the final version is being sold, 802.11n should be your default choice for a new wireless network.

Equipment supporting all four of these finalized standards — 802.11a, 802.11b, 802.11g, and 802.11n — can carry the Wi-Fi logo that's licensed for use by the Wi-Fi Alliance trade group based on equipment that passes interoperability testing. You absolutely want to buy only equipment that has been Wi-Fi certified, regardless of which 802.11 standard you're choosing.

The terms surrounding wireless networking can get complex. First, the order of lettering isn't really easily understandable because 802.11*b* was approved and hit the market before 802.11*a*. Also, you see the term *Wi-Fi* used frequently. (In fact, we thought about calling this book *Wi-Fi For Dummies* because the term is used so much.) Wi-Fi refers to the collective group of 802.11 specifications: 802.11a, b, g, and n. You may sometimes see this group also named *802.11x* networking, where *x* can equal a, b, g, or n. To make matters more confusing, a higher-level parent standard named 802.11 predates 802.11a, b, g, and n and is also used to talk about the group of the four standards. Technically, IEEE 802.11 is a standards group responsible for several other networking specifications as well. For simplicity in this book, we use 802.11 and Wi-Fi synonymously to talk about the four standards as a group. We could have used 802.11x, but we want to save a lot of *x*s (for our wives).

For the most part, 802.11a and 802.11b equipment is being phased out. If you're buying all-new gear, 802.11g or 802.11n are your real choices — and we're already starting to see 802.11g gear discontinued in favor of 802.11n. You can still find a few bits of 802.11a or b gear, but it's mostly sold to fit into older networks. If you already have some gear that's 802.11b, don't despair —

it still works fine in most cases, and you can upgrade your network to 802.11g or 802.11n-bit by bit (pun intended!) without worrying about compatibility. In this section, we still discuss 802.11a and b, even though they're increasingly not something you're likely to consider.

## Comparing the standards

The differences between these four standards fall into five main categories:

- ✔ **Data speed:** 802.11a and 802.11g networks are almost five times faster than the original 802.11b networks — 802.11n is five times faster still! For the most part, any current Wi-Fi gear (whether it be 802.11g or 802.11n) will be faster than the Internet connection into your house, but the extra speed of 802.11n may be worthwhile if you're trying to do things such as transfer real-time video signals around your home wirelessly.

- ✔ **Price:** 802.11g networking gear (the standard system today) has been on the market since the mid-2000s — accordingly, the price for this gear is quite low (less than $20 for an adapter). The new 802.11n adapters can cost about twice as much.

- ✔ **Radio signal range:** 802.11a wireless networks tend to have a shorter maximum signal range than 802.11b and g networks. The actual distances vary depending on the size and construction of your home. In most modern homes, however, all three of the older standards should provide adequate range. Because it uses a new technology called MIMO, 802.11n can have two or more times the range in your home, so if you have a big house, you might gravitate toward 802.11n.

- ✔ **Radio signal interference:** The radio frequency band used by both 802.11b and 802.11g equipment is used also by other home devices, such as microwave ovens and portable telephones, resulting sometimes in network problems caused by radio signal interference. Few other types of devices now use the radio frequency band employed by the 802.11a standard. 802.11n gear can use either frequency band (though not all gear does — some uses only the more crowded 2.4 GHz frequency range).

- ✔ **Interoperability:** Because 802.11a and 802.11b/g use different frequency bands, they can't communicate over the same radio frequency band. Several manufacturers, however, have products that can operate with both 802.11a and IEEE 802.11b/g equipment simultaneously. By contrast, 802.11g equipment is designed to be backward compatible with 802.11b equipment — both operating on the same frequency band. 802.11n is backward compatible with all three previous standards, though the 802.11a backward compatibility is available only on 802.11n gear that operates in the 5 GHz frequency range.

Think of dual-mode, multistandard devices as being in the same vein as AM/FM radios. AM and FM stations transmit their signals in different ways, but hardly anyone buys a radio that's only AM because almost all the receiving units are AM/FM. Users select which band they want to listen to at any particular time. With an 802.11a/b/g (or 2.4/5 GHz 802.11n) device, you can also choose the band that you want to transmit and receive in.

For a long time, wireless networks operating at the 2.4 GHz frequency range were most popular in the home, but the advent of 5 GHz capable 802.11n devices (such as Apple's popular AirPort Extreme with Gigabit Ethernet) have finally brought 5 GHz networks into lots of homes.

If you're starting your home wireless network from scratch, there's no compelling reason *not* to go with 802.11n. 802.11n gear doesn't cost that much more than the older 802.11g gear, and it provides a lot more networking capability. That said, if you have an existing 802.11g network in place, there's no reason to throw it away and move to 802.11n right away — unless you have some high bandwidth requirements like video.

# Planning Your Wireless Home Network

Installing and setting up a wireless home network can be ridiculously easy. In some cases, after you unpack and install the equipment, you're up and running in a matter of minutes. To ensure that you don't have a negative experience, however, you should do a little planning. The issues you need to consider during the planning stage include the ones in this list:

✔ Which of your computers will you connect to the network (and will you be connecting Macs and PCs or just one or the other)?

✔ Will all the computers be connected via wireless connections, or will one or more computers be connected by a network cable to the network?

✔ Which wireless technology — 802.11n or 802.11g — will you use?

✔ Which type of wireless adapter will you use to connect each computer to the network? And which of your computers already have one built-in?

✔ How many printers will you connect to the network? How will each printer be connected to the network — by connecting it to a computer on the network or by connecting it to a print server?

✔ Will you connect the network to the Internet through a broadband connection (cable or DSL) or dial-up? If you're sharing an Internet connection, will you do so with a cable/DSL/satellite/dial-up router or with Internet connection-sharing software?

✔ What other devices might you want to include in your initial wireless network? Do you plan on listening to MP3s on your stereo? How about downloading movies from the Internet (instead of running out in the rain to the movie rental store!)?

✔ How much money should you budget for your wireless network?

✔ What do you need to do to plan for adequate security to ensure the privacy of the information stored on the computers connected to your network?

We discuss all these issues and the entire planning process in more detail in Chapter 4.

# Choosing Wireless Networking Equipment

For those of us big kids who are enamored with technology, shopping for high-tech toys can be therapeutic. Whether you're a closet geek or (cough) normal, a critical step in building a useful wireless home network is choosing the proper equipment.

Before you can decide which equipment to buy, take a look at Chapter 4 for more information about planning a wireless home network. Chapter 5 provides a more detailed discussion of the different types of wireless networking equipment.

The following sections give you a quick rundown of what equipment you need, including an access point, network interface adapters, and wireless network interface adapters.

## Access point

At the top of the list is at least one wireless *access point* (AP), also sometimes called a *base station*. An AP acts like a wireless switchboard that connects wireless devices on the network to each other and to the rest of the network. You gotta have one of these to create a wireless home network. They range in price from about $30 to $200, with prices continually coming down. (Prices predominantly are in the $40–$60 range for 802.11g and in the $50–$175 range for 802.11n.) You can get APs from many leading vendors in the marketplace, including Apple (www.apple.com), D-Link (www.d-link.com), Cisco (http://home.cisco.com/en-us/wireless/), NETGEAR (www.netgear.com), and Belkin (www.belkin.com). We give you a long list of vendors in Chapter 20, so check that out when you buy your AP.

For wireless home networks, the best AP value is often an AP that's bundled with other features. The most popular APs for home use also come with one or more of these features:

✔ **Network hub or switch:** A hub connects wired PCs to the network. A *switch* is a "smarter" version of a hub that speeds up network traffic. (We talk more about the differences between hubs and switches in Chapter 2.)

✔ **DHCP server:** A Dynamic Host Configuration Protocol (DHCP) server assigns network addresses to each computer on the network; these addresses are required for the computers to communicate.

✔ **Network router:** A router enables multiple computers to share a single Internet connection. The network connects each computer to the router, and the router is connected to the Internet through a broadband modem.

✔ **Print server:** Use a print server to add printers directly to the network rather than attach a printer to each computer on the network.

In Figure 1-3, you can see an AP that also bundles in a network router, switch, and DHCP server. You may increasingly see more features added that include support for VoIP routing as well. We talk about more features for your AP in Chapter 5.

**Figure 1-3:**
Look for
an AP that
bundles a
network
router,
switch,
and DHCP
server.

## Network interface adapters

As we mention earlier in this chapter, home networks use a communication method *(protocol)* known as Ethernet. The communication that takes place between the components of your computer, however, doesn't use the Ethernet protocol. As a result, for computers on the network to communicate through the Ethernet protocol, each of the computers must translate between their internal communications protocol and Ethernet. The device that handles this translation is a *network interface adapter,* and each computer on the network needs one. Prices for network interface adapters are typically much less than $30, and most new computers come with one at no additional cost.

A network interface adapter that's installed inside a computer is usually called a *network interface card* (NIC). Virtually all computer manufacturers now include Ethernet capabilities, built right onto the PC motherboard as a standard feature with each personal computer.

## Wireless network interface adapters

To wirelessly connect a computer to the network, you must obtain a wireless network interface adapter for each computer. Prices range between $10 and $100. Most portable computers (laptops, netbooks, iPads, and so on) now come with a wireless network interface built in, as do many (but not all!) desktop computers. If your computer doesn't have a wireless NIC, don't worry. They're easy to install; most are adapters that just plug in.

The three most common types of wireless network interface adapters are

- ✔ **PC or Express Card:** This type of adapter is often used in laptop computers because most laptops have one or two PC Card slots. Figure 1-4 shows a PC Card wireless network interface adapter.

- ✔ **USB:** A Universal Serial Bus (USB) adapter connects to one of your computer's USB ports; these USB ports have been standard in just about every PC built since the turn of the millennium.

- ✔ **ISA or PCI adapter:** If your computer doesn't have a PC Card slot, or USB port, you have to install either a network interface card or a USB card (for a USB wireless network interface adapter) in one of the computer's internal peripheral expansion receptacles (slots). The internal expansion slots in modern PCs and Apple Macintosh computers follow the Peripheral Component Interconnect (PCI) standard.

Almost all smartphones, netbooks, laptops, and other portable devices are shipping with wireless already onboard, so you don't need an adapter of any sort. These devices just come with the wireless installed in them. We tell you how to get your wireless-enabled devices onto your wireless backbone in Part II.

**Figure 1-4:**
A PC Card
wireless
network
interface
adapter.

# Chapter 2

# From a to n and b-yond

*I*n the not-so-distant past, networked computers were connected only by wire: a special-purpose network cabling. This type of wiring has yet to become a standard item in new homes, but we're getting closer, with more people asking to have a home wired from the start. That's a different one of our books: *Smart Homes For Dummies* (also from Wiley and which we hope you consider when you're buying a new home). The cost of installing network cabling after a house is already built is understandably much higher than doing so during initial construction. By contrast, the cost of installing a wireless network in a particular home is a fraction of the cost of wiring the same residence — and much less hassle. As a result, because more and more people are beginning to see the benefits of having a computer network at home, they're turning to wireless networks. Just as most people can no longer recall life without wireless mobile phones, similarly, wireless computer networking has become the standard way to network a home.

That's not to say that it's easy, though. Face it: Life can sometimes seem a bit complicated. The average Joe or Jane can't even order a cup of java any more without having to choose between an endless array of options: regular, decaf, half-caf, mocha, cappuccino, latté, low fat, no fat, foam, no foam, and so on. You know what you want, but you don't know how to say it in a way that will get you what you want! Of course, after you get the hang of the lingo, you can order coffee like a pro. That's where this chapter comes in: to help you get used to the networking lingo that's slung about when you're planning, purchasing, installing, and using your wireless network.

Like so much alphabet soup, the prevalent wireless network technologies go by the names 802.11a, 802.11b, 802.11g, and now 802.11n; employ devices such as APs and Express cards; and make use of technologies with cryptic abbreviations (TCP/IP, DHCP, NAT, MIMO, WEP, and WPA). Pshew. Whether you're shopping for, installing, or configuring a wireless network, you will undoubtedly run across some or all of these not-so-familiar terms and more. This chapter is your handy guide to this smorgasbord of networking and wireless networking terminology.

If you're not the least bit interested in buzzwords, you can safely skip this chapter for now and go right to the chapters that cover planning, purchasing, installing, and using your wireless network. You can always refer to this chapter whenever you run into some wireless networking terminology that throws you. If you like knowing a little bit about the language that the locals speak before visiting a new place, read on.

# Networking Buzzwords You Need to Know

A computer *network* is composed of computers or network-accessible devices — and sometimes other peripheral devices, such as printers — connected in a way that they transmit data between participants. Computer networks have been commonplace in offices for well over 20 years, but with the advent of reasonably priced wireless networks, computer networks are now commonplace in homes. Now, we mere mortals can share printers, surf the Internet, play multiplayer video games, and stream video like the corporate gods have been doing for years.

A computer network that connects devices in a particular physical location, such as in a home or in a single office site, is sometimes called a *local area network* (LAN). Conversely, the network outside your home that connects you to the Internet and beyond is called a *wide area network* (WAN).

In a nutshell, computer networks help people and devices share *information* (files and e-mail) and expensive *resources* (printers and Internet connections) more efficiently.

## Workstations and servers

Each computer in your home that's attached to a network is a *workstation,* also sometimes referred to as a *client* computer. The Windows operating system (OS) refers to the computers residing together on the same local area network as a *homegroup.* A Windows-based computer network enables the workstations in a workgroup to share files and printers visible through *Network* (or *My Network Places* if you're using Windows XP). Home networks based on the Apple Macintosh OS offer the same capability. On a Mac, just use Finder to navigate to *Network.*

Some networks also have *servers,* which are special-purpose computers or other devices that provide one or more services to other computers and devices on a network. Examples of typical servers include:

✔ **Windows Home Server:** Microsoft and its hardware partners (companies such as HP) have created a new specification for hardware and software known as Windows Home Server. Essentially, Windows Home Server is a stripped-down version of the Windows OS that is designed to run on a small device that sits in your network and provides file and media storage for all the computers in your home (and remote access to your stuff over the Internet while you're out of the house). Windows Home Servers are a lot like the NAS (network attached storage) devices discussed in the next bullet point, but use a special Windows OS. You can read more at `www.microsoft.com/windows/products/winfamily/windowshome server/default.mspx`.

✔ **Network Attached Storage (NAS) Server:** A specialized kind of file server, an NAS device is basically a small, *headless* (it doesn't have a monitor or keyboard) computing appliance that uses a big hard drive and a special operating system (usually Linux) to create an easy-to-use file server for a home or office network. The Buffalo Technology LinkStation Network Storage Center (`www.buffalotech.com`) is a good example of an NAS device appropriate for a home network.

✔ **Print server:** A *print server* is a computer or another device that makes it possible for the computers on the network to share one or more printers. Traditionally, print servers were part of corporate — not home — networks, but many wireless networking access points now come with a print server feature built in, which turns out to be very handy.

✔ **E-mail server:** An *e-mail server* is a computer that provides a system for sending e-mail to users on the network. You may never see an e-mail server on a home network. Most often, home users send e-mail through a third-party service, such as America Online (AOL), Gmail, MSN Hotmail, and Yahoo!.

✔ **DHCP server:** Every computer on a network, even a home network, must have its own, unique network address to communicate with the other computers on the network. A Dynamic Host Configuration Protocol (DHCP) server automatically assigns a network address to every computer on a network. You most often find DHCP servers built into another device, such as a router or an AP.

You can find many types of client computers — network-aware devices — on your network, too. Some examples include:

✔ **Gaming consoles:** The Microsoft Xbox 360 (`www.xbox.com`), Sony PlayStation 3 (`www.playstation.com`), and Nintendo Wii (`www.nintendo.com`) have adapters for network connections or multi-player gaming and talking to other players while gaming. Cool! Read more about online gaming in Chapter 11.

✔ **Wireless network cameras:** The D-Link DCS-5300G (`www.dlink.com/products/?pid=342`) lets you not only view your home when you're away but also pan, tilt, scan, and zoom your way around the home. *That's* a nanny-cam.

✔ **Entertainment systems:** NETGEAR's EVA9150 Digital Entertainer Elite enables you to use wireless technology to stream music, video, movies, photos, and Internet radio stations from your computer or file server to your home stereo system. The system uses a computer on your home network as a source, which stores your CDs in the MP3 (or other) electronic format, and attaches just like a CD or DVD player to your home entertainment system.

Most consumer manufacturers are trying to network-enable their devices, so expect to see everything from your washer and dryer to your vacuum cleaner network-enabled at some point. Why? Because after such appliances are on a network, they can be monitored for breakdowns, software upgrades, and so on without your having to manually monitor them. Even power utilities are getting into the wireless game, installing wireless "smart meters" on the sides of people's homes to make meter reading faster and more accurate.

## Network infrastructure

Workstations must be electronically interconnected to communicate. The equipment over which the *network traffic* (electronic signals) travels between computers on the network is the *network infrastructure*.

### Network hubs

In a typical office network, a strand of wiring similar to phone cable is run from each computer to a central location, such as a phone closet, where each wire is connected to a network hub. The *network hub,* similar conceptually to the hub of a wheel, receives signals transmitted by each computer on the network and sends the signals out to all other computers on the network.

Figure 2-1 illustrates a network with a star-shaped *topology* (the physical design of a network). Other network topologies include *ring* and *bus*. Home networks typically use a star topology because it's the simplest to install and troubleshoot.

**Figure 2-1:**
It's all in the stars — a typical network star-shaped topology.

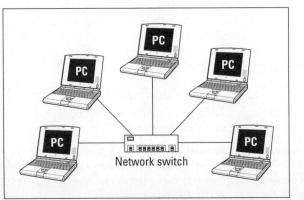

Network switch

### Bridges

A network *bridge* provides a pathway for network traffic between networks or segments of networks. A device that connects a wireless network segment to a wired network segment is a type of network bridge. In larger networks, network bridges are sometimes used to connect networks on different floors in the same building or in different buildings. In a wireless home network, the device that manages the wireless network, the *access point,* often acts as a bridge between a wireless segment of the network and a wired segment — even if the wired segment is simply a single wire running from a DSL or cable modem into the back of the access point.

### Hubs and switches

Networks transmit data in bundles called *packets.* Along with the raw information being transmitted, each packet also contains the network address of the computer that sent it and the network address of the recipient computer. Network hubs send packets indiscriminately to all ports of all computers connected to the hub — which is why you very rarely see them used any longer.

A special type of hub called a *switched hub* examines each packet, determines the addressee and port, and forwards the packet only to the computer and port to which it is addressed. Most often, switched hubs are just called *switches.* A switch reads the addressee information in each packet and sends the packet directly to the segment of the network to which the addressee is connected. Packets that aren't addressed to a particular network segment are never transmitted over that segment, and the switch acts as a filter to eliminate unnecessary network traffic. Switches make more efficient use of the available transmission bandwidth than standard hubs, and therefore offer higher aggregate throughput to the devices on the switched network.

### Routers

Over a large network and on the Internet, a *router* is analogous to a superefficient postal service — it reads the addressee information in each data packet and communicates with other routers over the network or Internet to determine the best route for each packet to take. In the home, a *home* or *broadband router* uses a capability called Network Address Translation (NAT) to enable all the computers on a home network to share a single Internet address on the cable or DSL network. The home router sits between your broadband modem and all the computers and networked devices in your house, and directs traffic to and from devices both within the network and out on the Internet.

So, the local area network in your home connects to the wide area network, which takes signals out of the home and on to the Internet.

The vast majority of wireless access points sold for the home market incorporate a router and a switch along with the access point — an all-in-one solution. Unless you already have a separate router and/or switch, you don't want to buy *just* an access point for your home wireless network, you'll want a *wireless router* or *Internet gateway,* as discussed in the next section.

Transmission Control Protocol/Internet Protocol (TCP/IP) is the most common protocol for transmitting packets around a network. Every computer on a TCP/IP network must have its own *IP address,* which is a 32-bit numeric address that's written as four groups of numbers separated by periods (for example, 192.168.1.100). Each number of these four sets of numbers is known as an *octet,* which can have a value from 0 to 255. The Internet transmits packets by using the TCP/IP protocol. When you use the Internet, the Internet service provider (ISP) — such as AOL, EarthLink, or your cable or DSL provider — assigns a unique TCP/IP number to your computer. For the period that your computer is connected, your computer "leases" this unique address and uses it like a postal address to send and receive information over the Internet to and from other computers.

A router with the Network Address Translation (NAT) feature also helps to protect the data on your computers from intruders. The NAT feature acts as a protection because it hides the real network addresses of networked computers from computers outside the network. Many WAN routers also have additional security features that more actively prevent intruders from gaining unauthorized access to your network through the Internet. This type of protection is sometimes described generically as a *firewall.* Good firewall software usually offers a suite of tools that not only block unauthorized access but also help you to detect and monitor suspicious computer activity. In addition, these tools provide you with ways to safely permit computers on your network to access the Internet.

### Internet gateways

These days, you can get a device that really does it all: a *wireless Internet gateway.* These devices combine all the features of an access point, a router, and a broadband modem (typically, cable or DSL, but this could also be a fiber-optic connection such as Verizon's FiOS or even another wireless connection). Some wireless Internet gateways even include a print server (which enables you to connect a printer directly to the gateway and use it from any networked PC), a dial-up modem, and even some Ethernet ports for computers and devices that connect to your network with wires.

For example, the 2Wire HomePortal 2000 series Internet gateways (www.2wire.com) include a built-in DSL modem, a router, a wireless access point, and other networking features such as a firewall and an easy-to-use graphical user interface (GUI) for configuring and setting up the gateway.

Generally, you can't buy these devices off-the-shelf at your local Best Buy, but you can get them directly from your broadband service provider.

The term *gateway* gets used a lot by different folks with different ideas about what such a device is. Although our definition is the most common (and, in our opinion, correct), you may see some vendors selling devices that they call Internet gateways that don't have all the functions we describe. For example, some access points and routers that don't have built-in broadband modems are also called gateways. We don't consider them to be Internet gateways because they link to the broadband modem. They're more of a modem gateway, but no one uses that term — it just isn't as catchy as an Internet gateway. We call them *wireless gateways* to keep everyone honest. Keep these subtle differences in mind when you're shopping.

## Network interface adapters

Wireless networking is based on radio signals. Each computer, or *station,* on a wireless network has its own radio that sends and receives data over the network. As in wired networks, a station can be a *client* or a *server.* Most stations on a wireless home network are personal computers with a wireless network adapter, but increasingly non-PC devices such as phones, entertainment systems, gaming consoles, and cameras have wireless networking capabilities too.

Each workstation on the network has a network interface card or adapter that links the workstation to the network (we discuss these in Chapter 1). This is true for wireless and *wireline* (wired) networks. In many instances the wireless functionality is embedded in the device, meaning the network interface adapter is internal and preinstalled in the machine. In other instances, these internal and external adapters are either ordered with your workstation or device or you add them during the installation process. We describe these options in the following subsections.

Figure 2-2 shows an external wireless networking adapter designed for attachment to a computer's Universal Serial Bus (USB) port, and Figure 2-3 shows an internal wireless networking adapter designed for installation in a desktop computer.

**Figure 2-2:**
A wireless network adapter that attaches to a computer's USB port.

**Figure 2-3:**
A wireless
network
adapter for
installation
inside a
desktop
computer.

## PC and Express Cards

When you want to add wireless networking capability to a laptop computer,
your first choice for a wireless network interface should probably be a
PC Card (see Figure 2-4). Nearly all Windows and some Mac laptops have
PCMCIA ports that are compatible with these cards.

**Figure 2-4:**
A PC Card
wireless
network
adapter.

A newer type of card called the *ExpressCard* has been slowly taking over
the role of the PC Card. The ExpressCard (`www.expresscard.org/web/
site`) is a slightly smaller and more capable version of the PC Card. The
ExpressCard uses less power, takes up less space, and provides faster connections to the internal circuitry of the device in which it is installed.

All wireless PC Cards must have an antenna so that the built-in radio can
communicate with an access point. Most have a built-in patch antenna
enclosed in a plastic casing that protrudes from the PC while the card is fully
inserted. You should always take care with this type of card because it's
likely to get damaged if it's not stored properly when not in use (or if your
dog knocks your laptop off the coffee table — don't ask!).

Many laptop computers use an internal Express card for wireless networking functionality. These cards don't slide into a slot on the side of the computer, but rather are installed at the factory and use an antenna built into the case of the computer.

### PCI adapters

Nearly all desktop PCs have at least one Peripheral Component Interconnect (PCI) slot. This PCI slot is used to install all sorts of add-in cards, including network connectivity. Most wireless NIC manufacturers offer a wireless PCI adapter — a version of their product that can be installed in a PCI slot (see Figure 2-5).

Some wireless PCI adapters are cards that adapt a PC Card for use in a PCI slot. The newest designs, however, mount the electronics from the PC Card on a full-size PCI card with a removable dipole antenna attached to the back of the card.

### USB adapters

The USB standard has, over the past several years, become the most widely used method of connecting peripherals to a personal computer. First popularized in the Apple iMac, USB supports a data transfer rate many times faster than a typical network connection, and is therefore a good candidate for connecting an external wireless network adapter to either a laptop or a desktop computer. Several wireless networking hardware vendors offer USB wireless network adapters. They're easy to connect, transport, and reposition for better reception.

**Figure 2-5:**
A wireless
PCI adapter.

Most computers built in the past ten years have at least two (and some have as many as eight) USB ports. If your computer has a USB port and you purchased a wireless USB network interface adapter, see Chapter 7 for more on setting up that adapter.

USB wireless NICs are sometimes a better choice than PC Cards or PCI cards because you can more easily move the device around to get a better signal, kinda like adjusting the rabbit ears on an old TV. If a desktop computer doesn't have a PC Card slot — most don't — but does have a USB port, you need to either install a PCI adapter or select a USB wireless network adapter.

If you're connecting an older computer via a USB NIC, check to see that that computer has a USB 2.0 *(Hi-Speed)* connection. The older, original, 1.0 version of USB has a much slower data transfer rate, and will potentially bog down your network connection. You can still use a USB 1.0 connection for a USB wireless NIC, but it's not an optimal method of connecting to your wireless network.

### Memory card wireless adapters

Most popular handheld personal digital assistant (PDA) computers and smartphones now come with wireless built right into them. If you still have an older PDA, you may be able to get it on your wireless network with a flash memory card wireless adapter. Many different kinds of flash memory cards are on the market (ask anyone who's shopping for a digital camera, and you'll be told more about SD, Micro SD, CF, Memory Stick, and the like than you'd ever want to hear). Most PDAs or smartphones use Compact Flash (CF) or Secure Digital (SD) cards, and you may be able to use that memory card slot to add wireless networking to your device.

Because wireless networking is being built into many of these devices, the market for memory card–style wireless adapters has shrunk, and many of the big manufacturers (such as Linksys) no longer make these products. You can still find CF or SD card wireless adapters from smaller specialty manufacturers, but they're typically a lot more expensive than the mainstream PC Card or USB adapters that you buy for a PC.

# Getting the (Access) Point

We want to talk some more about the central pivot point in your wireless network: the access point. Somewhat similar in function to a network hub, an *access point* in a wireless network is a special type of wireless station that receives radio transmissions from other stations on the wireless LAN and forwards them to the rest of the network. An access point can be a standalone device or even a computer that contains a wireless network adapter along with special access-point management software. Most home networks use a standalone AP, such as shown in Figure 2-6.

**Figure 2-6:**
A stand-
alone
access
point.

## Setting parameters to create your own personal network

Because many homes and businesses use wireless networking, a method is needed to distinguish one wireless network from another. Otherwise, your neighbor may accidentally send a page to the printer on your network. (That could be fun or that could be a little scary.) Three parameters can be used to uniquely identify each segment of a wireless network:

✔ **Network name:** When you set up your wireless network, you should assign a unique name to the network. Some manufacturers refer to the network name by one of its technical monikers — *service set identifier* (SSID) or perhaps *extended service set identifier* (ESSID). This can be confusing and comes up most often if you're using equipment from different manufacturers. Rest assured, however, that network name, SSID, and ESSID all mean the same thing.

If the AP manufacturer assigns a network name at the factory, it assigns the same name to every AP it manufactures. Consequently, you should assign a different network name to avoid confusion with other APs that may be nearby (like your neighbor's). *Note:* All stations and the AP on a given wireless network must have the same network name to ensure that they can communicate.

Assigning a unique network name is good practice, but don't think of the network name as a security feature. Most APs broadcast their network name, so it's easy for a hacker to change the network name on his or her computer to match yours. Changing the network name from the factory setting to a new name simply reduces the chance that you and your neighbor accidentally have wireless networks with the same network name.

✔ **Channel:** When you set up your wireless network, you have the option of selecting a radio channel. All stations and the access point must broadcast on the same radio channel to communicate. Multiple radio channels are available for use by wireless networks, and some of the newer wireless APs use multiple channels at once to increase the speed of the network. The number of channels available varies according to the type of wireless network you're using and the country in which you install the wireless network (due to differing regulations in each country). Wireless stations normally scan all available channels to look for a signal from an AP. When a station detects an AP signal, the station negotiates a connection to the AP.

✔ **Encryption key:** Because it's relatively easy for a hacker to determine a wireless network's name and the channel on which it's broadcasting, every wireless network should be protected by a secret encryption key unless the network is intended for use by the general public. Only someone who knows the secret key code can connect to the wireless network.

The most popular wireless network technology, *Wi-Fi,* comes with two types of security: Wired Equivalent Privacy (WEP) and Wi-Fi Protected Access (WPA). WEP uses the RC4 encryption algorithm and a private key phrase or series of characters to encrypt all data transmitted over the wireless network. For this type of security to work, all stations must have the private key. Any station without this key cannot get on the network. WPA, which is now built into all new Wi-Fi equipment and is a free upgrade on most older Wi-Fi equipment, is far more secure than WEP, and we recommend that you use it. WPA uses either Temporal Key Integrity Protocol (TKIP) or Advanced Encryption Standard (AES) encryption, which dynamically changes the security key as the connection is used. We talk about using both types of systems in Chapter 9, with our primary emphasis on WPA, and we promise we won't test you on these acronyms at all!

In the home, you'll most likely get your access point functionality through a *wireless home router* or a *wireless Internet gateway.* These devices combine the access point with a router, a wired Ethernet network switch, and (in the case of the gateway) a broadband modem. Similar devices may even throw in a print server. This Swiss Army knife–like approach is often a real bargain for use in a wireless home network. A standalone access point may be part of your network when you're adding a second wireless network to the mix (it would attach to one of the wired Ethernet ports on your router) or if you have some kind of fancy wired router in place (this isn't common, but some folks who telecommute from home may have a special router supplied by their company for accessing the corporate network).

We use the term *AP* throughout this chapter to mean either a standalone AP or the AP built into a wireless home router or gateway.

# Comparing infrastructure mode and ad hoc mode

Wireless networking devices can operate in one of two modes: infrastructure mode or ad hoc mode. The next two subsections describe the differences between these two modes.

### Infrastructure mode

When a wireless station (such as a PC or a Mac) communicates with other computers or devices through an AP, the wireless station is operating in *infrastructure mode*. The station uses the network infrastructure to reach another computer or device rather than communicate directly with the other computer or device. Figure 2-7 shows a network that consists of a wireless network segment with two wireless personal computers, and a wired network segment with three computers. These five computers communicate through the AP and the network infrastructure. The wireless computers in this network are communicating in infrastructure mode.

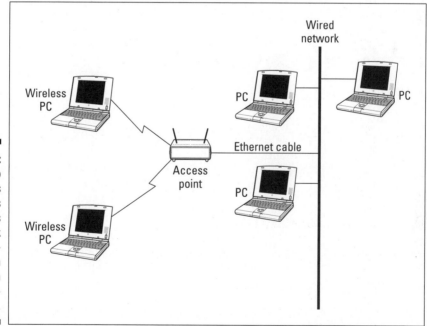

**Figure 2-7:**
The two wireless computers in this network communicate through the AP in infrastructure mode.

### Ad hoc mode

Whenever two wireless stations are close enough to communicate with each other, they're capable of establishing an *ad hoc network:* that is, a wireless network that doesn't use an AP. Theoretically, you could create a home network out of wireless stations without the need for an AP. It's more practical, however, to use an AP because it facilitates communication between many stations at once (as many as hundreds of stations simultaneously in a single wireless network segment, depending upon a particular AP's limitations). In addition, an AP can create a connection, or *bridge,* between a wireless network segment and a wired segment.

Ad hoc mode isn't often used in wireless home networks, but it could be used on occasion to connect two computers to transfer files where no AP is in the vicinity to create a wireless infrastructure.

We don't see any real advantage to using an ad hoc network in your home just to save a few bucks. You can buy a perfectly good wireless home router for under $50 (and even less when the sales are on!); the capabilities and ease-of-use you gain from this approach are well worth the minimal cost. And it's a heck of a lot easier to connect all of your computers to your Internet connection using the Infrastructure versus the ad hoc approach.

## Your Wireless Network's Power Station: The Antenna

The main interface between your access point or network interface card and the network is the antenna. Signals generated and received by your wireless gear are dependent on a high-quality antenna interface. To be smart in wireless networking, you need to know the basics about antennas. If you know how they work, you can better optimize your network.

The newest APs, which use the 802.11n standard (discussed in the later section titled "Exploring Industry Standards"), use a special technology called MIMO that uses advanced signal processing to "shape" the beam coming out of your antennas. These systems have a special antenna configuration optimized for this MIMO system; MIMO systems aren't designed to be modified with different antennas.

Access point antennas vary from manufacturer to manufacturer. Many APs have a single external antenna about 5 inches long. This type of antenna is a *dipole* antenna. Some APs have two external dipole antennas. Dual external antenna models should provide better signal coverage throughout the house. APs with dual antennas may transmit from only one of the antennas but receive through both antennas by sampling the signal and using whichever antenna is getting the strongest signal — a *diversity antenna system.*

Typical omnidirectional dipole antennas attach to the AP with a connector that enables you to position the antenna at many different angles; however, omnidirectional dipole radio antennas send and receive best in the vertical position.

The range and coverage of a Wi-Fi wireless AP used indoors is determined by these factors:

- **AP transmission output power:** This is the power output of the AP's radio, usually referred to as *transmission power,* or *TX power.* Higher power output produces a longer range. Wi-Fi APs transmit at a power output of less than 30 dBm (one watt). Government agencies around the world regulate the maximum power output allowed. APs for home use generally have power outputs in the range of 13 dBm (20 mW) to 15 dBm (31.6 mW). The higher the power rating, the stronger the signal and the better range your wireless network will have. Some wireless networking equipment manufacturers offer add-on amplifiers that boost the standard signal of the AP to achieve a longer range. We talk about boosters in Chapter 18.

- **Antenna gain:** The AP's antenna and the antennas on the other devices on the network improve the capability of the devices to send and receive radio signals. This type of signal improvement is *gain.* Antenna specifications vary depending on vendor, type, and materials. Adding a higher-gain antenna at either end of the connection can increase the effective range.

- **Antenna type:** Radio antennas both send and receive signals. Different types of antennas transmit signals in different patterns or shapes. The most common type of antenna used in wireless home networks, the dipole antenna, is described as *omnidirectional* because it transmits its signal in all directions equally. In fact, the signal from a dipole antenna radiates 360° in the horizontal plane and 75° in the vertical plane, to create a doughnut-shaped pattern. Consequently, the area directly above or below the antenna gets a very weak signal.

  Some types of antenna focus the signal in a particular direction and are referred to as *directional antennas.* In special applications where you want an AP to send its signal only in a specific direction, you could replace the omnidirectional antenna with a directional antenna. In a home, omnidirectional is usually the best choice, but that also depends on the shape of the home; some antennas are better for brownstones and multifloor buildings because they have a more spherical signal footprint rather than the standard flatish one.

- **Receive sensitivity:** The *receive sensitivity* of an AP or other wireless networking device is a measurement of how strong a signal is required from another radio before the device can make a reliable connection and receive data.

✔ **Signal attenuation:** A radio signal can get weaker as a result of interference caused by other radio signals because of objects that lie in the radio wave path between radios and because of the distance between the radios. The reduction in signal is *attenuation*. Read through Chapter 4 for a discussion of how to plan the installation of your wireless network to deal with signal attenuation.

To replace or add an antenna to an AP or other wireless device, you need to have a place to plug it in — as obvious a statement as that is, many antennas aren't detachable, and you can't add another antenna. Some access points use reverse TNC connectors that let optional antennas be used in 802.11b/g products.

Most 802.11n products handle the whole antenna situation differently than older 802.11g/b/a APs. That's because the 802.11n standard includes some new technologies that use multiple transmitters and antennas to increase range and speed. As a result, all the consumer-grade 802.11n APs we've seen do *not* include the ability to add on your own external antennas.

# Exploring Industry Standards

One of the most significant factors that has led to the explosive growth of personal computers and their effect on our daily lives has been the emergence of industry standards. Although many millions of personal computers are in use now around the world, only three families of operating system software run virtually all these computers: Windows, Mac OS, and Unix (including Linux). Most personal computers used in the home employ one of the Microsoft Windows or Apple Macintosh operating systems. The existence of this huge installed base of potential customers has enabled hundreds of hardware and software companies to thrive by producing products that interoperate with one or more of these industry-standard operating systems.

## Understanding antenna gain

Antenna gain is usually expressed in dBi units (which indicate, in decibels, the amount of gain an antenna has). An antenna with a 4 dBi gain increases the output power (the effective isotropic radiated power, or EIRP) of the radio by 4 dBm. The FCC permits IEEE 802.11 radios to have a maximum EIRP of 36 dBm when the device is using an omnidirectional antenna. The antennas included with wireless home networking equipment are typically omnidirectional detachable dipole antennas with gains of 2 dBi to 5 dBi. Some manufacturers offer optional high-gain antennas. (***Note:*** The maximum EIRP output permitted in Japan is 20 dBm; and the maximum output in Europe is only 10 dBm.)

# Understanding Wi-Fi channels

Now for a little talk about frequency bands used by the various Wi-Fi standards. In 1985, the FCC made changes to the radio spectrum regulation and assigned three bands designated as the industrial, scientific, and medical (ISM) bands. These frequency bands are

- **902 MHz–928 MHz:** A 26 MHz bandwidth

- **2.4 GHz–2.4835 GHz:** An 83.5 MHz bandwidth

- **5.15–5.35 GHz and 5.725 GHz–5.825 GHz:** A 300 MHz bandwidth

The FCC also opened some additional frequencies, known as Unlicensed National Information Infrastructure (U-NII), in the lower reaches of the five GHz frequencies.

The purpose of the FCC change was to encourage the development and use of wireless networking technology. The new regulation permits a user to operate, within certain guidelines, radio equipment that transmits a signal within each of these three ISM bands without obtaining an FCC license.

Wireless networks use radio waves to send data around the network. 802.11a uses part of the U-NII frequencies, and IEEE 802.11b and g use the ISM 2.4 GHz band. 802.11n can use either band, though not all 802.11n systems do (many use only the 2.4 GHz band).

An important concept when talking about frequencies is the idea of overlapping and non-overlapping channels. As we discuss in Chapter 18, signals from other APs can cause interference and poor performance of your wireless network. This happens specifically when the APs' signals are transmitting on the same (or sometimes nearby) channels. Recall that the standards call for a number of channels within a specified frequency range.

The frequency range of 802.11g, for example, is between 2.4 GHz and 2.4835 GHz, and it's broken up into fourteen equal-sized channels. (Only eleven can be used in the United States — any equipment sold for use here allows you to access only these eleven channels.) The problem is that these channels are defined in such a way that many of the channels overlap with one another — and with 802.11g, there are only three nonoverlapping channels. Thus, you wouldn't want to have channels 10 and 11 operating side by side because you would get signal degradation. You want noninterfering, nonoverlapping channels. So you find that people tend to use Channels 1, 6, and 11, or something similar. 802.11a doesn't have this problem because its eight channels, in the 5 GHz frequency band, don't overlap; therefore, you can use contiguous channels. As with 802.11b and g, however, you don't want to be on the same channel.

Computer hardware manufacturers recognize the benefits of building their products to industry standards. To encourage the adoption and growth of wireless networking, many companies that are otherwise competitors have worked together to develop a family of wireless networking industry standards that build on and interoperate with existing networking standards. As a result, reasonably priced wireless networking equipment is widely available from many manufacturers. You can feel safe buying equipment from any of these manufacturers because they're all designed to work together, with one important caveat: You need to make sure your gear can all "speak" using the same version of Wi-Fi.

The four major flavors of this wireless networking technology for LAN applications are IEEE 802.11a, 802.11b, 802.11g, and 802.11n — two of these, 802.11g and n are currently widely available. You just have to choose the flavor that best fits your needs and budget. (*Note:* There are other wireless standards, such as Bluetooth for short-range communications, for other applications in the home. We talk about these standards in Chapter 3 and elsewhere wherever their discussion is appropriate.)

## Wi-Fi history: 802.11b and 802.11a

In 1990, the IEEE adopted the document "IEEE Standards for Local and Metropolitan Area Networks," which provides an overview of the networking technology standards used in virtually all computer networks now in prevalent use. The great majority of computer networks use one or more of the standards included in IEEE 802; the most widely adopted is IEEE 802.3, which covers Ethernet.

IEEE 802.11 is the section that defines wireless networking standards and is often called *wireless Ethernet.* The first edition of the IEEE 802.11 standard, adopted in 1997, specified two wireless networking protocols that can transmit at either 1 or 2 megabits per second (Mbps) using the 2.4 GHz radio frequency band, broken into fourteen 5 MHz channels (eleven in the United States). IEEE 802.11b-1999 is a supplement to IEEE 802.11 that added subsections to IEEE 802.11 that specify the protocol used by Wi-Fi certified wireless networking devices.

The 802.11b protocol is backward compatible with the IEEE 802.11 protocols adopted in 1997, using the same 2.4 GHz band and channels as the slower protocol. The primary improvement of the IEEE 802.11b protocol was a technique that enabled data transmission at either 5.5 Mbps or 11 Mbps.

802.11b is an *old* standard. Most vendors no longer sell 802.11b equipment (or they sell one single line of products for customers who want to replace old gear). 802.11g, which we discuss in a moment, is compatible with 802.11b, but is much faster and not a penny more expensive. It has pretty much replaced 802.11b, particularly in the home networking market.

IEEE adopted 802.11a at the same time it adopted 802.11b. 802.11a specifies a wireless protocol that operates at higher frequencies than the 802.11b protocol and uses a variety of techniques to provide data transmission rates of 6, 9, 12, 18, 24, 36, 48, and 54 Mbps. 802.11a has 12 nonoverlapping channels in the United States and Canada, but most deployed products use only 8 of these channels.

Because it uses a different set of frequencies, 802.11a offers the following advantages over IEEE 802.11b:

✔ **Capacity:** 802.11a has about four times as many available channels, resulting in about eight times the network capacity: that is, the number of wireless stations that can be connected to the AP at one time and still be able to communicate.

✔ **Less competition:** Portable phones, Bluetooth, and residential microwave ovens use portions of the same 2.4 GHz radio frequency band used by 802.11b, which sometimes results in interference. By contrast, few devices other than IEEE 802.11a devices use the 5 GHz radio frequency band. *Note:* A growing number of cordless phones are starting to use this same frequency range, so the relative uncrowdedness of the 5 GHz spectrum isn't likely to last forever.

✔ **Improved throughput:** Tests show as much as four to five times the data link rate and throughput of 802.11b in a typical office environment. *Throughput* is the amount of data that can be transferred over the connection in a given period. (See the nearby sidebar, "Gauging your network's throughput.")

Like 802.11b, 802.11a has pretty much been superseded by newer technologies. (802.11n is significantly faster and can also use those higher frequencies used by 802.11a.) It's hard to find 802.11a wireless home routers or 802.11a network adapters on the market these days, with one exception. Some manufacturers carry *dual-band, dual-mode* networking gear that supports 802.11a *and* 802.11g in a single device — this equipment is often labeled *802.11a/b/g* because it also supports 802.11b equipment on the network. The idea behind this dual-band gear is that you can use the 802.11a frequencies for a fast channel for a specific purpose (such as sending audio and video from your PC to home theater) while using the 802.11g frequencies for all the normal Internet traffic in your network. 802.11n supports the same usage, with higher speeds, so many manufacturers have discontinued their a/b/g equipment. As we write in 2010, a few manufacturers (such as NETGEAR) still offer such wireless equipment.

# The outgoing standard: 802.11g

The third generation of IEEE standards-based products, which hit the streets 2003, is 802.11g. 802.11g is backward compatible with 802.11b wireless networking technology, but delivers the same transmission speeds as 802.11a — up to 54 Mbps — thus effectively combining the best of both worlds.

802.11g networking equipment is still widely available and can be considered a low-end approach to wireless networking. It's a bit cheaper than the newer 802.11n gear and is often included as standard in inexpensive new computers, netbooks, and so on.

## Gauging your network's throughput

Wi-Fi standards call for different speeds, up to 11 Mbps for 802.11b right on up to 300 Mbps for 802.11n. Radios attempt to communicate at the highest speed they can. If they encounter too many errors (dropped bits), the radio steps down to the next fastest speed and repeats the process until a strong connection is achieved. So, although we talk about 802.11n, for example, being up to 300 Mbps in speed, the reality is that unless you're very close to the AP, you're not likely to get that maximum rate. Signal fade and interference cut into your speeds, and the negotiated rate between the two devices drops.

That discussion represents just the speed. The actual throughput is another, related, matter. *Throughput* represents the rate at which the validated data flows from one point to another. It may take some retransmissions for that to occur, so your throughput is less than the negotiated speed of the connection. It may not be unusual for you to get only 40 to 50 percent of your maximum connection speed. In fact, that's rather normal.

 Although 802.11g works great, if you're considering doing more than just share Internet connections on your wireless network, you should consider investing in the newer 802.11n technology discussed in the next section. This newer standard provides speeds up to five times as fast as 802.11g or 802.11a, and can support both frequency ranges (the 2.4 GHz frequency supported by 802.11g as well as the 5 GHz frequency supported by 802.11a) — opening up more channels and decreasing the possibility that your neighbor's network will interfere with yours (a potential problem in urban and even suburban areas).

## *The next big thing: 802.11n*

After several years of deliberations (and to great cheering from us Wi-Fi geeks), the 802.11n was finalized in late 2009. But even before this standard was ratified, the folks at the Wi-Fi Alliance were busy certifying 802.11n gear. As we've mentioned before, certification is vitally important so that you can buy an 802.11n router from company X and an 802.11n network adapter from company Y and have full confidence that they'll work together. Figure 2-8 shows the Wi-Fi Alliance certification logo you'll find on 802.11n–compliant gear. (In this case, this gear is also compliant with 802.11b, a, and g.)

Here are a few key points to keep in mind about 802.11n:

   ✔ **Speed:** The theoretical maximum speed of 802.11n is 300 Mbps — five times faster than 802.11g. Real-world speeds have been measured in test centers at about 100 Mbps (still five times faster than 802.11g). With 802.11n, wireless can be a real alternative to wired networks, even for high-performance applications such as sending video around the home.

The 802.11n standard allows for a configuration that reaches a theoretical maximum speed of *600 Mbps*! (Wow!) This is done by utilizing wider radio channels (for the geek-friendly among us, 40 MHz channels instead of the standard 20 MHz), while simultaneously using four antennas at once. As we write, there's no 600 Mbps gear on the market, but we probably won't have to wait too long to see it appear. We can't wait, as you might imagine.

✔ **Distance:** 802.11n uses a special technology called *MIMO* (multiple inputs, multiple outputs) that modifies how signals are sent and received across your system's antennas. A MIMO system can send and receive data across more than one antenna at a time, and can use special signal processing to actually *beam form* the signal to extend its range and power in a certain direction. Although no one wants to quantify it exactly (or, to be more exact, everyone has a different figure), you can expect MIMO to extend the range of your wireless network by a factor of 2 or more.

The number of signals in use in an 802.11n MIMO system depends on the number of antennas in both the AP and the client device's 802.11n NIC. This is typically represented as a ratio like 3x2 (three antennas on the AP and 2 on the client). The fastest 802.11n systems in use today incorporate a 3x2 configuration; the potential 600 Mbps systems we discuss earlier will use a 4x4 configuration.

✔ **Channels:** 802.11n gear can use either the 2.4 or the 5 GHz channels, providing it with a considerably larger number of channels to choose from when looking for the best connection between stations on your wireless network (something 802.11n gear does automatically). The highest speeds of 802.11n also use something called *channel bonding*, where more than one channel is used at the same time (40 MHz of the radio airwaves instead of 20 MHz), to increase the amount of data sent across the network.

**Figure 2-8:**
Look for this logo on the box of your new 802.11n gear.

As a cost-saving measure, some 802.11n gear uses *only* 2.4 GHz frequencies. This equipment won't be able to use those relatively wide open 5 GHz channels but can still use the channel bonding feature for faster connections. Note that 802.11n gear that uses only the 2.4 GHz frequencies is *not* backward compatible with 802.11a (see the next bullet for more on this).

✔ **Backward compatibility:** 802.11n gear is backward compatible with any 802.11b or 802.11g gear, so your older network adapters will still work on a new 802.11n network. If your 802.11n router or access point works on the 5 GHz frequency range, it will also be backward compatible with 802.11a gear.

Adding 802.11a/b/g gear to an 802.11n network will *slow down* the whole network to a degree, but your network will still be faster than an 802.11a, b, or g network.

✔ **Cost:** Because it's a new technology, 802.11n equipment is about 50 percent more expensive than 802.11g equipment. The least expensive 802.11n gear available as we write is about $50 for a router supporting only the 2.4 GHz band — and closer to $100 for dual-band APs. You can expect these prices to drop rapidly as 802.11n becomes more mainstream, but 802.11n will still have a price premium over 802.11g for the next year or so.

As you shop for new wireless networking equipment, you'll have to make a decision between 802.11g and 802.11n. In general, we recommend that you strongly consider the 802.11n gear (the speed improvements are well worth the additional expense, in our minds). Regardless of the choice you make between 802.11g and n for your wireless *infrastructure* (routers and access points), we highly recommend that you select the 802.11n option when you're buying new computers (particularly laptops). There's not a big price difference here, and changing the internal networking cards on many computers (especially many laptops) isn't always a walk in the park — if you can get 802.11n put inside at the factory, so much the better. If you can't, well your device will be a bit slower than it can be on the network, but you can rest assured that it will definitely work — which is a very good thing.

# Understanding Wi-Fi Certifications

It's highly unlikely that every device on your network will be from the same manufacturer. Even if you're the world's biggest Apple fanatic or a major stockholder in HP, you're probably going to have something on your wireless network from another manufacturer, which means you can't rely on any single manufacturer to make sure that everything in your network works together properly. That's where standards and certifications fit into the wireless networking picture — they ensure that wirelessly outfitted devices work in the same way and can interoperate within a wireless home network no matter who makes them.

Two major groups do this for wireless home networks: the IEEE, who develop the technical standards that manufacturers follow when they design and build wireless gear, and the Wi-Fi Alliance, who test and certify interoperability of equipment within those technical standards. We discuss both groups in the following sections.

# The Institute for Electrical and Electronics Engineers (IEEE)

The Institute for Electrical and Electronics Engineers (IEEE) is a standards-making industry group that has for many years been developing industry standards that affect the electrical products we use in our homes and businesses. At present, products using the IEEE 802.11g and newer 802.11n standards are the overwhelming market leader in terms of deployed wireless networking products. Products that comply with this standard weren't the first wireless networking technology on the market — but they are now, by far, the dominant market-installed base.

# The Wi-Fi Alliance

In 1999, several leading wireless networking companies formed the Wireless Ethernet Compatibility Alliance (WECA), a nonprofit organization (`www.weca.net`). This group has recently renamed itself the Wi-Fi Alliance and is now a voluntary organization of more than 200 companies that make or support wireless networking products. The primary purpose of the Wi-Fi Alliance is to certify that IEEE 802.11 products from different vendors *interoperate* (work together). These companies recognize the value of building a high level of consumer confidence in the interoperability of wireless networking products.

The Wi-Fi Alliance organization has established a test suite that defines how member products will be tested by an independent test lab. Products that pass these tests are entitled to display the Wi-Fi trademark, which is a seal of interoperability. Although no technical requirement in the IEEE specifications states that a product must pass these tests, Wi-Fi certification encourages consumer confidence that products from different vendors will work together.

The Wi-Fi interoperability tests are designed to ensure that hardware from different vendors can successfully establish a communication session with an acceptable level of functionality. The test plan includes a list of necessary features. The features themselves are defined in detail in the IEEE 802.11 standards, but the test plan specifies an expected implementation.

# Chapter 3

# Exploring Bluetooth and Other Wireless Networks

Getting the most from computer technology is all about selecting the best and most dominant technology standards. The most dominant technology for wireless home networks is clearly the 802.11 (Wi-Fi) family of technologies defined by the 802.11a, 802.11b, 802.11g, and 802.11n standards (which we describe in Chapter 2). Wi-Fi is, simply, the reason why you're reading this book. It's the technology that has made wireless networks such a huge hit in the home.

But, Wi-Fi isn't the only game in town. You run into other home networking standards when you buy and install your Wi-Fi gear — standards that make it easier to get Wi-Fi where you want it.

Another popular wireless technology, which we discuss in this chapter, is *Bluetooth* (a short-range wireless networking system that's built into many cellular phones, cars, and those ubiquitous cordless headsets). Even if you intend to purchase and use only Wi-Fi wireless networking equipment, you should still be aware of Bluetooth. Who knows? It may come in handy.

In this chapter, we also talk about a few other key wired home networking standards (oops, did we say a dreaded word: *wired?*) such as *MoCA,* which builds networks over cable TV lines, and *HomePlug AV,* the standard for networking over your electrical power cables in your home. As surprising as it may seem, you can actually connect your computers, access points, and other devices over these existing in-wall cables. What's more, some wireless home routers come with these interfaces onboard to make it easier for you to install that AP wherever you want it. Isn't that nice? You betcha.

Finally, we talk about a few wireless networking standards that are designed not for *data* networking in the home, but rather for *control networks.* These standards, lead by ZigBee and Z-Wave, send signals around your home that let you automate and remotely control devices in the home. For example, you could use a ZigBee or Z-Wave system to turn on lights in remote locations, raise or lower drapes, or adjust your central heat or air conditioning. These are things that adventurous homeowners have been able to do for a long time by using wired solutions or unreliable powerline solutions such as X10; with these new wireless systems, anyone can get into home control and automation without a big wiring job and without the headaches of dealing with the AC powerlines.

# Who or What Is Bluetooth?

One of the most often talked about wireless standards, besides Wi-Fi, is *Bluetooth.* The Bluetooth wireless technology, named for the tenth-century Danish King Harald Blatand "Bluetooth," was invented by the L. M. Ericsson company of Sweden in 1994. King Harald helped unite his part of the world during a conflict around A.D. 960. Ericsson intended for Bluetooth technology to unite the mobile world. In 1998, Ericsson, IBM, Intel, Nokia, and Toshiba founded Bluetooth Special Interest Group (SIG), Inc., to develop an open specification for always-on, short-range wireless connectivity based on the Ericsson Bluetooth technology. Its specification was publicly released on July 26, 1999. In case you wonder how significant Bluetooth really is, take in this fact: Over 2 *billion* Bluetooth-equipped devices have been shipped since the technology hit the market about ten years ago. That ain't insignificant!

Sometimes a network of devices communicating via Bluetooth is described as a personal area network (PAN) to distinguish it from a network of computers often called a local area network (LAN).

The most common use of Bluetooth these days is in the world of mobile phones (and the geeky or cool — we'll leave the distinction up to you — Bluetooth hands-free headsets hanging off millions of ears out there). But there's more to Bluetooth than just phones. The following is a small sampling of existing Bluetooth products:

- ✔ Any of the *thousands* of mobile phones including Bluetooth
- ✔ Bluetooth wireless PC/Mac keyboards and mice
- ✔ Bluetooth hands-free headsets for mobile phones
- ✔ Bluetooth printers
- ✔ Bluetooth hands-free car kits that act as speakerphones in the car

Although intended as a wireless replacement for cables, Bluetooth is being applied to make it possible for a wide range of devices to communicate with each other wirelessly with minimal user intervention. The technology is designed to be low-cost and low-power to appeal to a broad audience and to conserve a device's battery life.

# Comparing Wi-Fi and Bluetooth

Wi-Fi and Bluetooth are designed to coexist in the network, and although they certainly have overlapping applications, each has its distinct zones of advantage.

The biggest differences between Wi-Fi and Bluetooth are

- ✔ **Distance:** Bluetooth is lower powered, which means that its signal can go only short distances (up to 10 meters, or a bit more than 30 feet). 802.11 technologies can cover your home, and in some cases more, depending on the antenna you use. Some Bluetooth devices operate under a high-powered scheme (called Class 1 Bluetooth devices), which can reach up to 100 meters. Most home Bluetooth devices don't have this kind of range, mainly because they're designed to be battery powered, and the shorter *Class 2* range of 10 meters provides a better trade-off between battery life and range.

- ✔ **Speed:** The latest versions of Wi-Fi can carry data at rates in the *hundreds* of megabits per second; the fastest existing Bluetooth implementations have a maximum data rate of 3 Mbps. So think of Wi-Fi as a networking technology that can handle high-speed transfers of the biggest files, and Bluetooth as something designed for lower speed connections (such as carrying voice or audio signals) or for the transfer or synchronization of smaller chunks of data (such as transferring pictures from a camera phone to a PC).

The current 3.0 version of Bluetooth incorporates a mode that allows data transfer speeds of up to 24 Mbps. It does this by using a Wi-Fi radio built into a Bluetooth 3.0 device, so the Bluetooth radio controls the transfer of the data, but the actual transfer occurs over Wi-Fi radio. We haven't seen any products hit the market with this feature (it was ratified in mid-2009), but we're keeping our eyes out.

- ✔ **Application:** Bluetooth is designed as a replacement for cables: that is, to get rid of that huge tangle of cables that link your mouse, printer, monitor, scanner, and other devices on your desk and around your home. In fact, the first Bluetooth device was a Bluetooth headset, which eliminated that annoying cable to the telephone that got in the way of typing. Many new cars are also outfitted with Bluetooth so that you can use your cellphone in your car, with your car's stereo speakers and an onboard microphone serving as your hands-free capability. Pretty neat, huh?

Wi-Fi (802.11a/b/g/n) and Bluetooth are similar in certain respects: They both enable wireless communication between electronic devices, but they're more complementary than direct competitors. Wi-Fi technology is most often used to create a wireless network of personal computers that can be located anywhere in a home or business. Bluetooth devices usually communicate with other Bluetooth devices in relatively close proximity.

The easiest way to distinguish Wi-Fi from Bluetooth is to focus on what each one replaces:

- **Wi-Fi is wireless Ethernet.** Wi-Fi is a wireless version of the Ethernet communication protocol and is intended to replace networking cable that would otherwise be run through walls and ceilings to connect computers in multiple rooms or even on multiple floors of a building.

- **Bluetooth replaces peripheral cables.** Bluetooth wireless technology operates at short distances — usually about 10 meters — and most often replaces cables that connect peripheral devices such as a printer, keyboard, mouse, or personal digital assistant (PDA) to your computer.

- **Bluetooth replaces IrDA.** Bluetooth can also be used to replace another wireless technology — Infrared Data Association (IrDA) wireless technology — that's already found in most laptop computers, PDAs, and even many printers. Although IR signals are secure and aren't bothered with radio frequency (RF) interference, IrDA's usefulness is hindered by infrared's requirement for line-of-sight proximity of devices. Just like the way your TV's remote control must be pointed directly at your TV to work, the infrared ports on two PDAs must be lined up to trade data, and your laptop has to be "pointing" at the printer to print over the infrared connection. Because Bluetooth uses radio waves rather than light waves, line-of-sight proximity isn't required.

Like Wi-Fi, Bluetooth can offer wireless access to LANs, including Internet access. Bluetooth devices can potentially access the Public Switched Telephone Network (PSTN: you know, the phone system) and mobile telephone networks. Bluetooth is able to thrive alongside Wi-Fi by making possible such innovative solutions as a hands-free mobile phone headset, print-to-fax, and automatic PDA, laptop, and cellphone/address book synchronization.

# Communicating with Bluetooth Devices: Piconets, Masters, and Slaves

Communication between Bluetooth devices is similar in concept to the ad hoc mode of Wi-Fi wireless networks (which we describe in Chapter 2). A Bluetooth device automatically and spontaneously forms informal WPANs, called *piconets,* with one to seven other Bluetooth devices that have the same Bluetooth profile. (A Bluetooth profile is simply a specific Bluetooth application — like a headset profile for attaching a wireless headset to a phone, or an audio profile for playing music over a wireless Bluetooth connection.) A capability called *unconscious connectivity* enables these devices to connect and disconnect almost without any user intervention.

Piconets get their name from merging the prefix *pico* (probably from the Italian word *piccolo,* which means small) and *net*work.

## Understanding Bluetooth connections

A particular Bluetooth device can be a member of any number of piconets at any moment in time (see Figure 3-1). Each piconet has one *master,* the device that first initiates the connection. Other participants in a piconet are *slaves.*

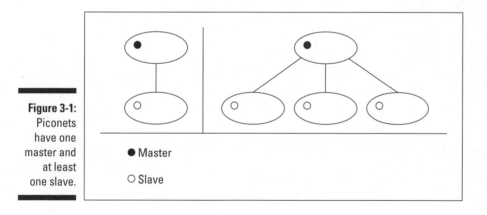

**Figure 3-1:**
Piconets
have one
master and
at least
one slave.

● Master

○ Slave

The three types of Bluetooth connections are

- ✔ **Data only:** When communicating data, a master can manage connections with as many as seven slaves.

- ✔ **Voice only:** When the Bluetooth piconet is used for voice communication (for example, a wireless phone connection), the master can handle no more than three slaves.

- ✔ **Data and voice:** A piconet transmitting both data and voice can exist between only two Bluetooth devices at a time.

Each Bluetooth device can join more than one piconet at a time. A group of more than one piconet with one or more devices in common is a *scatternet*. Figure 3-2 depicts a scatternet made up of several piconets.

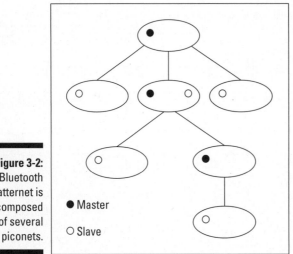

**Figure 3-2:**
A Bluetooth scatternet is composed of several piconets.

● Master
○ Slave

# *Transmitting data via Bluetooth*

Two things determine the data rate a connection can deliver: the amount of information sent in each packet over a Bluetooth connection and the type of error correction that's used. Bluetooth devices can send data over a piconet by using 16 types of packets. Sending more information in each packet (that is, sending longer packets) causes a faster data rate. Conversely, more robust error correction causes a slower data rate. Any application that uses a Bluetooth connection determines the type of packet used and, therefore, the data rate.

As mentioned, Bluetooth isn't nearly as fast as Wi-Fi — many Bluetooth devices reach a maximum data rate of 723 Kbps (compare that with 248 Mbps for 802.11n), but that's not usually important because Bluetooth is typically not used for transferring huge files and the like. The most common version of Bluetooth (Bluetooth 2.1) includes something called *EDR* (Enhanced Data Rate) that allows data transfers at speeds of up to 2.1 Mbps. (The raw speed is 3 Mbps; 2.1 is the actual data throughput rate.)

Both Wi-Fi (the 802.11b, g, and n versions) and Bluetooth use the 2.4 GHz frequency radio band, but note the significant differences in how these technologies use the band. Bluetooth radios transmit a signal strength that complies with transmission regulations in most countries and is designed to connect at distances from 10 centimeters to 10 meters through walls and other obstacles — although like any radio wave, Bluetooth transmissions can be weakened by certain kinds of construction material, such as steel or heavy concrete. Although Bluetooth devices can employ a transmission power that produces a range in excess of 100 meters, you can assume that most Bluetooth devices are designed for use within 10 meters of other compatible devices, which is fine for the applications for which Bluetooth is intended, such as replacing short-run cables.

## Understanding Bluetooth versions

Bluetooth has been around for a few years now and, like most technologies, has undergone some growing pains and revisions. In fact, multiple versions of Bluetooth-certified equipment are available, as newer and more capable variants of Bluetooth arrive on the market.

A common variant of Bluetooth is known as Bluetooth 1.2. This is basically a version of Bluetooth with all the bugs removed. Bluetooth 1.2 devices (most currently available devices, in other words) are *backward compatible* with earlier Bluetooth 1.0 and 1.1 devices. So, they work the same way, at the same speeds — just better. (Some technical advances in 1.2 allow most devices to have better real-world speeds.)

A growing number of Bluetooth devices support the *Bluetooth 2.1 + EDR* (extended data rate) standard. You can think of Bluetooth 2.1 + EDR versus the 1.x variants as being

similar to 802.11g versus 802.11b. It's faster (with a maximum speed three times as high — 2.1 Mbps versus around 700 Kbps for the EDR, or enhanced data rate), is better at resisting interference, and just basically works better all around. If you're shopping for something that may be sending larger files or requiring faster data transfers, such as a Bluetooth-equipped laptop (or a Bluetooth-enabled smartphone that can be used as a modem for your laptop), consider insisting on Bluetooth 2.1 and EDR.

Coming down the pike is the recently adopted Bluetooth 3.0 standard with potentially faster data transfer speeds — and the Bluetooth folks have adopted a new technology from Nokia called *Wibree* for the yet-to-be-ratified 4.0 version, which allows ultra-low-power implementations of Bluetooth for devices with limited battery or power supplies.

To make full use of the 2.4 GHz frequency radio band and to reduce the likelihood of interference, Bluetooth uses a transmission protocol that hops 1,600 times per second between 79 discrete 1 MHz-wide channels from 2.402 GHz to 2.484 GHz. Each piconet establishes its own random hopping pattern so that you can have many piconets in the same vicinity without mutual interference. If interference does occur, each piconet switches to a different channel and tries again. Even though Wi-Fi (802.11b, g, and n) and Bluetooth both use the 2.4 GHz band, both protocols use hopping schemes that should result in little, if any, mutual interference.

## Securing data in a Bluetooth network

To maintain the security of the data you send over a Bluetooth link, the Bluetooth standard includes several layers of security. First, the two Bluetooth devices that are connecting use *authentication* to identify each other. After the authentication process (sometimes called *pairing* in the Bluetooth world), the devices can begin sharing information. The data being sent across the radio link is *encrypted* (scrambled) so that only other authenticated devices have the key that can *decrypt* (unscramble) the data.

# Integrating Bluetooth into Your Wireless Network

Products that are the first to take advantage of Bluetooth technology include the following:

- ✔ Mobile phones
- ✔ Cordless phones
- ✔ PDAs
- ✔ Bluetooth adapters for PCs
- ✔ Bluetooth hands-free car kits
- ✔ Videocameras
- ✔ Videogaming consoles and controllers (the Nintendo Wii, for example)
- ✔ Digital still cameras
- ✔ Data projectors
- ✔ Scanners
- ✔ Printers

You can get a great idea of all the various ways that Bluetooth can be used in your network by going to the official Bluetooth products Web site at `www.bluetooth.com/products`, which lists over *10,000* products. We also go into great detail in Chapter 15 about some of the more common ways you use Bluetooth.

The current versions of Microsoft Windows, XP, Vista, and Windows 7, offer built-in support for Bluetooth devices, as do all versions of Mac OS (from 10.2 Jaguar on). And, of course, all the major smartphone OSs (iPhone OS, Windows Mobile, Nokia Symbian and Google Android) support Bluetooth.

In the following sections, we discuss how you can integrate Bluetooth into your wireless home network.

## Bluetoothing your mobile phone

One of the more interesting and most widely used applications of Bluetooth technology is for cellphones. In fact, nowadays it's hard to find a mobile phone that *doesn't* support Bluetooth. The most common use of Bluetooth in phones is providing hands-free operation, either using a Bluetooth headset or a hands-free Bluetooth system inside a car.

However, there's more to Bluetooth and your phone than just hands-free operation. Here are a few other ways that you can use Bluetooth in your wireless home network:

✔ **Synchronizing your phone with your PC or Mac.** Most smartphones (except the Apple iPhone, unfortunately) and many regular mobile phones (those in the industry call these feature phones) can use their Bluetooth connections to synchronize data from their PC. Bring your Bluetooth-enabled phone home, dock it in a power station near your PC, and it instantly logs on to your wireless home network via a Bluetooth connection to a nearby PC or Mac. Smartphones can update their address books, calendars, photos, music, and more with a Bluetooth PC — no cables required. All your events, to-do lists, grocery lists, and birthday reminders can be kept current just by bringing your Bluetooth-enabled product in range.

All you need is a Bluetooth adapter, like the one shown in Figure 3-3, for your PC (if it doesn't have Bluetooth built in already), some software from your phone manufacturer, and a few minutes of configuration, which we talk about in Chapter 15.

✔ **Tethering:** Another use of Bluetooth and mobile phones comes into play when your mobile phone includes a fast data plan (usually called *3G* networking, such as EV-DO, EDGE, or HSDPA, discussed in Chapter 13).

Most of these services can be used on your laptop computer when it's *tethered* to your mobile phone using Bluetooth (except, again unfortunately, the Apple iPhone — the phone supports it, but AT&T does not). The specifics on how this works vary from phone to phone and from mobile phone carrier to carrier, so we can't tell you exactly how to set this up for your particular situation, but your mobile phone carrier will provide instructions.

**WARNING!**

Many mobile phone providers charge an extra monthly fee (on top of your probably already high mobile data service fee) for tethering. Check your carrier's Web page for details before you do this.

**Figure 3-3:** Use a USB adapter to add Bluetooth capability to a desktop or laptop PC.

## *Wirelessly printing and transferring data*

Hewlett-Packard and other companies manufacture printers that have built-in Bluetooth wireless capability, which enables a computer that also has Bluetooth wireless capability to print sans printer cables. Bluetooth is used in other PC applications, such as wireless keyboards and wireless computer mice.

Another great use of Bluetooth wireless technology is to wirelessly transfer your digital photographs from your Bluetooth-enabled digital camera to your Bluetooth-enabled PC or Bluetooth-enabled printer — or even directly to your Bluetooth-enabled PDA. The newest wave of smartphones from several manufacturers includes wireless-enhanced models that have both Bluetooth and Wi-Fi built in. Wouldn't it be cool to carry your family photo album around on your Treo or iPhone to show off at the office?

# *Extending Your Wireless Home Network with "No New Wires" Solutions*

Wireless networking is great — so great that we wrote a book about it. But in many instances, wireless is just one way to do what you want; and often, wireless solutions need a hand from *wireline* (that is, wired) solutions to give you a solid, reliable connection into your home network.

A common application of wireline and wireless networking is a remote access point that you want to link back into your home network. Suppose that your cable modem is in your office in the basement, and that's where you have your main wireless router or access point. Now suppose that you want wireless access to your PC for your TV, stereo, and laptop surfing in the master bedroom on the third floor. Go for it! But don't be surprised to find that your AP's signal isn't strong enough for that application up there. How do you link one AP to the other?

You could install a wired Ethernet solution, which would entail running new CAT-5e/6 cables through your walls up to your bedroom. It's pretty messy if you ask us, but this approach certainly provides as much as 1,000 Mbps if you need it.

If you *can* run CAT-5e/6 cable and create an Ethernet network in your walls, you should, so by all means *do so!* But most folks can't do this, so these other solutions are the way to go.

A more practical way to get your cable modem up to the third floor is to run a *powerline* link between the two points. Think of this as one long extension cord between your router or AP in the first floor home office and your AP in your bedroom. Although not all of these powerline technology links can carry data as fast as an 802.11n Wi-Fi connection, they will likely exceed the speed of your Internet connection. If that's your primary goal, these are great, clean, and easy options for you.

The powerline networking concept takes a little getting used to. Most people are used to plugging an AC adapter or electrical cable into the wall and then another Ethernet cable into some other networking outlet for the power and data connections. With powerline networking, those two cables are reduced to one — the power cable! That electrical cord *is* your LAN connection — along with all the rest of the electrical cabling in your house. Cool, huh? To connect to your computer, you run an Ethernet cable from the powerline networking device (router, AP, and so on) to your computer, hub, or switch.

## Going hands-free in your car

Bluetooth technology is advancing into the arena of autos, too. Hands-free operation of mobile phones can be handy (pun intended) whenever you're talking on your phone, but when you're in a car it can be not only convenient but legally mandated. A number of cities and states in the U.S. (and beyond) ban cellphone use in a car unless a hands-free system is in place.

In response to interest by the automotive industry, the Bluetooth SIG formed the Car Profile Working Group in December 1999. This working group has defined how Bluetooth wireless technology will enable hands-free use of mobile phones in automobiles. Almost all car manufacturers now offer hands-free Bluetooth in their cars today. Using the Bluetooth in this car, you can pair your mobile phone and then use the steering wheel controls, navigation system screen and controller, and the car's audio system to control and make phone calls. Very cool. We talk about this topic more in Chapter 15.

If your car doesn't have built-in Bluetooth capabilities and you just can't imagine seeing yourself in the rear-view mirror with a Bluetooth headset jutting off your ear, you can install a hands-free kit in most cars without too much work. An even easier option is to consider a GPS navigation system; many aftermarket GPS systems now include Bluetooth and can use the speaker built into the GPS or connect to your car's stereo system for hands-free calling.

Networking on powerlines is no easy task. Powerlines are noisy, electrically speaking, with surges in voltage level and electrical interferences introduced by all sorts of devices both inside and outside the home. The state of the electrical network in a home is constantly changing, as well, when devices are plugged in and turned on. Because of this, powerline networking systems adopt a sophisticated and adaptive *signal-processing algorithm,* which is a technique used to convert data into electrical signals on the power wiring.

Powerline networking equipment is based on a standard called *HomePlug.* Most equipment available today, such as the NETGEAR XETB1001 Powerline Networking Kit (www.netgear.com, $120 retail), uses the original HomePlug standard (HomePlug 1.0), which offers speeds of 14 Mbps. (The WGX102 actually uses a proprietary version of HomePlug that is faster, offering speeds up to 85 Mbps.)

The HomePlug folks have developed a newer version, called HomePlug A/V, which supports speeds of over 200 Mbps, and products have started hitting the market using this faster standard. For example, the ZyXEL PLA450 (www.zyxel.com, about $120) is a wireless access point that uses this new HomePlug AV standard and can, under ideal conditions, reach this full 200 Mbps speed.

## Using other existing wires

Besides powerlines, your home will probably also have a number of phone lines and coaxial (cable TV) cables running through your walls. These wires can also potentially be used to extend the reach of your wireless network without installing new Ethernet cables in your home. We say *potentially* because although these wires definitely *can* do this job, no companies are currently shipping products to consumers that would let you use the wires this way.

In the past, a system called HomePNA (for Home Phoneline Networking Alliance) was widely available and did much the same thing that HomePlug and other powerline networking systems did, only leveraging the phone lines in your walls. Since the last edition of this book, HomePNA networking solutions have become unavailable in the consumer marketplace. That's too bad, because the technology has been greatly improved and works well. The companies behind the technology have, however, focused on the phone company market, rather than the consumer home networking market. HomePNA gear is found in many of the TV set-top boxes provided where phone companies offer television services — the technology is used to carry TV programming from a master set-top box to satellite set-top boxes throughout the home.

A similar technology, called MoCA (Multimedia over Coax) is used to carry TV programming and other data over the coaxial cables used for cable and satellite TV distribution. Again, like the current version of HomePNA, MoCA is a telephone (or cable) company technology — it's installed inside set-top boxes and not sold in the form of consumer equipment that can be purchased at the local Best Buy.

We think that this will change over time, and we hope that it does because phone lines and coaxial cables are better suited for carrying data than are powerlines. Keep your eyes peeled on these group's Web sites (www.homepna.org and www.mocalliance.org) to see when consumer products become available.

Although you can also buy powerline Ethernet bridge devices, which require a network cable connection to your PC or Mac, we highly recommend that you choose a powerline AP instead. In such a scenario, you connect one powerline Ethernet adapter to your main home wireless router (using an Ethernet cable) and plug that adapter into the wall. On the far end, you plug the powerline AP into the wall. And — *voilà!* — you have a fresh and nearby Wi-Fi signal in parts of your house that were previously out of reach from your main Wi-Fi access point.

# Controlling Your Home without Wires

Throughout this book, we talk about using wireless networks to send *data* around your home. This data could be what you traditionally think of as data (Web pages, e-mail, Word documents, and so on), or it could be different kinds of data (such as music MP3 files, digital photos, or video), but in the end it's all about getting one hunk of bits and bytes from one place in your home to another. The bits and the bytes — the *payload* of your networked communications — are the key here.

A completely different kind of wireless networking is control networking. In a *control network,* you aren't setting out to move data around the house; instead you are using a wireless network to send *commands* to devices in your home. In this instance you aren't sharing a data file with someone (or some device in your home) so much as telling it what to do (you bossy person you!).

## Understanding how home control networks work

Home control has been around a long time (we've been writing about it for over a decade, and it existed for decades before that), but traditional home control systems used complicated (and expensive) proprietary wiring systems or an old powerline networking system called X10.

The big news in home control, however, is the introduction of wireless networking into the mix. Wireless home control networks are designed around extremely low-power and low-cost chips that can (eventually) be built right into all sorts of appliances and electrical devices in the home.

Home control networks are *low-speed* networks. Because home control networks don't need to be concerned with carrying a big fat stream of high-definition data or the 80 megabyte Windows update du jour, they can get away with relatively puny data rates in the name of cost savings. (It doesn't take a lot of bandwidth to say "dim the lights in the hall.")

In another effort to trim expenses, home control networks are short range. (The chips can be smaller and cheaper if they don't transmit as much power as, for example, an 802.11n chip.) This may seem a bit counterintuitive — after all, home control systems won't work well if you can't reach the devices in your home that you want to control — but these networks overcome the issue of short range by using a *mesh topology.* Mesh means that each radio in the system can talk to every other radio, and in doing so they can retransmit the commands you send throughout the home. The most common metaphor here is the frog in the lily pond — the frog can't jump all the way across the pond in one fell swoop, but he can bounce from pad to pad until he finds his way across. A wireless home control network does the same thing, "organizing" itself and providing a route throughout the home for your control signals.

The network effect is in full effect in mesh networks like this. In case you're not familiar with it, the *network effect* states that the value of networked devices is exponentially related to the number of those devices. (For example, if only one fax machine existed in the world, it would be useless; if millions exist, they can be *very* useful.) A similar thing is true for mesh networked home control devices (called *modules*). One or two would work okay, if they were near each other, but when a home has dozens (or even hundreds), all sorts of devices can communicate with each other, and the whole network will perform significantly better.

## Exploring wireless networking standards: ZigBee and Z-Wave

The two main technology competitors for this marketplace are

- ✔ **ZigBee:** ZigBee is a wireless automation networking standard based on an international standard (called IEEE 802.15.4 — similar to the 802.11 standards used for Wi-Fi networks). As we mention earlier, ZigBee systems use a peer-to-peer networking infrastructure, called *mesh networking,* to reach throughout the home. ZigBee provides a data rate of 250 Kbps, while using chips that are inexpensive to manufacture. A group called the ZigBee Alliance (www.zigbee.org) — similar to the Wi-Fi Alliance — is helping manufacturers bring ZigBee products to market and helping ensure that the products work well together. As we write, only a few dozen ZigBee products are on the market, but dozens of manufacturers have joined the alliance.

- ✔ **Z-Wave:** A Danish semiconductor company called Zensys (www.zen-sys.com) has developed a competitor to ZigBee called Z-Wave. Z-Wave is a wireless, mesh, peer-to-peer automation networking protocol that's similar to ZigBee. Z-Wave systems operate at speeds of up to 9.6 Kbps (slower than ZigBee but still more than fast enough for home automation and control). Z-Wave products are still new to the market, but several major manufacturers, such as Leviton (www.leviton.com) and Wayne Dalton (www.wayne-dalton.com), are shipping products using Z-Wave.

ZigBee and Z-Wave are similar systems that *do not work together*. That is to say, a ZigBee chip and a Z-Wave chip can't talk to each other and work together in a home control network. But they can both be installed in the same home without causing interference nightmares. So while your ZigBee and Z-Wave networks can't directly interoperate, there's no problem with having both in your home (if you choose to do so) — for example, you could have a Z-Wave lighting control system and use ZigBee to control your heating and air-conditioning systems.

ZigBee and Z-Wave chips can be integrated directly into an appliance or electrical device (this will be more common in the future), or they can be integrated into a *control module* (a device that sits between your control network and the thing you want to control, and translates network commands into commands that the end device understands, such as on or off). In Chapter 14 we talk about some common ZigBee and Z-Wave devices, how they work, and how you can integrate them into your home.

# Part II
# Making Plans

The 5th Wave                    By Rich Tennant

"That's it! We're getting a wireless network for the house."

# In this part . . .

This part of the book helps you plan for installing your wireless home network — from deciding what you will connect to the network to making buying decisions and planning the installation of wireless networking equipment in your home. It used to be easy when there were only a few products on the market and only a few ways to get wireless into your house. Now, you can outfit your home in a myriad of ways, from devices that attach to your TV (or the TV itself!) to Wi-Fi–enabled cellphones to trusty old access points. We'll help you figure out a good, solid plan based on what you need — not what happens to be on sale at your local electronics store.

# Chapter 4

# Planning a Wireless Home Network

*W*e're sure that you've heard this sage advice: "He who fails to plan, plans to fail." On the other hand, management guru and author Peter Drucker says, "Plans are only good intentions unless they immediately degenerate into hard work." Because you're going to be spending your hard-earned money to buy the equipment necessary for your wireless network, we assume that you want to do a little planning before you start building your network. But, if you prefer to shoot first and aim later, feel free to skip this chapter and move on to Chapter 5.

In this chapter, we show you how to plan a wireless home network — from selecting the right wireless technology (there are several variants), to deciding what things to connect and where to connect them, to the all-important act of budgeting. You also find out about other issues you should consider when planning your home network, including connecting to the Internet; sharing printers, other peripherals, and fun, noncomputer devices; and security.

When you're ready to begin buying the wireless home networking parts (if you haven't done so already), head to Chapter 5, where we give detailed advice about buying exactly the equipment you need. In Part III, we show you how to set up and install your wireless home network.

# Deciding What to Connect to the Network

Believe it or not, some technogeeks have a computer in every room of their house. We have some close friends who fit into that category (including, well, ourselves). You may not own as many computers as we do (Danny has more than 20 in his house, and Pat lags behind with only 6, but for three people, how many do you really need?), but you probably own more than one, and we're guessing that you have at least one printer and some other peripherals. You're wirelessly networking your home for a reason, no matter whether it's to share that cool, new color inkjet printer (or scanner or digital video recorder), to play your computer-based video files on your new widescreen TV, or to give every computer in the house always-on access to the Internet. Whatever your reason, the first thing you must do when planning a wireless home network is to determine what you want connected to the network.

## Counting network devices

The first step to take in planning a network is to count the number of devices you want to attach to your network — that means any computer or device that you want attached to your broadband Internet connection, to your file servers, or to shared resources, such as printers. You almost certainly will connect to your network each of the computers you use regularly.

Next, consider devices that aren't necessarily computers in the traditional sense but that can benefit from a network connection — for example, the printers we mention in the preceding paragraph. You don't need to connect a printer directly to a single PC in a networked environment — you can connect it to a device known as a *print server* and let all your networked PCs access it. Similarly, you can connect devices such as *NAS* (Network Attached Storage), which let you store big files in a centralized location (or even do PC backups over the network). In Chapter 14, we talk about a whole big bunch of networkable devices that can go on your wireless LAN.

If you're an audiophile or just enjoy digital media, you should consider adding your home entertainment system to your network so that you can share MP3 files, play video games, and watch DVDs from anywhere in your house, wirelessly! (These cool gadgets are covered in Chapters 11 and 12.) Many portable/mobile devices have built-in Wi-Fi these days, too.

As you plan out your network and count devices, consider that some devices already have all the wireless network capabilities they need built in. For example, most laptop computers and some printers support at least 802.11g wireless networking — so you should put them on your list, but you don't need to spend any money to add them to your network.

Don't forget to count *all* the devices you're going to be connecting, even if a lot of them already have Wi-Fi built-in. You may not need to buy network adapters for these devices, but you're going to need to make sure that your AP (access point) can handle that many connections. You may be thinking, "Heck, there's no way I can get past the 30 or 40 (or higher) device limit on most APs." Well think again. Did you add in all of your networked gaming devices? Your networked Blu-ray disc player? That new LCD flat panel TV with built-in Wi-Fi? Oh yeah? Well, did you add in all of the iPhones, Blackberries, Android phones, Zunes, iPod touches, Nintendo DSs, iPads, and every other portable device under the sun? You should! A few otherwise great little APs (like Apple's very cost-effective Airport Express) have relatively low limits on the number of devices they can connect at once, and you could find yourself running out of room on the AP without really trying.

## Deciding what devices to connect with wires and what to connect wirelessly

After you know *what* you're networking, you need to choose *how* to network it. By that, we mean that you have to decide what to connect to your home's network with wires and what you should use wireless networking for. At first glance, this decision may seem obvious. You would expect us to always recommend using wireless because this book talks about wireless networks; however, using both wired and wireless connections can sometimes make the most sense.

Wireless network devices and wired network devices can be used on the same network. Both talk to the network and to each other by using a protocol known as Ethernet. (You should be getting used to that term by now if you've been reading from the beginning of the book. If not, read through Chapters 1 and 2 for more information about networking technology.)

The obvious and primary benefit of connecting to a network wirelessly is that you eliminate wires running all over the place. But, if two devices are sitting on the same desk or table — or are within a few feet of each other — connecting them wirelessly may be pointless. You can get Ethernet cables for $5 or less; an equivalent wireless capability for two devices may top $100 when everything is said and done.

## Selecting a wireless technology

After you know what you're networking *and* what will be on your wireless network, you have to decide how to network wirelessly. As we discuss extensively in Chapter 2, four main variants of wireless networking technologies exist: 802.11a, 802.11b, 802.11g and 802.11n.

Collectively, all these technologies are usually referred to as *Wi-Fi,* which isn't a generic term, but, rather, refers to a certification of *interoperability.* The folks at the Wi-Fi Alliance (www.wi-fi.org) do extensive testing of new wireless gear to make sure that it works seamlessly with wireless equipment from different manufacturers. When it works, it gets the Wi-Fi logo on the box, so you can rest assured that it will work in your network.

Wi-Fi certified gear works together — as long as it's of a *compatible* type. That means that any 802.11b, 802.11g, or 802.11n Wi-Fi certified gear works with any other equipment of that type; similarly, any 802.11a Wi-Fi certified gear works with any other 802.11a and 5 GHz capable 802.11n gear that has been certified. (Note that not all 802.11n gear is 5 GHz capable — if a particular piece of equipment supports this, it will say so and will also be 802.11a certified.) The 802.11b and g gear *does not* work with 802.11a gear, even if it has all been certified, because they work on different radio frequencies and cannot communicate with each other.

The discussion of wireless technology quickly degenerates into a sea of acronyms and technospeak. If you need a refresher on this alphabet soup — or to begin from square one — Chapter 2 is a primer on jargon, abbreviations, and other nuts-and-bolts issues.

For home users, the three most important practical differences among 802.11a, 802.11b, 802.11g, and 802.11n networks are speed, price, and compatibility:

✔ **802.11b** is an older standard that is no longer used. You would be hard pressed to find any 802.11b in your network, and only if you have been buying *legacy* equipment at flea markets or electronic junk yards.

✔ **802.11g** equipment has been the dominant standard in use for about seven years.

✔ **802.11a** can still be found in some special-use corporate environments, but it's no longer used in the home. It is as fast as 802.11g, costs much more, and has a shorter range.

✔ **802.11n** is five times faster than 802.11a and 802.11g and is 22 times faster than 802.11b.

- ✔ **802.11a and 802.11b** are *not* compatible.

- ✔ **802.11a and 802.11g** are *not* compatible.

- ✔ **802.11b and 802.11g** *are* compatible.

- ✔ **802.11n** is compatible with all other standards but at the cost of its higher speed — when you add 802.11a, b, or g gear to an 802.11n network, you slow down the ultimate *throughput* or speed of that network.

The 802.11n standard is compatible with all other standards, but not all 802.11n equipment supports both the 2.4 GHz (802.11b and g) and 5 GHz (802.11a) frequencies — many support only 2.4 GHz. An AP that includes 802.11n should work with any other device as well. So if you've got some legacy 802.11g gear around the house, you can confidently install an 802.11n AP.

Although 802.11g is fast enough (that is, faster than most Internet services), it's not as good at in-home services like sending video from place to place. So while you still *can* buy 802.11g APs, we recommend that you don't. The speed, range, and compatibility of 802.11n are more than worth the (only slightly larger) price tag.

## Choosing an access point

The most important and typically most expensive device in a wireless network is the *access point* (AP; also sometimes called a *base station*). An AP acts like a wireless switchboard that connects wireless devices on the network to each other and to the rest of the wired network; it's required to create a wireless home network. Figure 4-1 depicts three PCs connected wirelessly to each other through an AP.

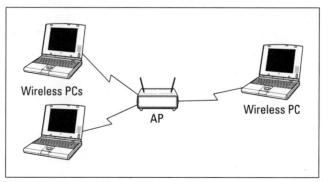

**Figure 4-1:**
Three PCs connected wirelessly to each other through an AP.

The vast majority of APs now available aren't just access points. Instead, most incorporate the functionality of a *broadband router* (which connects multiple computers to an Internet connection), a *network switch* (which connects multiple wired computers together), and even a *firewall* (which helps keep "bad guys" off your network). We call such APs *wireless routers*.

The most popular wireless routers for use in home networks are those that can do one or more of the following:

- **Connect wired PCs:** A *switch* is an enhanced version of a network hub that operates more efficiently and quickly than a simple hub. By building a switch inside the AP, you can use that one device to connect PCs to your network by using either wired network adapters or wireless adapters. We cover hubs and switches in more detail in Chapter 1.

- **Assign network addresses:** Every computer on a network or on the Internet has its own address: its Internet Protocol (IP) address. Computers on the Internet communicate — they forward e-mail, Web pages, and the like — by sending data back and forth from IP address to IP address. A Dynamic Host Configuration Protocol (DHCP) server dynamically assigns private IP addresses to the computers on your home network so that they can communicate. You could use a software utility in Windows (or Mac OS) to manually assign an IP address to each computer, but that process is tedious and much less flexible than automatic address assignment.

- **Connect to the Internet:** With a wireless router between a broadband modem and your home network, all computers on the network can access the Internet directly. (See the "Connecting to the Internet" section, later in this chapter, for more about the Network Address Translation feature that makes Internet sharing possible and for more on Internet connectivity.)

- **Add a print server:** A *print server* enables you to connect a printer directly to the network rather than connect it to one of the computers on the network. See the "Adding printers to the network" section, later in this chapter. Some wireless routers also let you use that same USB connector for other purposes, such as attaching an external hard drive as shared file storage on your network.

- **Provide firewall security:** A *firewall* is a device that basically keeps the bad guys off your network and out of your computers. We talk much more about firewalls in Chapters 9 and 10, but for now just know that a firewall is typically included in your access point to provide network security.

- **Be combined with a modem:** If you're a cable Internet or DSL subscriber, you may be able to use your own modem rather than lease one from your Internet service provider (ISP). In that case, consider purchasing a modem that's also a wireless AP. A cable or DSL modem combined with a wireless Internet gateway is the ultimate solution in terms of installation convenience and equipment cost savings.

You typically can't buy a modem/AP/router combination off the shelf (or at most Internet retailers) like you can buy a nonmodem AP/router. You get these all-in-one devices directly from your broadband service provider in almost all cases. It's worth noting, however, that broadband service providers don't want to have to support you if you need help configuring your wireless network (it costs them a lot of money to provide technical customer support), so the wireless devices they offer are usually very simple to set up, but also don't typically provide as much functionality (like print servers or guest networks) as separate AP devices. In fact, service provider–provided (say that fast three times) wireless devices will typically be set up to allow you as little flexibility as possible in terms of configuration and set up, so don't expect to be able to set them up in any way besides the factory default.

## Deciding where to install the access point

If you've ever experienced that dreaded dead zone while talking on a cellular phone, you know how frustrating poor wireless coverage can be. To avoid this situation within your wireless home network, you should strive to install your wireless network equipment in a way that eliminates dead wireless network zones in your house. Ideally, you determine the best placement of your AP so that no spot in your house is left uncovered. If that isn't possible, you should at least find any dead zones in your house to optimize your signal coverage.

To achieve optimum signal coverage, the best place to install an AP is near the center of your home. Think about where you will place the AP when you make your buying decision. All APs can sit on a shelf or table, but some APs can also be mounted to a wall or ceiling. When making your AP selection, ensure that it can be installed where it works best for the configuration of your house as well as stays out of reach of your little ones or curious pets.

The position of the access point is critical because your entire signal footprint emanates from the AP in a known way, centered from the AP's antennas. Sometimes, not enough consideration is given to the positioning of the access point because it so often works well out of the box, just sitting on a table.

Other people install the AP wrong in the first place. For example, probably one of the worst manufacturing decisions was to put mounting brackets on access points. People get the impression that you should then — duh — mount them on the wall. That's great except for the fact that, depending on the antenna, you may just kill most of your throughput. You see, when an antenna is flush up against a wall, as is typical in a wall-mount situation, the signals of the antenna reflect off the wall back at the antenna, causing interference and driving down throughput precipitously. Yech. (But you see, customers *want* a wall-mount bracket, so product managers at wireless LAN companies decided that they had to give it to them.) The best mounting is 6 or more inches off the wall.

The vertical positioning of the mounting point is important as well. Generally, you have more interference lower to the ground. If you did a cross section of your house in 1-foot intervals, when you get higher and higher, you would see less on your map. Thus, signals from an access point located on a shelf low to the ground will find more to run into than the ones that are mounted higher. Although this may sound like common sense, consider that most DSL and cable modems are installed by technicians who are used to installing phone and cable TV lines. How many of these are generally located 5 feet off the floor? They're not; they tend to be along the floorboards and low to the ground or in the basement. It's not surprising that a combined DSL access point router would be plugged in low to the ground, too.

See where we're going with this? You don't care where your cable modem is, but you should care where your AP is located. And, if you have an integrated product, you're probably tempted to swap out the cable modem for the cable modem access point. Simply moving that unit higher almost always does a world of good.

Moving an AP out of the line of sight of microwaves, cordless phones, refrigerators, and other devices is a good idea, too. Mounting the AP in the laundry room off the kitchen doesn't make a great deal of sense if you plan to use the AP primarily in rooms on the other side of the kitchen. Passing through commonly used interferers (all those metal appliances and especially that microwave oven when it's in use) generally isn't a smart move.

### Factors that affect signal strength

Many variables affect whether you get an adequate signal at any given point in your house, including these factors:

✔ **The distance from the AP:** The farther away from the AP, the weaker the signal. Wi-Fi 802.11g networks, for example, promise a maximum operating range of 100 feet at 54 Mbps to 300 feet at 1 Mbps. Indoors, a realistic range at 54 Mbps is about 60 feet. 802.11n networks have a significantly longer range outdoors of up to 750 feet and an indoor range up to 210 feet at 300 Mbps. The range differs from vendor to vendor as well.

✔ **The power of the transmitter:** Wi-Fi APs transmit at a power output of less than 30 dBm (one watt). So there's not much difference here between different vendors, but if you want to get out your slide rule and do some calculations, well . . . now you know what number to plug in.

✔ **The directivity or gain of the antennas attached to the AP and to wireless network adapters:** Different antennas are designed to provide different radiation patterns. That's a fancy way of saying that some are designed to send radio waves in all directions equally, but others concentrate their strength in certain directions. We talk more about this topic in Chapter 6, but the thing to keep in mind here is that different brands and models of access points have different kinds of antennas designed for different applications. Check out the specifications of the ones you're looking at before you buy them.

With MIMO-based 802.11n APs, you probably won't have an antenna that you can aim or even see, but many 802.11n APs use some highfalutin *beam forming* technologies to aim signals around your house. And even if your particular model doesn't do this, other characteristics of 802.11n (like the fact that most units use multiple antennas that each carry their own data stream over a physically separate signal path) mean you're likely to get significantly better range.

✔ **The construction materials used in the walls, floors, and ceilings:** Some construction materials are relatively transparent to radio signals, but other materials — such as marble, brick, water, paper, bulletproof glass, concrete, and especially metal — tend to reflect some of the signal, thus reducing signal strength.

✔ **Your house plan:** The physical layout of your house may not only determine where it's practical to position an AP but also affect signal strength, because the position of walls and the number of floors, brick fireplaces, basements, and so on can partially or even completely block the wireless network's radio signal.

✔ **Client locations:** Reception is affected by the distance from the AP to the rooms in your house where someone will need wireless network access.

✔ **Stationary physical objects:** Objects permanently installed in your home — such as metal doors, heating ducts, and brick fireplaces — can block some, or all, of the signal to particular spots in your house.

✔ **Movable physical objects:** Other types of objects, including furniture, appliances, plants, and even people, can block enough of the signal to cause the network to slow down or even to lose a good connection.

✔ **APs:** Interference can also be caused by the presence of other APs. In other words, if you have a big house (too big for a single AP to cover), you have to keep in mind that in parts of the house — like in the area that's pretty much directly between the two APs — you find that the radio waves from each AP can interfere with the other. The same is true if you live in a close-packed neighborhood in which a lot of people have APs for their home networks. Check out the following subsection for more information regarding this phenomenon.

# Wireless interference in the home

Probably the single biggest performance killer in your wireless home network is interference in the home. The Federal Communications Commission (FCC) set aside certain unlicensed frequencies that could be used for low-power wireless applications. In specific frequency bands, manufacturers can make (and you can use) equipment that doesn't require a license from the FCC for the user to operate. This is different from, for example, buying a 50,000-watt radio transmitter and blasting it over your favorite FM radio frequency band, which would be a major no-no because those bands are licensed for certain power levels.

As a result, all sorts of companies have created products (including cordless phones, wireless radio frequency [RF] remote controls, wireless speakers, TV set extenders, and walkie-talkies) that make use of these frequency bands. If you have lots of wireless devices already in your home, they may use some of the same frequency bands as your wireless home network.

Another form of wireless interference comes from devices that emit energy in the same bands, such as microwave ovens. If you have a cordless phone with its base station near a microwave and you notice that the voice quality degrades every time you use the microwave, that's because the micro (radio) waves are in the same radiation band as your cordless phone. Motors, refrigerators, and other home consumer devices do the same thing.

What's the answer? The good news is that you can deal with almost all these by knowing what to look for and being smart about where you place your equipment. If your access point is in the back office and you want to frequently work in the living room with your laptop — but your kitchen is in the middle — you may want to look at adding a second access point in the living room and linking it with the office via any of a number of alternative connections options (which we talk about in Chapter 3) that are immune to the problems we mention here.

Remember these specific things to look for when shopping. You see cordless phones operating primarily in the 900 MHz, 2.4 GHz, and 5 GHz frequencies. The 900 MHz phones pose no problems — but are also almost impossible to find these days — and the 2.4 GHz and 5 GHz phones interfere with your wireless network signals (in the 802.11b/g and 802.11a frequency ranges, respectively). Just know that cordless phones and wireless home networks really don't like each other much. You can find cordless phones that are designed not to interfere with your wireless network. These phones are usually labeled clearly that they're designed to work within and around wireless networks. We have tested a few, and while they do work much better — your network connection doesn't drop out when you answer the phone — they still cause enough interference that your connection will slow down a noticeable amount.

If you have problems with your cordless phone interfering with your wireless network (and not everyone does, so we don't want to overstate the issue), consider buying a cordless phone that uses the *DECT* (Digital Enhanced Cordless Telecommunications) system. These phones use completely different radio frequencies than any version of Wi-Fi (or Bluetooth, for that matter) and they're also — by the way — the longest range, best-sounding cordless phones that we've ever used.

You should attempt to keep a direct line between APs, residential gateways, and the wireless devices on your network. A wall that's 1.5 feet thick, at a 45 degree angle, appears to be almost 3 feet thick. At a 2 degree angle, it looks more than 42 feet thick. Try to make sure that the AP and wireless adapters are positioned so that the signal travels straight through a wall or ceiling for better reception.

### RF interference

Nowadays, many devices that once required wires are now wireless, and this situation is becoming more prevalent all the time. Some wireless devices use infrared technology, but many wireless devices, including your wireless network, communicate by using radio frequency (RF) waves. As a consequence, the network can be disrupted by RF interference from other devices sharing the same frequencies used by your wireless network.

Among the devices most likely to interfere with 802.11g and 802.11n networks are microwave ovens and cordless telephones that use the 2.4 GHz or 5 GHz band. The best way to avoid this interference is to place APs and computers with wireless adapters at least 6 feet away from the microwave and the base station of any portable phone that uses either band.

Bluetooth devices also use the 2.4 GHz band, but the hop pattern of the Bluetooth modulation protocol all but ensures that any interference is short enough in duration to be negligible.

Because relatively few devices are trying to share the 5 GHz frequencies used by some 802.11n devices, your network is less likely to experience RF interference if it's using 802.11n. If the 5 GHz frequency is the only clear band, 802.11n will work but at the cost of absolute distance.

You should also try to keep all electric motors and electrical devices that generate RF noise through their normal operation — such as monitors, refrigerators, electric motors, and universal power supply (UPS) units — at least 3 and preferably 6 feet away from a wireless network device.

### Signal obstacles

Wireless technologies are susceptible to physical obstacles. When deciding where best to place your APs, look at Table 4-1, which lists obstacles that can affect the strength of your wireless signals. The table lists common household obstacles (although often overlooked) as well as the degree to which the obstacle is a hindrance to your wireless network signals.

### Table 4-1     How Common Household Items Affect a Wi-Fi Signal

| Obstruction | Degree of Attenuation | Example |
|---|---|---|
| Open space | Low | Backyard |
| Wood | Low | Inner wall; door; floor |
| Plaster | Low | Inner wall (older plaster has a lower degree of attenuation than newer plaster) |
| Synthetic materials | Low | Partitions; home theater treatments |
| Cinder block | Low | Inner wall; outer wall |
| Asbestos | Low | Ceiling (older buildings) |
| Glass | Low | Nontinted window |
| Wire mesh in glass | Medium | Door; window |
| Metal tinted glass | Medium | Tinted window |
| Body | Medium | Groupings of people (dinner table) |
| Water | Medium | Damp wood; aquarium; in-home water treatments |
| Bricks | Medium | Inner wall; outer wall; floor |
| Marble | Medium | Inner wall; outer wall; floor |
| Ceramic (metal content or backing) | High | Ceramic tile; ceiling; floor |
| Paper | High | Stack of paper stock, such as newspaper piles |
| Concrete | High | Floor; outer wall; support pillar |
| Bulletproof glass | High | Windows; door |
| Silvering | Very high | Mirror |
| Metal | Very high | Inner wall; air conditioning; filing cabinets; reinforced concrete walls and floors |

You may want to consider reading Chapter 18 on troubleshooting before you finish your planning. Some good tips in that chapter talk about setting up and tweaking your network.

## The RF doughnut

The shape of the radio signal transmitted to the rooms in your home is determined by the type of antenna you have attached to the AP. The standard antenna on any AP is an *omnidirectional* antenna, which broadcasts its signal in a spherical shape. The signal pattern that radiates from a typical omnidirectional dipole antenna is shaped like a fat doughnut with a tiny hole in the middle. The hole is directly above and below the antenna.

The signal goes from the antenna to the floor above and the floor below, as well as to the floor on which the AP is located. If your house has multiple floors, try putting your AP on the second floor first. Most AP manufacturers claim a range of 200 feet indoors (at up to 300 Mbps for 802.11n and 54 Mbps for 802.11g). To be conservative, assume a range of 80 feet laterally and one floor above and below the AP. Keep in mind that the signal at the edges of the "doughnut" and on the floors below or above the AP are weaker than the signal nearer the center and on the same floor as the AP.

Because of this signal pattern, you should try to place the AP as close to the center of your house as is practically possible. Use a drawing of your house plan to locate the center of the house. This spot is your first trial AP location.

Draw a circle with an 80-foot radius on your house plan, with the trial AP location as the center of the circle. If your entire house falls inside the circle, one AP will probably do the job. Conversely, if some portion of the house is outside the circle, coverage may be weaker in that area. You need to experiment to determine whether you get an adequate signal there.

If you determine that one AP can't cover your house, you need to decide how best to place two APs (or even three, if necessary). The design of your house determines the best placement. For a one-level design, start at one end of the house and determine the best location for an 80-foot radius circle that covers all the way to the walls. The center of this circle is the location of the first AP. Then move toward the other end of the house, drawing 80-foot radius circles until the house is covered. The center of each circle is a trial location of an AP. If possible, don't leave any area in the house uncovered.

## *Adding printers to the network*

In addition to connecting your computers, you may want to connect your printers to the network. Next to sharing an Internet connection, printer sharing is perhaps the biggest cost-saving reason for building a network of home computers. Rather than buy a printer for every PC, everyone in the house can share one printer. Or maybe you have one color inkjet printer and one black-and-white laser printer. If both printers are connected to the network, all computers on the network can potentially print to either printer. Or perhaps you just want to sit by the pool with your wireless laptop and still be able to print to the printer up in your bedroom; it's easy with a network-attached printer.

You can also share other peripherals, such as network-aware scanners and fax machines. Leading manufacturers of digital imaging equipment (such as Hewlett-Packard) offer feature-rich, multiple-function peripherals that combine an inkjet or laser printer with a scanner, copier, telephone, answering machine, and fax machine. HP and Brother both offer wireless printers that make adding a shared printer to your network simple and quick. If you already have a printer, you can find wireless print servers such as the HP Jetdirect ew2500 802.11g Wireless Print Server to convert your wired printer to a wireless printer. These devices aren't cheap (about $300 list price for the HP), so they make more sense if you've got an expensive laser printer or graphics printer you want to set up wirelessly. If you've just got a plain old inkjet, it's probably cheaper to just buy a whole new printer with built-in wireless.

Here are three ways to share printers over a wired or wireless network:

- ✔ **Connect to a computer:** The easiest and cheapest way to connect a printer to the network is to connect a printer to one of the computers on the network. Windows enables you to share any printer connected to any Windows computer on the network. (For more on this topic, read Chapter 10.) The computer to which the printer is connected has to be running for any other computers on the network to use the printer. Similarly, if you're using Apple computers, any computer connected to the network can print to a printer that's connected to one of the computers on the network.

- ✔ **Use a wireless printer:** Many high-end printers even have print server options installed inside the printer cabinet. The cost for a home use, standalone network print server has come down a lot in the past few years, but printers with Wi-Fi built in tend to be at the high end of the price range. Although you can't expect wireless to be built-into the $89 special you found, don't be surprised to find printers and AIOs (*All-in-One* units that include a scanner and copier functionality) at prices starting around $150. And as long as you're going wireless with your printer, you might look for a model that also includes Bluetooth connectivity for smartphones, cameras, and other devices that can print via Bluetooth.

- ✔ **Use a print server:** Another way to add a printer is through a print server. As we mention earlier, several hardware manufacturers produce print server devices that enable you to connect one or more printers directly to the network. Some of these devices connect via a network cable, and others are wireless. Surprisingly, some manufacturers bundle a print server with their wireless router at little or no additional cost (meaning you plug the printer directly into a USB port on your wireless router). If you shop around, you can easily find a wireless AP, cable, or DSL router and print server bundled in one device.

You should be able to get your home network printer connections for free. Obviously, it doesn't cost anything to connect a printer to a computer that's already connected to the network. Several manufacturers also include a print server for free with other network devices. If you don't need one of those devices, just connect the printer you want to share to one of the computers on your home network.

Figure 4-2 depicts a home network with one printer connected to one of the PCs on the network and another printer connected to a wireless Internet *gateway,* which is a device that bundles a wireless AP and an Ethernet/cable/DSL router into a single unit. In this case, the wireless Internet gateway also has a connection for a printer and acts as a print server. Read through Chapters 1 and 5 for more information about these devices, what they do, and how to choose between them.

**Figure 4-2:** A wireless home network with a wireless Internet gateway and a bundled print server.

Connecting your printer to the wireless Internet gateway device is advantageous because a print server permits the printer to stand alone on the network, untethered from any specific computer. When you want to print to a printer that's connected directly to a computer on the network, that computer must be present and turned on; and, in many cases, you must have a user account and appropriate permission to access the shared printer. A print server makes its printers always available to any computer on the network — even from poolside.

Most folks don't mind having their printer connected to a computer or to a wireless router in their home — meaning that the computer is connected via peripheral cables to one of these devices. You may, however, want to make your printer *itself* wireless — so you can stick it *anywhere* in your house, even if that means that it's far away from any PCs or gateway devices. In this case, consider buying a *wireless print server* that can either be an internal part of your printer (in some cases, this is an optional module from the printer manufacturer) or sit next to your printer. In this case, your printer is completely decoupled from your wired network — the server is a wireless network *client* — as well as the hardware and software to run the printer itself.

Why would you spring for the extra money (about $80 to $100)? Here's an example. Pat had a spot (a closet) right in the middle of his house (literally!) where he wanted to hide a printer — but no wires and no PCs nearby. A wireless print server solved the problem and got his printer out of the way (and still in a convenient location).

## Adding entertainment and more

When you're planning your wireless network, don't forget to include a few gadgets for fun and relaxation. The wildly popular videogame consoles and handhelds from Sony, Microsoft, and Nintendo all offer network connectivity and Internet connectivity. Don't forget to consult with the gamers in your household when planning where you need network coverage in your home. And don't forget to take a look at Chapter 11 for the skinny about connecting your favorite console to your wireless network, as well as info on network-based, multiuser PC gaming.

An increasing number of consumer electronics devices, such as digital home entertainment systems, are network aware. Feature-packed home media servers can store thousands of your favorite MP3s and digital videos and make them available over the network to all the computers in your house. Several even include optional wireless networking connectivity. Connecting the sound and video from your PC to your home theater is even possible — really. Imagine surfing the Internet on a wide-screen TV! Jump to Chapter 12 for the details about connecting your A/V gear to your wireless home network.

Some of the coolest home electronic technology in recent years enables you to control the lights, heating, cooling, security system, home entertainment system, and pool right from your computer. Equally exciting technology enables you to use a home network to set up a highly affordable home video monitoring system. By hooking these systems to your wireless network and hooking the network to the Internet, you can make it possible to monitor and control your home's utilities and systems, even while away from home. Check out Chapter 14 for more about these smart home technologies as well as additional cool things you can network, such as connecting to your car or using your network to connect to the world.

# Connecting to the Internet

When you get right down to it, the reason why most people build wireless networks in their homes is to share their Internet connection with multiple computers or devices that they have around the house. That's why we first did it — and we bet that's why you're doing it. We've reached the point in our lives where a computer that's not constantly connected to a network and to the Internet is seriously handicapped. We're not exaggerating much here. Even things you do locally (use a spreadsheet program, for example) can be enhanced by an Internet connection; for example, in that spreadsheet program, you can link to the Internet to do real-time currency conversions. These days it's not uncommon to be using an online application such as Google Docs, working simultaneously with a handful of other people on a spreadsheet through your browser and Internet connection.

What a wireless network brings to the table is true whole-home Internet access. Particularly when combined with an always-on Internet connection (which we discuss in just a second) — but even with a regular dial-up modem connection (yes, some people still use modems) — a wireless network lets you access the Internet from just about every nook and cranny of the house. Take the laptop out to the back patio, let a visitor connect from the guest room, or do some work in bed. Whatever you want to do and wherever you want to do it, a wireless network can support you.

A wireless home network — or any home network, for that matter — provides one key element. It uses a NAT router (which we describe later in this section) to provide Internet access to multiple devices over a single Internet connection coming into the home. With a NAT router (which typically is built into your access point or a separate home network router), you can not only connect more than one computer to the Internet but also simultaneously connect multiple computers (and other devices, such as game consoles) to the Internet over a single connection. The NAT router has the brains to figure out which Web page or e-mail or online gaming information is going to which *client* (PC or device) on the network.

Not surprisingly, to take advantage of this Internet-from-anywhere access in your home, you need some sort of Internet service and modem. We don't get into great detail about this topic, but we do want to make sure that you keep it in mind when you plan your network.

Most people access the Internet from a home computer in one of these ways:

- Dial-up telephone connection
- Digital subscriber line (DSL)
- Cable Internet
- Fiber-optic service (such as Verizon's FiOS service)

- ✔ Broadband wireless services (like Clearwire, www.clearwire.com)
- ✔ Satellite broadband

DSL, cable, fiber-optic, broadband wireless and satellite Internet services are often called *broadband* Internet services, which is a term that gets defined differently by just about everyone in the industry. For our purposes, we define it as a connection that's faster than a dial-up modem connection (sometimes called *narrowband*) and is always on. That is, you don't have to use a dialer to get connected, but instead you have a persistent connection available immediately without any setup steps necessary for the users (at least after the first time you set up your connection).

Broadband Internet service providers are busily wiring neighborhoods all over the United States, but none of the services are available everywhere. (Satellite is available almost everywhere. But, as with satellite TV, you need to meet certain criteria, such as having a view to the south, that is, facing the satellites, which orbit over the equator.) Where it's available, however, growing numbers of families are experiencing the benefits of always-on and very fast Internet connectivity.

In some areas of the country, broadband wireless systems are beginning to become available as a means of connecting to the Internet. Most of these systems use special radio systems that are proprietary to their manufacturers. That is, you buy a transceiver and an antenna and hook it up on your roof or in a window. But a few are using modified versions of Wi-Fi to provide Internet access to people's homes. In either case, you have some sort of modem device that connects to your AP via a standard Ethernet cable, just like you would use for a DSL, fiber-optic, cable modem, or satellite connection.

For the purpose of this discussion of wireless home networks, DSL, fiber-optic, broadband wireless, and cable Internet are equivalent. If you can get more than one of these connections at your house, shop around for the best price and talk to your neighbors about their experiences. You might also want to check out www.broadbandreports.com, which is a Web site where customers of a variety of broadband services discuss and compare their experiences.

As soon as you splurge for a broadband Internet connection, the PC that happens to be situated nearest the spot where the installer places the DSL, fiber-optic, or cable modem is at a distinct advantage because it is the easiest computer to connect to the modem — and therefore to the Internet. Most DSL and cable modems connect to the PC through a wired network adapter card. FiOS uses a device called a router to connect to the PC via the same wired network adapter card. The best way, therefore, to connect any computer in the home to the Internet is through a home network.

You have two ways to share an Internet connection over a home network:

- ✔ **Software-based Internet connection sharing:** Windows XP, Windows Vista, and Mac OS X enable sharing of an Internet connection. Each computer in the network must be set up to connect to the Internet through the computer connected to the broadband modem. The disadvantage with this system is that you can't turn off or remove the computer connected to the modem without disconnecting all computers from the Internet. In other words, the computer connected to the modem must be on for other networked computers to access the Internet through it. This connected computer also needs to have two network cards installed — one card to connect to the cable/DSL modem or FiOS router and one to connect to the rest of the computer on your network via an AP or switch.

- ✔ **Broadband router:** A broadband router that is connected between the broadband modem and your home network allows all the computers on the network to access the Internet without going through another computer. The Internet connection no longer depends on any computer on the network. If the broadband router has Wi-Fi built in, it's a wireless router.

As we mention earlier in the chapter, nearly all APs now available for home networks have a built-in broadband router.

Read through Chapter 10 for details on how to set up Internet sharing.

Given the fact that you can buy a router (either as part of an access point or a separate router) for well under $60 these days (and prices continue to plummet), we think it's false economy to skip the router and use a software-based, Internet connection sharing setup. In our minds, at least, the advantage of the software-based approach (*very* slightly less money up front) is outweighed by the disadvantages (requiring the PC to always be on, lower reliability, lower performance, and a much bigger electric bill each month).

Both software-based, Internet connection sharing and cable or DSL routers enable all the computers in your home network to share the same network (IP) address on the Internet. This capability uses *Network Address Translation* (NAT). A device that uses the NAT feature is often called a *NAT router.* The NAT feature communicates with each computer on the network by using a private IP address assigned to that local computer, but the router uses a single public IP address in data it sends to computers on the Internet. In other words, no matter how many computers you have in your house sharing the Internet, they look like only one computer to all the other computers on the Internet.

Whenever your computer is connected to the Internet, beware the potential that some malicious hacker may try to attack your computer with a virus or try to break into your computer to trash your hard drive or steal your personal information. Because NAT technology hides your computer behind the NAT server, it adds a measure of protection against hackers, but you shouldn't rely on it solely for protection against malicious users. You should also consider purchasing full-featured firewall software that actively looks for and blocks hacking attempts, unless the AP or router you purchase provides that added protection. We talk about these items in more detail in Chapter 9.

As we recommend in the "Choosing an access point" section, earlier in this chapter, try to choose an AP that also performs several other network-oriented services. Figure 4-3 depicts a wireless home network using an AP that provides DHCP, NAT, a print server, and switched hub functions in a single standalone unit. This wireless router device then connects to the DSL or cable modem, which in turn connects to the Internet. Such a configuration provides you with connectivity, sharing, and a little peace of mind, too.

**Figure 4-3:** Go for a wireless router that combines AP, DHCP, NAT, print server, and switched hub functions in one unit.

If you already have a wired network and have purchased a cable or DSL router Internet gateway device without the AP function, you don't have to replace the existing device. Just purchase a plain old wireless access point. Figure 4-4 depicts the network design of a typical wired home network with an AP and wireless stations added. Each PC in the wired network is connected to the cable or DSL router, which is also a switch. By connecting the AP to the router, the AP acts as a bridge between the wireless network segment and the existing wired network.

**Figure 4-4:**
A wired
home
network
with an
AP and
wireless
stations
added.

# Budgeting for Your Wireless Network

Assuming that you already own at least one computer (and probably more)
and one or more printers that you intend to add to the network, we don't
include the cost of computers and printers in this section. In addition, the
cost of subscribing to an ISP isn't included in the following networking cost
estimates.

Wireless networking hardware — essentially APs and wireless network
adapters — is available at a wide range of prices. With a little planning, you
won't be tempted to bite on the first product you see. You can use the
following guidelines when budgeting for an AP and wireless network adapters.
Keep in mind, however, that the prices for this equipment will certainly
change over time, perhaps rapidly. Don't use this information as a substitute
for due diligence and market research on your part.

## Pricing access points

At the time this chapter was written, wireless access points for home use
ranged in price from about $35 (street price) to around $100.

*Street price* is the price at which you can purchase the product from a retail outlet, such as a computer-electronics retail store or an online retailer. The dreaded *suggested retail price* is often higher.

Multifunction access points that facilitate connecting multiple computers to the Internet — *wireless Internet gateways* if they contain modem functionality and *wireless gateways* or *routers* if they don't — range in price from about $50 to $200 for an 802.11n model (a bit less for one using the older 802.11g technology).

The differences in price between the cheapest APs and the more expensive models generally correspond to differences in features. For example, 802.11n APs that support both the 2.4 GHz and 5 GHz radio frequencies cost more than 2.4 GHz-only models — and models that let you use both frequency ranges at once (called *simultaneous dual band* APs) cost even more. We dig into this topic in Chapter 5.

## Pricing wireless network adapters

Wireless network adapters range from $25 to $125, depending on whether you purchase 802.11g or n technology and whether you purchase a PC Card, USB, or internal variety of adapter.

Most notebook computers sold are equipped with at least 802.11g wireless built into them, with 802.11n as an upgrade option. If you can get an upgrade to 802.11n when you're buying new PCs, you should do so.

## Looking at a sample budget

Table 4-2 shows a reasonable hardware budget to connect a laptop computer, and a home desktop computer, and a cable Internet connection to an 802.11n wireless home network.

### Table 4-2  A Hypothetical 802.11g Wireless Home Network Budget

| Item | Price Range | Quantity Needed |
|------|-------------|-----------------|
| Access point/wireless router | $35–$200 | 1 |
| Wireless network adapters | $25–$100 | 2 |
| Network cable | $5 | 1 |
| Cable or DSL modem (optional) | $75–$100 (or rented from your ISP) | 1 |

# Chapter 5

# Choosing Wireless Home Networking Equipment

*W*hen you're building something — in this case, a wireless home network — the time comes when you have to decide which building supplies to buy. To set up a wireless home network, you need, at minimum, an access point (AP) and a wireless networking adapter for each computer or other network-enabled device you want to have on the network. Getting this network online means you also need a router, which is typically part of a combined AP/router device (the wireless router). This chapter helps you evaluate and choose from among the growing number of APs and wireless networking adapters on the market.

Almost *all* computers sold today offer built-in wireless networking. In the case of laptop and netbook computers (portables, in other words), the figure is so close to 100% that it would be splitting hairs to discuss it. When it comes to desktop computers, wireless networking is almost always *available* and *often* standard, but the cheaper desktop computers will usually have wireless as an option rather than a standard feature. Most other computing/smartphone devices that you'll want to connect to your network have built-in Wi-Fi capabilities. The only devices that you'll probably have to buy separate network adapters for are older (say pre-1996) computers and peripheral devices like printers or gaming consoles. Otherwise, you'll probably find that everything you want to connect wirelessly is ready to go. These days, Wi-Fi is just about standard.

The advice in this chapter applies equally to PCs and Macs. You can use any access point for a Mac as long as it has a Web interface (that is, it doesn't require a Windows-only program to configure it). Despite that statement, if you have a Mac, you may want to consider using the Apple AirPort Extreme wireless router because it's easier to set up and use — in fact, we can recommend this wireless router for Windows users too, though it costs a bit more than equivalent routers from other manufacturers.

In this chapter, we use the term *AP* (access point) generically to refer to the base station of your wireless network. In most cases, it will be a part of a wireless router, but in some cases it will be a standalone AP. When it doesn't matter whether the AP is stand-alone or part of the router, we use the term *AP* or *access point*. When we're specifically talking about an AP that's integrated with a router, we use the term *wireless router*. Just to repeat ourselves, you'll probably be installing an AP that's part of a wireless router in your home, unless you've already got a home router in place. (Most people don't.)

## *Choosing an Access Point*

At the heart of each wireless home network is the access point (AP), also known as a base station. Depending on an AP's manufacturer and included features, the price of an AP suitable for home use ranges from about $35 to $175. Differences exist from model to model, but even the lowest-price units are surprisingly capable.

For most wireless home networks, the most important requirements for a wireless access point are as follows (sort of in order of importance):

- ✔ Certification and standards support (Wi-Fi certification)
- ✔ Security
- ✔ Performance (range and coverage) issues
- ✔ Manageability
- ✔ Compatibility and form factor
- ✔ Bundled server and router functionality
- ✔ Operational features
- ✔ Price
- ✔ Warranties
- ✔ Customer and technical support

With the exception of pricing (which we cover in Chapter 4), we explore the selection of access point products in depth in terms of these requirements throughout the following sections of this chapter.

In Chapter 4, we describe how to plan the installation of a wireless home network, including how to use your AP to determine the best location in your house as well as the number of APs you need. If you can determine a location that gives an adequate signal throughout your entire house, a single AP obviously is adequate. If some areas of your home aren't covered, you need one or more additional APs or a more powerful AP (and we tell you how to extend your network coverage in Chapter 18). Fortunately, most residences can be covered by the signal from a single AP, particularly when that AP uses the further-reaching 802.11n standard (discussed in Chapter 3).

# Understanding Certification and Standards

We talk in Chapter 2 about the Wi-Fi Alliance and its certification process for devices. At a minimum, you should ensure that your devices are Wi-Fi certified. (You can see the logo right on the box and in the product's data sheet.) This certification provides you with the assurance that your wireless LAN equipment has been through the wringer of interoperability and compliance testing and meets all the standards of 802.11b, g, a, or n.

In fact, there's even more to Wi-Fi certification than just meeting the 802.11b, g, a, and n standards. Wi-Fi certification means that a piece of equipment has been thoroughly tested to work with other similar Wi-Fi equipment, regardless of brand. This is the interoperability part of the certification, and it means that you can plug a D-Link adapter into your desktop computer, use a built-in Intel adapter in your notebook, and install a NETGEAR AP as the hub of your network, and everything will work.

Back in the early days of wireless networking, this interoperability was *not* assured, and you needed to buy all your equipment from the same vendor — and then you were locked in to that vendor. Wi-Fi certification frees you from this concern.

The Wi-Fi Alliance certifies the following:

✔ **General Wi-Fi certification:** For 802.11a, b, g, and n equipment (as well as *multimode* equipment that supports more than one standard at a time — such as 802.11n gear that also supports 802.11a, b, and g), this certification simply lets you know that a given piece of Wi-Fi certified gear will connect to another piece of gear using the same standard.

This certification is the bottom-line "must have" that you should look for when you buy a wireless LAN system. We recommend that you choose products certified 802.11n unless you have a tight budget (in which case you should feel just fine about choosing an older 802.11g system).

✔ **Security certification:** This certification ensures the equipment can work with the WPA (Wi-Fi Protected Access) and WPA2 security systems. (See Chapter 9 for more on this topic.) WPA-certified equipment can be certified by the Wi-Fi Alliance for any of these types of WPA:

- *WPA and WPA2 Personal:* This is the minimum you should look for — equipment that has been certified to work with the WPA Personal (or WPA-PSK) system described in Chapter 9.

  If you can help it, don't buy any Wi-Fi gear that isn't certified for at least WPA2 Personal. We think that this is the minimum level of security you should insist on with a Wi-Fi network.

- *WPA/WPA2 Enterprise:* This business-oriented variant of WPA provides the ability to use a special 802.1x or RADIUS server (explained in Chapter 9) to manage users on the network. For the vast majority of wireless home networkers, this capability is overkill, but it doesn't hurt to have it. (Any WPA/WPA2 Enterprise certified system also supports WPA/WPA2 Personal.)

- *WPS: Wi-Fi Protected Setup* certification is increasingly common on new equipment, but still rather new as we write this. WPS, which we discuss in detail in Chapter 9, is a user-friendly front end to WPA2 Personal and allows you to set up network security simply by pushing buttons (or entering preassigned PIN codes) on your AP/router and network clients.

- *EAP: Extensible Authentication Protocol* is part of the WPA Enterprise/802.1x system used in business wireless LANs. EAP provides the mechanism for authenticating users (or confirming that they are who they say they are). A number of different EAP types can be used with WPA Enterprise — each type can be certified by the Wi-Fi Alliance. You don't need to worry about this unless you're building a WPA Enterprise security system for your network.

✔ **WMM:** *Wi-Fi Multimedia* certification can be found on a number of audio/video and voice Wi-Fi equipment (these items are discussed in Chapters 12 and 13, respectively). WMM-certified equipment can provide on your wireless LAN some *Quality of Service* (QoS), which can give your voice, video, or audio data priority over other data being sent across your vnetwork. We talk about WMM where appropriate in Chapters 12 and 13.

Back around 2006, WMM was the "next big thing" in Wi-Fi, but as the raw speed of wireless networks has gone through the roof with the advent of 802.11n, we've heard less and less about WMM. If you have a device that you know could use WMM (like a Wi-Fi phone), look for a WMM-certified AP. Otherwise, WMM is probably not that important to you.

## What to look for in 802.11n gear

The 802.11n standard has a bit more variation in its specifications than previous 802.11 standards such as 802.11g. What this means is that although all 802.11n gear can work at a certain (very high) baseline of performance, some gear may be more capable than others.

The biggest variation in the category of 802.11n gear revolves around the frequencies used. All 802.11n gear works within the 2.4 GHz band that was also used by 802.11b and 802.11g. Some — but far from all — 802.11n equipment also works in the 5 GHz frequency range that was previously the sole domain of the 802.11a standard. This higher frequency range is less crowded with other wireless gear (such as cordless phones and Bluetooth devices), so you're less likely to face interference. Additionally, the 5 GHz band has more channels (the frequency band is divided into a number of channels), making it even easier to find an uncrowded frequency.

Most of this *dual-band* (2.4 and 5 GHz) 802.11n gear today works in either one or another of the frequency bands at a time. What this means is that if you have any legacy 802.11b or g equipment on your network, the 5 GHz capability of your AP or router will not come into play. Some of the more expensive wireless routers on the market have the capability to operate in both bands *simultaneously*. This is a great capability to have in a mixed 802.11g/802.11n network, because your old gear can happily hum along at 802.11g speeds by using the 2.4 GHz radio in your router, while your fancy new 802.11n gear can reach maximum 802.11n speeds in the 5 GHz band.

The final thing to look for when choosing 802.11n systems is the capability of the equipment to perform *channel bonding*. All Wi-Fi systems use 20 MHz wide channels to transmit and receive data across the network airlink; many 802.11n systems can *bond* two adjacent channels together to form one bigger 40 MHz channel. (For this reason, channel bonding is sometimes referred to as *40 MHz channel width*.) This bigger, bonded channel can carry more data and allow your system to reach the higher (200+ Mbps) speeds promised by 802.11n.

By the way, significantly more channels are available for bonding in the 5 GHz frequency range, which is another reason to choose a dual-band system.

# Considering Compatibility and Form Factor

When choosing an AP, make sure that the AP and its setup program are compatible with your existing components, check its form factor, and determine whether wall-mountability and outdoor use are important to you:

> ✔ **Hardware and software platform:** Make sure that the device you're buying supports the hardware and software platform you have. Certain wireless devices support only Macs or only PCs — it's not that they won't work with different computer platforms, but that their configuration software requires a particular operating system (OS). And some devices support only certain versions of system software. Luckily, most APs use

a Web browser for configuration, so they can work with any PC type and any operating system that supports 802.11 and Web browsing (which is to say all current operating systems).

✔ **Setup program and your computer's operating system:** Make sure that the setup program for the AP you plan to buy runs on your computer's operating system and on the next version of that operating system (if it's available — meaning if you're using Vista, look for Windows 7 support too, should you ever decide to upgrade). Setup programs run only on the type of computer for which they were written. A setup program designed to run on Windows doesn't run on the Mac OS, and vice versa. Again, most vendors are moving toward browser-based configuration programs, which are much easier to support than standalone configuration utilities.

✔ **Form factor:** Make sure you're buying the correct *form factor* (that is, the shape and form of the device, such as whether it's external or a card). For example, don't assume that if you have a tower PC, you should install a PCI card. It's nice to have the more external and portable form factors, such as a Universal Serial Bus (USB) adapter, because you can take it off if you need to borrow it for something or someone else, or if you just want to reposition it for better reception.

USB comes in two versions: USB 1.1 and USB 2.0 (also known as High Speed USB). If your computer has a USB 1.1 port, it has a maximum data-transfer speed of 12 Mbps. USB 2.0 ports can transfer data at 480 Mbps, which is 40 times faster than USB 1.1. If you plan to connect an 802.11g or n device to a USB port, it must be USB 2.0.

Many brands of PC Cards include antennas enclosed in a casing that is thicker than the rest of the card. The card still fits in the PC Card slot, but the antenna can block the other slot. For most users, this shouldn't pose a serious problem; however, several manufacturers offer wireless PC Cards that have antenna casings no thicker than the rest of the card. If you actively use both PC Card slots (perhaps you use one for a FireWire card for your camcorder), make sure that the form of the PC Card you're buying doesn't impede the use of your other card slot.

✔ **Wall-mountability:** If you plan to mount the device on the wall or ceiling, make sure that the unit is wall mountable, because many are not. We don't necessarily recommend that wall mount your AP, but a lot of people make this choice for aesthetic reasons, and who are we to judge?

✔ **Outdoor versus indoor use:** Some devices are designed for outdoor — not indoor — use. If you're thinking about installing it outside, look for devices hardened for environmental extremes.

# Looking for Bundled Functionality: Servers, Gateways, Routers, and Switches

You can find and buy wireless APs that perform only the AP function; but for home use, APs that bundle additional features are much more popular, for good reason. In most cases, you should shop for an AP that's also a network router and a network switch — a wireless home router like the one we describe in Chapter 2. To efficiently connect multiple computers and to easily share an Internet connection, you need devices to perform all these functions, and purchasing one multipurpose device is the most economical way to accomplish that.

## DHCP servers

To create an easy-to-use home network, your network should have a Dynamic Host Configuration Protocol (DHCP) server. A *DHCP server* dynamically assigns an IP address to each computer or other device on your network. This function relieves you from having to keep track of all the devices on the network and assign addresses to each one manually.

Network addresses are necessary for the computers and other devices on your network to communicate. Because most networks now use a set of protocols (Transmission Control Protocol/Internet Protocol, or TCP/IP) with network addresses (Internet Protocol, or IP, addresses), we refer to network addresses as *IP addresses* in this book. In fact, the Internet uses the TCP/IP protocols, and every computer connected to the Internet must be identified by an IP address.

When your computer is connected to the Internet, your Internet service provider (ISP), such as Time Warner Road Runner or Verizon FiOS, assigns your computer an IP address. However, even when your computer isn't connected to the Internet, it needs an IP address to communicate with other computers on your home network.

The DHCP server can be a standalone device, but it's typically a service provided by either a computer on the network or a network router. The DHCP server maintains a database of all the current DHCP clients — the computers and other devices to which it has assigned IP addresses — issuing new addresses as each device's software requests an address.

## Bring your network back to life in the right order

Your home network is comprised of many parts. If you're smart, you've consolidated them as much as possible, because having fewer devices means easier installation and troubleshooting. But suppose that you have a cable modem, a router, a switch, and an access point — not an unusual situation if you grew your network over time. Now suppose that the power goes out. Each of these devices resets at different rates. The switch will probably come back fairly quickly because it's a simple device. The cable modem will probably take the longest to resync with the network, and the AP and router will come back up probably somewhere in-between.

The problem that you, as a client of the DHCP server (which is likely in the router in this instance), have is that not all the elements are in place for a clean IP assignment to flow back to your system. For example, the router needs to know the IP address assigned to your cable modem for you to have a good connection to the Internet. If the cable modem hasn't renegotiated its connection, it cannot provide that to the router. If the AP comes back online before the router, it cannot get its DHCP from the router to provide connectivity to the client. Different devices react differently when something isn't as it should be on startup.

Our advice: If you have a problem with your connectivity that you didn't have before the electricity went out and came back on, follow these simple steps. Turn everything off, start at the farthest point from the client (usually this is your broadband modem), and work back toward the client, to let each device get its full start-up cycle complete before moving to the next device in line — ending with rebooting your PC or other wirelessly enabled device.

## *NAT and broadband routers*

A *wireless router* is a wireless AP that enables multiple computers to share the same IP address on the Internet. This fact would seem to be a contradiction because every computer on the Internet needs its own IP address. The magic that makes an Internet gateway possible is Network Address Translation (NAT). Most access points you buy now are wireless gateways — you actually need to seek out those that have *only* AP functionality.

Vendors sometimes call these wireless routers *wireless broadband routers* or perhaps *wireless cable/DSL routers*. What you're looking for is the word *router* somewhere in the name or description of the device itself. Standalone access points (without the router functionality) usually are called just an access point, so sometimes it's easier to look for something *not* called that!

In addition to providing NAT services, the wireless routers used in home networks also provide the DHCP service. The router communicates with each computer or other device on your home network via private IP addresses —

the IP addresses assigned by the DHCP server. (See the section "DHCP servers," earlier in this chapter.) However, the router uses a single IP address — the one assigned by your ISP's DHCP server — in packets of data intended for the Internet.

In addition to providing a method for sharing an Internet connection, the NAT service provided by a broadband router also adds a measure of security because the computers on your network aren't directly exposed to the Internet. The only computer visible to the Internet is the broadband router. This protection can also be a disadvantage for certain types of Internet gaming and computer-to-computer file transfer applications. If you find that you need to use one of these applications, look for a router with *DMZ* (for *demilitarized zone*) and *port forwarding* features, which expose just enough of your system to the Internet to play Internet games and transfer files. (Read more about this topic in Chapter 11.)

A *wireless Internet gateway* is an AP that's bundled with a cable, fiber-optic, or DSL modem or router. By hooking this single device to a cable connection or DSL line (or to the termination of your fiber-optic connection), you can share an Internet connection with all the computers connected to the network, wirelessly. By definition, all wireless Internet gateway devices also include one (and typically, several) wired Ethernet port that enables you to add wired devices to your network as well as wireless devices.

## Switches

Wireless routers, available from nearly any manufacturer, include from one to eight (most commonly, four) Ethernet ports with which you can connect computers or other devices via Ethernet cables. These routers are not only wireless APs but are also wired switches that efficiently enable all the computers on your network to communicate either wirelessly or over Ethernet cables.

 Make sure that the switch ports support at least *100BaseT* Ethernet — which is the 100 Mbps variant of Ethernet. You should also ensure that the switch supports the *full-duplex* variant of 100BaseT — meaning that it supports 100 Mbps of data in both directions at the same time. If you're looking for the ultimate in performance, you should strongly consider paying a bit more for a router that supports *Gigabit Ethernet* (1000BaseT).

Even though you may intend to create a wireless home network, sometimes you may want to attach a device to the network through a more traditional network cable. For example, we highly recommend that when you configure a router for the first time, you attach the router to your computer by a network cable (rather than via a wireless connection).

## *Print servers*

A few multifunction wireless routers have a feature that enables you to add a printer to the network: a print server. Next to sharing an Internet connection, printer sharing is one of the most convenient (and cost-effective) reasons to network home computers because everyone in the house can share one printer. Wireless print servers have become much more economical in the past few years. However, when the print server is included with the wireless router, it's suddenly *very* cost effective.

The disadvantage of using the print server bundled with the AP, however, is apparent if you locate your AP in a room or location other than where you would like to place your printer. Consider a standalone print server device (discussed in Chapter 10) if you want to have your printer wirelessly enabled but not near your AP.

# *Exploring Operational Features*

Most APs share a common list of features, and most of them don't vary from one device to the next. Here are some unique, onboard features that we look for when buying wireless devices — and you should, too:

- **Wired Ethernet port:** Okay, this one seems basic, but having a port like this saves you time. We tell you time and again to first install your AP on your wired network (as opposed to trying to configure the AP via a wireless client card connection) and then add the wireless layer (like the aforementioned client card). You can save yourself lots of grief if you can get your AP configured on a direct connection to your PC because you reduce the things that can go wrong when you add the wireless clients.

- **Auto channel select:** Some access points, typically more expensive models designed for office use, offer an automatic channel-selection feature. That's nice because, as you read in Chapter 6 and in the troubleshooting areas of Chapter 18, channel selection can try your patience. (You may wonder why professional users pay more for more business-class access points — this feature, which adds to the expense of an AP, is a good reason.)

- **Detachable antennas:** In most cases, the antenna or antennas that come installed on an AP are adequate for good signal coverage throughout your house. However, your house may be large enough or may be configured in such a way that signal coverage of a particular AP could be significantly improved by replacing a stock antenna with an upgraded version. Also, if your AP has an internal antenna and you decide that the signal strength and coverage in your house are inadequate, an external antenna jack allows you to add one or two external antennas. Several manufacturers sell optional antennas that extend the range of the standard antennae; they attach to the AP to supplement or replace the existing antennae.

The FCC requires that antennas and radios be certified as a system. Adding a third-party, non-FCC-certified antenna to your AP violates FCC regulations and runs the risk of causing interference with other radio devices, such as certain portable telephones.

Detachable antennas are a potentially big benefit for 802.11g (and earlier 802.11a and b) systems, but not so much for 802.11n. Because of the very tight integration between hardware and antenna in a MIMO 802.11n system, most 802.11n routers don't offer detachable antennas and wouldn't benefit from them if they did.

✔ **Uplink port:** APs equipped with internal three- and four-port hub and switch devices are also coming with a built-in, extra uplink port. The *uplink port* — also called the crossover port — adds even more wired ports to your network by uplinking the AP with another hub or switch. This special port is normally an extra connection next to the last available wired port on the device, but it can look like a regular Ethernet jack (with a little toggle switch next to it). You want an uplink port — especially if you have an integral router or DSL or cable modem — so that you can add more ports to your network while it grows. (And it will grow.)

# Knowing What Security Features You Need

Unless you work for the government or handle sensitive data on your computer, you probably aren't overly concerned about the privacy of the information stored on your home network. Usually it's not an issue anyway because someone would have to break into your house to access your network. But if you have a wireless network, the radio signals transmitted by your network don't automatically stop at the outside walls of your house. In fact, a neighbor or even someone driving by on the street in front of your house can use a computer and a wireless networking adapter to grab information right off your computer, including deleting your files, inserting viruses, and using your computer to send spam — unless you take steps to protect your network.

The original security technology for Wi-Fi equipment was Wired Equivalent Privacy (WEP). Perhaps the most well-publicized aspect of Wi-Fi wireless networking is the fact that the WEP security feature of Wi-Fi networks can be *hacked* (broken into electronically). Hackers have successfully retrieved secret WEP keys used to encrypt data on Wi-Fi networks. With these keys, the hacker can decrypt the packets of data transmitted over a wireless network. Since 2003, the Wi-Fi Alliance has been certifying and promoting a replacement security technology for WEP: Wi-Fi Protected Access (WPA and the newer but closely related WPA2). WPA/WPA2 is based on an IEEE standard effort known as 802.11i (so many 802.11s huh?). This technology makes cracking a network's encryption key much more difficult and is standard in just about all Wi-Fi access points and network adapters available now. As discussed earlier in this chapter, in the section "Understanding Certification and Standards," look for Wi-Fi Alliance certifications for WPA equipment.

Any Wi-Fi gear that you buy should support the latest security certification — WPA2. Don't accept any less and don't forget to turn on your network's security.

Other useful security features to look for when buying an AP include

- ✔ **Network Address Translation** (NAT), which we discuss earlier in this chapter
- ✔ **Virtual Private Network** (VPN) pass-through that allows wireless network users secure access to corporate networks
- ✔ **Monitoring software** that logs and alerts you to computers from the Internet attempting to access your network
- ✔ **Logging and blocking utilities** that enable you to log content transmitted over the network as well as to block access to given Web sites

We talk much more about security in Chapter 9. We encourage you to read that chapter so that you can be well prepared when you're ready to install your equipment.

# Examining Range and Coverage Issues

An AP's functional *range* (the maximum distance from the access point at which a device on the wireless network can receive a useable signal) and *coverage* (the breadth of areas in your home where you have an adequate radio signal) are important criteria when selecting an AP. Wi-Fi equipment is designed to have a range of hundreds of meters when used outdoors without any obstructions between the two radios. Coverage depends on the type of antenna used.

Just like it's hard to know how good a book is until you read it, it's hard to know how good an AP is until you install it. Do your research before buying an AP, and then hope that you make the right choice. Buying ten APs and returning the nine you don't want is simply impractical. (Well, maybe not impractical, but rather rude.) The key range and coverage issues, such as power output, antenna gain, or receive sensitivity (which we cover in Chapter 2), aren't well labeled on retail boxes. Nor are these issues truly comparable among devices because of the same lack of consistent information. Because many of these devices are manufactured using the same chipsets, performance usually doesn't vary extensively from one AP to another. However, that is a broad generalization, and some APs do perform badly. Our advice: Read the reviews and be forewarned! Most reviews of APs and wireless routers do extensive range and throughput (speed) testing — look at sites such as CNET (www. cnet.com) or ZDNet (www.zdnet.com).

In Chapter 2, we talk about the differences between the 2.4 and 5 GHz frequency bands that different Wi-Fi systems use (802.11b and g use 2.4 GHz, 802.11a uses 5 GHz, and 802.11n can use either). In that chapter, we also talk about the fact that higher frequencies (that is, 5 GHz compared to 2.4 GHz) tend to have shorter ranges than lower frequencies (all things equal, which they're not in the case of 802.11n; more on that in a moment). In general, 2.4 GHz systems have a longer reach, but they also operate in a more crowded set of frequencies and are therefore more prone to interference from other systems (other Wi-Fi networks *and* other devices such as phones and microwaves). In an urban environment, you may very well find that a 5 GHz system has a better range simply due to this lack of interference.

The 802.11n systems on the market use multiple antennas and special techniques to boost, or focus, the antenna power and greatly increase the range of the AP versus a standard 802.11g model. Even when operating in the 5 GHz frequency range, you should find that an 802.11n system has a range several times greater than that of an 802.11g system.

# Controlling and Managing Your Device

When it comes to installing, setting up, and maintaining your wireless network, you rely a great deal on your device's user interface, so check reviews for this aspect of the product. In this section, we discuss the many different ways to control and manage your devices.

## Web-based configuration

APs, wireless clients, and other wireless devices from all vendors ship with several utility software programs that help you set up and configure the device. An important selling feature of any wireless device is its setup process. The ideal setup procedure can be accomplished quickly and efficiently. Most available APs and devices can be configured through either the wired Ethernet port or a USB port.

Our favorite setup programs enable you to configure the device by connecting through the Ethernet port and accessing an embedded set of Web (HTML) pages. Look for an AP with one of these. This type of setup program — often described as *Web-based* — can be run from any computer that is connected to the device's Ethernet port and has a Web browser. Whether you're using Windows, the Mac OS, or Linux, you can access any device that uses a Web-based configuration program.

## Software programming

If you think that using a Web configuration program might be difficult for you, look for an AP with an automated setup program.

Several AP manufacturers provide setup software that walks you step by step through the process of setting up the AP and connecting to your network. Windows automated setup programs are typically called *wizards*. If you're new to wireless technology, a setup wizard or other variety of automated setup program can help you get up and running with minimum effort.

Even if an AP comes with a setup wizard, it also ships with configuration software that permits you to manually configure all the available AP settings. For maximum flexibility, this configuration software should be Web based (refer to the preceding section).

## Upgradeable firmware

Wireless networking technology is constantly evolving. As a result, many features of Wi-Fi access points are implemented in updateable software programs known as *firmware*. Before you decide which AP to buy, determine whether you can get feature updates and fixes from the vendor and whether you can perform the updates by upgrading the firmware. (See the nearby sidebar, "Performing firmware updates," for some pointers.) Check also for updated management software to match up with the new or improved features included in the updated firmware.

## Performing firmware updates

Most firmware updates come in the form of a downloadable program you run on a computer connected to the AP (or other device) by a cable (usually Ethernet, but sometimes USB). Make sure that you carefully read and follow the instructions that accompany the downloadable file. Updating the firmware incorrectly can lead to real headaches. Here are a few tips:

✔ Make sure that you make a backup of your current firmware before performing the update.

✔ Never turn off the computer or the AP while the firmware update is in progress.

✔ If something goes wrong, look through the AP documentation for instructions on how to reset the modem to its factory settings.

You may feel that frequent firmware updates are evidence of faulty product design. However, acknowledging that wireless technology will continue to be improved, buying a product that can be upgraded to keep pace with these changes without the need to purchase new equipment can save you money in the long run.

# Taking Price into Account

Although we can't say much directly about price (except that the least expensive item is rarely the one you want), we should mention other things that can add to the price of an item. Check out which cables are provided. (Yes, wireless devices need cables, too!) In an effort to trim costs, some companies don't provide the Ethernet cable for your AP that you need for initial setup.

Also, before you buy, check out some of the online price comparison sites, such as CNET (http://shopper.cnet.com), Retrevo (www.retrevo.com), and Yahoo! Shopping (http://shopping.yahoo.com). Internet specials pop up all the time.

# Checking Out Warranties

There's nothing worse than a device that dies one day after the warranty expires. The good news is that because most of these devices are solid state, they work for a long time unless you abuse them by dropping them on the floor or something drastic. In our experience, if your device is going to fail because of some manufacturing defect, it generally does so within the first 30 days or so.

You encounter a rather large variance of warranty schedules among vendors. Some vendors offer a one-year warranty; others offer a lifetime warranty. Most are limited in some fashion, such as covering parts and labor but not shipping.

When purchasing from a store, be sure to ask about its return policy for the first month or so. Many stores give you 14 days to return items, and after that, purchases have to be returned to the manufacturer directly, which is a huge pain in the hind end, as Pat would say. If you only have 14 days, get the device installed quickly so that you can find any problems right away.

Extended service warranties are also often available through computer retailers. (We never buy these because by the time the period of the extended warranty expires, they're simply not worth their price given the plummeting cost of the items.) If you purchase one of these warranties, however, make sure that you have a clear understanding of the types of problems covered as well as how and when you can contact the service provider if problems arise. As we mention earlier in this chapter, if you don't purchase a warranty, you probably need to contact the product manufacturer for support and warranty service rather than the store or online outlet where you purchased the product.

# Finding Out about Customer and Technical Support

Good technical support is one of those things you don't appreciate until you can't get it. For support, check whether the manufacturer has toll-free or direct-dial numbers for support as well as its hours of availability. Ticklish technical problems seem to occur at the most inopportune times — nights, weekends, holidays. If you're like us, you usually install this stuff late at night and on weekends. (We refuse to buy anything from anyone with only 9 a.m.–5 p.m., Monday–Friday hours for technical support.) Traditionally, only high-end (that is to say, expensive) hardware products came with 24/7 technical support. However, an increasing number of consumer-priced computer products, including wireless home networking products, offer toll-free, around-the-clock, technical phone support.

# Part III
# Installing a Wireless Network

The 5th Wave                    By Rich Tennant

"Oh, Arthur is very careful about security on the Web. He never goes online in the same room on consecutive days."

# In this part . . .

*N*ow comes the work: installing a wireless network in your home and getting it up and running. Whether you're a Mac user or have PCs running a Windows operating system — or both — this part of the book explains how to install and configure your wireless networking equipment. No doubt you're also interested in sharing a single Internet connection and, of course, making your home network as secure as possible. (You don't want your nosy neighbors getting on your network, do you?) This part helps you get the most out of your home's wireless network — by getting it installed right, the first time.

# Chapter 6

# Installing Wireless Access Points in Windows

*I*n this chapter, we describe the installation and configuration of your wireless home network's access point (AP). We explain how to set up and configure the access point so that it's ready to communicate with any and all wireless devices in your home network. In Chapter 7, we describe the process for installing and configuring wireless network adapters.

Chapters 6 and 7 deal solely with Windows-based PCs. For specifics on setting up and installing wireless home networking devices on a Mac, see Chapter 8.

## Before Getting Started, Get Prepared

Setting up an AP does have some complicated steps where things can go wrong. You want to reduce the variables to as few as possible to make debugging any problems as easy as possible. Don't try to do lots of different things all at once, such as buying a new PC, installing Windows 7, and adding a router, an AP, and wireless clients. (Go ahead and laugh, but lots of people try this.)

We recommend that you follow these general steps when setting up an AP:

1. **Get your PC set up first on a standalone basis.**

   If you have a new computer system, it probably shouldn't need much setup because it should be preconfigured when you buy it. If you have an older system, make sure that no major software problems exist before you begin. If you have to install a new operating system (OS), do it now. *Bottom line:* Get the PC working fine on its own so that you have no problems when you add functionality.

2. **Add a broadband Internet connection for that one PC.**

   Ensure that everything is working on your wired connection first. If you have a broadband modem, get it working on a direct connection to your PC. Make sure you can surf the Web (go to a number of sites that you know work) to ascertain that the information is current (as opposed to coming from cache memory from earlier visits to the site).

3. **Share the broadband connection with your router and add your home network routing option.**

   This step entails shifting your connection from your PC to your router; your router will have instructions for doing that. When that's working, make sure you can add another PC or other device, if you have one, by using the same instructions for your router. Make sure that your PC can connect to the Internet and that the two devices can see each other on the local area network. This action establishes that your logical connectivity among all your devices and the Internet is working.

   Because you may be installing an AP on an existing broadband network, we're covering the AP installation first; we cover the installation of the router and Internet sharing in Chapter 10.

4. **Try adding wireless to the equation: Install your wireless AP and wireless NICs (if they're not built-in) and disconnect the Ethernet cable from each computer to see whether they work — one at a time is always simpler.**

   By now, any problems that occur can be isolated to your wireless connection. If you need to fall back on logging on to your manufacturer's Web site, you can always plug the wired connection in and do so.

If your AP is in an all-in-one cable modem/router/AP combo, that's okay. Think about turning on the elements one at a time. If a wizard forces you to do it all at once, go ahead and follow the wizard's steps; just recognize that if all goes wrong, you can reset the device to the factory settings and start over. (It's extreme, but it usually saves time.)

# Setting Up the Access Point

Before you install and set up a wireless network interface adapter in one of your computers, you should first set up the wireless access point (also called a *base station*) that will facilitate communication between the various wireless devices on your network. In the following sections, we describe how to set up a typical AP.

## Preparing to install a wireless AP

The procedure for installing and configuring most wireless APs is similar from one manufacturer to the next . . . but not exactly the same. You're most likely to be successful if you locate the documentation for the AP you've chosen and follow its installation and configuration instructions carefully.

As we discuss in Chapter 5, when deciding which AP to purchase, consider ease of setup. By far, the easiest network configurations we have experienced have been with those APs that support WPS (or Wi-Fi Protected Setup, discussed in more detail in Chapter 9). Many WPS APs/routers support *pushbutton* configuration, where you literally push a physical button on the AP and click a virtual software button on your PC; in doing so, you associate the computer with the AP, complete with security in place. The WPS PIN method, where you find the PIN number printed on a label on your AP and enter it in a software program on your PC, does the trick equally well. If you're using a WPS setup, you can follow the quick setup instructions that came with your AP and pretty much ignore what we're saying in this chapter. Apple's AirPort Extreme wireless routers have a similarly simple setup for Mac users (and include software for Windows-only users).

Because having a network makes it easy to share an Internet connection, the best time to set up the AP for that purpose is during initial setup. In terms of setting up a shared Internet connection, you will already have a wired computer on your broadband (cable or DSL). This is very helpful as a starting place for most AP installations because most of the information you need to set up your AP is already available on your computer. If you don't have a wired computer on your Internet connection — that is, if this is the first computer you're connecting — first collect any information (special login information, such as username or password) that your Internet service provider (ISP) has given you regarding using its services.

Before you begin plugging things in, make sure that you've done your research:

- **Ensure that your computer has a standard wired Ethernet connection.** Most AP configurations require wired access for their initial setup. An Ethernet port is normally found on the back of your computer; this port looks like a typical telephone jack, only a little bit wider.

- **Collect your ISP's network information.** You need to know the following information; if you have a hard time figuring the following things out, ask the tech support folks at your ISP or check the support pages of the ISP's Web site:

  - *Your Internet protocol (IP) address:* This is the equivalent of your network's phone number. Your IP address identifies your network on the Internet and enables communications. It's always four 1- to 3-digit numbers separated by periods (125.65.24.129, for example).

  - *Your Domain Name System (DNS) or service, or server:* This special service within your ISP's network translates domain names into IP addresses. *Domain names* are the (relatively) plain English names for computers attached to the Internet. The Internet however, is based on IP addresses. For example, www.wiley.com is the domain name of the Web server computers of our publisher. When you type **www.wiley.com** into your Web browser address bar, the DNS system sends back the proper IP address for your browser to connect to.

  - *Whether your ISP is delivering all this to you via Dynamic Host Configuration Protocol (DHCP):* In almost all cases, the Internet service you get at home uses DHCP, which means that a *server* (or computer) at your ISP's network center automatically provides all the information listed in the preceding bullet, without you needing to enter anything manually. It's a great thing!

In the vast majority of cases, your ISP *does* use DHCP, and you don't have to worry about any of this information. If your service is Verizon's FiOS, your ISP is delivering an Ethernet connection to a firewall box that may or may not have wireless already built in. Verizon gives you the access information to this box when it's installed, and you can find all the information about your network connection from this box.

✔ **Collect the physical address of the network card used in your computer** *only if you're already connected directly to a cable/DSL modem.* Many ISPs used to use the physical address as a security check to ensure that the computer connecting to its network was the one paying for the service. Because of this security check, many AP manufacturers have added a feature called *MAC address cloning* to their routers. MAC address cloning allows home users to pay for only one connection from their ISP while having many devices able to get to the Internet. Most AP and Internet access devices available today permit you to change their physical addresses (Media Access Control [MAC] addresses) to match the physical address of your computer's existing network card. How you do this varies from system to system, but typically you'll see a list of MAC addresses (in a pull-down menu) for all devices connected to your AP. Simply select the MAC address you're looking to clone and click the button labeled Clone MAC address (or something similar).

Because some providers still track individual machines by MAC address, it's best to be prepared by writing down the MAC address of your computer's NIC in case you need it. How will you know that your ISP is tracking MAC addresses? Well, unfortunately, it's not always obvious — you might not see a big banner on the ISP's Web site telling you that MAC address tracking is in effect. But if you switch from a direct connection to your PC to a Wi-Fi router connection and you can't get online, MAC address tracking may indeed be the issue. The first step in troubleshooting such a problem is to unplug *everything* from the power supply (router/AP, broadband modem, and PC), and then turn everything back on starting with the modem and slowly working your way back to the PC(s). If you're still not getting online, call your ISP's technical support line. If MAC tracking is the issue, you can get around it by cloning your PC's MAC address in your router as discussed in the preceding paragraph.

## Installing the AP

If you're connecting your first computer with your ISP, the ISP should have supplied you with all the information we list in the preceding section except for the physical address of the network card (which you don't need if you aren't already connected).

Before you install your wireless gear, buy a 100-foot Ethernet cable. If you're installing your AP at a distance farther than that from your router or Internet-sharing PC, get a longer cable. Trust us: This advice comes with having done this a lot. You need a wired backup to your system to test devices and debug problems. To do that (unless you want to keep moving your gear around, which we don't recommend), you need a long cable. Or two. Anyone with a home network should have extra cables, just like you have electrical extension cords around the house. You can get good-quality 100-foot CAT-5e/6 patch cables online at places like Deep Surplus (www.deepsurplus.com) or a host of other online retailers for around $15.

When you're ready to do the AP installation, follow these steps:

1. **Gather the necessary information for installing the AP (see the preceding bulleted list) by following these steps:**

   In Windows XP:

   a. **Choose Start⇨Programs⇨Accessories⇨Command Prompt.**

   This step brings up the command prompt window, which is a DOS screen.

   b. **Type** IPCONFIG /ALL **and then press Enter.**

   The information scrolls down the screen. Use the scroll bar to slide up to the top and write down the networking information we list earlier in this chapter (physical address, IP address, default gateway, subnet mask, DNS servers) and whether DHCP is enabled.

   In Windows Vista/Windows 7:

   a. **Choose Start⇨Network⇨Network and Sharing Center.**

   The Network and Sharing Center appears, which gives you access to all network adapters and their properties.

   b. **From the Network and Sharing Center, click the View Status link.**

   A pop-up status window appears with all the information you need. Write this down on a piece of paper in case your AP configuration program asks for it as you move forward.

2. **Run the setup software that accompanies the AP or device containing your AP, like a wireless router.**

   The software probably starts when you insert its CD-ROM into the CD drive. In many cases, this software detects your Internet settings, which makes it much easier to configure the AP for Internet sharing and to configure the first computer on the network. For example, Figure 6-1 shows the Linksys Wireless-G Setup Wizard that accompanies the Linksys WAP54G Wireless-G Access Point, which is a wireless gateway from Linksys, a division of Cisco Systems, Inc.

**Figure 6-1:**
The Linksys
Wireless-G
Access
Point Setup
Wizard.

If your computer is using Windows Vista or Windows 7, you will see a lot of security dialog box pop-ups. The enhanced security in Vista/7 asks for your permission every time the installation software tries to do anything. As long as you have administration rights on your user account, you can keep saying yes to these security pop-ups and move through your AP setup. Be sure to look at the top left of the pop-up window so you know when you are saying yes to a security warning and when you are saying yes to the install. Even though Vista/7 dims the rest of the screen when a security warning pops up, it's confusing with the number of pop-ups you can run into. Just read the top left of the window and you'll always know what you're working in.

3. **When you're prompted by the setup software to connect the AP (see Figure 6-2), unplug the network cable that connects the broadband modem to your computer's Ethernet port and plug this cable into the Ethernet port that's marked *WAN* or *Modem* on your network's cable or DSL router or Internet gateway.**

   If you're using an Internet or wireless gateway, run a CAT-5e/6 cable from one of its Ethernet ports to the computer on which you're running the setup software. (*CAT-5e/6 cable* is a standard Ethernet cable or patch cord with what look like oversized phone jacks on each end. You can pick one up at any computer store or Radio Shack, if one didn't come with your AP.)

   If you're using a separate AP and router (in other words, if your AP *is not* your router), you need to connect a CAT-5e/6 cable between the AP and one of the router's Ethernet ports. Then connect another cable from another one of the router's Ethernet ports to the computer on which you're running the setup software.

**Figure 6-2:**
It's time to
connect the
AP or wire-
less router.

Most new APs try to obtain an IP address automatically and configure
themselves for you by choosing the channel and setting default parameters
for everything else (see Figure 6-3). In most cases, you need to manually
configure the security and some of the other information you collected
in Step 1, so have that information handy.

**Figure 6-3:**
What the AP
can find on
its own.

4. **Make note of the following access point parameters:**

   - Service set identifier (SSID)

   - Channel — if you're using an 802.11n AP, this should be set to Auto

   - WEP key or WPA2 passphrase (see Chapter 9 for more details on this subject), if your system doesn't use WPS

   - Router pin, if your system *does* use WPS (again, see Chapter 9 for more details on Wi-Fi Protected Setup)

   - Admin username and password

   - MAC address

   - Dynamic or static wide area network (WAN) IP address

   - Local IP address

   - Subnet mask

   - PPPoE (Point-to-Point Protocol over Ethernet) — sometimes found on DSL connections, and rarely for cable modems

   The preceding list covers the AP parameters you most often encounter and need to configure, but the list isn't comprehensive. (Read more about them in the next section.) You need this information if you plan to follow the steps for modifying AP configuration, which we cover in the later section "Changing the AP Configuration." (What did you expect that section to be called?) Other settings you probably don't need to change include the transmission rate (which normally adjusts automatically to give the best throughput), RTS/CTS protocol settings, the beacon interval, and the fragmentation threshold.

5. **Complete the software installation, and you're finished.**

   After you complete the AP setup process, you have a working access point ready to communicate with another wireless device.

## Configuring AP parameters

Here's a little more meat on each of the access point parameters you captured in Step 4 of the preceding section:

✔ **Service set identifier (SSID):** The SSID (sometimes called the *network name, network ID,* or *service area*) can be any alphanumeric string, including upper- and lowercase letters, up to 30 characters long. The AP manufacturer may set a default SSID at the factory, but you should change this setting. Assigning a unique SSID doesn't add much security; nonetheless, establishing an identifier that's different from the factory-supplied SSID makes it a little more difficult for intruders to access your wireless network. And, if you have a nearby neighbor with a wireless AP of the same type, you won't get the two networks confused.

When you configure wireless stations, you need to use the same SSID or network name that's assigned to the AP. It's also a good idea to turn off the SSID broadcast, a feature whereby the AP announces itself to the wireless world in general. Turning this off helps hide your AP from the bad guys who might want to hang off your network. However, hiding your SSID by no means absolutely hides your network (think of it as a mechanism for keeping out casual intruders to your network — dedicated intruders won't be stopped by a hidden SSID).

✔ **Channel:** This is the radio channel over which the AP communicates. If you plan to use more than one AP in your home, you should assign a different channel (over which the AP communicates) for each AP to avoid signal interference. If your network uses the IEEE 802.11g protocols, 11 channels — which are set at 5 MHz intervals — are available in the United States. However, because the radio signals used by the IEEE 802.11g standard are spread across a 22 MHz-wide spectrum, you can only use as many as three channels (typically 1, 6, and 11) in a given wireless network. If you have an 802.11n AP, you will want to have this set to Auto so that the AP and the wireless network card can switch between channels and use the ones with the least interference.

You can use other channels besides 1, 6, and 11 in an 802.11g network, but those three channels are the ones that are *noninterfering.* In other words, you could set up three APs near each other that use these channels and they wouldn't cause any interference with each other.

If you're setting up an 802.11n router that supports the 5 MHz frequency range, you have somewhere between 12 and 23 channels from which to choose (depending upon which country you live in). These channels don't overlap (like the 2.4 GHz channels do), so you can use them all without interference, while you can use only three without interference in the 2.4 GHz band. If you operate only one AP, all that matters is that all wireless devices on your network be set to the same channel. If you operate several APs, give them as much frequency separation as possible to reduce the likelihood of mutual interference.

Most 802.11g access points, such as some from Linksys, default to Channel 6 as a starting point and detect other access points in the area so that you can determine which channel to use. 802.11n access points will dynamically switch channels and choose the channels with the least interference automatically, which is cool.

A number of less-expensive 802.11n APs available today use only the 2.4 GHz frequency range. They can use multiple channels in this range, switching dynamically between channels if they find too much interference. The 2.4 GHz range is also the same frequency as Bluetooth devices. All new 802.11n APs have the option to work in a default mode, using only 20 MHz of bandwidth inside the 2.4 GHz channel space (a single channel), or they can use a combined pair of channels (providing 40 MHz of bandwidth). Using combined (or *bonded*) channels allows your 802.11n gear to reach greater data speeds and has the fringe benefit of helping your network avoid interference with Bluetooth devices. If you use a lot of Bluetooth devices around your computer — such as a Bluetooth headset, mouse, keyboard, and camera — make sure you are in combined mode so that your 802.11n connection does not affect your Bluetooth devices and vice versa.

When you have multiple access points set to the same channel, sometimes roaming doesn't work when users move about the house, and the transmission of a single access point blocks all others that are within range. As a result, performance degrades significantly (you see this when your *throughput,* or speed of file and data transfers, decreases noticeably). Use different, widely separated channels for 802.11g; because the 5 GHz 802.11n channels are inherently not overlapping, you don't have to worry about choosing widely separated channels in this case.

✔ **WPA2:** Wi-Fi Protected Access (WPA2) is one of the best solutions in Wi-Fi security. Two versions of WPA are available:

  • *WPA2 Personal, or Pre-Shared Key (PSK),* gives you a choice of two encryption methods: TKIP (Temporal Key Integrity Protocol), which utilizes a stronger encryption method and incorporates Message Integrity Code (MIC) to provide protection against hackers, and AES (Advanced Encryption System), which utilizes a symmetric 128-bit block data encryption. TKIP was the only system available in the first version of WPA; WPA2 added the ability to use AES, a stronger encryption system.

  • *WPA2 Enterprise, or RADIUS (Remote Authentication Dial-In User Service)* utilizes a RADIUS server for authentication and the use of dynamic TKIP, AES, or WEP. RADIUS servers are specialized computer devices that do nothing but authenticate users and provide them with access to networks (or deny unauthorized users access). If you don't know what a RADIUS server is all about, chances are good that you don't have one.

We talk about both types of WPA2 in much greater detail in Chapter 9. WPA2 Enterprise is, frankly, overkill for the home environment and much more difficult to set up. We recommend that you use WPA2 Personal instead — it gets you 99 percent of the way there in terms of security and is much easier to set up and configure.

✔ **WEP keys:** You should always use some security on your wireless network, and if your network cannot support WPA, you should use, at minimum, Wired Equivalent Privacy (WEP) encryption. Only a determined hacker with the proper equipment and software can crack the key. If you don't use WEP or some other form of security, any nosy neighbor with a laptop, wireless PC Card, and range-extender antenna may be able to see and access your wireless home network. Whenever you use encryption, all wireless stations in your house attached to the wireless home network must use the same key. Sometimes the AP manufacturer assigns a default WEP key. Always assign a new key to avoid a security breach. Read Chapter 9 for great background info on WEP and WPA2.

✔ **WPS:** *Wi-Fi Protected Security* works with WPA2 and makes it considerably easier to set up WPA2 security on your network by automating the process. As we discuss in Chapter 9, you can implement WPS in two ways:

  • *PIN code:* You can turn on WPA2 by simply entering a PIN code printed on your Wi-Fi hardware (usually on a label).

  • *Pushbutton:* You can press a button on your Wi-Fi router (a physical button or a virtual button on a screen on the router). When you push the button, your devices can automatically connect to the router and automatically configure WPA2 in 2 minutes. Simply push the button(s) and let things set themselves up with no further intervention.

✔ **Router PIN:** This is the PIN number used for rapid implementation of network encryption and security using the WPS (Wi-Fi Protected Setup) system that many new APs include — and as we mention at the beginning of this chapter. Your PIN should also be printed on a label on the side, back, or bottom of your AP. See Chapter 9 for details.

✔ **Username and password:** Configuration software may require that you enter a password to make changes to the AP setup. The manufacturer may provide a default username and password (see the user documentation). Use the default password when you first open the configuration pages, and then immediately change the password to avoid a security breach. (*Note:* This isn't the same as the WPA2 shared key, which is also called a *password* by some user interfaces.) Make sure that you use a password you can remember and that you don't have to write down. Writing down a password is the same as putting a sign on the equipment that says "Here's how you hack into me." If you ever lose the password, you can always reset a device to its factory configuration and get back to the point where you took it out of the box.

✔ **MAC address:** The *Media Access Control (MAC) address* is the physical address of the radio in the AP. This number is printed on a label attached to the device. You may need to know this value for troubleshooting, so write it down. The AP's Ethernet (RJ-45) connection to the wired network also has a MAC address that's different from the MAC address of the AP's radio.

✔ **Dynamic or static wide area network (WAN) IP address:** If your network is connected to the Internet, it must have an IP address assigned by your ISP. Most often, your ISP dynamically assigns this address. Your router or Internet gateway should be configured to accept an IP address dynamically assigned by a DHCP server. It's possible, but unlikely, that your ISP will require a *set* (static) IP address.

✔ **Local IP address:** In addition to a physical address (the MAC address), the AP also has its own network (IP) address. You need to know this IP address to access the configuration pages by using a Web browser. Refer to the product documentation to determine this IP address. In most cases, the IP address is 192.168.*xxx.xxx*, where *xxx* is between 1 and 254. It's also possible that an AP could choose a default IP that's in use by your cable or DSL router (or a computer that got its IP from the cable or DSL router's DHCP server). Either way, if an IP conflict arises, you may have to keep the AP and cable or DSL routers on separate networks while configuring the AP.

✔ **Subnet mask:** In most cases, this value is set at the factory to 255.255.255.0. If you're using an IP addressing scheme of the type described in the preceding paragraph, 255.255.255.0 is the correct number to use. This number, together with the IP address, establishes the subnet on which this AP will reside. Network devices with addresses on the same subnet can communicate directly without the aid of a router. You really don't need to understand how the numbering scheme works except to know that the AP and all the wireless devices that will access your wireless network must have the same subnet mask.

✔ **PPPoE:** Many DSL ISPs still use Point-to-Point Protocol over Ethernet (PPPoE). The values you need to record are the username (or user ID) and password. The DSL provider uses PPPoE as a means of identifying and authorizing users.

# Changing the AP Configuration

Each brand of AP has its own configuration software you can use to modify the AP's settings. Some products provide several methods of configuration. The most common types of configuration tools for home and small-office APs are

✔ **Software-based:** Some APs come with access point setup software you run on a workstation to set up the AP over a wireless connection, a USB cable, or an Ethernet cable. You don't see this much any longer except in professional high-end equipment that needs remote management not meant to work over the local network. One big exception here is Apple's AirPort Extreme and AirPort Express (discussed in Chapter 8), which use software built into Apple's OS X operating system (or a downloadable software client for Windows) instead of a Web-based configuration system.

✔ **Web-based:** Most APs intended for home and small-office use have a series of HTML forms stored in firmware. You can access these forms by using a Web browser over a wireless connection or over a network cable to configure each AP. In many cases when you're setting up your AP, you simply open the Web browser on the machine you have connected to the wired port on the AP; the browser automatically takes you to the AP setup wizard. This is so much simpler than the old days of having to load software on your machine just to set up your AP.

To access your AP's management pages with a Web browser, you need to know the local IP address for the AP. Most APs use the first address available on the network, such as 192.168.2.1. Note the last digit is almost always 1 to show the first of a possible 254 addresses in that last position. If you didn't note the IP address when you initially set up the AP, refer to the AP's user guide to find this address. If you're using a wireless router/Internet gateway, you can also run `ipconfig` (Windows XP) or open the Network and Sharing Center (Windows Vista or 7), as we describe in Chapter 7. The Internet gateway's IP address is the same as the default gateway.

Some APs and wireless routers have their administrative and configuration Web page IP addresses printed on labels on the back or bottom of the AP. If yours doesn't, we recommend that you get a label maker and print your own. There's nothing worse than looking for the user manual at an inopportune time when you need to be online now!

When you know the AP's IP address, follow these steps to access the AP management utility:

1. **Run your Web browser software.**

2. **Type the IP address for the AP on the Address line and then press Enter or click the Go button.**

   You'll probably see a screen that requests a password.

3. **Enter the password that you established during the initial setup.**

   This is the password that prevents unauthorized individuals from making changes to your wireless AP's configuration.

   After you enter the password, the AP utility displays an AP management screen. If you're not using a Web-based tool, you need to open the application that you initially installed to make any changes.

Bookmark your AP's configuration page in your Web browser for easier access in the future.

Within the AP's management utility, you can modify all the AP's settings, such as the SSID, channel, and WEP encryption key. The details of how to make these changes vary from manufacturer to manufacturer. Typically, the AP management utility also enables you to perform other AP management operations, such as resetting the AP, upgrading its firmware, and configuring any built-in firewall settings.

AP manufacturers periodically post software on their Web sites that you can use to update the AP's firmware, which is stored in the circuitry inside the device. Many new APs have the ability to automatically update the firmware directly from the manufacturer's site. We don't recommend that you set this up because most of the time you aren't going to need it, and upgrading firmware is serious business. If you decide to install a firmware upgrade, follow the provided instructions very carefully. ***Note:*** Do *not* turn off the AP or your computer while the update is taking place.

The best practice is to modify AP settings only from a computer that's directly connected to the network or the AP by a network cable. If you must make changes over a wireless connection, think through the order that you will make changes; otherwise, you could orphan the client computer. For example, if you want to change the wireless network's WPA2 key, change the key on the AP first and make sure that you write it down. As soon as you save the change to the AP, the wireless connection is effectively lost. No data passes between the client and the AP, so you can no longer access the AP over the wireless connection. To reestablish a useful connection, you must change the key on the client computer to the same key you entered on the AP.

# Chapter 7

# Setting Up a Wireless Windows Network

. . . . . . . . . . . . . . . . . . . . . . . . . . . . . . . . . . . . . . . . . . .

*In This Chapter*

▶ Installing wireless network interface adapters

▶ Modifying your adapter's settings

▶ Connecting with ease with Windows XP

▶ Setting up your network with Windows Vista

▶ Setting up a Windows 7 network

▶ Keeping track of your network's performance

. . . . . . . . . . . . . . . . . . . . . . . . . . . . . . . . . . . . . . . . . . .

*I*n this chapter, we describe the installation and configuration of wireless devices on Windows computers. To that end, we explain how to set up and configure the wireless network interface adapter in each of your computers (and other wireless devices) so that they can communicate with the access point (AP) and with one another. We also include special coverage for installing and configuring wireless network adapters in computers running Windows XP, Vista, and 7 (it's amazingly easy) and in handheld computers running one of the Microsoft mobile operating systems.

Read through Chapter 6 for information about physically installing APs, and see Chapter 8 for a discussion of setting up a Mac-based wireless network. If you find yourself lost in acronyms, check out Chapter 2 for the background on this equipment.

# Setting Up Wireless Network Interface Adapters

 Unless you have an older Windows computer that didn't come with built-in wireless (almost all new computers have wireless built-in and set up from the factory these days), you can safely ignore this section. These instructions tell you how to configure Windows to recognize your wireless adapter when you install it yourself. Otherwise, feel free to skip ahead to the individual sections regarding Windows XP, Vista, or Windows 7.

After you have the AP successfully installed and configured (see Chapter 6), you're ready to install and set up a wireless network interface adapter in each client device. Wireless network adapters all require the same information to be installed, although the installation on different platforms may vary to some degree. From most manufacturers, the initial setup procedure differs somewhat depending on the operating system that's running your computer.

In this section, we walk you through installing device drivers and client software before addressing the typical setup procedure for various wireless network interface adapters.

 The installation procedure for most types of PC devices consists of installing the hardware (the device) in your computer and then letting Windows detect the device and prompt you to supply a driver disc. With most wireless network adapters, however, you should install the software provided with the wireless networking hardware *before* installing the hardware.

## Installing device drivers and client software

Whenever you install an electronic device on your Windows PC, including a wireless network interface adapter, Windows needs to know certain information about how to communicate with the device. This information is a *device driver.* When you install a wireless network adapter, depending on which version of Windows you're using, you may be prompted to provide the necessary device driver. Device driver files typically accompany each wireless networking device on an accompanying CD. Most wireless device manufacturers also make the most up-to-date device driver files available for free download from their technical support Web sites.

When you install the wireless adapter into your computer, Windows uses the device driver files to add the adapter to your computer's hardware configuration. The new network adapter's driver also must be configured properly for it to communicate with other computers over the Windows network.

Even if you receive a driver CD with your wireless network interface adapter, we still recommend checking the manufacturer's Web site for the most recent software. Check the manufacturer's Web site and see whether you need to download the newest driver software as well as the newest *firmware,* which is the special software that resides in the flash memory of your network adapter and enables it to do its job.

The exact procedure for installing the drivers and software for the wireless network adapters varies from manufacturer to manufacturer, so read the documentation that accompanies the product you're installing *before* you begin. Although the details may differ from the instructions that accompany your product, the general procedure is in the following set of steps.

Because some antivirus programs often mistake installation activity for virus activity, shut down any antivirus programs you may have running on your PC *before* you begin any installation of software or hardware. (Remember to turn it back on when you're done!) In Windows XP, Vista, or Windows 7, you must have an account with administrator access to install any software on the device. Normally this is the default account you set up for yourself when you first configured the computer.

To install the software, follow these steps:

1. **Insert the CD that accompanies the wireless network adapter.**

   If the CD's startup program doesn't automatically begin, choose Start➪Run or use Windows Explorer to run the Setup.exe program on the CD.

2. **Install the software for configuring the network adapter by following the instructions on your screen.**

   Typically, you follow along with an installation wizard program.

   Don't insert the network adapter until you're prompted to do so by the installation software, as shown in Figure 7-1. In some cases, you may be prompted to restart the computer before inserting the adapter. For some older versions of Windows, you're prompted to insert your Windows CD in order for the setup program to copy needed networking files.

**Figure 7-1:**
Don't
connect
your
wireless
network
adapter
until you're
prompted
by the setup
software.

Because you installed the wireless network adapter's drivers and configuration software before inserting the adapter, the operating system should be able to automatically locate the driver and enable the new adapter.

If Windows can't find the driver, it may start the Found New Hardware Wizard (or Add/Remove Hardware Wizard or even New Hardware Wizard — it depends on which OS you're using). If this does happen, don't panic. You can direct Windows to search the CD-ROM for the drivers it needs, and they should be installed without issues (although you may have to reboot again).

After you insert or install your wireless network adapter — and restart the computer, if prompted to do so — the OS might prompt you to configure the new adapter. In most cases the configuration is handled through the OS automatically, but if it's not, keep reading. If you just get a message that your hardware is installed and ready to use, you can skip Step 3 and move on.

3. **If the software prompts you to configure the new adapter, you need to make sure that the following settings, at minimum, match those of your network's wireless AP:**

   • *SSID (network name or network ID):* Most wireless network adapter configuration programs display a list of wireless networks that are in range of your adapter. In most instances, you see only one SSID listed. If you see more than one, it means that one (or more) of your neighbors also has a wireless network that's close enough for your wireless adapter to "see." Of course, it also means that your neighbor's wireless adapter can see your network too. This is one good reason to give your wireless network a unique SSID (network name), and it's also a compelling reason to use encryption.

- *WPA2 passphrase (or WEP key):* Enter the same key or passphrase you entered in the AP's configuration. We discuss this concept in greater detail in Chapter 9.

- *Device PIN:* If your Wi-Fi gear supports the new WPS security configuration system, you can skip entering the passphrase and just enter the PIN for connecting to your AP. Typically the PIN is located on a label attached to your network adapter. We discuss WPS in greater detail in Chapter 9.

After you configure the wireless network adapter, the setup program may announce that it needs to reboot the computer.

As a bonus, most wireless adapters — as part of their driver installation package — include a bandwidth monitor. This handy tool is used to debug problems and inform you of connection issues. Almost all these tools are graphical and can help you determine the strength of the signal to your AP device as well as the distance you can travel away from the device before the signal becomes too weak to maintain a connection.

## PC Cards and mini-PCI cards

Nearly all Windows laptops and some Mac laptop computers have PC Card ports that are compatible with these cards. Belkin, Linksys, NETGEAR, D-Link, and others offer an 802.11n/g PC Card wireless network interface adapter. Most such devices already come preinstalled in portable computers and in some desktop computers. Many new laptops have DisplayPort adapters that are similar to PC Card slots. Don't confuse the two; even though they look the same, you don't want to jam a PC Card into a DisplayPort socket.

Most PC Card wireless network adapters require that you install the software drivers *before* inserting the PC Card for the first time. This is very important. Doing so ensures that the correct driver is present on the computer when the operating system recognizes that you've inserted a PC Card. Installing the drivers first also ensures that you can configure the wireless network connection when you install the device.

If you're installing a PC Card in a Windows-based computer with a PC Card slot, use the following general guidelines and don't forget to refer to the documentation that comes with the card for detailed instructions. (See Chapter 8 if you're a Mac user.)

Even if you received a CD with the PC Card, check the manufacturer's Web site for the most recent drivers and client station software. Wireless networking technology is continually evolving, so we recommend that you keep up with the changes.

To install a wireless PC Card in your computer, follow these steps:

1. **Insert the CD that accompanies the PC Card.**

   If the setup program doesn't automatically start, choose Start⇨Run (in Windows) or open Windows Explorer to run the Setup.exe program on the CD.

2. **Install the wireless client software.**

   During this installation, you may be asked to indicate the following:

   - Whether you want the PC Card set to infrastructure (AP) mode or to ad hoc (peer-to-peer) mode. Choose infrastructure mode to communicate through the AP. We talk about the difference between infrastructure and ad hoc modes in Chapter 2.

   - The SSID (network name).

   - Whether you will use a network password (which is the same as WPA2 encryption).

3. **After the wireless client software is installed, restart the computer if the install tells you to do so.**

4. **While the computer restarts, insert the PC Card wireless network adapter into the available PC Card slot.**

   Windows XP comes with generic drivers for many wireless PC Cards to make installation simpler than ever. Some PC Cards, which are made specifically for XP and certified by Microsoft, have no software included and rely on XP to take care of it. Even so, we recommend that you follow the directions that come with your PC Card and check whether your card is compatible with XP. Later in this chapter, we discuss the Windows XP Wireless Zero Configuration tools, which provide software for many Windows XP compliant and noncompliant cards.

   Windows Vista and Windows 7 don't have many built-in generic drivers, but they do have large built-in libraries of device-specific drivers that will automatically be installed when you connect your network adapter. To take advantage of these driver libraries, you will want to be sure that your PC Card has certified Vista drivers. At a minimum, the card should have a gray box on the package that says "Works with Windows Vista" and the Microsoft logo for Vista or a blue Microsoft logo saying "Compatible with Windows 7" for Windows 7.

   When Windows finds the driver, it enables the driver for the card, and you're finished.

# PCI and PCIx cards

If you purchase a wireless networking adapter that fits inside your PC, you must make sure that you have the right type for your computer. Most desktop computers built in the past five years contain PCI slots. The type of slot your computer has is most likely standard PCI. If you have a newer computer that uses PCIx, you're all set because PCIx is fully backward compatible. That means that you can use standard PCI cards in PCIx slots. The only difference you see is that the card doesn't fill the slot — the PCIx card slot is almost twice the length of the older standard PCI slot. Refer to your computer's documentation to determine which type of slot is inside your computer and then purchase a wireless network interface adapter to match.

Most manufacturers choose to mount a PC Card on a standard PCI adapter. Some of the newest PCI adapters consist of a mini-PCI adapter mounted to a full-size PCI adapter. In either of these configurations, a black rubber dipole-type antenna, or another type of range-extender antenna, is attached to the back of the PCI adapter.

Most PCI cards come with specific software and instructions for installing and configuring the card. We can't tell you exactly what steps you need to take with the card you buy, but we can give you some generic steps. Don't forget to read the manual and follow the onscreen instructions on the CD that comes with your particular card.

Follow these general guidelines for installing a PCI adapter card:

1. **Insert into the CD-ROM drive the CD that accompanied the adapter.**

   If necessary, choose Start➪Run (in Windows) or open Windows Explorer to run the Setup.exe program on the CD.

2. **Select the option for installing the PCI card driver software.**

   At this point, the driver is only copied to the computer's hard drive. The driver is added to the operating system in Step 4.

3. **If you're prompted to restart the computer, select No, I Will Restart My Computer Later and then click the Next (or Finish) button.**

   During the install process, many Windows-based computers prompt you to restart the computer by displaying a pop-up box with a question similar to "New drivers have been installed, do you want to restart for the changes to take effect?" The normal reaction may be to do what it asks and click OK — but *don't do it!* The software installation needs to be fully completed before the computer can be restarted. You know that it's completed because the installation wizard (not a Windows pop-up) prompts you for your next step. After the software has completed its installation process, *it* prompts you in its own software window to restart your computer, or it informs you that you need to restart to complete the installation.

4. **While the wireless station software is being installed, you may need to indicate whether you want the PC Card to be set to infrastructure (AP) mode or to ad hoc (peer-to-peer) mode. Choose infrastructure mode. You may also need to provide the SSID (network name) and indicate whether you'll use WEP/WPA or WPA2 encryption.**

   We recommend WPA2 because it's the most secure encryption for your wireless network.

5. **After the PCI card driver is installed, shut down the computer.**

6. **Unplug the computer and install the PCI card in an available slot.**

7. **Plug in the computer and restart it.**

   Windows recognizes that you have installed new hardware and automatically searches the hard drive for the driver. When Windows finds the driver, it enables the driver for the adapter, and you're finished.

# USB adapters

If you purchased a USB adapter, it's easy to install in your USB port. All new PCs and laptops come with at least one USB port (and usually more). Most USB adapters attach to the USB port via a USB cable. Many come with a base and an extension cable that allow you to move the USB adapter into a better position for its antenna. (See Chapter 8 if you're a Mac user.)

Here are the general guidelines for installing a USB wireless NIC:

1. **Insert into the CD-ROM drive the CD that accompanied the USB adapter.**

   If the CD's AutoRun feature doesn't cause the setup program to start, use the Run command from the Start button (in Windows) or open Windows Explorer to run the `Setup.exe` program on the CD.

2. **Install the driver software for the device.**

   In most cases, the software asks you to attach the USB device as soon as the drivers are installed. When finished, you see a confirmation in the notification area in the lower-right corner in Windows letting you know your USB network card has been installed and configured for use with Windows.

3. **After the wireless station software is installed, restart the computer if the installation software requires it.**

   You see the wireless adapter as a new network adapter in your system, and you have a new icon in your task tray indicating that the wireless is working correctly.

# Connecting to a Wireless Network with Windows XP

If you know that you'll use your computer to connect to several different wireless networks — perhaps one at home and another at work — Windows XP enables you to configure the wireless adapter to automatically detect and connect to each network on-the-fly, without further configuration.

To configure one or more wireless networks for automatic connection, follow these steps:

1. **In the notification area of the status bar, at the bottom of the screen, click the Network icon to display the Wireless Network Connection dialog box, and then click the Properties button.**

2. **In the Wireless Network Connection Properties dialog box that appears, click the Wireless Networks tab, as shown in Figure 7-2.**

**Figure 7-2:**
The Wireless Network Connection Properties dialog box.

Unless you've set it up with the SSID broadcast turned off (which we don't recommend because it doesn't really provide much of a security benefit — as discussed in Chapter 9), you'll see your network listed here. If your computer is in range of other wireless networks, their SSIDs will also be listed.

3. **To add another network to the list, click the Add button on the Wireless Networks tab.**

4. **In the Wireless Network Properties dialog box that appears, type the Network Name in the text box labeled Network Name (SSID).**

This is the name of the wireless network AP to which you will connect your computer.

You may want to enter the network name (SSID) for the wireless network at your office, for example.

5. **If you're connecting to a wireless network at your office, make sure that you have appropriate authorization and check with the network administrator for encryption keys and authorization procedures that he or she has implemented.**

If the network administrator has implemented a system for automatically providing users with WEP/WPA2 keys, click OK.

If the wireless network to which you plan to connect doesn't have an automatic key distribution system in place, do this:

    *a. Deselect the check box labeled The Key Is Provided for Me Automatically.*

    *b. Enter the WPA passphrase.*

    *c. Click OK to save this network SSID.*

6. **Move on to the next network (if any) that you want to configure.**

Notice the Key Index scroll box near the bottom of the dialog box. By default, the key index is set to 1. Your office network administrator knows whether you need to use the key index. This feature is used if the system administrator has implemented a *rotating key system,* which is a security system used in some office settings. You don't need to mess with this feature unless you're setting up your computer to use at work — it's not something you use in your wireless home network.

7. **After adding all the necessary wireless networks, click OK on the Wireless Networks tab of the Wireless Network Connection Properties dialog box.**

Windows XP now has the information it needs to automatically connect the computer to each wireless network whenever the wireless station comes into range.

# Connecting to a Wireless Network with Windows Vista

Windows Vista has wireless networking built right into the OS. Everything takes place in the Network and Sharing Center. From this one location, you can work with any of your network connections and get any information about those connections — from your IP address and your available bandwidth to troubleshooting connections with problems.

Before you get started, make sure you have the SSID and the WEP/WPA2 passphrase you set up in your AP handy — or your AP's router PIN if your AP supports WPS.

To set up a wireless network with the Vista Network and Sharing Center, follow these steps:

1. **Click the Windows Start icon in the lower-left corner of the screen. Select Network in the right column.**

   The Network dialog box appears.

2. **Click Network and Sharing Center in the links bar (just below the menu at the top of the screen).**

   The Network and Sharing Center appears, as shown in Figure 7-3. The default network you see is your wired network if you've previously been connected to one (such as plugging your computer directly into your broadband modem).

3. **To connect to your wireless network, click the Manage Network Connections link on the left menu.**

   The list is blank by default because if have not set up a wireless connection at this point.

4. **Click the Add button to begin the process of creating a wireless network connection.**

5. **In the How Do You Want to Add a Network window, select one of the following options for setting up your network:**

   • *Add a Network That Is in Range of This Computer:* Windows searches for any available wireless networks. Find your network and double click on its name to select it.

   • *Manually Create a Network Profile:* If you have turned off the broadcast of the SSID on your AP, you need to use the manual setup in Vista to add your AP to the list. Vista's manual Add wizard walks you through the process to get you connected.

**Figure 7-3:**
The
Windows
Vista
Network
and Sharing
Center.

- *Create an Ad Hoc Network:* An Ad Hoc network is one where two computers communicate with each other without an access point in the middle. Typically, you'd choose this option if you were trying to share files with another person and you were out of range of an AP-based wireless network (called an *Infrastructure* network). For most folks, this is a very rare occurrence. To create an ad hoc network, click this option and follow the wizard's steps. (Microsoft has a good tutorial at http://windows.microsoft.com/en-US/windows-vista/Set-up-a-computer-to-computer-ad-hoc-network.)

  You can also create an ad hoc network to use Windows Internet Connection Sharing (ICS), which allows a computer with both a wired and wireless network adapter to act like an AP for other wireless computers. This works in a pinch, but given that APs cost about $35 and have a lot of advantages (easier to set up, better performance, always-on, and so on), we don't recommend that you use this kind of network.

6. **Enter the WEP/WPA2 key and then click Connect.**

   The New Connection Wizard tests the connection. If your AP supports WPS, the wizard asks for your AP PIN number.

7. **To configure the connection, choose whether this is a Public or Private connection and then click Next.**

   After your AP has been discovered, or set up, you are asked to configure the connection to the AP. In Vista, security has been tightened on all network connections, so you must choose whether this is a Public or Private network connection. If you want to share anything from your Vista machine, choose Private, as shown in Figure 7-4. After you complete the selection, you return to the Manage Wireless Networks window, where you see your connection in the list.

**Figure 7-4:**
Setting the
network
location.

Set Network Location

Customize network settings

Network name:    Belkin_N1_0383C

Location type:    ○ **Public**
                 Discovery of other computers and devices will be limited, and
                 the use of the network by some programs may be restricted.

                 ● **Private**
                 This allows you to see computers and devices, while making
                 your computer discoverable.

                 Help me choose

Network Icon:    [ Change ]

Merge or delete network locations

[ Next ]  [ Cancel ]

If you're not sure you want to share anything from your Vista machine, you can gain a lot more security by choosing Public — you can always change it to Private later. When the connection is classified as Public, the Windows firewall is set with its strongest security, and many programs are restricted from using the connection — all programs to which you have not specifically granted access to an Internet connection are blocked from using this network connection. Vista security asks for permission to do everything, so any virus that's trying to use the connection will trigger the security to pop up and alert you.

8. **Close the Manage Wireless Networks window.**

    You return to the Network and Sharing Center, which shows the new wireless connection. Now that you have added your wireless network to your system, you can disconnect your Ethernet connection and try out your network.

You can discover and learn a lot more about your new wireless connection by using the tools in the Network and Sharing Center. In Figure 7-5, we have our Belkin AP set up as a Private network. From here, we can click the View Status link to see all the details of our connection. Clicking the Details button brings up all the information you might need about the speed, the amount of data that has been passed over the connection, the IP address, and pretty much everything else you may want to know about your connection. If you're having problems with your connection, the View Status pop-up also has a Diagnose button that can help determine the cause of your connection problem.

**Figure 7-5:** The Network and Sharing Center shows the new wireless network.

The Network and Sharing Center includes a helpful Signal Strength meter (which you can see from the View Status screen). We found in our tests that the Windows meter is not as fast to respond as some of the vendors' software that comes with your wireless network card. But if your vendor does not give you a signal meter, this one works fine to find weak coverage areas in your house.

# Connecting to a Wireless Network with Windows 7

The latest (and definitely, in our experience) greatest version of Windows is Windows 7. Like Windows Vista before it, Windows 7 makes connecting to wireless networks a snap. The built-in wireless networking configuration system is super slick, and we believe that there's no reason to ever use the software that might come with a network adapter when you're using Windows 7.

The big addition in Windows 7 is the *View Available Networks* feature. This feature lets you quickly find all of the available wireless networks in your location, wherever you may be — at home, in the office, near a wireless hot spot, and so on.

To use this feature to set up your network connection in Windows 7, follow these steps:

1. **Click the View Available Networks icon on the far right in the Windows taskbar.**

   Windows displays a list of available networks, as shown in Figure 7-6.

**Figure 7-6:**
Click here
to find your
wireless
network in
Windows 7.

2. **Select the network you want to join by clicking its name (SSID) in the resulting list. If you plan to connect to this network regularly (for example, if this is your home network), select the Connect Automatically check box. Then click the Connect button.**

3. **If you're connecting to a secured (WEP or WPA) network, Windows prompts you to enter the password. Enter the WEP or WPA password in the Security Key box, as shown in Figure 7-7, and then click OK.**

**Figure 7-7:**
Enter your
security key
(WPA or
WEP pass-
phrase) in
this box.

Your computer connects to the network, and you're all set. If you selected the Connect Automatically option in Step 2, your computer will always connect to this network whenever it's within range.

If you're having difficulties connecting to the network, click the Open Network and Sharing Center link at the bottom of Figure 7-6 and follow the steps we discuss in the preceding section, "Connecting to a Wireless Network with Windows Vista," to establish a network connection. But you really should never need to do this unless you're dealing with something problematic like a network with a "hidden" SSID that you need to enter manually.

# Tracking Your Network's Performance

When you have your network adapters and APs installed and up and running, you may think that you've reached the end of the game — wireless network nirvana! And, in some ways you have, at least after you go through the steps in Chapter 9 and get your network and all its devices connected to the Internet. But part of the nature of wireless networks is the fact that they rely on the transmission of radio waves throughout your home. If you've ever tried to tune in to a station on your radio or TV but had a hard time getting a signal (who hasn't had this problem — besides kids who've grown up on cable TV and Internet radio, we suppose), you probably realize that radio waves can run into interference or just plain peter out at longer distances.

The transmitters used in Wi-Fi systems use very low power levels — at least compared with commercial radio and television transmitters — so the issues of interference and range that are inherent to any radio-based system are even more important for a wireless home network.

Luckily, client software — usually in the form of a link test program — comes with some wireless network adapters, and signal meters are built into the Windows XP, Vista, and Windows 7 system trays. These tools enable you to look at the performance of your network. With most systems (and client software), you can view this performance-monitoring equipment in two places:

- ✔ **In your system tray:** Most wireless network adapters install a small signal-strength meter on the Windows system tray (usually found in the lower-right corner of your screen, although you may have moved it elsewhere on your screen). This signal-strength meter usually has a series of bars that light up in response to the strength of your wireless network's radio signal. It's different with each manufacturer, but most that we've seen light up the bars in green to indicate signal strength. The more bars that light up, the stronger your signal.

- ✔ **Within the client software itself:** The client software you installed along with your network adapter usually has a more elaborate signal-strength system that graphically (or using a numerical readout) displays several measures of the quality of your radio signal. This is often called a *link test* function, although different manufacturers call it different things.

(Look in your manual or in the online help system to find it in your network adapter's client software.) The link test usually measures several things:

- *Signal strength:* Also called *signal level* in some systems, this is a measure of the signal's strength in dBm. The higher this number, the better, and the more likely that you can get a full-speed connection from your access point to your PC.

- *Noise level:* This is a measure of the interference that's affecting the wireless network in your home. Remember that electronics in your home (such as cordless phones and microwaves) can put out their own radio waves that interfere with the radio waves used by your home network. Noise level is also measured in dBm, but in this case, lower is better.

- *Signal to Noise Ratio (SNR):* This is the key determinant to the performance of your wireless network. This ratio is a comparison of the signal (the good radio waves) with the noise (the bad ones). SNR is measured in dB, and a higher number is better.

Many link test programs not only provide a snapshot of your network performance, but also give you a moving graph of your performance over time. This snapshot can be helpful in two ways. First, if you have a laptop PC, you can move it around the house to see how your network performance looks. Second, it can let you watch the performance while you turn various devices on and off. For example, if you suspect that a 2.4 GHz cordless phone is killing your wireless LAN, turn on your link test and keep an eye on it while you make a phone call. Figure 7-8 shows the signal meter that is included with the Intel PROSet wireless adapters included from the factory with many Windows laptops. (Search in your applications folder for Intel PROSet System Tools.)

**Figure 7-8:**
Checking out your signal levels with a signal meter.

When you grow more comfortable with your wireless LAN — and start using it more and more — you can leverage these tools to tweak your network. For example, you can have your spouse or a friend sit in the living room watching the link test results while you move the access point to different spots in the home office. Or you can use the link test with a laptop to find portions of your house that have weak signals and then use these results to decide where to install a second access point.

# Chapter 8

# Setting Up a Wireless Mac Network

*I*f you're an Apple Macintosh user and you've just decided to try wireless networking, this chapter is for you. We talk about wireless networking equipment as it relates to the Mac and how to set up and configure one of Apple's wireless routers (the AirPort Extreme). We focus on Mac OS X versions 10.5 (Leopard) and 10.6 (Snow Leopard) because they're the most current versions of the Mac operating system at the time of this writing, but the advice we offer in this chapter gets you up and running with *any* version of OS X. Along the way, Apple has added a few new features to its wireless networking software (such as, in OS X 10.5, the ability to rapidly see which networks have encryption turned on), but by and large, the Wi-Fi connectivity in OS X has been the same in all versions.

*Note:* Apple stopped developing its previous operating system, OS 9, in 2002 and stopped building computers that supported that OS in 2006, so we don't talk about OS 9 here. If you have an older Mac that still runs only OS 9, you're not out of luck — OS 9 Macs can support and connect to AirPort and other Wi-Fi networks, but not all the features we discuss in this chapter apply.

We focus on the Apple AirPort system in this chapter simply because Apple has its own (robust and easy to use) Wi-Fi home router hardware that's tightly integrated into the OS X system software — and many Mac users prefer sticking with an all-Apple network. However, this doesn't mean that Apple computers *must* use AirPort routers; they can connect to any standards-based Wi-Fi router using the 802.11b, g, or n standard — both Danny and Pat use Macs with non-Apple routers every day. Also, *other* computers and devices can use an AirPort system as their Wi-Fi router (given a common Wi-Fi standard). Again, Pat and Danny both use Windows computers on AirPort networks every day.

# Exploring Your AirPort Hardware Options

In 1999, Apple Computer had a product launch for the iBook notebook (remember the multicolored curvy ones that looked a lot like a toilet seat?), and part of that big dog-and-pony show (*all* Apple product launches are extravaganzas!) was the introduction of the AirPort Wi-Fi wireless networking system. AirPort was the first mainstream, consumer-friendly, consumer-focused wireless networking system. Over the years, AirPort (which has gone through a few name changes and design upgrades, as we discuss) has become an integral part of the Apple product lineup and is installed (or available) in *all* of Apple's desktop and notebook computers.

The AirPort product line includes

- ✔ **Client adapters** — known as *AirPort cards* — which are installed inside Apple computers at the factory
- ✔ **Wireless routers** — known as *AirPort base stations* — that act as the base station for a Wi-Fi network

Apple's current AirPort products use the newest Wi-Fi 802.11n technology, which is (as we write) the state of the art in the wireless LAN world. Apple computers equipped with AirPort Extreme cards can connect to any Wi-Fi compatible 2.4 GHz 802.11b, g, or n wireless network, as well as 5 GHz 802.11a and 802.11n networks — regardless of whether the network uses Apple equipment or wireless equipment from any other Wi-Fi certified vendor. Apple also includes 802.11g or n networking in all of its iPhones, iPads, and iPod touch devices.

The current generation of AirPort products (dubbed AirPort Extreme and AirPort Express) is compatible with the 802.11n standard. You may also run into some older generations of AirPort equipment (just plain *AirPort* by name, as well as earlier editions of the AirPort Extreme) that are compatible with the older 802.11b or g standards but don't support 802.11n or a. If you're buying an AirPort Extreme router from eBay or some other merchant, make sure that you're buying the latest version by looking for the *AirPort Extreme Base Station with simultaneous dual-band support.* It's a mouthful, but it's the one you want!

## Getting to know the AirPort card

The current AirPort Extreme card is a mini-PCI Card (well, it's the same size and shape but designed to fit *only* in AirPort slots in Macs). It fits inside an Apple computer, such as several recent PowerBook G4s, iBooks, and iMacs, but doesn't fit in the original AirPort slot in older Macs — and isn't required for any of the Macs built since 2005 (all of which already have Wi-Fi built in).

Because Apple hasn't sold any consumer computers (MacBooks, MacBook Pros, iMacs and Mac Minis) without built-in Wi-Fi since 2005, the AirPort Extreme card isn't something you can just pick up at the Apple store. Instead, if you need one, you need to bring your Mac to a Mac repair store (such as an Apple Store or another authorized service center) and have them install one for you. For the vast majority of readers, this is a non-issue because their Macs are already Wi-Fi equipped.

## Apple AirPort Extreme–ready computers

Apple has been including Wi-Fi capability as a standard feature of all its computers for a few years — so any Mac laptop or desktop purchased since mid-to-late 2005 has at least 802.11g Wi-Fi capability built in. The only exceptions are the MacPro desktop machines, which are most often used in business environments (where wired Ethernet connections are common); these computers have the AirPort capability as an option in some lower-priced configurations.

All Apple computers sold since mid-to-late 2006 have been capable of supporting 802.11n as well, including the following:

- ✔ iMac with Intel Core 2 Duo (except the 17-inch 1.83 GHz iMac)
- ✔ MacBook with Intel Core 2 Duo
- ✔ MacBook Pro with Intel Core 2 Duo
- ✔ Mac Pro with AirPort Extreme card option

Some older Macintosh computers may not have an AirPort Extreme card installed but can be equipped with one (as discussed in the preceding section). You can find a list of these computers at `http://support.apple.com/kb/HT3024?viewlocale=en_US`. This Web page also includes a link to another Apple Web page that lists all Macintosh computers that can use the older AirPort card as well (though, as we mention in the nearby sidebar, good luck finding one!).

Apple computers that are equipped for installation of an AirPort Extreme card have an antenna built into the body of the computer. When you install the AirPort Extreme card, you attach the card to the built-in antenna. (All radios need an antenna to be able to send and receive radio signals, and wireless networking cards are no exception.)

If your older Mac doesn't support AirPort or AirPort Extreme, you can try using a standard Wi-Fi network adapter with the drivers found at `www.ioxperts.com/devices/devices_80211b.html`.

## The amazing disappearing AirPort card

The original AirPort card — the one that fits into all the older G3 and Titanium G4 PowerBooks, original iBooks, and original iMacs — has been discontinued by Apple. Not because they aren't good guys and not because they don't want to sell such cards to their customers. The problem is that the 802.11b chips inside these cards are no longer available. (The chip vendors are spending all their time building 802.11n chips like those found in the AirPort Extreme card.)

The result is that cards for these Macs are extremely rare — the only real source of these cards is the small number that have been stockpiled by folks who repair Macs as service parts. Think back to Econ 101, and you can see how this situation may drive up prices. We've seen these older cards (which originally cost about $100) for more than $150 on eBay and on various reseller Web sites. (They're nowhere to be found on Apple's own site.)

The only other alternative is to find a third-party Wi-Fi adapter that can work with your older Mac. For notebook computers such as the PowerBook, it's a PC Card adapter (see Chapter 2 for more on this), and for desktop Macs (such

as Power Macs), it's a PCI card. The AirPort software built into Mac OS X doesn't work with these devices (and almost none of them have a set of Mac *driver* software). The solution is to mate a card with some specialized software that works with a Macintosh.

The most popular solution here is to find an 802.11b PC or PCI card that works with the IOXpert 802.11b driver for Mac OS X ($19.95 after a free trial period). This software works with a large number of 802.11b cards and all versions of OS X (including the current Tiger version). Go to `www.ioxperts.com/devices/devices_80211b.html` to find out more, to see a list of compatible (and incompatible) cards, and to download the trial version.

Another option for an older Mac without wireless is to use a USB WI-FI network adapter (we discuss these in Chapter 4). Although there are dozens and dozens of such adapters available on the market, we've found that only a few include software that will let them work on a Mac. Before you buy such an adapter, verify on the box (or the manufacturer's Web site) that Mac software is indeed included.

## *"Come in, AirPort base station. Over."*

Apple currently sells two wireless routers, which they call *base stations*, as well as two versions of the wireless router with a built-in hard drive (for computer backups and network-attached storage) called the *Time Capsule*. (We discuss the Time Capsule in more detail in the section "Backing up with Time Capsule," later in this chapter.)

The main Apple AirPort product is the AirPort Extreme base station with simultaneous dual-band support. This $179 base station is fully compatible with the 802.11n standard (see Chapter 3) and includes the following features:

✔ **High-speed networking:** Using 802.11n on the wireless side of the house and full Gigabit (1,000 Kbps) wired Ethernet connections for three devices, this router provides connections as fast as any on the market.

✔ **True dual-band capabilities:** The AirPort Extreme has two radios that let you set up your network to provide 802.11n (or a, b, or g) networks on both the 2.4 GHz and 5 GHz radio bands *at the same time.* (See Chapter 5 for more on this.) You can configure your network for maximum throughput and range no matter what mix of network client devices you connect to the network.

✔ **A USB port:** You can configure the USB port to provide

- *A printer connection* (using the built-in print server). You can share just about any USB printer over the network, so you can send print jobs from your Macs or Windows computers to a central printer.

- *A shared storage device* (called AirPort Disk), using a USB hard drive. You simply plug in any USB external hard drive and enable the AirPort Disk feature by using Apple's software, and Macs and Windows computers can share the hard drive space for backups, storage of media files (such as digital music), and more.

- *A USB hub feature* (you need to provide your own hub), with which you can "double up" your AirPort Extreme base station's USB port, attaching more than one printer and/or hard drive at once.

✔ **Up-to-date security support:** The AirPort Extreme base station with Gigabit Ethernet supports WPA and WPA2 encryption, as well as support for business-grade security standards such as RADIUS and 802.1x.

✔ **Guest network support:** A very cool feature available on the AirPort Extreme (and a few other routers) is its *guest network* feature, which you set up in the AirPort Utility software on either a Mac or a PC. (See the later section "Configuring the AirPort base station on OS X" for details on setting up guest network.) A guest network can be completely separate (logically) from your primary network (so users on that network can't "see" your PCs and other devices), can have its own password for security purposes, and more. If you have a lot of house guests who want to get on your wireless network with their laptops, iPhones, and the like, this is a very handy feature to have.

Figure 8-1 shows the AirPort Extreme base station with simultaneous dual-band support.

**Figure 8-1:**
Going
802.11n
Apple style.

## Getting aboard the AirPort Express

The AirPort Extreme isn't the only Apple entry in the AP space (and, in fact, it's not even the most interesting!). Apple also has a small form factor (about the size of a deck of cards) access point known as the AirPort Express (shown in Figure 8-2).

**Figure 8-2:**
The AirPort
Express is
a jack of all
trades.

This $99 device can fulfill a bunch of different roles in your wireless life, including the following:

- **A full-fledged AP and router:** The AirPort Express can do pretty much everything any full-size AP can do — you can build your entire wireless LAN around an AirPort Express.

- **A travel router:** A cool new category of APs are those designed for use on the road — travel routers that you can pack up and plug into any broadband access (like that available in most hotels) and provide yourself with an instant Wi-Fi hot spot. You might use a travel router if your hotel doesn't have Wi-Fi (only wired broadband), or if you've got more than one device you want to get online and you don't want to have to pay the $14 a day many hotels charge for each Wi-Fi connection. The small size of the AirPort Express lets you stick it in your laptop bag and bring it wherever you go. Pat wrote this chapter in a hotel room in Vegas using his AirPort Express — a pretty sad commentary on his after-hours life these days!

- **A WDS repeater:** The Apple AirPort system supports the WDS (wireless distribution system) standard, which allows you to extend your network throughout even a *huge* house by having your wireless signals hop from AP to AP until they reach your distant clients.

- **A USB print server:** You can plug a USB printer into the AirPort Express and get printer access from the entire network.

- **An AirTunes player:** Perhaps our favorite feature of the AirPort Express is its support for AirTunes. AirTunes is the Apple software system that lets you listen to the music in your iTunes collection (and from your iPod) throughout your network. The AirPort Express has analog and digital audio connectors that you plug into a stereo or home theater. Although Apple's fancy AppleTV is an even better way of doing this, it costs four times as much as the AirPort Express; so if your focus is on music more than TV, you might consider choosing the AirPort Express.

Like the AirPort Extreme base station, the AirPort Express uses the 802.11n standard and can work with any type of Wi-Fi certified 802.11a, b, g, or n client. Note, however, that the AirPort express is *not* a simultaneous dual-band router, so it doesn't work on both the 2.4 and 5 GHz frequency bands at the same time. If you choose to use the 5 GHz band, you will be able to connect only 802.11a or n equipment that uses that frequency. Your 802.11 b and g gear will not be able to connect to the network unless you choose to use the 2.4 GHz frequencies only. (The setting in the AirPort Utility you'll want to choose if you've got g or b gear is *802.11n [802.11b/g compatible]*.)

There are three big differences between the AirPort Extreme and AirPort Express:

- The Airport Express supports only ten clients at once — which, as we discuss in Chapter 2, is an easy number to reach when you start adding wireless-enabled smartphones, iPods, gaming consoles, and entertainment devices to your network.

✔ The Airport Express doesn't support the *simultaneous* dual-band feature that the full-sized AirPort Extreme supports. So you can't have a 5 GHz *and* a 2.4 GHz network going at the same time in your home like you can with an AirPort Extreme.

✔ The AirPort Express USB port doesn't support attachment of a hard drive, so you can't use the AirPort Express for AirPort disk network-based storage for your home.

If you know that you're going to have some heavy-duty wireless networking needs, don't build your network around an AirPort Express. But if you live in an apartment or condo or smaller home and don't have a lot of devices to attach to the network, it's a great (and inexpensive) way to get started. And if your needs grow and you need to update to an AirPort Extreme, you'll still find the AirPort Express useful as a WDS repeater, for AirTunes or as a remote print server (Pat uses his for the latter two purposes and loves it!).

## Backing up with Time Capsule

Apple launched some great new backup software with OS 10.5 called Time Machine. With Time Machine activated, your Mac automatically and continually backs itself up as you use it. (You *do* back up your computer don't you? You sure as heck should!) Although Time Machine works great with an external hard drive plugged into your Mac's USB port, that strategy isn't all that convenient for users of laptop computers — and of course, *most* Macs sold these days are laptops.

What makes Time Machine really cool is its ability to do automatic, continuous background backing-up over a wireless connection. And to make this work, you need a *Time Capsule.* A Time Capsule is nothing more — and nothing less — than an AirPort Extreme base station with a built-in hard drive. All the features of a regular AirPort Extreme base station are included: the simultaneous dual-band support, the Gigabit Ethernet wired switch, the guest network support, all of it.

You can buy a Time Capsule for $299 for a 1 terabyte version (1,000 gigabytes, in other words) and $499 for a 2 terabyte version. And the storage space isn't *just* for Time Machine backups. Any Mac or Windows PC on your network can access it and use it as shared storage for all computers on the network.

The Time Capsule is the *only* device that Apple *officially* supports for Time Machine backups across a wireless network. Only game in town, in other words. That having been said, many people successfully use Time Machine on AirPort Disks and on other Network Attached Storage (NAS — see Chapter 10 for more on this topic) devices. This is *not* a task for the uninitiated, but you can find threads discussing this topic on sites such as Mac OS X Hints (www.macosxhints.com — a *great* site for Mac geeks) if you want to try!

The Time Capsule is very cool because it's all highly integrated and a snap to set up and it supports Time Machine. But for the $120 premium of a 1 terabyte version (over a plain AirPort Extreme base station), you can *easily* buy a 2 terabyte external hard drive and plug it into the AirPort Extreme for use as an AirPort Disk. And if the hard drive gets too small or, even worse, fails (which they do tend to do more often than you'd hope, but far less often than you'd fear), an external drive is much easier to replace, upgrade, or supplement with a second disk than is the disk built into the Time Machine (which is not user accessible). Of course, as we mention earlier, Apple doesn't support Time Machine backups to an AirPort Disk, so you'll have to jury rig such a setup.

# Using AirPort with OS X Macs

Apple makes it exceptionally easy to configure an AirPort Extreme base station or an AirPort Express. All Mac OS X computers that are capable of working with an AirPort system include one or two bits of software installed in the Utilities folder (found in your Applications folder):

- For OS X 10.4 and earlier, you find two bits of software:
  - AirPort Setup Assistant and
  - AirPort Admin Utility
- For OS X 10.5 (Leopard) and 10.6 (Snow Leopard), there's just a single program called AirPort Utility that incorporates the two previous apps in one.

The primary mode of Airport Utility (and Setup Assistant on older versions of OS X) is a "follow along with the steps" program (like the wizard programs often used on Windows computers) that guides you through the setup of an AirPort system by asking you simple questions. The Manual Setup mode of Airport Utility (or OS X 10.4 and earlier's Admin Utility) is used for tweaking and updating your settings later, after you already have everything set up. Most people can just use the primary mode of Airport Utility (or the Setup Assistant) for all their configuration needs — though we recommend that you occasionally run the manual setup mode/Admin Utility program to upgrade the *firmware* (the underlying software inside your AirPort), as we discuss later in the "Upgrading AirPort base station firmware on OS X" section.

## Configuring the AirPort base station on OS X

After you've purchased a new AirPort Extreme base station or an AirPort Express that you will use as a base station, you use the Airport Utility to set it up for use in your wireless home network.

Before running the AirPort Utility, it's a good idea to make sure that your Internet connection is up and running by connecting your Mac directly to your broadband modem by using an Ethernet cable. Check with your ISP for instructions on getting connected.

Follow these steps to configure the AirPort base station:

1. **Connect your AirPort to your broadband modem by using an Ethernet cable and plug your AirPort into the wall (power).**

2. **Click the Applications folder on the Dock.**

3. **When the Applications folder opens, double-click the Utilities folder icon.**

4. **In the Utilities folder, double-click the AirPort Utility icon to display the AirPort Utility window, shown in Figure 8-3.**

   The software searches for your new AirPort (and any existing AirPorts you have in range).

**Figure 8-3:** The OS X AirPort Utility window finds your AirPort(s).

> AirPort Utility
>
> Base Station 5fa9d7
>
> Base Station a6af6a
>
> AirPort Utility found an AirPort Extreme (Simultaneous Dual–Band) with default settings.
>
> AirPort Extreme Name: Base Station a6af6a
>
> IP Address: 10.0.1.1
>
> Version: 7.4.2
>
> AirPort ID: 00:24:36:A6:AF:6A
>
> If this isn't the AirPort wireless device you want to set up, you can select another from the list on the left. If you don't see it, make sure it is plugged in and in range of your computer.
>
> Click Continue to set up this AirPort Extreme.
>
> Manual Setup          Go Back     Continue

5. **Click the name of the AirPort in the left panel and then click the Continue button.**

   Your network will have its name assigned at the factory, similar to *Apple Network xxxxxx,* where *xxxxxx* is a six-digit hexadecimal number.

6. **In the next panel (shown in Figure 8-4), fill in the following information about your AirPort and then click the Continue button:**

   • *AirPort Extreme Name:* Enter a name for your network (something like "Danny's Network" or "Pat's Super Secret Wi-Fi Clubhouse" — any name you can remember). Note that this setting is labeled *AirPort Express Name* for an Airport Express.

- *(Optional) AirPort Extreme Password:* We recommend that you put a password on your network so no one can accidentally (or maliciously) change your settings. Note that this password is *not* the password for your network's WPA security, but rather the admin password for the AirPort base station itself. Note that this setting is named *AirPort Express Password* for an AirPort Express.

**Figure 8-4:**
Give your network a name.

7. **Tell your AirPort what you want to do with it by selecting one of the options shown in Figure 8-5. Then click Continue.**

   The first time you set up a network, select the I Want to Create a New Wireless Network option.

**Figure 8-5:**
Set up a new network.

8. **On the wireless security settings screen shown in Figure 8-6, enter a name for your wireless network and then select one of the following options for the security level of your network:**

   - *WPA2 Personal:* We *highly* recommend that you choose the WPA2 Personal option and then choose a password combining both alphabetical and numeric characters. Check the Remember This Password in My Keychain check box so you don't have to re-enter the password each time your computer connects to the network.

   - *No Security:* If you select this option, your network is not password-protected, and any wireless device can connect to your network. We don't recommend selecting this option (see Chapter 9 for the reasons why), but if you feel confident that you don't need security on your network — maybe you live miles away from your neighbors or you're just not worried if someone gets access to your broadband connection or network — you can choose this option.

9. **Click Continue to move to the next step.**

Figure 8-6:
Set your
wireless
security. Be
sure to use
WPA2!

10. **If you want to establish a guest network (as described earlier), fill in the fields shown in Figure 8-7 and select the Enable Guest Network check box.**

    *Note:* This option is for the AirPort Extreme only and not for the AirPort Express.

11. **Click Continue.**

    Your AirPort detects your Internet connection and prompts you to perform any setup required. If you use a standard residential broadband connection, you see a screen like the one in Figure 8-8.

**Figure 8-7:**
Create a
guest net-
work to let
visitors get
access to
the Internet
but stay off
your private
network.

**Figure 8-8:**
Confirm
your
Internet
connection.

12. **Most broadband connections automatically connect to your AirPort and assign it an IP address via DHCP; in this case, select the I Connect to the Internet with a DSL or Cable Modem Using DHCP check box. Then click Continue.**

    In rare cases (some DSL modems), you need to enter some additional information that you'll be prompted for by the AirPort Utility — information that should have been provided to you by your broadband provider.

13. **On the final screen, review your settings and then click Update.**

    This step writes your settings into the memory of the AirPort and restarts the AirPort. When the restart is completed, your Mac automatically connects to the AirPort, and you and your network are all set.

## Upgrading AirPort base station firmware on OS X

In this section, we explain how to upgrade the firmware of an AirPort base station. Upgrading the firmware on your AirPort Extreme base station through a direct Ethernet cable connection is easiest. Use an Ethernet cable (either a straight-through cable or a crossover cable; the base station automatically detects the type of cable you're using) to connect your computer's Ethernet port to the base station's LAN port. You can also do the upgrade over a wireless connection.

To upgrade the firmware of a new AirPort base station that you're setting up for the first time, follow these steps:

1. **On the Dock, click the Applications folder.**

2. **When the Applications folder opens, double-click the Utilities folder.**

3. **Double-click the AirPort Utility icon to display the Select Base Station window.**

4. **Highlight the base station name and then select Upload Firmware from the Base Station menu.**

   Your AirPort connects to Apple's servers and checks for updated firmware. A pop-up window (as shown in Figure 8-9) lists both your current firmware version and the latest available version.

5. **If a newer version of the firmware is available, select it and click OK to apply it.**

**Figure 8-9:**
Choose which firmware version to use here.

Choose the firmware version you want to upload to your AirPort wireless device, or choose Other... to browse for another version.

Current Version  7.4.2

Upload Version  [ 7.4.2                    ▲▼ ]

Updating firmware will cause any computer on the wireless network to be disconnected.

( Cancel )    ( OK )

6. **A message pops up, stating that uploading the software will cause the wireless network to be disconnected. Click OK.**

   The new firmware is copied to the base station.

7. **When you see a message that says the system is waiting for the base station to restart and that the base station has been successfully updated, click OK.**

8. **When the AirPort Utility indicates that the firmware upgrade is done, close the application.**

## Connecting another Mac to your AirPort network on OS X

When you set up your AirPort base station by following the directions in the earlier section "Configuring the AirPort base station on OS X," you also set up the AirPort card in the computer you used to configure the base station. However, you need to configure the AirPort cards in the other Mac computers in your house to enable them to connect to the AirPort network. Follow these steps:

1. **Click the Apple Menu and select System Preferences, and then select the Network preference pane.**

2. **When the Network preference pane opens, select AirPort, as shown in Figure 8-10.**

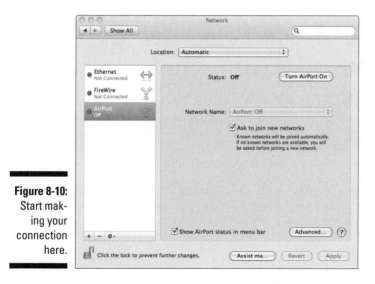

**Figure 8-10:** Start making your connection here.

3. **Make sure that the AirPort Power is on — if it's not, click the Turn AirPort On button.**

4. **In the Network Name pull-down menu, select the AirPort network you created.**

5. **Select the Show AirPort Status in Menu Bar check box.**

   This step streamlines the process the next time you want to get connected to this network. If you've turned on Encryption for your AirPort network, you're prompted to enter a password.

6. **Select the appropriate type of encryption and then type your password in the Password text box. Select the Remember Password in My Keychain check box to retain the password for future use.**

   See Chapter 9 for more on encryption.

7. **Click OK.**

8. **When the Network preference pane indicates that you're connected to the AirPort network, you can close the window.**

After you've gone through these steps, you have an AirPort icon on your menu bar. The next time you want to connect to this AirPort network, simply go up to the menu bar, click the AirPort icon, and select the network name. That's it!

# Adding a Non-Apple Computer to Your AirPort Network

One reason why wireless home networking has become so popular is the interoperability between wireless networking equipment from different vendors. Because it adheres to the standards and is Wi-Fi certified, Apple wireless networking equipment is no exception. You can even use a Windows or Linux computer to connect to an Apple AirPort base station.

From the user perspective (yours, in other words), the instructions we give in Chapter 7 for connecting to any wireless network work for connecting a non-Apple computer to an Apple AirPort network. Use Window's built-in wireless configuration software or the software that came with your wireless network adapter, find your AirPort network, enter your WPA password, and you're set. That's all there is to it. Wi-Fi is truly a cross platform system.

# Connecting to Non-Apple-Based Wireless Networks

One scenario you may encounter in a home network is the need to connect a Macintosh computer to a non-Apple-based network. Follow the procedures outlined in this earlier section titled "Connecting another Mac to your AirPort network on OS X" for adding a computer to a wireless network — using the Network preference pane in your Mac's System Preferences, the procedure should be identical. If you have any trouble, it almost certainly relates to the network password. Here are a few troubleshooting tips to resolve password issues:

- **Try turning off encryption on the wireless network:** If you can successfully connect your Mac to the network without the need of a password, you can be sure that the password was the problem. Don't leave the network unprotected, however. Read on.

- **Check the password configuration:** When you turn on the access point's encryption, determine whether the password is an alphanumeric value or a hexadecimal number. Some hardware vendors provide configuration software that has you enter a passphrase, but the software then generates a hexadecimal number. You have to enter the hexadecimal number, not the passphrase, in the AirPort software.

- **Watch for case sensitivity:** If the Windows-based access point configuration software enables you to enter an alphanumeric password, keep in mind that the password is case sensitive. For WEP, the password should be either exactly 5 characters (letters and numbers) for 64-bit encryption or 13 characters for 128-bit encryption. You should then enter exactly the same characters in the Password text box in the AirPort pane of Internet Connect.

- **Use current software:** Make sure that you're using the most current version of AirPort software. The most up-to-date software makes it easier to enter passwords connecting to a Windows-based wireless network. The new software automatically distinguishes between alphanumeric and hexadecimal passwords. With earlier versions of the software, to connect to a WEP-encrypted Windows-based network, you have to type quotation marks around alphanumeric values and type $ in front of hexadecimal numbers.

These guidelines should help you get your Mac connected to a Windows wireless network, including the capability to share the Internet. Keep in mind, however, that other factors determine whether you can also share files, printers, and other resources over the wireless network.

# Chapter 9

# Securing Your Home Network

*I*f you read the news — well, at least if you read the same networking news sources that we do — you've probably seen and heard a thing or two (or a hundred) about wireless local area network (LAN) security. In fact, you really don't need to read specialized industry news to hear about this topic. Many major newspapers and media outlets — *The New York Times,* the *San Jose Mercury News,* and *USA Today,* among others — have run feature articles documenting the insecurity of wireless LANs. Most of these stories have focused on *wardrivers,* folks who park in the lots in front of office buildings, pull out their laptops, and (way too) easily get onto corporate networks.

In this chapter, we talk a bit about these security threats and how they may affect you and your wireless home network. We also (helpful types that we are) give you some advice on how you can make your wireless home network more secure. We talk about a system called Wi-Fi Protected Access (WPA), which can make your network secure to most attacks, and also an older system called Wired Equivalent Privacy (WEP), which doesn't do such a good job but may be the best you can do in many cases.

 The advice we give in this chapter applies to any 802.11 wireless network, whether it uses a, b, g, or n, because the steps you take to batten down the hatches on your network are virtually identical, regardless of which version of 802.11 you choose. (If you missed our discussion on 802.11 basics, jump back to Chapter 2.)

No network security system is absolutely secure and foolproof. And, as we discuss in this chapter, Wi-Fi networks have some inherent flaws in their security systems, which means that even if you fully implement the security system in Wi-Fi (WPA or especially WEP), a determined individual could still get into your network. We're not trying to scare you off here. In a typical residential setting, chances are good that your network won't be subjected to some sort of determined attacker like this. Follow our tips, and you should be just fine.

# Assessing the Risks

The biggest advantage of wireless networks — the fact that you can connect to the network just about anywhere within range of the base station (up to 300 feet, or even longer with the new 802.11n technology) — is also the biggest potential liability. Because the signal is carried over the air via radio waves, anyone else within range can pick up your network's signals, too. It's sort of like putting an extra RJ-45 jack for a wired LAN out on the sidewalk in front of your house: You're no longer in control of who can access it.

One thing to keep in mind is that the bad guys who are trying to get into your network probably have bigger antennas than you do. Although you may not pick up a usable signal beyond a few hundred feet with that antenna built into your laptop PC, someone with a big directional antenna that has much more gain than your PC's antenna (*gain* is a measure of a circuit's ability to increase the power of a signal) may be able to pick up your signals — you would never know it was happening.

## General Internet security

Before we get into the security of your wireless LAN, we need to talk for a moment about Internet security in general. Regardless of what type of LAN you have — wireless or wired or using powerlines or phone lines or even none — when you connect a computer to the Internet, some security risks are involved. Malicious *crackers* (the bad guys of the hacker community) can use all sorts of tools and techniques to get into your computers and wreak havoc.

For example, someone with malicious intent could get into your computer and steal personal files (such as your bank statements you've downloaded by using Quicken) or mess with your computer's settings — or even erase your hard drive or use it to store illicit files. Your computer can even be hijacked (without your knowing it) as a jumping off point for other people's nefarious deeds; as a source of an attack on another computer (the bad guys can launch these attacks remotely using your computer, which makes them that much harder to track down); or even as a source for spam e-mailing.

What we're getting at here is that you need to take a few steps to secure *any* computer attached to the Internet. If you have a broadband (DSL, satellite, fiber-optic, or cable modem) connection, you *really* need to secure your computers. The high-speed, always-on connections that these services offer make it easier for a cracker to get into your computer. We recommend that you take three steps to secure your computers from Internet-based security risks:

✔ **Use and maintain antivirus software.** Many attacks on computers don't come from someone sitting in a dark room, in front of a computer screen, actively cracking into your computer. They come from viruses (often scripts embedded in e-mails or other downloaded files) that take over parts of your computer's operating system and do things you don't want your computer doing (such as sending a copy of the virus to everyone in your e-mail address book and then deleting your hard drive). Choose your favorite antivirus program and use it. Keep the *virus definition files* (the data files that tell your antivirus software what's a virus and what's not) up to date. And for heaven's sake, use your antivirus program!

If you use a Mac, you can safely ignore this part — you don't need antivirus software.

✔ **Use a personal firewall on each computer.** *Personal firewalls* are programs that basically look at every Internet connection entering or exiting your computer and check it against a set of rules to see whether the connection should be allowed. After you've installed a personal firewall program, wait abut a day and then look at the log. You may be shocked and amazed at the sheer number of attempted connections to your computer that have been blocked. Most of these attempts are relatively innocuous, but not all are. If you have broadband, your firewall may block hundreds of these attempts every day.

We like ZoneAlarm (`www.zonealarm.com`) for Windows computers as well as the firewall built into Windows Vista and Windows 7, and we use the built-in firewall on our Mac OS X computers.

✔ **Turn on the firewall functionality in your router.** Whether you use a separate router or one integrated into your wireless access point, it will have at least some level of firewall functionality built in. Turn this function on when you set up your router or access point. (It's an obvious option in the configuration program and may well be turned on by default.) We like to have both the router firewall and the personal firewall software running on our PCs. It's the belt-and-suspenders approach, but it makes our networks more secure.

In Chapter 11, we talk about some situations (particularly when you're playing online games over your network) where you need to disable some of this firewall functionality. We suggest that you do this only when you must. Otherwise, turn on that firewall — and leave it on.

Some routers use a technology called *stateful packet inspection* (SPI) firewalls, which examine each packet (or individual chunk) of data coming into the router to make sure that it was truly something requested by a computer on the network. If your router has this function, we recommend that you try using it because it's a more thorough way of performing firewall functions. Others simply use Network Address Translation (NAT, which we introduce in Chapter 2) to perform firewall functions. This strategy isn't quite as effective as stateful packet inspection, but it works quite well.

## Airlink security

The area we focus on in this chapter is the aspect of network security that's unique to wireless networks: the airlink security. These security concerns have to do with the radio frequencies beamed around your wireless home network and the data carried by those radio waves.

Traditionally, computer networks use wires that go from point to point in your home (or in an office). When you have a wired network, you have physical control over these wires. You install them, and you know where they go. The physical connections to a wired LAN are inside your house. You can lock the doors and windows and keep someone else from gaining access to the network. Of course, you have to keep people from accessing the network over the Internet, as we mention in the preceding section, but locally it would take an act of breaking and entering by a bad guy to get on your network. (It's sort of like it was on Danny's old favorite TV show *Alias,* where they always seem to have to go deep into the enemy's facility to tap into anything.)

Wireless LANs turn this premise on its head because you have absolutely no way of physically securing your network. Of course, you could join the tinfoil hat brigade ("The NSA is reading my mind!") and surround your entire house with a Faraday cage. (Remember those from physics class? We don't either, but they have something to do with attenuating electromagnetic fields.) But, really, you're not going to do that, are you?

Some access points have controls that let you limit the amount of power used to send radio waves over the air. This solution isn't perfect (and it can dramatically reduce your reception in distant parts of the house), but if you live in a small apartment and are worried about beaming your Wi-Fi signals to the apartment next door, you may try limiting the amount of power. It doesn't keep a determined cracker with a supersize antenna from grabbing your signal, but it may keep honest folks from accidentally picking up your signal and associating with your access point.

## No security!

A lot of wireless LAN gear (access points and network cards, for example) is shipped to customers with all the security features turned off. That's right: zip, nada, zilch, no security. A wide-open access point sits there waiting for anybody who passes by (with a Wi-Fi equipped computer, at least) to associate with the access point and get on your network.

This isn't a bad thing in and of itself; initially configuring your network with security features turned off and then enabling the security features after things are up and running

is easier than doing it the other way 'round. Unfortunately, many people never take that extra step and activate their security settings. So a huge number of access points out there are completely open to the public (when they're within range, at least).

We should add that some people *purposely* leave their access point security turned off to provide free access to their neighborhoods. (We talk about this topic in Chapter 16.) But we find that many people don't intend to do so.

Basically, what we're saying here is that the radio waves sent by your wireless LAN gear will leave your house, and there's not a darned thing you can do about it. Nothing. What you can do, however, is make it difficult for other people to tune into those radio signals, thus (and more importantly) making it difficult for those who can tune into them to decode them and use them to get onto your network (without your authorization) or to scrutinize your e-mail, Web surfing habits, and so on.

You can take several steps to make your wireless network more secure and to provide some airlink security on your network. We talk about these topics in the following sections, where we discuss both easy and more complex methods of securing your network.

# Getting into Encryption and Authentication

Two primary (and interrelated) security functions enable you to secure your network:

- **Encryption:** Uses a cryptographic *cipher* to scramble your data before transmitting it across the network. Only users with the appropriate *key* can unscramble (or decipher) this data.

✔ **Authentication:** Simply the act of verifying that a person connecting to your wireless LAN is indeed someone you want to have on your network. With authentication in place, only authorized users can connect with your APs and gain access to your network and to your Internet connection.

With most wireless network systems, you take care of both functions with a single step — the assignment of a network *key* or *passphrase.* (We explain later in this chapter, in the section "Enabling encryption," where to use each of these.) This key or passphrase is a secret set of characters (or a word) that only you and those you share it with know.

The key or passphrase is often known as a *shared secret* — you keep it secret but share it with that select group of friends and family whom you want to allow access to your network. With a shared secret (key or passphrase), you perform both of these security functions:

✔ You authenticate users because only those who have been given your supersecret shared secret have the right code word to get into the network. Unauthenticated users (those who don't have the shared secret) cannot connect to your wireless network.

✔ Your shared secret provides the mechanism to encrypt (or scramble) all data being sent over your network so that anyone who picks up your radio transmissions sees nonsensical gibberish, not data that they can easily read.

The two primary methods of providing this authentication and encryption are

✔ Wired Equivalent Privacy (WEP)

✔ Wi-Fi Protected Access (WPA)

Note that there are two versions of WPA — WPA and WPA2 — but we refer to them jointly as WPA except when discussing their differences.

We talk about the WEP and WPA security systems in more detail in the remaining parts of this chapter. WEP, an older system, provides only a limited amount of security because certain flaws in its encryption system make it easy for crackers to figure out your shared secret (the *WEP key*) and therefore gain access to your network and your data.

 WPA is the current, up-to-date, security system for Wi-Fi networks (there are several variants, which we discuss later in this chapter), and it provides you with much greater security than does WEP. If you have the choice, *always* use WPA on your network rather than WEP.

The shared secret method of securing a network is by far the most common and the easiest method. But it doesn't provide truly bulletproof user authentication, simply because having to share the same secret passphrase or key with multiple people makes it a bit more likely that somehow that secret will get into the wrong hands. (In fact, some experts would probably hesitate to even call it an authentication system.)

For most home users, this *isn't* a problem (we don't think that you have to worry about giving Nana the passphrase for your network when she's in town visiting her grandkids), but in a busy network (such as in an office), where people come and go (employees, clients, customers, and partners, for example), you can end up in a situation where just too many people have your shared secret.

When this happens, you're stuck with the onerous task of changing the shared secret and then making sure that everyone who needs to be on the network has been updated. It's a real pain.

These kinds of busy networks have authentication systems that control the encryption keys for your network and authorize users on an individual basis (so that you can allow or disallow anyone without having to start from scratch for *everyone*, like you do with a shared secret).

If you have this kind of busy network, you may want to consider securing your network with a system called *WPA Enterprise* and *802.1x*. See the sidebar "802.1x: The corporate solution" later in this chapter, for more information on this topic.

# Introducing Wired Equivalent Privacy (WEP)

The original system for securing a wireless Wi-Fi network is known as *WEP*, or *Wired Equivalent Privacy*. The name comes from the admirable (but, as we discuss, not reached) goal of making a wireless network as secure as a wired one.

In a WEP security system, you enter a *key* in the Wi-Fi client software on each device connecting to your network. This key must match the key you establish when you do the initial setup of your access point or wireless router (which we describe in Chapter 7).

WEP uses an encryption protocol called *RC4* to secure your data. Although this protocol (or *cipher*) isn't inherently bad, the way that it's implemented in WEP makes it relatively easy for a person to snoop around on your network and figure out your key. And after the bad guys have your key, they can access your network (getting into PCs and other devices attached to the network or using your Internet connection for their own purposes) or stealthily intercept everything sent across the wireless portion of your network and decode it without your ever knowing!

It doesn't take superhacker skills to do this either — anyone running Windows, Linux, or Mac with wireless capabilities can download free and readily available software from the Web and, in a short time, figure out your key.

### Understanding how WEP works

WEP encrypts your data so that others can't read it unless they have the key. That's the theory behind WEP, anyway. WEP has been a part of Wi-Fi networks from the beginning. (The developers of Wi-Fi were initially focused on the business market, where data security has always been a big priority.) The name itself belies the intentions of the system's developers; they wanted to make wireless networks as secure as wired networks.

To make WEP work, you must activate it on all the Wi-Fi devices on your network via the client software or configuration program that came with the hardware. And every device on your network must use the same WEP key to gain access to the network. (We talk a bit more about how to turn on WEP in the later section, "Clamping Down on Your Wireless Home Network's Security.")

For the most part, WEP is WEP is WEP. In other words, it doesn't matter which vendor made your access point or which vendor made your laptop's PC Card network adapter — the implementation of WEP is standardized across vendors. Keep this one difference in mind, however: WEP key length. Encryption keys are categorized by the number of bits (1s or 0s) used to create the key. Most Wi-Fi equipment these days uses *128-bit* WEP keys, but some early gear (such as the first generation of Apple AirPort equipment) supported only a 64-bit WEP key.

Many access points and network adapters on the market support even longer keys — for example, many vendors support a 256-bit key. The longest standard key, however, is 128 bits. Most equipment enables you to decide how long to make your WEP key; you can often choose between 64 and 128 bits. Generally, for security purposes, you should choose the longest key available. If, however, you have some older gear that can't support longer WEP key lengths, you can use a shorter key. If you have one network adapter that can handle only 64-bit keys but have an access point that can handle 128-bit keys, you need to set up the access point to use the shorter, 64-bit key length.

### Deciding whether to use WEP

WEP sounds like a pretty good deal, doesn't it? It keeps your data safe while it's floating through the ether by encrypting it, and it keeps others off your access point by not authenticating them. But, as we mention earlier in this chapter, WEP isn't all that secure because flaws in the protocol's design make it not all that hard for someone to crack your WEP code and gain access to your network and your data. For a typical home network, a bad guy with the right tools could capture enough data flowing across your network to crack WEP in a matter of hours.

We don't know of a single AP or wireless router, or network adapter being sold today that doesn't support the newer (and much more secure) WPA protocol. And, almost any computer with Windows XP or later (Vista or Windows 7) or any version of Macintosh OS X will also have built-in support for WPA. So there are many good reasons to skip WEP entirely and just go with WPA — and no good reasons to not do so unless you really, *really* need to.

But (there's often a *but* in these situations) at times you may need to consider using WEP encryption. You run into this situation with certain pieces of Wi-Fi gear because with most APs you can't have "mixed" encryption methods on the same network. In other words, you can't have laptop A connected to the Wi-Fi AP using WPA and laptop B (which doesn't support WPA) connected using WEP. It's often one security system or the other.

We say earlier in this chapter that almost all PCs support WPA, but the dirty little secret of the Wi-Fi business is that not all non-PC devices support WPA yet. A good example here is the original Nintendo DS handheld gaming device (luckily the newer DSi *does* support WPA). Before you buy any of these devices, check the product specs and make sure you see WPA (or even better, WPA2) listed on that long list of acronyms of supported protocols and features.

If you *know* that you're going to have non-WPA devices on your network (like one of those aforementioned original Nintendo DSs), you have two primary choices: 1.) Downgrade your entire network to WEP (boo!), or 2.) choose an AP or wireless router that supports the simultaneous use of more than one type of encryption (rare, but not uncommon on fancier APs). A third (and in our mind, better) option is to use an AP that lets you create a *guest network* (see Chapter 5 for more on this) — like Apple's Airport Extreme and Cisco's Valet wireless routers. In this case, you can create a strongly secured WPA network for all of your WPA-capable devices and then create a second, segregated network for those devices that only support WEP.

# Opting for a better way: WPA

If you can use WPA — meaning if your access point or wireless router and the wireless clients on your network support it — you should enable and use WPA as the airlink security system on your network. WPA is significantly more secure than WEP and keeps the bad guys off your network much more effectively than any implementation of WEP.

Two variants of WPA are available: WPA and WPA2. The major difference between these two is the *cipher,* or *encryption,* system used to encode the data sent across the wireless network. WPA2 — which is the latest and most powerful wireless security system — uses a system called Advanced Encryption Standard (AES), which is pretty much uncrackable by mere mortals. But even the original WPA version (that's just WPA to you and us), with its Temporal Key Integrity Protocol (TKIP), is much more secure than WEP.

WPA2 is also known as 802.11i. 802.11i is simply the IEEE (the folks who make the standards for wireless LANs) standard for advanced Wi-Fi security. WPA was a step toward 802.11i set by the Wi-Fi Alliance. WPA2 incorporates all the security measures included in 802.11i.

What's better about WPA?

- ✔ **More random encryption techniques:** WPA has basically been designed as an answer for all the current weaknesses of WEP, with significantly increased encryption techniques. One of WEP's fatal flaws is that because its encryption isn't sufficiently random, an observer can more easily find patterns and break the encryption. WPA's encryption techniques are more random — and thus harder to break.

- ✔ **Automatic key changes:** WPA also has a huge security advantage in the fact that it automatically changes the key (although you, as a user, get to keep using the same passcode to access the system). So, by the time a bad guy has figured out your key, your system has already moved on to a new one, and he can't do anything with that knowledge.

  It's possible to use an 802.1x system, as described in the sidebar "802.1x: The corporate solution," later in this chapter, to provide automatic key changes for WEP systems. This is *not* something you would find in anyone's home network, but some businesses use it, and it does indeed minimize the effect of WEP's fixed keys.

- ✔ **More user friendly:** WPA is easier for consumers to use because there's no hexadecimal stuff to deal with — just a plain text password. The idea is to make WPA much easier to deal with than WEP, which takes a bit of effort to get up and running (depending on how good your access point's configuration software is).

The type of WPA (and WPA2) we're talking about here is often called *WPA Personal* or *WPA PSK* (preshared key). The more complex (and not suitable for the home) version of WPA/WPA2 that is often used by businesses is *WPA Enterprise.* We talk about WPA Enterprise in the sidebar titled "802.1x: The corporate solution."

# Clamping Down on Your Wireless Home Network's Security

Well, that's enough of the theory and background, if you've read from the beginning of this chapter. It's time to get down to business. In this section, we discuss some of the key steps you should take to secure your wireless network from intruders. None of these steps is difficult, will drive you crazy, or make your network hard to use. All that's required is the motivation to spend a few minutes (after you have everything up and working) battening down the hatches and securing for sea. (Can you tell that Pat used to be in the Navy?)

The key steps in securing your wireless network, as we see them, are the following:

1. Change all the default values on your network.

2. Enable WPA.

3. Close your network to outsiders (if your access point supports this).

In Chapter 16, we talk about using a *virtual private network* (VPN) to secure your wireless connection when you're away from home and when using public Wi-Fi hot spots. A virtual private network encrypts *all* the data that you send and receive through your computer's network connection by creating a secure and encrypted network *tunnel* that runs from your computer to an Internet gateway (which could be in your office's network or run by a service provider on the Internet). If you really wanted to be as secure as possible, you could use a VPN from a service provider such as Witopia (www.witopia.net) to encrypt your traffic at home too. The added benefit of a VPN, beyond security, is anonymity. To folks on the Internet, you will "look" like you're surfing the Internet from that Internet gateway and not your home — which makes it harder for folks to track your comings and goings on the Internet. A VPN isn't required to have a secure Wi-Fi network, but if you have one and your WEP or WPA security is broken by a bad guy, your communications will be secured by another layer of encryption — although a VPN won't necessarily ensure that files on your computer can't be accessed if you have file sharing turned on.

Hundreds of different access points and network adapters are available. Each has its own unique configuration software. (At least each vendor does; and often different models from the same vendor have different configuration systems.) You need to RTFM (Read the Fine Manual!). We give you some generic advice on what to do here, but you really, really, really need to pick up the manual and read it before you enable security on your network. Every vendor has slightly different terminology and different ways of doing things. If you mess up, you may temporarily lose wireless access to your access point. (You should still be able to plug in a computer with an Ethernet cable to gain access to the configuration system.) You may even have to reset your access point and start over from scratch. Follow the vendor's directions (as painful at that may be). We tell you the main steps you need to take to secure your network; your manual gives you the exact line-by-line directions on how to implement these steps on your equipment.

Most access points also have some wired connections available — Ethernet ports you can use to connect your computer to the access point. You can almost always use this wired connection to run the access point configuration software. When you're setting up security, we recommend making a wired connection and doing all your access point configuration in this manner. That way, you can avoid accidentally blocking yourself from the access point when your settings begin to take effect.

## Getting rid of the defaults

It's incredibly common to go to a Web site like Wigle.net, look at the results of someone's Wi-Fi reconnoitering trip around their neighborhood, and see dozens of access points with the same service set identifier (SSID, or network name; refer to Chapter 2). And it's usually Linksys because Linksys is the most popular vendor out there (though NETGEAR, D-Link, and others are also well represented). Many folks bring home an access point, plug it in, turn it on, and then do nothing. They leave everything as it was set up from the factory. They don't change any default settings.

Well, if you want people to be able to find your access point, there's nothing better (short of a sign on the front door) than leaving your default SSID broadcasting out there for the world to see. In some cities, you could probably drive all the way across town with a laptop set to `Linksys` as an SSID and stay connected the entire time. (We don't mean to just pick on Linksys here. You could probably do the same thing with an SSID set to `default`, the D-Link default, or any of the top vendors' default settings.)

When you begin your security crusade, the first thing you should do is to change all the defaults on your access point. You should change, at minimum, the following:

✔ Your default SSID

✔ Your default administrative password

If you don't change the administrative password, someone who gains access to your network can guess at your password and end up changing all the settings in your access point without your knowing. Heck, if they want to teach you a security lesson — the tough love approach, we guess — they could even block you out of the network until you physically reset the access point (by pressing the "reset" button typically found on the back of the AP). These default passwords are well known and well publicized. Just look on the Web page of your vendor, and we bet you can find a copy of the user's guide for your access point available for download. Anyone who wants to know them does know them.

When you change the default SSID on your access point to one of your own making, you also need to change the SSID setting of any computers (or other devices) that you want to connect to your LAN. To do this, follow the steps we discuss in this part's earlier chapters. In other words, if you initially connected your PC to a network called "Default," that network will no longer be available under that name, so you'll need to look for — and connect with — the new network name.

This tip really falls under the category of Internet security (rather than airlink security), but here goes: Make sure that you turn off the Allow/Enable Remote Management function (it may not be called this exactly) if you don't need it. This function is designed to allow people to connect to your access point over the Internet (if they know your IP address) and do configuration stuff from a distant location. If you need this turned on (perhaps you have a home office and your IT gal wants to be able to configure your access point remotely), you know it. Otherwise, it's just a security hole waiting to be opened, particularly if you haven't changed your default password. Luckily, most access points have this function set to Off by default, but take the time to make sure that yours is set to Off.

## Enabling encryption

After you eliminate the security threats caused by leaving all the defaults in place (see the preceding section), it's time to get some encryption going. Get your WPA (or WEP) on, as the kids say.

We've already warned you once, but we'll do it again, just for kicks: Every access point has its own system for setting up WPA or WEP, and you need to follow those directions. We can give only generic advice because we have no idea which access point you're using.

To enable encryption on your wireless network, we suggest that you perform these generic steps:

1. **Open your access point's configuration screen.**

2. **Go to the Wireless, Security, or Encryption tab or section.**

   We're purposely being vague here; bear with us.

3. **Select the option labeled Enable WPA or WPA PSK (or, if you're using WEP, the one that says Enable WEP or Enable Encryption or Configure WEP).**

   You should see a menu similar to the one shown in Figure 9-1. (It's for a NETGEAR access point or router.)

4. **If you're using WEP, select the check box or pull-down menu option for the appropriate WEP key length for your network. If you're using WPA, skip this step.**

   We recommend 128-bit keys if all the gear on your network can support it. (See the earlier section "Understanding how WEP works" for the lowdown on WEP keys.)

**Figure 9-1:**
Setting up WPA on a NETGEAR access point.

5. **For WPA, create a passphrase that will be your network's shared secret. For WEP, create your own key if you want (we prefer to let the program create one for us):**

    a. **Type a passphrase in the Passphrase text box.**

    b. **Click the Generate Keys (or Apply or something similar) button.**

*Remember the passphrase.* Write it down somewhere, and put it someplace where you won't accidentally throw it away or forget where you put it. Danny likes to tape his passphrase to the box that his Wi-Fi gear came in so that he can always track it down.

Whether you create your own key or let the program do it for you, a key should now have magically appeared in the key text box. ***Note:*** Some systems allow you to set more than one key (usually as many as four keys). In this case, use Key 1 and set it as your default key by using the pull-down menu.

*Remember this key!* Write it down. You'll need it again when you configure your computers to connect to this access point.

Some access points' configuration software doesn't necessarily show you the WEP key you've generated — just the passphrase you've used to generate it. You need to dig around in the manual and menus to find a command to display the WEP key itself. (For example, the Apple AirPort software shows just the passphrase; you need to find the *Equivalent Network Password* in the Airport Admin application to display the WEP key — in OS X, this is in the Base Station menu.)

For WEP, the built-in wireless LAN client software in Windows XP numbers its four keys from 0–3 rather than 1–4. So, if you're using Key 1 on your access point, select Key 0 in Windows XP.

6. **Click OK to close the WPA or WEP configuration window.**

    You have finished turning on WPA or WEP. Congratulations.

Can we repeat ourselves again? Will you indulge us? The preceding steps are *very* generic. Yours may vary slightly (or, in rare cases, significantly). Read your user's guide. It tells you what to do.

After you configure WPA or WEP on the access point, you must go to each computer on your network, get into the network adapter's client software (as we describe in Chapters 7 and 8), turn on WPA or WEP, and enter the passphrase or the WEP key. Typically, you find an Enable Security dialog box containing an option to turn on security and one to four text boxes for entering the key. Simply select the option to enable WEP or WPA, enter your key or passphrase in the appropriate text box, and then click OK. For Windows 7, all you need to do is enter the WEP or WPA password in the Security Key text box, as shown in Figure 9-2.

**Figure 9-2:**
Entering a
WPA pass-
phrase in
Windows 7.

Connect to a Network

Type the network security key

Security key: ●●●●●●●●

☑ Hide characters

OK    Cancel

## Closing your network

The last step we recommend that you take in the process of securing your wireless home network (if your access point allows it) is to create a *closed network* — a network that allows only specific, predesignated computers and devices onto it. You can do two things to close down your network, which makes it harder for strangers to find your network and gain access to it:

✔ **Turn off SSID broadcast:** By default, most access points broadcast their SSID out onto the airwaves. This makes it easier for users to find the network and associate with it. If the SSID is being broadcast and you're in range, you should see the SSID on your computer's network adapter client software and be able to select it and connect to it — that is, assuming you have the right WEP key or WPA password, if encryption is configured on that access point. When you create a closed network, you turn off this broadcast so that only people who know the exact name of the access point can connect to it.

You can find access points even if they're not broadcasting their SSIDs (by observing other traffic on the network with a network *sniffer* program), so this security measure is an imperfect one — and no substitute for enabling WPA. But it's another layer of security for your network. Also, if you're in a situation where you'll have lots of people coming into your home and wanting to share your connection, you may not want to close off the network, so you'll need to balance convenience for your friends against the small exposure of a more open network.

✔ **Set access control at the MAC layer:** Every network adapter in the world has assigned to it a unique number known as a Media Access Control (MAC) address. You can find the MAC address of your network adapter by looking at it (it's usually physically printed on the device) or using software on your computer:

  • In Windows Vista or 7, open a command window (click the Start button and type **cmd** in the search text box) and then enter the getmac /v command (note the space between getmac and /v). You then see a list of all the network adapters installed in your computer with their MAC addresses..

- Look in the Network Control Panel or System Preference on a Mac.

With some access points, you can type the MAC addresses of all the devices you want to connect to your access point and block connections from any other MAC addresses.

Again, if you support MAC layer filtering, you make it harder for friends to log on when visiting. If you have some buddies who like to come over and mooch off your broadband connection, you need to add their MAC addresses as well, or else they can't get on your network. Luckily, you need to enter their MAC addresses only one time to get them "on the list," so to speak — at least until you have to reset the access point (which shouldn't be that often).

Neither of these "closed" network approaches is absolutely secure. MAC addresses can be *spoofed* (imitated by a device with a different MAC address, for example), and hidden SSIDs can be seen (with the right tools), but both are ways to add to your overall security strategy.

## Dealing with the WEP hex and ASCII issues

One area that is consistently confusing when setting up a WEP key — and often a real pain — is the tendency of different vendors to use different formats for the keys. The most common way to format a key is to use *hexadecimal* (hex) characters. This format represents numbers and letters by using combinations of the numbers 0–9 and the letters A–F. (For example, the name of Pat's dog, Opie, would be represented in hexadecimal as *4f 70 69 65*.) A few other vendors use *ASCII*, which is simply the letters and numbers on your keyboard.

Although ASCII is an easier-to-understand system for entering WEP codes (it's really just plain text), most systems make you use hexadecimal because it's the standard. The easiest way to enter hex keys on the computers connecting to your access point is to use the passphrase we discuss in the section "Enabling encryption." If your network adapter client software lets you do this, do it! If it doesn't, try entering the WEP key you wrote down when you generated it. (It's probably hexadecimal.) If that doesn't work either, you may have to dig into the user's manual and see whether you need to add any special codes before or after the WEP key to make it work. Some software requires you to put the WEP key inside quotation marks; other software may require you to put an *0h* or *0x* (that's a zero and an *h* or an *x* character) before the key or an *h* after it (both without quotation marks).

# Taking the Easy Road

We hope that the preceding section has shown you that enabling security on your wireless network isn't all that hard. It's straightforward, as a matter of fact. But a percentage of folks are always going to want things to be even easier (count us in that group!). So the Wi-Fi Alliance and Wi-Fi equipment manufacturers have developed a new standard (yeah, another standard!) called *Wi-Fi Protected Setup,* or WPS.

WPS (in its early days of development, WPS was called *Simple Config*) is an additional layer of hardware or software or both built into Wi-Fi APs, routers, and network adapters that makes it easier for users to set up WPA in their network and easier to add new client devices to the network.

Not all Wi-Fi equipment on the market supports the WPS system — it's optional, and not all manufacturers have chosen to adopt it. But based on what WPS brings to the table, it's an attractive system that we suspect will be made available more widely over time.

So what *does* WPS do? Well, it essentially automates the authentication and encryption setup process for WPA by using one of two methods:

- ✔ **A PIN:** All WPS certified equipment will have a PIN (personal information number) located on a sticker. When a WPS-certified router or AP detects a new wireless client on the network, it will prompt the user to enter this PIN — either through the management software or Web page for the router, or directly on the router itself using an interface (such as an LCD screen) located on the router. If the correct PIN is entered, the network will automatically configure WPA and allow that device to join the network. That's all there is to it!

- ✔ **A button:** The other mechanism for using WPS is called *PBC* (or push button configuration). As the name implies, a button (either a physical button or a virtual one on a computer screen or LCD display) is used — there's a button on both the AP/router and the client hardware. When the router or AP detects a new Wi-Fi client wanting to join the network, vsion to join the network, you simply press the buttons on both the router/AP and the client; configuration is automatic at this point.

- ✔ **USB:** The final method for using WPS involves USB flash drives (the little stick memory cards so many folks carry around these days). WPS can allow a user to simply "carry" the network credentials to a client on a flash drive; simply plug the flash drive into the AP/router and then into the network client, and configuration is automatic.

To be a bit pedantic about it, the USB method of setting up WPS is not an actual part of the Wi-Fi Alliance's WPS specification — it's just a nifty trick that some manufacturers have come up with on their own. But hey, it works, so who are we to split hairs?

WPS takes the drudgery out of setting up WPA and makes the process pretty much foolproof. WPS *doesn't* change the actual level of security you're getting on your network — all it does is turn on WPA (WPA2, to be exact). One thing to keep in mind about WPS is that you need to have WPS capabilities on both ends of the connection — the AP/router and the network client — to use the system, but you can *still use* the old-fashioned manual configuration process described in the preceding section to add non-WPS capable gear to your network.

As WPS becomes more widespread, the Wi-Fi Alliance folks have another trick up their sleeves to make things even easier. These tricks come in the form of an additional way of using WPS called *NFC* (near field communications). NFC is an extremely short-range (think centimeters, not feet) radio system (similar, and related, to the RFID tags now in use in warehouses and other logistics systems). With NFC, you would simply put the WPS client and AP/router in very close proximity, and they'd automatically configure network access and security. Pretty cool.

The NFC method of configuring WPS is *optional* in the WPS standard — while the PIN and button are mandatory (found in all WPS certified devices).

As we mention at the outset, WPS is still just a few years old, but you can see the growing list of WPA-compliant products at the Wi-Fi Alliance Web site at www.wi-fi.org/wifi-protected-setup. (Just scroll down to the link titled Products Certified for Wi-Fi Protected Setup.)

# Going for the Ultimate in Security

Setting up your network with WPA security keeps all but the most determined and capable crackers out of your network and prevents them from doing anything with the data you sent across the airwaves (because this data is securely encrypted and appears to be just gibberish).

But WPA has a weakness, at least the way it's most often used in the home: the preshared key (your shared secret or passphrase) that allows users to connect to your network and that unlocks your WPA encryption.

Your preshared key can be vulnerable in two ways:

- ✔ **If it's not sufficiently difficult to guess (perhaps you used the same word for your passphrase as you used for your network's ESSID):** You would be shocked by how many people do that! Always try to use a passphrase that combines letters (upper- and lowercase is best) and numbers and doesn't use simple words from the dictionary.

- ✔ **If you've given it to someone to access your network and then they give it to someone else:** For most home users, this isn't a big deal, but if you're providing access to a large number of people (maybe you've set up a hot spot), it's hard to put the genie back in the bottle when you've given out the passphrase.

Neither of these two circumstances is usually a problem for the typical home — WPA-PSK (WPA Home) is more than sufficient for most users. But if you want to go for the ultimate in security, you may consider using an AP (and wireless clients) that supports *WPA Enterprise.*

WPA Enterprise uses a special server, known as a *RADIUS* server, and a protocol called 802.1x (see the nearby sidebar, "802.1x: The corporate solution"), which provide authentication and authorization of users using special cryptographic keys. When a RADIUS server is involved in the picture, you get a more secure authorization process than the simple shared secret used in WPA Home. You also get a new encryption key created by the RADIUS server on an ongoing basis — which means that even if a bad guy figured out your key, it would change before any damage could be done.

Now you *can* create and operate your own RADIUS server on a spare computer in your home (see the commercial software available at www.lucidlink. com, or the free software at www.freeradius.org), but that topic is beyond the scope of this book.

You can use a hosted RADIUS service on the Internet. Such services charge a small monthly fee (about $5 per month) and let you use a RADIUS server that's hosted and maintained in someone's data center. All you need to do is pay your monthly bill and follow a few simple steps on your access point and PCs to set up RADIUS authentication and WPA Enterprise.

You need to have an AP that supports WPA Enterprise — check the documentation that came with yours because not all APs support it.

Several services provide WPA Enterprise RADIUS support. An example is the *McAfee Wireless Home Security* product (www.mcafee.com), which offers WPA Enterprise support for a one-time fee of about $50.

## 802.1x: The corporate solution

Another security standard that's quite popular in the corporate Wi-Fi world is 802.1x. This isn't an encryption system but, rather, an authentication system. An 802.1x system, when built into an access point, allows users to connect to the access point and gives them only extremely limited access (at least initially). In an 802.1x system, the user could connect to only a single network port (or service). Specifically, the only traffic the user could send over the network is your login information, which is sent to an authentication server that would exchange information (such as passwords and encrypted keys) with the user to establish that he or she was allowed on the network. After this authentication process has been satisfactorily completed, the user is given full access (or partial access, depending on what policies the authentication server has recorded for the user) to the network.

802.1x is *not* something we expect to see in any wireless home LAN any time soon. It's a business-class kind of thing that requires lots of fancy servers and professional installation and configuration. We just thought we would mention it because you no doubt will hear about it when you search the Web for wireless LAN security information.

# Part IV
# Using Your
# Wireless Network

The 5th Wave          By Rich Tennant

"Wait a minute...This is a movie, not a game?! I thought I was the one making Keanu Reeves jump kick in slow motion."

# In this part . . .

*A*fter you get your wireless home network installed
and running, you probably can't wait to use it, in
both practical and fun ways. In this part, we cover the
basics on what you can do with your network, such as
share printers, files, folders, and even hard drives. But
you can do many other cool things over a wireless network, too, such as play multiuser computer games, access
your music collection, see what's happening in your front
yard from anywhere in the world, and operate various
types of smart-home conveniences. We even help you figure out how to use your high-speed mobile phone service
to create a network that goes where you do. How cool is
that? Of particular interest to many is our full chapter on
using Bluetooth-enabled devices such as printers, cameras, and phones. (Bluetooth and Wi-Fi are like chocolate
and peanut butter — they go great together.)

# Chapter 10

# Putting Your Wireless Network to Work

**R**emember that old Cracker Jack commercial of the guy sitting in the bed when the kid comes home from school? "What did you learn in school today?" he asks. "Sharing," says the kid. And then, out of either guilt or good manners, the old guy shares his sole box of caramel popcorn with the kid.

Just as you shouldn't hog your caramel popcorn, you shouldn't hog your network resources. We're going to help you share your Cracker Jacks now! (After all, that's kinda the purpose of a network, right?) You have a wireless network installed. It's secure. It's connected. Now you can share oodles of devices with others in your family — not just your Internet connection, but also printers, disk drives, gaming consoles, and A/V controls.

In this chapter, we give you a taste of how you can put your wireless network to work. We talk about accessing shared network resources, setting up user profiles, accessing peripheral devices across the network (such as network printing), checking out network shares on other PCs, and other such goodies.

 Entire books have been written about sharing your network. *Home Networking For Dummies* (by Kathy Ivens); *Mac OS X All-in-One Desk Reference For Dummies* (by Mark L. Chambers, Erick Tejkowski, and Michael L. Williams); and *Windows XP For Dummies, Windows Vista For Dummies,* and *Windows 7 For Dummies* (by Andy Rathbone), all from Wiley, include some details about networking. These books are all good. In fact, some smart bookstore should bundle them with *Wireless Home Networking For Dummies* because they're complementary. In this chapter, we expose you to the network and what's inside it (and there's probably a free prize among those Cracker Jacks some-where, too!). That should get you started. But if you want to know more, we urge you to grab one of these more detailed books.

It's one thing to attach a device to the network — either directly or as an attachment — but it's another to share it with other people. Sharing your computer and devices is a big step. You not only open yourself up to lots of potential unwanted visitors (such as bad folks sneaking in over your Internet connection), but you also make it easier for friendly folks (like your kids) to erase stuff and use things in unnatural ways. That's why you can (and should!) control access by using passwords or by allowing users to only read (open and copy) files on your devices rather than change them. In Windows XP, security is paramount, and you must plan how, what, and with whom you share. Windows Vista and Windows 7 take that security to the next level by securing who can allow sharing in the first place. Definitely take the extra time to configure your system for these extra security layers. We tell you in this chapter about some of these mechanisms; the books we mention previously go into these topics in more detail.

# A Networking Review

Before we get too far into the concept of file sharing, we want to review some basic networking concepts (which we touch on in earlier chapters of this book), such as what a network is and how it works.

Simply defined, a *network* is something that links computers, printers, and other devices. A *protocol* is the language that devices use to communicate with each other on a network. These days, the standard protocol used for most networking is Ethernet.

For one device to communicate with another under the Ethernet protocol, the transmitting device needs to accomplish a few things. First, it must announce itself on the network and declare which device it's trying to talk to. Then it must authenticate itself with that destination device by confirming that the sending device is who it says it is. This is done by sending a proper name, such as a domain or homegroup name, and also a password that the receiving device accepts.

For our purposes, when we talk about networking, we're talking about sharing devices on a Windows-based network.

With the latest Vista and Windows 7 operating systems, Microsoft has taken a simple, intuitive approach that looks surprisingly like Mac OS X when you use the Details view. In Vista and Windows 7, you just have Network, and under Network, you can see all the computers and resources that you can access shares on within your network. All the domain and homegroup information is in the easily accessible Network and Sharing Center, shown in Figure 10-1. You can expand this view by clicking the See Full Map link on the top-right side of the window in Windows 7. (Vista shows all the devices in this window by default, whereas Windows 7 hides some devices to stick with the basics in the initial view.)

**Figure 10-1:**
View your
network
details in
Windows 7.

# Getting to Know the Windows 7 Network and Sharing Center

"Hello! I'm here!" When a computer attached to a network is turned on, it broadcasts its name to every other device on the network and asks every device to broadcast as well. If that computer is sharing something, such as a folder or a printer, the other devices can see it. By asking the other devices to broadcast, the computer can then see all of them. This process is repeated (on average) every 15 minutes on most networks with Windows computers attached to them.

The "Hello, I'm here" process is a great way to add devices to a network. Unfortunately, it's not too great at detecting whether a device falls off or is disconnected from that network. If a machine or shared device seems to be visible on your network but doesn't respond when you try to access it, the problem may not be on your computer. Devices that get disconnected from your network don't immediately appear to be disconnected on some of your other computers. They usually get removed from the list of available networked computers only if they fail to answer the every-15-minutes "Hello" calls from the other machines.

The Network control panel (which you can access from the Windows 7 Start menu) is your ticket to the network and to see what shared resources are available, such as servers, other computers, and printers, as shown in Figure 10-2. (The risk versus reward of sharing these types of items just makes sense. The chances of a bad guy getting into your printer and printing documents are rather low — there's not much reward for doing that.)

You can see what's shared with you on your network by checking out your PC's homegroup. Click the Start button and then click your name in the Start menu. In the Explorer window that opens, click Homegroup in the left navigation menu to see all the shared folders and libraries in your homegroup that you can access.

If you want to be able to quickly access these shares from within one of your own libraries (such as Documents), just right-click the shared folder/library and drag it to the library on your computer where you want to have access to the shared folder/library. When you drop the shared folder/library on your library, select the Include in Library option from the menu that pops up. After you've done that, you can access the files in that folder/library from within your own library, as if they were on your own hard drive.

Regardless of the operating system, devices that are set up to share are always represented by small computer icons. If you double-click one of these icons, you can see any shared printers, folders, or other devices represented by the appropriate icons. Sometimes you have to *drill down* (continue to double-click icons) to find all the shared items on your network.

In general, you see two types of devices on your network:

- ✔ **Standalone network devices:** These are computers, storage devices, gaming devices, and so on that have a network port and are on the network in their own right.

- ✔ **Attached devices:** These are peripherals, drives, or other devices that are on the network because they're attached to something else, such as a PC.

Just double-click your homegroup to see all your home computers and other networked devices. Click any to see what you can share within them.

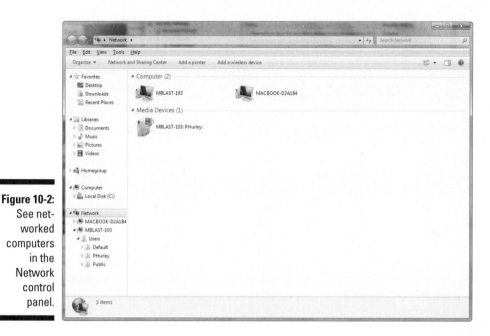

**Figure 10-2:**
See net-
worked
computers
in the
Network
control
panel.

All this mouse clicking can be a pain. Save your wrist and create a shortcut to your shared resources by right-clicking the item and choosing Create Shortcut. Shortcuts are especially handy for people who have networked devices that they visit often on the Internet, such as File Transfer Protocol (FTP) sites.

If you find a computer that you expect to be on the network but it's not, make sure that its homegroup name is the same as the other machines — this is a common mistake. (See the later section "Setting up a homegroup in Windows 7.")

In Windows 7, the best way to visualize what's on your computer and your network is to view the Network Map available in the Network and Sharing Center. Simply load the Network and Sharing Center and then click the See Full Map link on the top-right side of the window. Figure 10-3 shows the map view of your available network resources.

Just because you see a device in the Network and Sharing Center network map doesn't mean that you can *share* with that device — where *share* means that you can view, use, copy, and otherwise work on files and resources on that device. The devices need to be set up for sharing for that to happen. (Think of it like your regular neighborhood, where you can see many of the houses, but you can't go in some of them because they're locked.) To set up sharing, see the next section.

**Figure 10-3:**
Viewing the
full map
of your
networked
devices.

# Sharing in Windows 7 — I Can Do That!

*File sharing* is a basic feature of any home network. Whether sharing MP3 files on a computer with other devices (including your stereo, as we discuss in Chapter 12) or giving access to financial files for Mom and Dad to access on each other's computers, sharing files is a way to maintain one copy of something and not have a zillion versions all over the network.

Previous versions of Windows (like XP) made it difficult for anyone without the title "certified network engineer" underneath the name on his or her business card to get a home network with sharing set up and running.

With the advent of Windows 7, the folks at Microsoft really topped themselves in terms of making sharing easy with the advent of the *homegroup*. The homegroup (which replaces all the complicated workgroup stuff in previous versions of Windows) rolls up all of your Windows PC sharing needs in one *extremely* easy-to-configure control panel setting. If you've seen the Windows 7 "I made that" ads on TV where people talk about how easy it is for them to share media and files with their new Windows 7 computers, you've seen the homegroup in action.

## Choosing what to share

Before you begin the process of setting up sharing on your networked homegroup computers, you need to figure out exactly what you want to share. Within Windows 7, you have several options:

- Pictures
- Music
- Videos
- Documents
- Printers
- Media Sharing

The first five items are pretty self-explanatory: You can share pictures, music, videos, documents that reside on your computer, and printers attached to your computer via a USB or other direct connection (such as a parallel or serial printer). The Media Sharing feature is a bit different because it doesn't just let other users access your media files (pictures, music, and video), but in fact allows you to *stream* files from one computer to another (or to a Windows 7 UPNP-compatible media device like those we talk about in Chapter 12). By streaming, we mean that you can have a media file stored on your computer and play it back (display a picture, listen to a song, or watch a video) on another computer or media device (like an Xbox 360).

Windows 7 provides secure file sharing for file transfers — other users must have your common, shared homegroup password to connect and read or write files to and from your computer. Media Sharing is an exception here. Any Windows 7 computers and media player devices attached to your network will be able to access your media (for playback purposes only), without your password. Your media files can't be downloaded or changed, but they can be accessed. There's no real security risk here — as long as you don't mind people seeing your media — and this is a necessary evil to make media streaming work easily, especially with media player devices.

By default — meaning when you first turn on sharing in your homegroup — documents are shared with *Read* access, which means other users can view (and download) your files, but they can't change them on your computer or transfer other files onto your computer. In the following sections, we talk about how to turn on homegroup sharing on your computers and then customize the level of access you allow on a library-by-library basis on your computer.

# *Setting up a homegroup in Windows 7*

To create a homegroup and turn on sharing on a Windows 7 computer, just follow these steps:

1. **Click the Start button and select Control Panel.**

2. **Within the Control Panel window that appears, open the Network and Sharing Center.**

   You see a control panel window similar to the one shown in Figure 10-4.

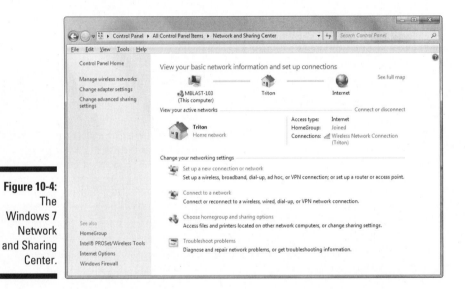

Figure 10-4:
The
Windows 7
Network
and Sharing
Center.

3. **Click the Choose Homegroup and Sharing Options link.**

4. **In the Control Panel window that appears, select Create a Homegroup.**

   The Create a Homegroup window opens, as shown in Figure 10-5.

5. **Choose what items you want to share and then click Next.**

   You can choose to share documents, music, videos, pictures, and printers.

   After you click Next, a new window appears, giving you the password you need when you access your new network share on other Windows 7 computers. (See Figure 10-6.)

6. **Write down your password — you'll need it!**

   You're given an option to print the password and instructions. If you have a printer hooked up to your Windows 7 PC, do this!

**7. Click Finish.**

You're all set.

See how easy that is? We think Microsoft really knocked this one out of the park — and if your existing Windows Vista PCs can support it, we highly recommend that you upgrade to Windows 7!

**Figure 10-5:**
Choose
what you
want to
share in
Windows 7.

**Figure 10-6:**
Write this
password
down or,
better yet,
print it out.

## You can never be too protected

The number of ways that someone can get on your network multiplies with each new technology you add to your network. We note in Chapter 9 that wireless local area networks (LANs) seep out of your home and make it easy for others to log in and sniff around. If someone does manage to break into your network, the most obvious places to snoop around and do damage are the shared resources. Sharing your C: drive (which is usually your main hard drive), your Windows directory, or your Documents library makes it easier for people to get into your machine and do something you would rather they not do.

You see, sharing files broadcasts to the rest of the network the fact that something is shared, telling everyone who has access your computer's name on the network and how to find it. Sharing can broadcast that availability across firewalls, proxies, and servers. Certain types of viruses and less-than-friendly hackers look for these specific areas (such as your shared C: drive) in broadcast messages and follow them back to your machine.

If you're going to share these parts of your system on your network, run a personal firewall or the Windows Firewall on your machines for an added layer of security. Get virus software. Protect your machine and limit your exposure. (And, by all means, be sure to follow our advice in Chapter 9 for securing your wireless network.)

## *Sharing specific libraries*

As we mention earlier in the chapter, when you enable homegroup sharing on your computer, all libraries (documents, music, video, and photos) are shared at a read-only level. For most folks, this is a good balance between security and convenience — other computers in your home network can access each other's files without having permission to actually overwrite, delete, or modify them.

You may want, however, to modify these settings for a particular library. Perhaps you want to allow your family to *write* to your photos library so that they can transfer pictures to your PC. Or maybe you want to keep the Documents library on your home office PC private so no one else on your home network can access your confidential Word documents. Well, you can do that — and do it easily — in Windows 7. And you don't have to do it just on a library basis; in fact, you can customize sharing down to the level of folders within a library or even on a file-by-file basis.

Unless you set a specific sharing level for them, all files and folders within a library share that library's access level. For example, if you share your Documents library at the *read/write* level on your homegroup, all the files and folders within that library are also shared at that level. If you have specific items within a library that you want to share differently from the rest of the library, set your sharing preference for the library (as outlined in the following steps) and then select the item you want to change and repeat the same steps with your preferred sharing level.

To customize the sharing setting for a library, a folder, or an individual file, simply do the following:

1. **From the Start menu, select the library for which you want to modify sharing settings. If you're modifying settings for a specific folder or file, navigate to it within your library.**

   If the library is not on you Start menu, open a Windows Explorer window and navigate to the library you're looking for.

2. **Right-click on the name of the library and select Share With and choose your preferred setting.**

   If you're working with folders or files within a single library, you can select multiple files and/or folders by Ctrl-clicking on them and apply your settings *en masse*.

   Here's a rundown of your sharing options:

   • *Nobody:* No one on your network can open, download, or modify this library, folder, or file.

   When you set a folder to Nobody, the folder icon appears with a lock on it, giving you quick visual confirmation that your change was executed.

   • *Homegroup (Read):* This is the default setting. Users on other networked PCs within your homegroup can access this library and the folders/files within it by opening it remotely or transferring it to their computer.

   • *Homegroup (Read/Write):* Users on other networked PCs within your homegroup can modify files and folders within this library, or transfer their own files into the library or folders within it.

   • *Specific People:* This setting lets you specify exactly who can access a library/folder/file. If you choose this setting, you're prompted to choose users from the users on your computer (the user accounts you set up when you configured Windows, in other words) or to add user accounts from other computers in your homegroup. You can specify exactly what level (read or read/write) you want to give the user account you're adding. If you need to create a user account for someone you'd like to specifically give access to a library, folder, or file on your computer, follow the steps in the next section.

## *Adding users*

For others to get access to what resources you have shared, you need to give them permission. You do that by giving them a logon on your computer — essentially adding them to the network as a user. The group is then given certain rights within the folder you have shared; every user in the group has access only to what the group has access to. (For more details on this process, we strongly recommend that you use the Windows Help file to discover how to set up new users and groups on your system.)

In Windows 7, creating user accounts and adding them to groups requires you to have an Administrator account. We're guessing that you're the administrator of your home-networked computer (it's your network, right?), so you have access to an Administrator account logon.

Unless you're very sure you know what you're doing, you should never give new user accounts an Administrator account. Instead, give these users a Standard account. Keep in mind that by creating these accounts, you're also creating a logon that can be used to turn on and access your computer directly. For the purposes of sharing files and peripherals, a Standard user account provides all the access that any individual on the network would normally need.

To add users to your network, follow these steps:

1. **From the Start menu, select Control Panel and double-click the User Accounts icon.**

   This step displays the Users Accounts control panel window.

2. **Click the Manage Another Account link, and then in window that appears, click the Create a New Account link.**

   The Create New Account control panel window appears, as shown in Figure 10-7.

3. **In the New Account Name text box, enter the desired name for the user account.**

4. **Make sure the Standard User radio button is selected and then click the Create Account button.**

   You're done. If you share a library/folder/file using the Share with Specific People option, you can now share with this user by selecting that person's name from the menu.

**Figure 10-7:**
Create a
new user
account
here.

## Accessing shared files

Whether drives, folders, or single files are set up for sharing on your wireless home network, you access the shared thing in pretty much the same way. On any networked PC, you simply log on to the network, head for Network (or My Network Places, as the case may be), and navigate to the file (or folder or drive) you want to access. It's really as easy as that.

Just because you can *see* a drive, folder, or file on the network doesn't necessarily mean that you have *access* to that drive, folder, or file. It all depends on set permissions.

## Be Economical: Share Your Printer

Outside of the fact that there's only so much space on your desk or your kitchen countertop, you simply don't need a complete set of peripherals at each device on your network. For example, digital cameras are quite popular, and you can view pictures on your PC, on your TV, and even in wireless picture frames around the house. But you probably need only one color printer geared toward printing high-quality photos for someone to take home (after admiring your wireless picture frames!).

The same is true about many peripherals: business card scanners, backup drives (such as USB hard drives and NAS — *network attached storage* — boxes), and even cameras. If you have one device and it's network enabled, anyone on your wireless home network should be able to access that device for the task at hand.

The most common shared peripheral is a printer. Setting up a printer for sharing is easy, and using it is even easier. You may have several printers in your house, and different devices may have different printers — but they all can be shared. You may have the color laser printer on your machine, a less-expensive one (with less-expensive consumables such as printer cartridges, too) for the kids' computer, and a high-quality photo printer near the TV set plugged into a USB port of a networkable A/V device. Each of these printers can be used by a local device — if it's properly set up.

Here are the steps you need to take to share a printer:

1. Enable printer sharing in the operating system of the computer to which the printer is attached.

2. Set up sharing for the installed printer. We say *installed* printer because we assume that you've already installed the printer locally on your computer or other device.

3. Remotely install the printer on every other computer on the network.

4. Access the printer from any PC on the network!

You perform the third step on every other PC in the house. Basically, you install the printer on each of these computers, but in a logical way — *logically* as opposed to *physically* installing and connecting the printer to each computer. You install the printer just like any other printer except that you're installing a *network* printer, and the printer installation wizard searches the network for the printers you want to install.

The process you use varies depending on your operating system and the type of printer you're trying to install. In every case, read the printer documentation before you start because some printers require their software to be partially installed before you try to add the printer. We've seen this a lot with multifunction printers that support scanning, copying, and faxing.

## *Installing a printer in Windows XP*

With Windows XP, the easiest way to start the installation of a printer is to look inside My Network Places, find the computer sharing the printer, and double-click the shared printer. This action starts the Add Printer Wizard, which takes you through the process of adding the printer. This wizard works like any good wizard — you make a few selections and click Next a lot. If you didn't add the drivers to the shared printer already, you may be asked for the printer drivers. Just use the Browse button to direct the wizard to look in the shared folder or CD-ROM drive where you put the printer software on the computer that the printer is attached to.

You have two options for installing a network printer:

- **From your Printers folder:** Choose Start⇨Settings⇨Printers and Faxes (or simply Start⇨Printers and Faxes, depending on how your Start menu is configured).

- **From My Network Places:** Double-click the computer that has the printer attached. An icon appears, showing the shared printer. Right-click the icon and then choose Connect from the pop-up menu that appears.

If the necessary driver is already installed on the print server, simply select the printer, and it's ready to go. If the driver is not yet installed, either route leads you to the Add Printer Wizard, which guides you through the process of adding the network printer.

Don't start the Add Printer Wizard unless you have installed the proper drivers to the shared printer or you have the installation CD for your printer handy. The Add Printer Wizard installs the printer *drivers* (software files that contain the info required for Windows to talk to your printers and exchange data for printing). The wizard gets these from the CD that came with your printer. If you don't have the CD, go to the Web site of your printer manufacturer and download the driver to your desktop and install from there. Don't forget to delete the downloaded files from your desktop when you've finished installing them on the computer.

Note also that the wizard allows you to browse your network to find the printer you want to install. Simply click the plus sign next to the computer that has the printer attached, and you should see the printer below the computer. (If not, make sure that printer sharing is enabled on that computer.)

At the end of the wizard screens, you have the option to print a test page. We recommend that you do this. You don't want to wait until your child has to have a color printout for her science experiment (naturally, she waits until 10 minutes before the bus arrives to tell you!) to find out that the printer doesn't work.

## Installing a printer in Vista and Windows 7

Windows 7 and Vista are the easiest versions of Windows yet when it comes to installing peripheral devices. For the vast majority of devices, "plug and play" is just that — and not the "plug and pray" it was often derided as in older versions of the OS. So installing a printer is as simple as turning on the printer, plugging it into a USB jack on your computer, and sitting back. You can watch while Windows identifies the printer, obtains the drivers from the Internet (or from its internal library of printer drivers), and completes the process. In the case of literally every printer we've ever installed, that's all you have to do.

If, however, this doesn't work for you (and, hey, it could happen . . . though usually only for printers without USB — those using the older parallel or serial ports, which is exceedingly rare these days), Windows 7 and Vista have a process very similar to the ones used in older versions of Windows. Just do the following:

1. **From the Start button, select Devices and Printers.**

2. **Click the Add a Printer link.**

   The Add Printer Wizard opens.

3. **Select Add a Local Printer.**

   Windows prompts you to choose a printer port.

4. **Choose the Use an Existing Port option and keep the default port recommended by Windows and then click Next.**

5. **In the Install the Printer Driver window that appears, select the model and manufacturer for your printer; then click Next.**

   If you can't find your printer in this list, do the following:

   a. Click Windows Update and let Windows connect to the Internet to check for more drivers.

   b. If this process still doesn't find your driver, dig out the installation CD that came with it, click the Have Disk link, and follow the instructions on screen.

6. **Depending upon the particular printer you're using, the wizard may prompt you for further steps; follow them and then click Finish.**

## *Accessing your shared printers*

After you have the printers installed, how do you access them? Whenever your Print window comes up (which you summon by pressing Ctrl+P in most applications), you see a field labeled Name for the name of the printer accompanied by a pull-down menu of printer options. Use your mouse to select any printer — local or networked — and the rest of the printing process remains the same as though you had a printer directly plugged into your PC.

You can even make a networked printer the default printer by right-clicking the printer and then choosing Set As Default Printer from the pop-up menu that appears.

# Sharing Other Peripherals

Sharing any other peripheral is similar to sharing printers (as described in the preceding section). You need to make sure that you're sharing the device on the computer it's attached to. Then you need to install that device on another PC by using that device's installation procedures. Obviously, we can't be specific about such an installation because of the widely varying processes that companies use to install devices. Most of the time — like with a printer — you need to install the drivers for the device you're sharing on your other computers.

Note that some of the devices you attach to your network have integrated Web servers in them. This is getting more and more common. Danny's AudioReQuest (www.request.com) music server, for example, is visible on his home network and is addressable by any of his PCs. Thus, he can download music to and from the AudioReQuest server and sync it to other devices he wants music on. Anyone else in the home can do the same — even remotely, over the Internet. We talk more about the AudioReQuest system in Chapter 12.

Danny has also set up a virtual CD server in his home to manage all the CDs his kids have for their games. This server is shared on the home network. By using Virtual CD software from H+H Zentrum GmbH (www.virtualcd-online.com, $69.95 for a five-user license), Danny has loaded all his CDs and many of his DVDs onto a single machine so that his kids (he has four) can access those CDs from any of their individual PCs. (He has four *spoiled* kids.) Rather than look to the local hard drive for the CD, any of the kids' PCs looks to the server to find the CD — hence, the name *virtual CD*. Now those stacks of CDs (and moans over a scratched CD!) are gone.

# Sharing Files between Macs and Windows-Based PCs

If you have an Mac OS X computer (using OS X versions 10.2 right on through to the current 10.6), you don't need to do anything special to get your Mac connected to a PC network for file sharing. All these versions of OS X support Windows networking protocols right out of the box, with no add-ons or extra software required.

## Bonjour, madam!

One cool feature that Apple has added to its latest versions of Mac OS — Mac OS versions 10.2 and beyond — is a networking system named Bonjour. Bonjour, previously known as Rendezvous, is based on an open Internet standard (IETF, or Internet Engineering Task Force, Zeroconf) and is being adopted by a number of manufacturers outside of Apple.

Basically, Bonjour (and Zeroconf) is a lot like Bluetooth (which we discuss in Chapter 15) in that it allows devices on a network to discover each other without any user intervention or special configuration. Bonjour is slowly being incorporated into many products, such as printers, storage devices (basically, networkable hard drives), and even household electronics such as TiVo.

Here's one great feature about Bonjour: On Macs equipped with Apple AirPort network adapter cards, it lets two (or more) Macs in range of each other — in other words, within Wi-Fi range — *automatically* connect to each other for file sharing, instant messaging, and other tasks without going through any extra steps of setting up a peer-to-peer network.

Bonjour is enabled automatically in Mac OS version 10.2/3/4/5/6 computers if you enable Personal File Sharing (found in System Preferences; look for the Sharing icon) or use Apple's iChat Instant Messaging program, Apple's Safari Web browsers, or any Bonjour-capable printer connected to your AirPort network.

## Getting on a Windows network

To connect to your Windows PCs or file servers, simply go the OS X Finder and then choose Go⇨Connect to Server (⌘+K). In the dialog box that appears, type the IP address or host name of the server you're connecting to and then click the Connect button. Alternatively, click the Browse button in the dialog box to search your local network for available servers and shares.

## Letting Windows users on your Mac network

To let Windows users access your Mac, you simply turn on file sharing in your Mac's System Preferences. To do so in OS X versions 10.4 and earlier, follow these steps:

1. **Open System Preferences (click the System Preferences icon on your Mac's dock).**

2. **Click the Sharing tab to view your file-sharing options. Make sure that the Services tab is open.**

3. **Select Windows Sharing in the services listing and then click the Start button to activate it.**

4. **Close the Sharing dialog box.**

If you're using the latest versions of OS X (10.5 Leopard and 10.6 Snow Leopard), just do the following:

1. **Open System Preferences and click the Sharing tab (as described in the preceding steps).**

2. **Select the File Sharing check box.**

3. **Click the Options button.**

4. **In the dialog box that appears, select the Share Files and Folders Using SMB check box.**

5. **Click Done.**

That's it! Your Mac automatically turns on Windows sharing and opens the appropriate holes (ports) in your firewall. If you haven't already enabled accounts on your Mac for sharing, you're prompted by OS X to do so now. Simply click the Enable Accounts button and, in the dialog box that opens, select the accounts (or users) of your Mac that you want to allow access to. To do this, select the check box next to each name you want to enable and then click Done. That's all there is to it.

If you want to connect to your LAN from a Windows computer, simply browse your Network in Windows 7 or Vista (or Neighborhood Network in Windows XP), and then enter your network's address on an Explorer address bar. It's something like the following:

```
\\192.168.1.3\username
```

Substitute your Mac's IP address and your OS X username for *username,* of course!

# Chapter 11

# Gaming Over Your Wireless Network

*I*n case you missed it, gaming is huge. We mean *huge*. The videogaming industry is, believe it or not, bigger than the entertainment industry generated by Hollywood. Billions of dollars per year are spent on PC game software and hardware and on gaming consoles such as Wii, PlayStation, and Xbox. You probably know a bit about gaming — we bet that you at least played Minesweeper on your PC or Pong on an Atari when you were a kid. What you may not know is that videogaming has moved online in a big way. For that, you need a network.

All three of the big gaming console vendors — Sony (www.us.playstation.com), Microsoft (www.xbox.com), and Nintendo (www.nintendo.com) — have made it easy for you to connect your console (and, in the case of Sony and Nintendo, handheld gaming device) to a broadband Internet connection, such as a cable or DSL, to play against people anywhere in the world. Online PC gaming has also become a huge phenomenon, with games such as World of Warcraft attracting millions of users.

A big challenge for anyone getting into online gaming is finding a way to get consoles and PCs in different parts of the house connected to your Internet connection. For example, if you have an Xbox 360, it's probably in your living room or home theater, and we're willing to bet that your cable or DSL modem is in the home office. Lots of folks string a CAT-5e/6 Ethernet cable down the hall and hook it into their game machine — a great approach if you don't mind tripping over that cable at 2 a.m. when you let the dogs out.

Enter your wireless home network, a much better approach to getting these gaming devices online.

In this chapter, we talk about some of the hardware requirements for getting a gaming PC or game console online. There's good news here: Wireless is built into Nintendo's and Sony's current consoles. In fact, Nintendo's Wii is so wireless friendly that you have to pay extra for a *wired* network connection, and a low-cost optional accessory for the Xbox 360. We also talk about some steps you need to take to configure your router (or the router in your access point, if they're the same box in your wireless local area network) to get your online gaming up and running.

Our focus here is on wireless *networking* connections. Keep in mind that gaming consoles have also become unwired in terms of the connections that their controllers use. All three of the current consoles (the Wii, the PlayStation 3, and the Xbox 360) use wireless technologies such as Bluetooth (see Chapter 3 for more on Bluetooth) to connect their controllers to the console. The Xbox 360 can even work with wireless headsets, so you can wirelessly yell "I'm ripping your head off right now" to the gamer on the far end of the connection. (You Seth Rogen fans out there know what we're talking about here!)

# PC Gaming over a Wireless Home Network

We should preface this section of the book by saying that this book isn't entitled *Gaming PCs For Dummies.* Thus, we don't spend any time talking about PC gaming hardware requirements in any kind of detail. Our gamer pals will probably be aghast at our brief coverage here, but we really just want to give you a taste of what you may want to think about if you decide to outfit a PC for online gaming. In fact, if you're buying a PC for this purpose, check out the class of computers called *gaming PCs,* optimized for this application. Throughout this chapter, we use the term *gaming PC* generically to mean any PC in your home that you're using for gaming — not just special-purpose gaming PCs.

Your best resource, we think, is to check out an online gaming Web site that has a team of experts who review and torture-test all the latest hardware for a living. We like CNET's www.gamespot.com and www.gamespy.com.

In the following sections, we discuss the hardware and networking requirements for PC gaming over a wireless network.

## Getting the right hardware

At the most basic level, you need any modern multimedia PC (or Macintosh, for that matter) to get started with PC gaming. Just about any PC or Mac purchased since 2002 or so will have a fast processor and a decent graphics or video card. (You hear both terms used.) If you start getting into online gaming, think about upgrading your PC with high-end gaming hardware or building a dedicated gaming machine. Some key hardware components to keep in mind are the following:

- ✔ **Fast processor:** Much of the hard work in gaming is done by the video card, but a fast Intel Core 2 or Core i3/i5/i7 (or the AMD equivalent) central processing unit (CPU) is always nice to have.

- ✔ **Powerful video card:** The latest cards from ATI and nVIDIA (`www.nvidia.com`) contain incredibly sophisticated computer chips dedicated to cranking out the video part of your games. If you get to the point where you know what frames per second (fps) is all about and you start worrying that yours are too low, it's time to start investigating faster video cards.

  We're big fans of the ATI (`www.ati.com`) Radeon HD 5800 and 5900 graphics processors, but then we're suckers for fast hardware that can crank out the polygons (the building blocks of your game video) at mind-boggling speeds.

- ✔ **Fancy gaming controllers:** Many games can be played by using a standard mouse and keyboard, but you may want to look into some cool specialized game controllers that connect through your PC's Universal Serial Bus (USB). For example, you can get a joystick for flying games or a steering wheel for driving games. Check out Creative Technologies (`www.creative.com`) and Mad Catz (`www.madcatz.com`) for some cool options.

- ✔ **Quality sound card:** Many games include a *surround sound* soundtrack, just like DVDs provide in your home theater. If you have the appropriate number of speakers and the right sound card, you hear the bad guys creeping up behind you before you see them on the screen. *Très* fun.

## Examining networking requirements

Gaming PCs may (but don't have to) have some different innards than regular PCs, but their networking requirements don't differ in any appreciable way from the PC you use for Web browsing, e-mail, or anything else. You shouldn't be surprised to hear that connecting a gaming PC to your wireless network is no different from connecting any PC.

You need some sort of wireless network adapter connected to your gaming PC to get it up and running on your home network (just like you need a wireless network adapter connected to *any* PC running on your network, as we discuss in Chapter 5). These adapters are almost always built right into your PC. If your PC doesn't have a network adapter, you can fit one in the Express or PC Card slot (of a laptop computer, for example), add one internally (in your desktop PC) using a PCI or PCI Express card, or connect the adapter to a USB or Ethernet port of a desktop computer. If you have a Mac that you're using for gaming, you'll use the built-in AirPort Extreme card (which we discuss in Chapter 8). There's nothing special you need to do, hardware-wise, with a gaming PC.

When it comes to *playing* online games, you may need to do some tweaking to your home network's router — which may be a standalone device or part of your access point. In the upcoming sections "Dealing with Router Configurations to Get a PC or Console Online" and "Setting Up a Demilitarized Zone (DMZ)," we discuss these steps in further detail.

Depending on which games you're playing, you may not need to do any special configuring. Most games play just fine without any special router configurations — particularly if your PC isn't acting as the *server* (which means that other people aren't connecting to your PC from remote locations on the Internet).

# Getting Your Gaming Console on Your Wireless Home Network

Although PC gaming can be really cool, we find that many people prefer to use a dedicated game console device — such as a PlayStation 3 (PS3), a Wii, or an Xbox 360 — to do their gaming.

In the following sections, we explore some of the advantages to using a console, what wireless networking gear you need, and how to sign up for an online gaming service.

## Exploring the advantages to using a console over a PC

And, although hardcore gamers may lean toward PC platforms for their gaming (often spending thousands of dollars on ultra-high-end gaming PCs with the latest video cards, fastest processor and memory, and the like), we think that for regular gamers, consoles offer these compelling advantages:

- ✔ **They're (relatively) inexpensive.** Although they're more expensive than the previous generation of consoles, today's current consoles are cheaper than a PC — the Wii and Xbox 360 start below $200, and the PS3 starts at about $300. Even if you dedicate an inexpensive PC for gaming, you'll probably spend closer to $500 — and even more if you buy the fancy video cards and other equipment that gives the PC the same gaming performance as a console.

✔ **They're simple to set up.** Although it's not all that hard to get games running on a PC, you're dealing with a more complicated operating system on a PC. You have to install games and get them up and running. On a game console, you simply shove a disc into the drawer and you're playing.

✔ **They're in the right room.** Most folks don't want PCs in their living rooms or home theaters, although some really cool models are designed just for that purpose. A game console, on the other hand, is relatively small and inconspicuous and can fit neatly on a shelf next to your TV.

✔ **They work with your biggest screen.** Of course, you can connect a PC to a big-screen TV system (using a special video card). But consoles are designed to plug right into your TV or home theater system, using the same cables you use to hook up a VCR or DVD player. In the case of the Xbox 360 and PS3, you get a full HD (1080p) picture with digital surround sound to boot.

✔ **They can replace your Blu-ray and/or DVD player.** The PS3 and Xbox 360 (as well as the previous Xbox and PlayStation 2) can play DVD videos on your big screen. The PS3 even includes a built-in Blu-ray disc player for high-definition movies (which makes it a great deal, because some standalone Blu-ray players cost almost as much as the PS3 itself).

Today's game consoles offer some awesome gaming experiences. Try playing the Xbox 360 game Halo 3 on a big-screen TV with a surround sound system in place — it's amazing. You can even get a full HDTV picture on the Xbox 360 and PlayStation 3. And, because these gaming consoles are really nothing more than specialized computers, they can offer the same kind of networking capabilities that a PC does; in other words, they can fit right into your wireless home network.

## Connecting your console to your network

Getting your console onto your wireless network is possible (and easy) with almost all current or recent gaming consoles. The equipment you need depends on which console you have.

 People who own the most current generation of consoles are pretty much all set. Nintendo Wii and Sony PlayStation 3 have built-in Wi-Fi capabilities. If you're using an Xbox 360, you need to pick up the Xbox 360 Wireless N Networking Adapter ($99, www.xbox.com/en-US/hardware/x/xbox360wirelessnnetadapter).

Owners of the older PlayStation 2 or original Xbox need to add some hardware to their systems to get online via a wireless network. Both of these consoles include a built-in Ethernet port but no Wi-Fi.

Early PS2 units (before the "slim" case design was introduced in 2004) do *not* have built-in Ethernet. Sony used to offer a *PlayStation Network Adapter* that provided this feature, but it is no longer available. If you have one of these older PS2s and don't have the adapter, search sites like eBay and Craigslist for a used adapter.

To connect one of these Ethernet-only consoles to your wireless network, you need a special Wi-Fi adapter known as a *Wi-Fi Ethernet bridge*. A *bridge* is simply a device that connects two segments of a network. Unlike hubs or switches or routers or most other network equipment (we talk about much of this stuff in Chapters 2 and 5), a bridge doesn't do anything with the data flowing through it. A bridge basically passes the data straight through without manipulating it, rerouting it, or even caring what it is. A wireless Ethernet bridge's sole purpose is to send data back and forth between two points. (It's not too tough to see where the name came from, huh?)

Although we're discussing wireless Ethernet bridges in terms of game console networks, these handy devices can be used for lots of different applications in your wireless LAN. Basically, any device that has an Ethernet port — such as a personal video recorder (PVR), a Blu-ray disc player, and even an Internet refrigerator (such as the Samsung Internet Refrigerator) — can hook into your wireless home network by using a wireless Ethernet bridge.

The great thing about wireless Ethernet bridges, besides the fact that they solve the problem of getting noncomputer devices onto the wireless network, is that they're the essence of plug-and-play. You may have to spend three or four minutes setting up the bridge itself (to get it connected to your wireless network), but you don't need to do anything special to your game console other than plug in the bridge. All the game consoles we discuss in this chapter (at least when equipped with the appropriate network adapters and software) "see" your wireless Ethernet bridge as just a regular Ethernet cable. You don't need any drivers or other special software on the console. The console doesn't know (nor does it care in its not-so-little console brain) that there's a wireless link in the middle of the connection. It just works!

If you have encryption (such as WPA) set up on the network, you need to complete one step before plugging your wireless bridge into your gaming console's Ethernet port. Plug the bridge into one of the wired Ethernet ports on your router and access the bridge's built-in Web configuration screens; there, you enter your WPA passphrase (or WEP key if you're using WEP for some reason) and network name (or ESSID). After you've made these settings, you're ready to plug the bridge into your console and get online. It's that simple!

Here are some examples of wireless Ethernet bridges ("gaming adapters," as some vendors name them):

✔ **D-Link DGL-3420 wireless 108AG gaming adapter:** D-Link (www.dlink. com) has developed the DGL-3420 wireless 108AG ($99 list price) with gaming consoles in mind. D-Link even has its own online GamerLounge site with lots of great gaming information (http://games.dlink.com). The DGL-3420 (see Figure 11-1) doesn't need any special drivers or configuration. It does include a Web-browser-based configuration program that enables you to do things like enter your Wi-Fi Protected Access (WPA) passphrase. (Check out Chapter 9 for more information on this topic.)

The DGL-3420 is a loaded Ethernet bridge that supports both 802.11a and 802.11g (most folks use 802.11g) and even supports the higher-speed Super G 108 Mbps variant of 802.11g — if your router also supports it.

There's even some special "secret sauce" for making gaming faster: the D-Link GameFuel prioritization technology, as discussed in the sidebar, "Optimizing your router for gaming."

✔ **SMC SMCWEBT-G EZ Connect g wireless Ethernet bridge:** The SMC Network SMCWEBT-G wireless Ethernet bridge is an inexpensive Swiss Army knife of an Ethernet bridge. First, it's an 802.11g wireless Ethernet bridge with a theoretical 108 Mbps maximum speed. (You need a router that also supports the Super G protocol.) Like the D-Link bridge we discuss in the preceding section, the SMCWEBT-G supports WPA encryption, which means that it plays nicely on your secured wireless network.

There's more to it, though: The SMCWEBT-G can be configured to work as an access point all on its own (so that you can plug it into a stand-alone router to provide wireless access) and even as a *WDS repeater* that can extend the range of your network if your primary router is one of the SMC wireless routers. For only $79.99, it's a relative bargain and well worth checking out.

**Figure 11-1:**
The D-Link
DGL-3420
gaming
adapter.

When we wrote the last edition of this book three years ago, no manufacturers offered 802.11n versions of these adapters. We expected by now (mid 2010) to see *tons* of these devices; however, that's not the case. The problem (and it's not really a problem, *per se*) is that Wi-Fi is being built right into so many devices that there's less of a reason to build new versions of these bridges. We did find one new 802.11n bridge in our searches: Buffalo Technology's Nfiniti Wireless-N Dual Band Ethernet Converter (`www.buffalotech.com/products/wireless/client-adapters/nfiniti-wireless-n-dual-band-ethernet-converter-wli-tx4-ag300n`). The Nfiniti bridge has a street price of about $100, and it includes *four* Ethernet ports. This makes it a perfect companion for your family/media room — there's room to plug in not only your gaming console, but also other devices like networked TVs, Blu-ray disc players, or even a home theater PC. Pretty cool.

## Signing up for console online gaming services

Having the hardware to bring your console online is only half the battle — you also need to sign up for an online gaming service. Each of the big console manufacturers offers an online gaming service, providing head-to-head network game play as well as fun stuff like game downloads (both demos and full-blown games), text and voice chat, shopping, and Web browsing.

Not all console games are designed for online play. Each service has dozens (if not hundreds) of online-capable games, but just as many games are not network-enabled.

In this chapter, we're talking about the network gaming services offered by the three major console manufacturers. For the most part, these services are the way you will access most online games for each of the consoles. Some games, however, might use their own network, or are accessed via the console manufacturer's network but require an additional subscription to use.

### Living large with Xbox Live

The Microsoft online gaming service Xbox Live (`www.xboxlive.com`) is the longest running of the three console online gaming networks, launched right after the original Xbox was put on market in late 2001to early 2002. Xbox Live has over 8 million subscribers worldwide, as we write in late 2007, so it should always be easy to find someone to play with!

Xbox Live isn't just about playing against someone else; it's almost a new lifestyle. With Xbox Live, you can

- Communicate in real time during games.
- Set up chats with your friends.
- Meet gamers from all over the world and put together a posse of your favorite teammates to go after others.
- Set up your own clans and start competitions with Xbox Live features.

✔ Join Xbox Live tournaments.

✔ Download cool new stuff for your favorite games that's available only online — new maps, missions, songs, skins, vehicles, characters, quests, and more. You can even download entertainment content (such as movies and music) for your Xbox 360.

✔ Play games against hot celebs that Microsoft courts online.

With the discontinuation of the original Xbox and the focus on the Xbox 360, Xbox Live has been mainly focused on users of the new console. There *is* still service available for the original Xbox, but we devote most of our discussion here to the Xbox 360.

There are two levels of service for Xbox Live:

✔ **Silver:** This is a free service; anyone with an Xbox 360 can sign up for it and access game content (like additional levels), and get the ability to create a *gamertag* (online identity) and participate in online chats with friends. What you can't do with the free silver service is participate in multiplayer online games; to do that, you need to be a gold member (read on!).

✔ **Gold:** This is the subscription (in other words, pay) service in Xbox Live. You get to play online games against friends (and strangers) and get additional features such as access to an online marketplace and enhanced friends list functionality. There are a number of different plans for signing up for Xbox Live Gold; the most common is a $49.99 plan, which provides a year's worth of service and includes a headset for live voice chat during gaming.

## PSP: Your passport to Wi-Fi gaming

If you're into handheld gaming devices, the Sony PSP (PlayStation Portable) may be just the ticket. Sony offers two versions: the PSP Go and PSP 3000. The PSP Go is the newer of the two and costs a bit more ($250 versus $170 list price for the PSP 3000). Both systems offer a similar set of features — including Skype phone calling, pictures and videos, audio playback, and, of course, gaming. The older PSP 3000 also supports the *UMD* (Universal Media Disk) format; a small optical disc upon which you can buy major studio movies and TV shows for playback on your PSP.

And of course, the PSP has had built-in Wi-Fi support since the very first PSP. This continues with the Go and 3000, both of which include an 802.11b adapter that lets you connect to any 802.11b, g or n Wi-Fi network. The initial PSPs shipped with support for only WEP encryption, but a firmware upgrade in 2005 lets you connect even the older models to a properly secured WPA network, and all current PSPs support WPA. When connected via Wi-Fi, you can play online games against others on your network or over the Internet. There's even a built-in Web browser, so that when your thumbs need a break from all that hot gaming action, you can surf your favorite Web sites.

## Going Wi-Fi and portable with Nintendo DS

Nintendo has a nifty handheld gaming console called the Nintendo DS (it's Nintendo's competitor to the Sony PSP) that features, among many things, *two screens.* (Imagine driving in a race while looking simultaneously out your windshield and at a bird's-eye view of your car on the track.)

Like the PSP, the DS has built-in support for Wi-Fi network connectivity. This connectivity is now used for hooking up with other nearby DS users — using a feature of the DS called *PictoChat,* which allows you to share drawings and have text chats.

To make it even easier to get your DS online, Nintendo has its *free* Nintendo Wi-Fi Connection service. This service allows you to connect the DS to your home Wi-Fi network to play a number of online games being launched

with the service (just as you can connect your Wii to your home Wi-Fi network).

The coolest part of this service is that Nintendo has partnered with several Wi-Fi public hotspot providers to offer *free* Nintendo DS-accessible hot spots around the United States to connect to online gaming when you're on the road. The biggest issue you'll face with the DS on the road (and this is true for a lot of portable devices, as we discuss in Chapter 16) is that you can't log in to Wi-Fi hot spots that require you to sign in on a Web page for full access. Nintendo's own hot spots (they aren't actually building their own, but rather have partnered with some hot spot providers) don't have this limitation. (You'll be able to log in automatically.) Go to `www.nintendo.com/games/wifi/hotspot` to find out where Nintendo has hot spots near you.

Microsoft doesn't provide the broadband service for Xbox Live (none of the gaming companies do) — just the gaming service itself. Thus, you need to already have a cable, fiber-optic, or DSL modem set up in your home.

If you're going to play Xbox Live, you need to make sure that your router is Xbox Live–compatible. Go to `http://support.xbox.com/support/en/us/xbox360/XboxLive/GetConnected/CompatibleNetworkEquipment/CompatibleNetworkingEquipment.aspx`. On this page, Microsoft lists routers that don't work with its Live service, so be sure to check the list before you buy. If your router isn't on the Works or Does Not Work list, it's in a huge gray area of "we have no clue, but don't blame us if it doesn't work." Microsoft always loves a scapegoat!

If your current router isn't on this list, don't despair. Check the router manufacturer's Web site. Often, it has specific steps, such as installing a *firmware* update (updating the router's software), that make the router work just fine. Some routers work just as they are, but they simply haven't been certified for some reason.

### *Playing online with PlayStation Network*

Sony's previous game console, the PlayStation 2 (PS2), was the most successful console ever, with over 120 million (say that really slowly in a Dr. Evil voice for full effect) consoles sold by 2007. This older console, as we mentioned, had some networking capabilities, and indeed over 200 network-capable games have been released over the years, with millions of users taking advantage of them. But Sony never put together an integrated competitor to Microsoft's Xbox Live with the PS2 — essentially the gaming software companies themselves set up online portals for their individual games.

With the new PS3 console, however, Sony has pulled out all the stops and launched the PlayStation Network. The *PlayStation Network,* a free service for PS3 and PSP (PlayStation Portable) owners, provides the following services:

- ✔ **PlayStation Store:** You can shop online for downloadable games (they get stored on your PS3's hard drive), demos of new games, and high-definition trailers of new games and movies.

- ✔ **Online game play:** Registered users can participate in free online head-to-head gaming. PlayStation Network also supports online gaming for some specific titles that require additional subscriptions (typically directly with the game software company itself) — so while the PlayStation service is free, you may have to pay a subscription fee for certain games.

- ✔ **Online community:** As is the case with Xbox Live, when you register with PlayStation Network, you can establish an online identity and participate in message boards and live text or voice chats with your gaming buddies over your wireless network.

- ✔ **Web browsing:** Not actually part of the PlayStation Network (in other words, you don't need to register to do this) but neat nonetheless. The PS3 has a built-in Web browser so you can surf the Web on your big-screen TV.

You can find more information about PlayStation Network online gaming at the Sony site (`http://us.playstation.com/ps3/features/ps3featuresnetwork.html`).

### Wii? No, wheeeeeee!

The best selling of the three new-generation gaming consoles is Nintendo's Wii — fueled by a lower price and especially by the absolutely cool Wiimote, which uses motion control in addition to buttons to control game action. With the Wii, Nintendo has pulled out all the online stops — the Wii includes built-in Wi-Fi, a Web browser, loads of online games, and an online ecosystem for you to enjoy using your motion-controlled gaming controllers.

Nintendo's Wi-Fi Connection service provides free online gaming for the Wii and also for Nintendo's DS handheld gaming device (both have built-in Wi-Fi). As is the case with the PS3, most networked Wii games can be played online for free, but some titles require you to purchase a subscription with the game's software vendor.

The Wii also includes an Internet Channel — which is Wiispeak for a Web browser (specifically the Opera Web browser) that allows you to surf the Web on your TV. Additionally, like the other gaming consoles, the Wii includes an online store for buying games, downloading game demos, and more.

# Dealing with Router Configurations to Get a PC or Console Online

So far in this chapter, we talk a bit about the services and hardware you need to get into online gaming using your wireless network. What we haven't covered yet — getting online and playing a game — is either the easiest or the hardest part of the equation. The difficulty of this task depends on two things:

- ✔ **The platform you're using:** If you're trying to get online with a PC (whether it's Windows-based or a Mac), well, basically there's nothing special to worry about. You just need to get it connected to the Internet as we describe in Chapter 9. For certain games, you may have to do a few fancy things with your router, which we discuss later in this chapter. If you're using a gaming console, you may have to adjust a few things in your router to get your online connection working, but when you're using a game console with many routers, you can just plug in your wireless equipment and go.

- ✔ **What you're trying to do:** For many games, after you establish an Internet connection, you're ready to start playing. Some games, however, require you to make some adjustments to your router's configuration. If you're planning to host the games on your PC (which means that your online friends will be remotely connecting to your PC), you definitely have to do a bit of configuration.

Don't sweat it, though. It's usually not all that hard to get gaming set up, and it's getting easier every day because the companies that make wireless LAN equipment and home routers realize that gaming is a growth industry for them. They know that they can sell more equipment if they can help people get devices such as game consoles online.

You need to accomplish two things to get your online gaming — well, we can't think of a better term — online:

1. **Get an Internet Protocol (IP) address.**

   Your access point needs to recognize your gaming PC's or console's network adapter and your console's wireless Ethernet bridge, if you have one in your network configuration. If you have WEP or, better yet, WPA configured (refer to Chapter 9), your game machine needs to provide the proper passphrase or key. Your router (whether it's in the access point or separate) needs to provide an IP address to your gaming machine.

2. **Get through your router's firewall.**

   The part that takes some time is configuring the firewall feature of your router to allow gaming programs to function properly.

## Getting an IP address

For the most part, if you've set up your router to provide IP addresses within your network using DHCP (as we discuss in Chapters 5 and 6), your gaming PC or gaming console automatically connects to the router when the device is turned on and sends a Dynamic Host Configuration Protocol (DHCP) request to the router, asking for an IP address. If you've configured your gaming PC, as we discuss in Chapters 7 and 8, your computer should get its IP address and be online automatically. Or, as we like to say about this kind of neat stuff, aut*omagically.* You may need to go into your operating system's network control panel to select an access point and enter your WPA passphrase, but otherwise it should just work without any intervention.

If you have a game console with a wireless Ethernet bridge, the process should be almost as smooth. The first time you use the bridge, you may need to use a Web browser interface on one of your PCs to set up WEP keys or WPA passphrases; otherwise, your router should automatically assign an IP address to your console.

Before you get all wrapped around the axle trying to get your game console connected to your router, check out the Web site of your console maker *and* your router manufacturer. We have no doubt that you can find lots of information about how to make this connection. In many cases, if you're having trouble getting your router to assign an IP address to your console, you need to download a firmware upgrade for your router. *Firmware* is the software that lives inside your router and tells your router how to behave. Most router vendors have released updated firmware to help their older router models work with gaming consoles.

Some older router models simply don't work with gaming consoles. If online gaming is an important part of your plans, check the Web sites we mention earlier in this chapter *before* you choose a router.

In most cases, if your console doesn't get assigned an IP address automatically, you need to go into your router's setup program — most use a Web browser on a networked PC to adjust the configuration — and manually assign a fixed IP address to the console. Unlike DHCP-assigned IP addresses (which can change every time a computer logs on to the network), this fixed IP address is always assigned to your console.

## Optimizing your router for gaming

A few vendors have begun to sell wireless routers (or gateways, depending on their terminology) tweaked to support gaming. A wireless router manufacturer can do two things to ensure that gaming works well:

✔ **Make it easier to support online game play:** Routers can be designed to work specifically with online gaming applications. For example, a router may include more built-in game application support in its Web configuration, so you can easily "turn on" game support in the firewall and NAT routing functionality, without having to go through lots of trouble setting up port forwarding and DMZs (discussed in the final two sections of this chapter). Many gaming-specific routers support Universal Plug and Play (UPnP), also discussed in those sections, which makes the configuration of game applications automatic.

✔ **Provide *prioritization* to game applications:** For the ultimate in gaming experience, some routers prioritize gaming

applications over other traffic flowing through the router. Therefore, if two (or more) different applications are trying to send traffic through your router at the same time (such as your game and your spouse's e-mail application sending a work document to the server), the router makes sure that the gaming data gets through to the Internet first. This concept can reduce the *latency* (or delay) you experience in playing online games and make the experience better. (You can blow up the other guy faster!)

An example of this kind of wireless router is the D-Link DGL-4500 Xtreme N Wireless Gaming Router (`www.dlink.com/products/?pid=643`, $199.99). This router includes the D-Link *GameFuel* prioritization technology, an 802.11n AP (promising raw speeds, when used with D-Link's own adapters, of up to 300 Mbps), and a wired switch supporting Gigabit (1000BaseT) connections for your wired PCs and consoles.

Every router has a slightly different system for doing this, but typically you simply select an IP address that isn't in the range of DHCP addresses that your router automatically assigns to devices connected to your network.

You need to assign an IP address that isn't in the range of your router's IP address pool but is within the *same subnet*. For example, if your router uses DHCP to assign addresses in the range of 192.168.0.0 to 192.168.0.32 for computers connected to the network, you want to choose an IP address such as 192.168.0.34 for your console. Every router's configuration program is different, but you typically see a box that reads something like DHCP Server Start IP Address (with an IP address next to it) and another box that reads something like DHCP Server Finish IP Address with another box containing an IP address. (Some routers may just list the start address, followed by a *count,* which means that the finish address is the last number in the start address plus the count number.)

The key thing to remember is that you have to come up with only the last number in the IP address, the number after the third period in the IP address.

The first three (which are usually 192.168.0) don't change. All you need to do to assign this IP address is to choose a number between 1 and 254 that is *not* in the range your router uses for DHCP. (Most routers use the .1 address, so you should use a number between 2 and 254.)

# Getting through your router's firewall

After you've assigned an IP address to your gaming PC or game console and are connected to the Internet, you may well be ready to start playing games. Our advice: Give it a try and see what happens. Depending on the games you play, any additional steps may not be needed.

The steps we're about to discuss shouldn't be required for a game console. And, although we haven't checked out every single game out there, we haven't run into any incidences where you need to get involved with the port forwarding, which we're about to discuss, with a game console. If you have an older router that doesn't work well with console games, you may consider putting your console on the router's DMZ, as we discuss in the upcoming section "Setting Up a Demilitarized Zone (DMZ)."

### Understanding port forwarding

If your games don't work, you may need to get involved in configuring the firewall and Network Address Translation (NAT). As we discuss in Chapter 5, home network routers use a system called NAT to connect multiple devices to a single Internet connection. Basically, NAT translates between public Internet IP addresses and internal IP addresses on your home's network. When a computer or other device is connected to your home network (wirelessly or even a wired network), the router assigns it an internal IP address. Similarly, when your router connects to the Internet, it's assigned its own public IP address: that is, its own identifying location on the Internet. Traffic flowing to and from your house uses this public IP address to find its way. After the traffic (which can be gaming data, an e-mail, a Web page, whatever) gets to the router, the NAT function of the router figures out to which PC (or other device) in the house to send that data.

One important feature of NAT is that it provides firewall functionality for your network. NAT knows which computer to send data to on your network because that computer has typically sent a request over the Internet for that bit of data. For example, when a computer requests a Web page, your NAT router knows which computer made the request so that when the Web page is downloaded, it gets sent to the right PC. If no device on the network has made a request — meaning that an unrequested bit of data shows up at your public IP address — NAT doesn't know where to send it. This process provides a security firewall function for your network because it keeps this unrequested data (which could be some sort of security risk) off your network.

NAT is a cool thing because it lets multiple computers share a single public IP address and Internet connection and helps keep the bad guys off your network. NAT can, however, cause problems with some applications that may require this unrequested data to work properly. For example, if you have a Web server on your network, you would rightly expect that people would try to download and view Web pages without your PC sending them any kind of initial request. After all, your Web server isn't clairvoyant. (At least ours isn't!)

Gaming can also rely on unrequested connections to work properly. For example, you may want to host a game on your PC with your friends, which means that their PCs will try to get through your router and connect directly with your PC. Even if you're not hosting the game, some games send chunks of unrequested data to your computer as part of the game play. Other applications that may do this include audio- and videoconferencing programs (such as Windows Messenger) and remote control programs (such as pcAnywhere).

To get these games (or other programs) to work properly over your wireless home network and through your router, you need to get into your router's configuration program and punch some holes in your firewall by setting up NAT port forwarding.

Of the many routers out there, they don't all call this process *port forwarding.* Read your manual. (Really, we mean it. Read the darn thing. We know it's boring, but it can be your friend.) Look for terms such as *special applications support* or *virtual servers.*

### Setting up port forwarding

Port forwarding effectively opens a hole in your firewall that not only allows legitimate game or other application data through, but may also let the bad guys in. Set up port forwarding only when you have to, and keep an eye on the logs. (Your router should keep a log of whom it lets in — check the manual to see how to find and read this log.) We also recommend that you consider using personal firewall software on your networked PCs (we like ZoneAlarm, www.zonelabs.com) and keep your antivirus software up to date.

Some routers let you set up *application-triggered* port forwarding (sometimes just called *port triggering*), which basically allows your router to look for certain signals coming from an application on your computer (the triggers) and then enable port forwarding. This option is more secure because when the program that requires port forwarding (your game, in this case) isn't running, your ports are closed. They open only when the game (or other application) requires them to be open.

When you set up port forwarding on your router, you're selecting specific ports (ports are subsegments of an IP address — a computer with a specific IP address uses different numbered ports to connect different applications to the network) and sending all incoming requests using those ports to a specific computer or device on your network. When you get involved in setting up port forwarding, you notice two kinds of ports: TCP (Transmission Control

Protocol) and UDP (User Datagram Protocol). These names relate to the two primary ways in which data is carried on the Internet, and you may have to set up port forwarding for both TCP and UDP ports, depending on the application.

Every router or access point will have its own unique system for configuring port forwarding. Generally speaking, you find the port forwarding section of the configuration program and simply type into a text box on the screen the port numbers you want to open. For example, Figure 11-2 shows port forwarding being configured on a NETGEAR WPN824 router/access point.

**Special Applications** — Microsoft Internet Explorer

File　Edit　View　Favorites　Tools　Help

## Special Applications

Special Applications can only be used by 1 user at any time.

|  | Name | Incoming Ports | | | Outgoing Ports | | |
|---|---|---|---|---|---|---|---|
| On |  | Type | Start | Finish | Type | Start | Finish |
| 1. ☐ | dialpad | udp ▾ | 51200 | 51201 | udp ▾ | 51200 | 51201 |
| 2. ☐ | paltalk | udp ▾ | 2090 | 2091 | udp ▾ | 2090 | 2091 |
| 3. ☐ | quicktime | udp ▾ | 6970 | 6999 | tcp ▾ | 554 | 554 |
| 4. ☑ | starcraft | udp ▾ | 6112 | 6112 | tcp ▾ | 6112 | 6112 |
| 5. ☐ |  | udp ▾ |  |  | udp ▾ |  |  |
| 6. ☐ |  | udp ▾ |  |  | udp ▾ |  |  |

Save　Cancel

Help　Close

Done　　Internet

**Figure 11-2:**
Setting
up port
forwarding.

As we mention earlier in this chapter, ports are assigned specific numbers. To get some gaming applications to work properly, you need to open (assign) port forwarding for a big range of port numbers. The best way to find out which ports need to be opened is to read the manual or search the Web page of the game software vendor. You can also find a relatively comprehensive list online at http://practicallynetworked.com/sharing/app_port_list.htm.

If your router is UPnP enabled (Universal Plug and Play, a system developed by Microsoft and others that, among other things, automatically configures port forwarding for you) and the PC game you're using uses Microsoft DirectX gaming, the router and the game should be able to talk to each other and automatically set up the appropriate port forwarding. Just make sure that you enable UPnP in your router's configuration system. Usually you simply select a check box in the router's configuration program.

# Setting Up a Demilitarized Zone (DMZ)

If you need to do some special port forwarding and router tweaking to get your games working, you may find that you're spending entirely too much time getting it all up and running. Or you may find that you open what *should* be the right ports — according to the game developer — and that things still just don't seem to be working correctly. It happens; not all routers are equally good at implementing port forwarding.

Here's another approach you can take: Set up a *demilitarized zone* (DMZ). This term has been appropriated from the military (think the North and South Korean borders) by way of the business networking world, where DMZs are used for devices such as Web servers in corporate networks. In a home network, a DMZ is a virtual portion of your network that's completely outside your firewall. In other words, a computer or device connected to your DMZ accepts all incoming connections — your NAT router forwards all incoming connections (on any port) to the computer connected to the DMZ. You don't need to configure special ports for specific games because everything is forwarded to the computer or device you have placed on the DMZ.

Most home routers we know of set up a DMZ for only one of your networked devices, so this approach may not work if you have two gaming PCs connected to the Internet. However, for most people, a DMZ does the trick.

Although setting up a DMZ is perhaps easier to do than configuring port forwarding, it comes with bigger security risks. If you set up port forwarding, you lessen the security of the computer that the ports are being forwarded to — but if you put that computer on the DMZ, you've basically removed all the firewall features of your router from that computer. Be judicious when using a DMZ. If you have a computer dedicated only to gaming, a game console, or a kid's computer that doesn't have any important personal files configured to be on your DMZ, you're probably okay — but you run a risk that even that computer can be used to attack the others on your network. DMZs are perfectly safe for a console, but they should be used for PCs and Macs only if you can't make port forwarding work.

Depending on the individual router configuration program that comes with your preferred brand of router, setting up a DMZ is typically simple. Figure 11-3 shows a DMZ being set up on a Siemens SpeedStream router/access point. It's a dead-simple process. In most cases, you need only select a check box in the router configuration program to turn on the DMZ and then use a pull-down menu to select the computer you want on the DMZ.

**Figure 11-3:**
Setting up a
DMZ.

# Chapter 12

# Networking Your Entertainment Center

*B*eyond the normal computer stuff (connecting PCs and Macs with the Internet, each other and peripheral devices like printers), our favorite use of wireless home networking is as the media for transporting audio and video around the house. With the right equipment, you can easily get music and video from your PC, your mobile phone, and the Internet into your home theater or home audio system and beyond — far beyond, in fact, as wireless systems can extend your audio/video throughout your home.

## Understanding How Wireless Networking Can Fit Into Your Entertainment System

What can you do with wireless networking of your audio and video? Well here are just a few of the things you can make happen without wires:

✔ Get music or video from your PC or Mac and play it on your home theater or A/V (audio/video) gear.

✔ Play the music stored on your iPod, cellphone, or smartphone on your home theater or A/V gear.

✔ Put your media (music, video, or photographs) on a wirelessly enabled server and share it with devices throughout the house.

✔ Access audio and video from Internet sources and play it on your home theater or A/V gear.

✔ Extend your A/V equipment's reach wirelessly — doing anything from adding speakers in the back of your home theater to creating a whole home audio system that fills your home with music.

In this chapter, we talk about the (mainly inexpensive) devices that you can add to your wireless home network to do one or all of these things. Audio/video networks used to be hard to create and expensive to implement. No more. Wireless makes it easy, and you'll find that an increasing amount of A/V equipment is coming with wireless (typically Wi-Fi for whole home A/V applications, but also Bluetooth for connecting to mobile devices) built right-in.

You may be thinking, "Whoa, wait a minute, I thought wireless was just for data. Are you telling me that I need to move my PC to my living room and put it next to my TV?" Rest assured: We're not suggesting that, although some people do exactly that — you could indeed put your PC next to your TV, link it with a video cable, and run your Internet interconnection to the living room. But, you don't need to do this with a wireless network in place. Instead, everything (PCs, stereo gear, and so on) can stay exactly where it is and use the wireless network to move songs and movies around your home.

The revolution we're talking about — and are just getting started with in this chapter and the ones that follow — is the whole-home wireless revolution, where that powerful data network you install for your PCs to talk to one another and the Internet can also talk to lots of other things in your home. You hear us talk a great deal about your *whole-home audio network* or a *whole-home video network*. That's our code for "you can hear (view) it throughout the house." You built that wireless network (in Part III), and now other devices will come and use it. And coming they are, indeed — by the boxful. Be prepared to hear about all these great devices — things you use every day, such as your stereo, refrigerator, and car — that want to hop onboard your wireless home highway.

# *Wirelessly Enabling the Gear in Your Home Entertainment System*

If you're like most folks, your home entertainment system probably consists of a TV, a stereo or surround sound receiver, some components (such as a Blu-ray or DVD player, a TV set top box, and so on), and a few speakers. For most parties, this setup is enough to make for a memorable evening!

And, if you're like most people, you have a jumble of wires linking all this audio/visual (A/V) gear together. The mere thought of adding more wiring to the system — to link your receiver to your computer to play some digital music files, for example — is a bit much.

We have some good news for you. Regardless of whether you have a $250 television set or a $25,000 home theater, you can wirelessly enable almost any type of A/V gear you have. In the following sections, we discuss the wireless bandwidth requirements for the two major applications for your entertainment system: audio and video. Then we get into the specific options available on the market.

## Understanding bandwidth requirements for audio and video

Here are the two predominant ways that audio and video files are handled with your entertainment/computer combo:

- ✔ **Streaming:** The file is accessed from your PC's hard drive, a server, or networked hard drive or from a server on the Internet and sent via a continuous signal to your entertainment hardware for live playback. This is the way that most media content is handled in home networks today.

  Streaming applications are *real-time* applications, meaning that what you are hearing or seeing, or both, is what's being streamed over the network *right now*. Any problems with the network, such as not having enough bandwidth to support the media you're playing, have a noticeable effect in your playback experience (for example, dropped audio or blocky video).

  Unlike with file transfer (discussed in the next bullet), a streaming application is sensitive to network delays and lost data packets. You tend to notice a bad picture pretty quickly. With streaming, you need to get the packets right the first time because most of the transmission protocols don't allow for retransmission, even if you want to. You just get clipped and delayed sound, which sounds bad.

- ✔ **File transfer:** The file is sent from your PC's hard drive, a server, or networked hard drive or from a server on the Internet to a storage device connected directly to your stereo system components, where it's stored for later playback. File transfers can pretty much work over *any* network connection.

  With file transfer, lots of transmissions take place in the background. For example, many audio programs allow for automatic synchronization between file repositories, which can be scheduled during off hours to minimize the effect on your network traffic when you're using your home network. And, in these cases, you're not as concerned with how long it takes as you would be if you were watching or listening to it live while it plays.

  Unlike with streaming, a file transfer is not sensitive to network delays and lost packets. Any lost data can be retransmitted when its loss is detected.

A good-quality 802.11g signal is fine in most instances for audio or video file transfers and is also more than adequate for audio streaming. Whether it's okay for *video streaming* depends a great deal on how the video was encoded and the size of the file. The larger the file size for the same amount of running time, the larger the bandwidth that's required to transmit it for steady video performance. Video is a bandwidth hog; whereas audio streaming might require a few hundred Kbps of bandwidth (or maybe one or two Mbps for uncompressed audio), video can require much more. Low-resolution Internet video (for example, YouTube videos) doesn't require a lot of bandwidth; it also doesn't look all that great on your TV. If you want to send DVD-quality video across your wireless network, you need several Mbps's worth of wireless bandwidth to do so — HDTV can require as much as 20 Mbps.

The high bandwidth requirements of video were one of the driving forces behind the development of 802.11n. 802.11g may have a nominal bandwidth of 54 Mbps, but in the real world, users can expect less than 20 Mbps of real throughput across the whole network. A single channel of HDTV would stop the entire network dead.

If you're considering streaming high-quality video across your wireless network, you should definitely build (or upgrade to) an 802.11n network. Again, remember, if you're just doing audio streaming, 802.11g is more than adequate, so there's no need to upgrade an existing wireless router just for this purpose.

## Exploring your equipment options

You can choose from a number of different options when you build a wireless entertainment network, as described in the following sections. Later in the chapter, we take a deeper dive into these product categories and talk about how you can get audio and video onto your wireless network.

Almost all the entertainment networking equipment we discuss in this chapter includes wired Ethernet connections in addition to Wi-Fi networking. So if your whole-home network consists of both wired and wireless network infrastructure, and the wired part of your network reaches your entertainment system, you can use Ethernet instead of Wi-Fi to connect your audio/video gear — we recommend that you do so if the cables are there!

When you shop for a wireless entertainment device of any sort, it's important to make sure it's certified not only for the variant of 802.11 you're using (g or n), but also for the level of wireless networking security you're using. (See Chapter 9 for more on this.) Most new devices support all current Wi-Fi security standards (up to and including WPA2 Personal), but traditionally this category of product lagged behind computer networking products in terms of security. Remember that you can't have a mix of WEP and WPA/WPA2 on the same network — we recommend walking away from a product that supports only WEP unless you're comfortable reducing the security on your entire network.

### Media adapters

The most basic (but by no means unsophisticated) wireless media systems are known as *media adapters*. These devices have no storage themselves, so they're strictly for streaming media. A media adapter does exactly what its name says it does: It converts (or adapts) a streaming audio or video file coming from your computer (such as an MP3 music file) to an analog or digital audio (or video) format that your TV or audio equipment understands. A media adapter connects to your wireless network on the computer side using Wi-Fi, and connects to your home entertainment gear using standard audio and video cables. A good example of such a device is Apple's AirPort Express (`www.apple.com/airportexpress/`) which also doubles as a travel router. (See Chapter 8 for more on the Airport Express.)

In the early days of Wi-Fi, media adapters were the primary mechanism for connecting PCs and A/V equipment. Since then, we've seen the development of sophisticated media players (discussed in the next section) as well as the incorporation of wireless digital media support in other devices like A/V receivers and game consoles. As a result, there are very few wireless media adapters left on the market. If your needs are simple, however — like just getting music from a PC to a stereo — a media adapter can do the job for the least amount of money.

### Media players/servers

Media players or servers add storage to the mix. Typically, these devices have a built-in hard drive that lets you locally store entertainment content for playback, so you don't have to rely as much on the performance of your wireless network. Most media players also will stream content from your computer network (and the Internet), so you can think of them as a media adapter with a hard drive. Examples include Apple's AppleTV (`www.apple.com/appletv`), which retails for $229, and D-Link's MediaLounge players (such as the DPG-1200, `www.dlink.com/products/?pid=655`, which retails for $229.99).

There's no Ministry of Naming Esoteric Wireless Entertainment Gear. (If there were, we think it would be right next door to the Ministry of Banning Common Household Items from Airplanes, but that's another story entirely!) What we mean by this statement is that not all vendors use exactly the same terms we're using here to delineate the difference between an *adapter* and a *player/server*. The bottom line is that an adapter has no local storage and is a streaming-only device, whereas a player/server has a hard drive (or other storage) and can work independently of your PC's hard drive (syncing the content and then playing it back whenever, even when your spouse has the laptop at work).

### Media center extenders

A specialized category of media adapters/players, *media center extenders* work specifically with Windows XP, Vista, and Windows 7 computers running Microsoft's Windows Media Center software. A media center extender essentially replicates the Media Center user interface on your TV and lets you access all the content stored on your Media Center PC remotely. A media center extender may have a hard drive for local content storage, but it is primarily a streaming solution, with the content you're accessing all coming from your Media Center PC. The primary Media Center Extender device is Microsoft's Xbox 360 gaming console (discussed in Chapter 11). Companies such as Linksys and HP have offered standalone media center extender devices in the recent past, but as we write in mid-2010, these products have been discontinued with no replacements.

### Networked audio/video gear

Some audio/video gear has the networking built right in. This could be a home theater receiver with networking capabilities that let you stream audio from your computer directly into the receiver (without requiring a stand-alone media adapter), or it could be a purpose-built wireless entertainment system that uses Wi-Fi to distribute audio (and to a lesser degree, video) around your home. A good example of the former is Denon's AVR-4310CI home theater receiver, with built-in Wi-Fi (`http://usa.denon.com/ProductDetails/5130.asp`); an example of the latter is the Sonos Digital Music System (`www.sonos.com`), which uses Wi-Fi to create a multiroom, whole-home audio distribution system. (For more on Sonos, see the section "Choosing equipment with built-in Wi-Fi," later in this chapter.)

You can also find networked A/V equipment that provides access to specific Internet-based services like Netflix on-demand movies — most Blu-ray disc players being sold today offer this feature, and many include built-in Wi-Fi (from manufacturers like Samsung and LG).

Most networked home theater receivers do *not* have built-in Wi-Fi but instead provide only a wired Ethernet connection. You can use a *Wi-Fi Ethernet bridge* (discussed in the section "Adding Wi-Fi to Ethernet A/V gear," later in the chapter) to connect these devices to your wireless network.

### Home theater PCs

You can bring content right to your home theater or media room by installing a home theater PC. These are purpose-built PCs designed to function as your home theater's DVR (digital video recorder), DVD player, and general jack-of-all-trades content source.

## Internet-connected A/V devices

There are two big trends in the world of consumer Audio/Video (A/V) gear right now. The first of these trends is *3D*, which is kind of cool (provided you don't mind wearing the dorky glasses) and totally outside the bounds of this particular book. The second is *Internet-connected* A/V gear. You can find Internet-connected flat panel TVs (plasma or LCD TVs, in other words), Internet-connected A/V home theater receivers, and Internet-connected Blu-ray disc players — using either built in Wi-Fi or an external Wi-Fi adapter (or an Ethernet cable for a wired connection).

As the name implies, these systems allow you to connect to Internet-provided services. That could mean connecting to your Netflix account to watch on-demand movies; connecting to YouTube to watch videos; connecting to Picasa or Flickr albums for photo slide shows. You can even find *widgets* that let you check the weather, news, or stocks prices. (Widgets are similar to the modules you might be familiar with from a My Yahoo! or iGoogle home page on your PC's Web browser.) Blu-ray disc players will also use their network connection to access BD-Live content (special extra content related to the Blu-ray disc you're playing at the time — to learn more about BD-Live check out this site: `www.sonypictures.com/homevideo/bluray/bdlive.html`).

Most Internet-connected A/V equipment does not, however, connect to your own in-home stores of digital music files and digital videos on your PCs or external storage devices. So, in most cases, you're not going to replace a digital media adapter or player with an Internet-connected Blu-ray disc player or TV. You may find, however, that a networked A/V home theater receiver will have the ability to connect to your PCs and access your digital music files. This capability varies from receiver to receiver, so you have to read the specs closely before you buy.

We like to think of Internet-connected A/V gear as just another awesome application that can use your home network, rather than as a replacement for a media adapter/player for accessing your personal content.

# Getting Media from Computers to Traditional (Non-Networked) A/V Equipment

The most common question we're asked in the realm of wireless entertainment is, "How do I play the thousands of digital songs stored on my computer on the high-quality audio system in my family room?" The *second* most common question we're asked is, "How do I take all those videos on my computer and play them on my big-screen TV?"

Well, these are questions we can answer. In fact, this entire chapter is designed to answer those questions and variants thereof. But we start off with the simplest answer to these simple questions: Get a digital media adapter or player (as described in the previous section "Exploring your equipment options"). If audio is your biggest concern (and for most folks it is), a digital media adapter can be an easy-to-configure and inexpensive route between point A (your computer) and point B (your A/V system). Adding video to the equation means you'll have to spend a bit more money (and will probably benefit from the *local storage* contained in a digital media player instead of an adapter).

What should you look for when choosing a media adapter or player? We think the following things are important:

- **Network compatibility and performance:** Any media adapter or player you choose should be Wi-Fi certified and support at least 802.11g. If you're choosing a system that supports video as well, we strongly recommend that you choose an 802.11n system. Finally, you should ensure that your adapter or player supports the Wi-Fi security system you're using on your network. (We recommend that you use WPA2.)

Even if your requirements are for audio only, if your AP or wireless router uses 802.11n, you should choose an 802.11n media player or adapter simply because mixing 802.11g and 802.11n on the same network decreases the overall speed of the network. Keep your network all n to maximize throughput for any use of the network. Or, if you have a simultaneous dual-band wireless router (see Chapter 5), you can put your entertainment networking on one band (typically the 5GHz band) and keep your computers on the other band (the 2.4 GHz band).

- **Software requirements:** Some media adapters and players require the installation of software on your PC or Mac. This software acts like Windows Media Player or iTunes does on your computer, and it indexes all the media on your computer and streams (or forwards) it to your adapter or player. Many media adapters or players actually use iTunes and/or Windows Media Player (which you probably already have installed on your PC), which simplifies matters greatly.

Look at the specs for the equipment you're buying to see whether it claims to be Windows Media– or iTunes-compatible. It's a lot easier to use what you've already got than to add even more media software to your PCs and Macs.

- **User interface:** The user interface is simply the mechanism that you use to control your media player. For some simple media adapters (such as Apple's multipurpose AirPort Express — which can also be used as a router or as a print server), the interface is on your computer; this means you have to use the software on the computer to control the media adapter, which isn't convenient. Other adapters and players have a simple remote control that lets you skip forward and back through songs or video programs, pause, and stop and start the program. Some adapters and players even include their own touch screen remotes or let you use an app on a smartphone like an iPhone or Android phone to control them.

✓ **Display:** Your media player or adapter's display is part of its user interface, but we're mentioning it separately simply because not all media adapters and players even have a display — which is inconvenient to say the least. For media adapters and players that do have a display, you'll find two distinct mechanisms:

  • *LCD/LED screens on the device itself:* Many media players or adapters have a small text display on the device, which can display your playlists, the title or song name currently playing, and more. Keep in mind that you don't want this display to be too small, because you're likely to be trying to read it from across the room.

  • *TV onscreen displays:* These are typical for media players and adapters that can handle video content. An onscreen menu (similar to the one that your cable or satellite set-top box offers) lets you view and browse all your PC-based media on the big screen. An onscreen display is sexy and a lot easier to use from across the room than a smaller screen on the device itself, but an onscreen display does require you to have your TV turned on, even when you're only listening to music — so you might consider a player/adapter that offers *both* an onscreen display and a built-in display.

An adapter without a screen isn't necessarily completely inconvenient. For example, Pat uses Apple's AirPort Express for playing music on his home office stereo system. Because he always has at least one of his Apple laptop computers in that room, he can simply open iTunes and choose music. Or he can use Apple's *Remote* iPhone app to control iTunes on his computer or on his Apple TV.

✓ **File format support:** You can use a number of file formats for storing audio and video on a computer. Examples in the audio world include MP3, WMA (Windows Media Audio), and AAC (used by iTunes). The video world includes formats such as WMV (Windows Media Video), MPEG-2, and MPEG-4. Most media adapters and players support the most common file formats (particularly widely used standards such as MP3 and MPEG), but you should pay close attention to the formats you actually use to make sure that your adapter or player matches up with them.

✓ **DRM support:** DRM (or *digital rights management*) is a blanket term to describe various copy protection and usage restriction systems used by online music and video stores to control how customers use music and videos that they download or purchase. DRM is, at its essence, an effort to keep digital music and video downloads off the Internet and off file-sharing services (such as peer-to-peer networks). Unfortunately for consumers, most DRM is overly restrictive and makes it hard to distribute your purchased music and video not only to strangers over the Internet but also to *yourself* over your home network. If a lot of the music and video that you have on your computers is from an online store, check carefully to see whether your media adapter or player can support the variant of DRM that the store uses — oftentimes the answer is no.

✔ **Support for subscription services and Internet radio:** Although most music and video obtained online is downloaded to a PC and stored there for future playback, some online services support a streaming model (often called a subscription service). With these services (an example is Rhapsody, www.rhapsody.com), you don't actually own a song or album, but you can access any of millions of songs on demand (as long as your subscription is current). Some media adapters and players allow you to *directly* access these services, so you can completely bypass your computer and listen to (or watch) this online content through your wireless network and broadband Internet connection.

In addition to subscription services such as Rhapsody, hundreds of Internet *radio stations* play their own chosen music playlists (like traditional radio stations). You can't choose which songs to listen to with Internet radio (like you can with a subscription service), but you don't have to pay anything either. Many media adapters and players can tune into Internet radio stations — without requiring you to use your computer to tune in.

✔ **Audio and video outputs:** Remember again that media adapters and players are designed to sit in between your computer(s) and your audio/video gear and to covert digital music and video files into a format that your A/V gear can understand. To connect your adapter or player to that A/V gear, you need to use some standard audio/video cables. As a baseline, you should expect your adapter/player to have a stereo pair of analog audio outputs (RCA cables, just like the ones that connect DVD players, tape decks, and the like). More advanced models have digital audio outputs (TOSLINK or coaxial) for connecting to a home theater receiver.

On the video side, at a minimum you should have a composite video connection (the yellow video cable found on VCRs). If you want to get a high-definition picture from your adapter or player, expect to find either a set of analog *component video* outputs (three cables, like the ones found on many DVD players) or an HDMI (High Definition Multimedia Interface) digital video connector like the connectors found on Blu-ray disc players. HDMI can actually carry both video *and* digital audio on one cable.

# Choosing Networked Entertainment Gear

The digital media adapters and players we discuss in the preceding section make a connection between your computer network and traditional (non-networked) A/V gear. Not all A/V gear is incapable of being networked though. In fact, a growing number of home theater receivers and even televisions are being outfitted with network capabilities.

Most networked A/V gear (be it a Blu-ray disc player or a TV) simply provides access to Internet entertainment services (as we discuss in the sidebar in this chapter titled "Internet-connected A/V Devices"). However, in some cases (mainly with "networked" A/V receivers), these devices have a built-in digital media adapter (or the functionality of one) — providing you with the ability to access digital media files across your home network. Almost all of these network-enabled receivers and TVs are Ethernet devices and *not* Wi-Fi enabled.

You can also find whole-home wireless audio distribution systems that can connect to your computers, but that also can be self-contained wireless entertainment systems. We talk about both types of systems in this section.

## Adding Wi-Fi to Ethernet A/V gear

In the future, we expect that most networked entertainment gear will have built-in Wi-Fi. And in fact, several high-end receivers and TVs do have built-in Wi-Fi today. (An example of this is Denon's AVR-4310CI receiver, which retails for $2,999 and includes built-in 802.11g networking.) Manufacturers have been reluctant to incorporate Wi-Fi due to the rapid pace of technological change (for example this nearly 3 grand receiver includes only 802.11g, which is now being replaced by 802.11n). Rather than be caught with outdated wireless technology, many manufacturers have skipped wireless entirely.

Unfortunately for us as consumers, nothing is worse than having a great piece of entertainment gear that you want to get onto your home network, but the nearest outlet is yards away and you don't have a cable long enough to plug it in. So, you can imagine Danny's face when he had his brand-new, networking-capable AudioReQuest system (www.request.com) with no Ethernet connection near to plug it into. Argh!

To get this gear on your network, you need a wireless *bridge*. Here are some excellent options that are available:

- ✔ **NETGEAR's Universal WiFi Internet Adapter WNCE2001** (www.netgear. com/ConnectWiFi, $79.99). This device connects to any 802.11b, g, or 2.4 GHz n network, supports WPA2 and easy configuration with WPS. (See Chapter 9 for more on WPS.)

- ✔ **Apple Airport Express** (www.apple.com/airportexpress, $89). This 802.11n device is a great little multipurpose product. It's a media adapter, a wireless Ethernet bridge, a travel router, an access point, and a print server all in one slick white package. It can't do all these things at once, but it can be configured for any of these uses. Oh, and it can play music purchased at the iTunes store, and it supports WPA2.

- ✔ **Cisco/Linksys' WET610N Wireless N Bridge** (http://homestore. cisco.com/en-us/adapters/linksys-wrt610n-wirelessn-gaming_stcVVproductId65221232VVcatId552009VVviewprod. htm, $99.99). It costs a few bucks more, but it supports connections to 5 GHz 802.11n networks, which can be very handy if you're using a dual-band network in your home.

These wireless bridges may be labeled or marketed as *gaming adapters,* simply because that was the first primary use for such devices — connecting gaming consoles without wireless connections to a wired network. There's no magic in the name; they work just fine for entertainment, too.

You'll also find a number of bridges on the market that support 802.11g only. Wi-Fi equipment manufacturers have been slow to roll out 802.11n networking in these sorts of devices, which is disappointing but just a fact of life you'll have to live with for a while longer.

Here are a couple of tips for buying wireless bridges:

- ✔ **Look for 802.11n for this application.** You need the bandwidth, and 802.11n is where you'll find it. Video doesn't work well at 802.11g speeds, but if you're doing music-only, 802.11g will be fine.

- ✔ **Make sure the security matches your network security needs.** All the wireless bridges we mention in this chapter support WPA/WPA2 security on the network, but other products on the market don't. Remember that security in a wireless network is a least-common-denominator concept: If even one of your devices supports only WEP and not WPA, your entire network will run using the (not-so-secure) WEP security system.

## Choosing equipment with built-in Wi-Fi

Some manufacturers are building whole-home wireless entertainment systems (typically focused on music-only applications) that let you set up a centralized, remotely controlled multiroom audio system without wires or complicated installations. Essentially, you can use Wi-Fi to get a whole-home audio system like the really rich folks have in their mansions with $200,000 custom-installed wiring systems. Wireless power to the people!

We focus on a leading-edge wireless media server product, the Sonos Music System (www.sonos.com, about $999 for a two-room system called the Bundle 250), as shown in Figure 12-1. This technogeek's dream system consists of a controller (the brains of the system) and two "zone" players (the endpoints of the system where all the speaker and system interfaces are housed, as well as a four-port switch so that you can network other items in the vicinity — nice!). Connect one zone player to your home theater receiver and the other to a pair of speakers (or buy matching speakers from Sonos for another $250) in another room, and you're ready to go.

Most buyers of the Sonos also buy a local network attached storage (NAS) hard drive because the Sonos itself doesn't have one — a non-NAS system just plays music found elsewhere, such as on your PC. You can also have more than one Sonos zone player; the players talk to each other and the controller in a mesh-like fashion, so if you have a really large house, you can still use the Sonos system. In such instances, the Sonos system synchronizes the music so that it all plays at the same time, avoiding any weird echo-type sounds around the house. Sonos uses 802.11g for its wireless protocol and creates its own mesh network hopping from Sonos to Sonos throughout your home.

**Figure 12-1:**
The Sonos Music System is advanced stuff!

If you want to connect your Sonos system to your existing wireless network (and to your Internet connection, for playing Internet radio stations), you can add in the $99 Sonos Zonebridge, which plugs into an Ethernet port on your home router and automatically bridges your PC and Sonos wireless networks.

If the nearly $1,000 starting price for a Sonos system is a bit more than you want to pay, consider the Logitech Squeezebox Touch system ($299 per module, www.logitech.com/speakers-audio/wireless-music-systems/devices/5745). This system uses a touchscreen interface (like that found on an iPhone or Android phone) and connects to the music stored on computers, NAS server devices, or even streamed over the Internet, and it plugs into your audio equipment or a pair of powered speakers. The Squeezebox Touch works on any 802.11g-compatible wireless network and supports all of the latest security protocols like WPA2, so it's ready to plug into just about any home network (unless you're using a 5 GHz-only 802.11n network, which is rare). You can use as many Squeezebox Touches as you'd like, so a two-room system similar to the base Sonos system would cost you $598 (a good bit cheaper!). When you've got more than one Squeezebox Touch, you can choose to play different music at each station, or synchronize your music so the same thing is playing throughout the house.

If you need a good set of cheap but high-quality powered speakers to attach to a Sonos or Squeezebox Touch system, we've heard nothing but praise for the

Audioengine 2 system ($199 for a stereo pair, `http://audioengineusa.com/Store/Audioengine-2`). These speakers can be plugged directly into a PC or Mac, into the output of an iPod, or connected to your wireless music system. A great price and some great sound can be yours for not too much money.

# Putting a Networked PC in Your Home Theater

When you talk about your home entertainment center, you often talk about *sources:* devices such as tape decks, AM/FM receivers, phono players, CD units, DVD players, and other consumer electronics devices that provide the inputs of the content you listen to and watch through your entertainment system.

When you think about adding a networked PC to your entertainment mix, the PC becomes just another high-quality source device attached to your A/V system — albeit wirelessly. To connect your PC to your entertainment system, you must have some special audio/video cards and corresponding software to enable your PC to "speak stereo." When the PC is configured like this, you effectively have a *home theater PC* (or *HTPC,* as the cool kids refer to them). In fact, if you do it right, you can create an HTPC that funnels audio and video into your system at a higher-quality level than many moderately priced, standalone source components. HTPC can be that good.

 You can either buy a ready-to-go HTPC right off the shelf or build one yourself. We don't recommend that you build an HTPC unless you have a fair amount of knowledge about PCs. If that's the case, have at it. Another obvious point: It's much easier to buy a ready-to-go version of an HTPC off the shelf. You can find out more about HTPCs in *Home Theater For Dummies* (we wrote that one, too). What we include here is the short and sweet version of HTPC.

You can find a wide range of HTPCs that vary in processor speed, storage capabilities, and more — for example some folks want to be able to do hard-core gaming on their HTPCs, in which case they'd need even more RAM, greater processor speed, and the fastest possible video cards. Regardless of your needs, a home theater PC needs ample hard drive space to store audio and video files and the appropriate software. (See the following section.) Here's a rundown of what an HTPC can do:

- ✔ **Store audio (music) files:** Now you can easily play your MP3s anywhere on your wireless network.

- ✔ **Store video clips:** Keeping your digital home video tapes handy is quite the crowd pleaser — you can have your own *America's Funniest Home Videos* show.

- ✔ **Play CDs and DVDs:** The ability to play DVDs is essential in a home theater environment.

✔ **Act as a DVR (digital video recorder):** This optional (but almost essential, we think) function uses the HTPC's hard drive to record television shows like a TiVo (www.tivo.com). (See the nearby sidebar, "Checking out PC DVRs," for the lowdown on PC-based DVRs.)

✔ **Let you play video games on the big screen:** With the right hardware, PCs are sometimes even better than gaming consoles (which we cover in Chapter 11).

✔ **Tune in to online music and video content:** Grab the good stuff off the Internet (yes, and pay for it) and then enjoy it on the big screen with good audio equipment.

✔ **Provide a high-quality, progressive video signal to your TV video display:** This is behind-the-curtain stuff. Simply, an HTPC uses special hardware to display your PC's video content on a TV. Sure, PCs have built-in video systems, but most are designed to be displayed only on PC monitors, not on TVs. To get the highest possible video quality on your big-screen HDTV, you need a special video card that can produce a high-definition, progressive-scan video signal. (This investment also gives you better performance on your PC's monitor, which is never bad.)

You're probably going to want an HTPC that supports an HDMI output for connecting your TV. We'd go so far as to say that this is almost mandatory for newer TVs, especially if you want to play high definition Blu-ray discs.

✔ **Decode and send HDTV content to your high-definition TV display:** HTPCs can provide a cheap way to decode over-the-air HDTV signals and send them to your home entertainment center's display. You just need the right hardware (an HDTV-capable video card and a TV tuner card). If you have HDTV, this is a cool optional feature of HTPC.

## Checking out PC DVRs

Using the HTPC's hard drive to record television shows like the way a TiVo does is an optional (but almost essential, we think) function. And using an HTPC as a DVR is a standard feature in a Windows XP/Vista Media Center PC — and something that we think you should consider adding to your home-built HTPC. Even if this were the only thing you wanted to do with your HTPC, it would be worth it. You can simply install a PC DVR kit and skip much of the other stuff (such as the DVD player, decoder, and software).

*Tip:* Because the biggest limitation to any DVR system is the amount of space on your hard drive for storing video, consider a hard drive upgrade regardless of your other HTPC intentions.

PC DVR kits on the market include the ATI TV Wonder Tuners (www.amd.com/us/products/pctv/tv-wonder-tuners), SnapStream Beyond TV (www.snapstream.com), and Hauppauge WinTV HVR products (www.hauppauge.com).

From our perspective, the best bet for a home theater PC is a *small form factor* PC with an HDMI output something like an Apple Mac Mini (www. apple.com/macmini) or a Dell Zino HD (the URL is way too long for us to print out for you; go to www.dell.com and search for Zino HD). Both of these PCs are tiny (smaller than a standard Blu-ray disc player), include HDMI connections, special software for displaying on a TV screen (Windows Media Center for the Dell, Apple's Front Row software for the Mac Mini), and plenty of computing horsepower and storage. The Zino HD has the added advantages of optional Blu-ray disc player and a TV tuner, if you haven't already got a DVR and Blu-ray disc player.

If you have a Windows XP, Vista, or Windows 7 PC with Microsoft's Windows Media Center software included, you can put it anywhere in your home and use it as an HTPC through a Windows Media Extender — as long as you also have an Xbox 360 gaming console. Other manufacturers — specifically, Linksys and HP — also manufactured Media Center Extenders, but they've discontinued these products (in our opinion because they didn't offer any more functionality than just using an Xbox 360, weren't any cheaper, and you couldn't play games on them).

## Other wireless ways (where there's a will . . . )

We're obviously biased toward the 802.11 technologies because we believe in a wireless home network backbone. We think that with all the focus on standards, costs will decrease, new features will evolve, and the overall capability will continue to get better. Collectively, it simply gives you more options for the home.

That doesn't mean, however, that standards are the only way to go. Plenty of proprietary 900 MHz, 2.4 GHz, and 5 GHz approaches — as well as other frequency bands — are popular because they're cheap to manufacture and cheap to implement. For example, check out the Audiovox Terk (www.audiovox.com, $99) Leapfrog Series Wireless A/V System (Model LF-30S, for example), which uses the same 2.4 GHz frequency spectrum as 802.11b

and 802.11g to carry audio and video around the house. The gear we've tested in this space, like the X10 Entertainment Anywhere and various Radio Shack 900 MHz models, has been somewhat of a disappointment, but it does work.

So, 802.11 isn't the only way, but we prefer it based on experience. Just remember: The more signals you put in the 2.4 GHz and 5 GHz ranges to compete with your 802.11 signals, the more problems you have. The 802.11 products are building in new quality-of-service capabilities designed to deal with multiple simultaneous audio and video transmissions, and over time will be more robust, accessible, and reliable, we think. Look for the Wi-Fi icon when you buy.

# Wirelessly Connecting Inside Your Home Theater

Our main focus in this chapter has been on how to connect your TV and/or audio equipment (your home theater, if you call it that) to the Internet and to the computers in your house, wirelessly. We focus on that because we think that's the best use of wireless in the A/V realm.

That having been said, we know that sometimes wireless can come in very handy within the home theater room. (We call that room our "family room" or "den," but maybe we're just not being fancy enough!) In particular, there are two places where wireless can come in very handy in that room (no matter what you call yours):

- ✔ Connecting speakers that you'd have a hard time running wires to. Specifically, we're talking about the *surround* speakers in a five (or more) channel surround sound system — by surround speakers, we mean *back* speakers.

- ✔ Getting a video signal to a flat panel TV mounted on a wall or somewhere where hiding cables is difficult.

Although there are "wireless" solutions for both of these situations, it's important to remember that they're not truly wireless. Speakers and TVs have a common need, and that need is power. These wireless solutions can eliminate the signal cables that run to a TV or a speaker, but they can't replace the need to get power to those devices. So they're really solutions that use *fewer* wireless, and not solutions that use *no* wires.

## Unwiring speakers

If you've ever installed a multichannel home theater system, you probably know what the biggest pain in the rear end part actually is. And no, it's not connecting all of those myriad cables on the back of the receiver (yeah, that's not fun either); it's trying to get a pair (or two pairs) of speaker wires from the front of the room to the back where your back and/or side surround speakers are located. And it's just going to get worse as new generations of home theater gear go from 5.1 (five speakers and a subwoofer) to 6.1, 7.1, and beyond.

So it's nice to think about not running that extra 100 feet (or more, when you combine them all up) of speaker wire and trying to keep it out of site (so your spouse doesn't make you sleep in the dog house). Well you can do that with wireless speakers. You have two options here:

- ✔ You can buy a surround sound system that comes with wireless speakers. In this case, wireless is built in to both the receiver and the speakers, and you just turn it on!

- ✔ You can buy wireless adapters that connect to the outputs of your receiver and send a signal to another wireless adapter connected to each of your surround speakers. This can work great, but it's expensive and complex.

It's probably obvious, but we like the former solution much more. Most major manufacturers of home theater equipment (Sony, Samsung, Panasonic, and so on) sell home theater systems consisting of a receiver (often with a Blu-ray or DVD player built-in), a subwoofer, wired front speakers, and a pair of wireless speakers for the surrounds. All you need to do is find a power outlet in the back of your room for the surrounds and you're all set. Easy peasy.

If you want to get a bit fancier and select all of your own components (your favorite receiver and your preferred brand of non-wireless speakers) you can do that, too. You just need to purchase and install a wireless audio adapter kit. Such a kit consists of two components: a *transmitter* (or sender) that connects to your audio source (such as one of the outputs of your home theater receiver) and a *receiver* that connects to your speakers.

Seems pretty simple? But actually it's not, because the receiver module also needs to include an *amplifier* to actually power your speakers (unless you're using powered speakers with built-in amplifiers, which is relatively rare for surround sound speakers).

A good (and inexpensive) example of such a system is the Rocketfish Universal Wireless Rear Speaker Kit ($109.99, www.rocketfishproducts.com). This system connects to the surround speaker cables coming out of your A/V receiver and sends a signal up to 100 feet to the Rocketfish receiver. The receiver, in turn contains an amplifier that supports two speakers (with simple speaker wire connections). Yes, you'll need to run a small amount of speaker wire, and you'll need to plug the Rocketfish receiver into the wall, but you'll avoid that long run from the front to the rear of the room. For some folks, that's just the trick. Other manufacturers, like Bose (www.bose.com), offer similar systems.

## Cutting the video cable

The other big "uh oh" that lots of people face when wiring their home theaters comes to light when they go to the trouble of mounting a new fancy flat panel plasma or LCD TV on the wall and then realize they have to get some big fat HDMI, component video, and other video cables into the back of the TV. Hiding the power cable is bad enough, but what happens when you have three or four thick cables to hide? It's enough to send the most self-confident person running into the arms of a professional installer.

Well, wireless technologies can help you with this problem by carrying those video signals over radio waves instead of cables. But we have to warn you right now: It's probably not going to be any cheaper than paying someone to hide the cables in the wall. At the time of this writing, we're still in the early days of wireless video transmission. Systems that can transmit full HD (high definition) HDMI signals cost around $600 and go up from there. And there's still not a single agreed-upon standard for doing so. Oh yeah, and there's no getting around the power cable that your TV will need. So even with wireless, there's still a cable to hide.

But there is good news on this front: Manufacturers are starting to build wireless video connections right into their TVs and related equipment (like home theater A/V receivers). At the International Consumer Electronics show in January 2010, several manufacturers announced such products, and they're starting to slowly make their way to market. When wireless is built into hundreds of thousands of TVs and receivers, the price will come *way* down. For example, LG (www.lg.com) has started selling flat panel TVs with wireless HDMI built in, and it sells a transmitter device for about $350 that connects to all your video sources and sends their outputs to the TV.

Today, if you want to make a wireless video connection, you have to buy a transmitter/receiver pair of equipment, like the surround speaker transmitter/receiver pairs discussed in the previous section. A good example of such a device is Gefen's Wireless HDMI Extender (www.gefen.com/kvm/dproduct.jsp?prod_id=4318, $999). This kit does exactly what its name implies: extends an HDMI connection without wires.

At the time we're writing this book in mid-2010, we think that wireless video is something worth waiting a while longer on. If you have a special situation (like brick walls that can't hide cables at all), and you can afford it, go for it — the solutions we've seen all work very well. And if you're buying a new TV and it has wireless video connectivity built-in, well that's a no brainer. Otherwise, we think you'll find that this will be much cheaper and easier in a couple of years.

# Chapter 13

# Extending Your Mobile Network

· · · · · · · · · · · · · · · · · · · · · · · · · · · · · · · · · · · · · · · · ·

· · · · · · · · · · · · · · · · · · · · · · · · · · · · · · · · · · · · · · · · ·

*I*n all the years we've been tracking the comings and goings of the wireless world, we've never seen anything like the absolute explosion of activity, product development, and just plain general (and we mean *general* — not just industry insiders but kids and grandmas and everyone in between) interest in broadband mobile wireless — 3G — and the devices that connect to these networks.

Just about everyone we know has heard of 3G, which stands for the *third generation* of mobile (cellular) wireless systems. Even those few people who haven't have heard about the iPhone or any of the hot Android phones or the Blackberry have heard of 3G. The smartphone (or, as David Pogue of the *New York Times* has dubbed them, "app phones") revolution has captured the interest and imagination of the general public to the point that new phone launches make the front page of newspapers, and a relatively minor antenna issue (we're talking about you, iPhone 4) seems to cause an entire nation to hold its breath.

We guess you're probably nodding your head right now thinking, "Well, duh guys, I already know all this, what does it have to do with *home* wireless networks?" Well, stick with us. Because while, in the past, your home network and the mobile network didn't have much to do with each other, now they do.

In this chapter, you find out how you can use mobile broadband to bring your wireless network with you. With the right gear (and the right account from your mobile provider), you can create an on-the-go *hot spot* of Internet-connected Wi-Fi that you can use with any Wi-Fi equipped gear you own. So your car, your hotel room, your seat on the train, your picnic bench at the park, and even your beach towel can have fast Wi-Fi access for your laptop or netbook computer, your handheld computing devices, and your iPod touch or iPad.

Also in this chapter, we talk about how you can better extend the mobile network into your home. It's a sad fact that as awesome as 3G wireless is, coverage is still an issue for many folks. And coverage *inside* the house is usually even worse than it is outside. If you've ever had to go stand on the patio or in the driveway to keep a mobile call from dropping, you know what we're talking about. We discuss new devices called *femtocells* that connect to your home broadband (cable, DSL, and so on) connection and create what is, in effect, a personal cell tower for you. Five bars in the house! Finally!

# Building Your Own Hot Spots with 3G

In Chapter 16, we discuss Wi-Fi hot spot networks, which are designed to let you get your laptop or netbook computer online when you're away from home. However, you don't *need* to be in a hot spot to get online without wires away from your home or office; you can use wireless WAN services — the so-called 3G and 4G networks offered by companies like AT&T, Verizon Wireless, and Sprint in the U.S. and hundreds of other countries. With a portable Wi-Fi router or a smartphone (such as an iPhone, a Blackberry, a Palm, or an Android phone) and a connection to a broadband wireless network, you can *always* be online wherever you are (except maybe in the middle of the desert or on top of a mountain). So you might not even need to pull your laptop out if you just want to tweet about your latest activity or e-mail a photo of the kids to grandma.

If you're not familiar with the term *hot spot,* check out Chapter 16, where we talk in detail about this concept. Essentially it's a public-access Wi-Fi network that you can access when you're in the vicinity.

In the following sections, we discuss broadband wireless networks in more detail as well as give you some options for getting multiple devices online without buying multiple data plans.

## Exploring wireless WAN services

Wireless WAN services enable you to get online without wires away from your home or office. These *wireless wide area network services* are offered by cellular carriers worldwide providing data services over the same cell towers used to make calls and send text messages.

Wireless WAN services come in different flavors depending on the technology each carrier is deploying and where each flavor is available. Some of the most common of these connections are

✔ **GSM UMTS:** This is the 3G (third generation) version of the GSM (Global System for Mobile Communications), which is the world's predominant mobile phone system (the UMTS stands for Universal Mobile Telephone System). The current version of GSM 3G is the variant of UMTS called *HSPA* (High Speed Packet Access). In the U.S., carriers such as AT&T and T-Mobile offer this service.

✔ **CDMA EV-DO:** CDMA is the competing mobile system developed by Qualcomm (right here in Pat's town, San Diego). The 3G version of CDMA, EV-DO (Evolution Data Only) is roughly equivalent to the UMTS 3G services offered on GSM networks. EV-DO service offered in the U.S. by Sprint and Verizon.

You'll hear lots of advertising by competing cellphone carriers about which is better: GSM or CDMA. Well, the fact is that the current 2010 version of GSM is slightly faster than its CDMA competitor. But the actual speed is based on more than just the underlying technology — factors like who has the most (and best-located) cell towers has just as much weight as the technology itself. We think, all things considered, that the technology isn't really the deciding factor. One thing to keep in mind, however, if you travel a lot internationally, is that you're likely to find 3G GSM networks wherever you go. A 3G CDMA network? Not so much.

✔ **4G:** Technology never stands still — especially in the wireless world — so the *next* generation of wireless WAN is already being built. Two main alternatives are in development:

• *WiMAX:* WiMAX (Worldwide Interoperability for Microwave Access) is *much* faster than existing 3G: It can hit speeds of up to 70 Mbps — though real world speeds are typically much less. WiMAX is so fast that it can actually be used as a replacement for a wired DSL or cable modems, though it's primarily being marketed as a mobile service today. In the U.S. just one carrier (Sprint and its partner Clearwire) offers WiMAX and only in a limited number of locations.

• *LTE:* LTE, or Long Term Evolution, is exactly what its name implies: an evolutionary step from today's GSM or CDMA systems. LTE is designed to work with both of these systems, so carriers can evolve (there's that word again) their networks into 4G without losing compatibility with existing equipment. In the U.S., both Verizon and AT&T have committed to installing LTE, though we're still a year or two away from seeing this on the market.

3G (and the emerging 4G) services are being built right into all sorts of devices. For example, you can get built-in 3G in the following devices:

✔ Cellphones and smartphones

✔ Netbook computers

✔ Laptop computers

✔ Tablet computers (like the Apple iPad)

You can also install a 3G *aircard* (essentially, a 3G network adapter like the Wi-Fi network adapters we talk about in Chapter 3) into your PC or Mac laptop or netbook computer. Aircards are available (you buy them directly from your wireless carrier) in both ExpressCard and USB formats (just like Wi-Fi network adapters), depending on what kinds of ports are available on your computer. You'll typically pay about $100 for an aircard, though most carriers offer significant discounts (up to 100 percent) if you buy them along with a service contract.

Using these data services on your portable computer is easy. You just plug your ExpressCard or USB aircard into your laptop and launch your carrier's cellular access program. You're online, surfing away. For the privilege, you'll pay about $40 to $60 per month, depending upon the carrier and your data plan. That's on top of whatever you pay for your mobile service plans for your phone, of course.

The problem with an aircard is that it works on only one device at a time. However, there are ways to get multiple devices online without breaking the bank, as we discuss in the next section.

## Getting multiple devices online without buying multiple service plans

What happens when you have a smartphone *and* an iPad *and* a laptop or netbook computer and you want to get them all online at once? Well, you can pay for 3G services for each of these devices (ugh), or you can find a better solution. In this section, we discuss some of those better solutions that will get more than one device — even a whole minivan's worth of devices — online without buying multiple 3G service plans. What we're talking about, of course, is to create your own hot spot on the go!

You have several options here: You can buy a mobile router, you can *tether* (explained a bit later) your laptop or other device to your 3G (or 4G) mobile phone, or you can find a mobile phone with a built-in Wi-Fi hot spot. All these options require you to pay an extra $20 to $50 per month on top of your mobile bill, but if you're a real road warrior, the expense may very well be worthwhile to you.

Many 3G data service plans have monthly bandwidth limits — you pay extra for every bit and byte you transfer across it after a set limit. Most folks don't exceed their service plan limits when they send e-mails and Facebook updates and pictures from their smartphones. But when you mix in a couple of laptops and start watching TV shows on Hulu or your favorite YouTube videos, your bandwidth usage can go *way* up. And the *overage* charges many wireless carriers charge when you exceed your bandwidth limitations can be stupendously expensive. So if you start down this path, pay close attention to your current data plan, alternative plans you might want to move up to, and (most of all) your monthly bills!

### MiFi'ing yourself a hot spot

The easiest solution for getting several devices online on the road is to purchase a mobile hot spot device. (Everyone we know calls this device a *MiFi* — which is the brand name of the most popular device in this category.)

The leader in this category is the Novatel's MiFi family (www.novatel wireless.com). About the size of a deck of cards, the MiFi includes a built-in aircard and a Wi-Fi router/access point. (The 2200 model, used for North American EV-DO 3G networks is pictured in Figure 13-1.) The MiFi connects to your carrier's 3G mobile network and lets you connect up to five devices (smartphones, laptops, iPads, whatever) to its built-in Wi-Fi router. Easy as pie.

**Figure 13-1:**
Car trips are much quieter when everyone's connected to the MiFi.

The only drawback is the price. A MiFi 2200 lists for about $269 (though discounts are *definitely* available if you sign a 2-year contract), and you'll pay $40 or more a month for a service plan. (The more you pay, the more data you can download using the MiFi in a given month.) So a MiFi isn't cheap, but when compared to the price of buying aircards and multiple data service plans, it can be economical. In the U.S., Verizon offers the MiFi on its EV-DO network, and Sprint is launching a similar product (from a different vendor, Sierra Wireless, www.sierrawireless.com) that works on Sprint's 3G and 4G (WiMAX) networks.

### Tethering

If you already have a 3G smartphone or cellphone and you don't need to get several other devices online at one time, a solution worth checking out is *tethering*. Tethering is the act of connecting a laptop or netbook computer to the Internet using the 3G data service built into a 3G phone. You can tether via Bluetooth (if both your phone and computer have Bluetooth and support this feature) or via a USB cable (if they don't).

Bluetooth tethering is wire-free and kinda, well, sexy (heck, you can leave your phone sitting in your backpack while you tether your laptop or netbook), but USB tethering has one distinct advantage: In most cases, your laptop will keep your phone charged over the USB cable, so you don't have to worry about having a dead battery when you're done with your tethering session.

Unfortunately, tethering isn't something that you just do — you can't turn on your phone and your laptop/netbook and magically have tethering set up. Instead, there has been one *huge* obstacle to tethering, and that's your wireless carrier. While tethering has been technically possible for a long time, and available throughout the world for several years, it wasn't until late 2009 (later for some carriers) that U.S. carriers would actually even *allow* you to set up tethering. The good news here is most carriers now do allow tethering, for a price — about $20 per month on top of your existing data plan.

After you've established a tethering service plan with your wireless carrier, you can configure tethering on your phone and on the computer you're trying to connect to the Internet. Now this is the point where we're going to have to leave you on your own a bit; there are a lot of permutations in the exact set-up procedure, because it's dependent on what model of phone and computer you are tethering together. So forgive us for abandoning you here and saying "follow the instructions from your carrier," but that's what we have to do.

That said, in general, you'll do the following:

1. Turn on tethering service with your carrier. (Call the carrier or access its Web site if you can modify your account online.) Make sure you get explicit instructions (or the address of the Web page that contains them) when you do so.

2. Turn on tethering within your phone's setup menus. (For example, on an iPhone, go to Settings➪General➪Network and find the Set Up Internet Tethering menu item.)

3. Connect your phone to your computer with a USB docking cable or via Bluetooth. (If you're using Bluetooth, you need to *pair* the devices, as we discuss in Chapter 15.)

4. Set up your tethered phone in your computer's network control panel or preferences pane. (In Windows, this is in the Network and Sharing Center in the Control Panel; on a Mac, this is in the Network preference pane of System Preferences.)

Tethering is a relatively economical way of adding *one* device (at a time — you can tether multiple devices, but not simultaneously) to your existing 3G data plan. It isn't as flexible as a MiFi, nor as fast and cheap as using a hot spot, but if it's just you, your smartphone, and your laptop on the road, it's a great solution.

## An iReady hot spot from Clearwire

Clearwire, Sprint's 4G partner, recently launched a new mobile hot spot device that's aimed squarely at their rival AT&T: the iSpot (www.clear.com/spot/ispot). This $99 4G mobile hot spot comes in the same white color as all manner of Apple "i" products and is designed specifically for providing Wi-Fi service to Apple products. In fact the marketing materials are explicit on this front: "Didn't think your iPad, iPhone, or iPod touch could get even better? Guess again, my friends, guess again."

In fact, the iSpot is *not* a general-purpose mobile hot spot device. It's designed specifically to work with Apple devices, so if you're planning on mixing in your Windows 7 laptop or netbook computers, it's not the device for you. But if you have iPod touches, iPads, or even iPhones that don't have 3G built-in or that don't get good network coverage in your area, the iSpot is for you. In fact, if you're thinking about buying an iPad, Clearwire has priced the iSpot with you in mind. The price of the iSpot is the same as the premium Apple charges for 3G iPads over same-spec Wi-Fi only iPads, and the $25 monthly service charge is comparable to the AT&T 3G plan for the iPad. If you're like Danny, with a car full of teenagers with iPod touches (you can connect up to eight devices to the iSpot at once), the iSpot may be just what you need!

### Hot spot in a phone

There's a third option to getting devices online away from home (and away from hot spots) that's essentially a combination of tethering and the MiFi: using your 3G (or 4G) smartphone as a portable hot spot. Like tethering, your phone is the center of the action, and like a MiFi, you can connect multiple devices over a Wi-Fi connection.

As we write, only a few phones and wireless carriers support this smartphone-as-hot-spot functionality.

- ✔ **Palm Pre Plus and Pixi Plus phones:** The Palm Pre Plus and Pixi Plus smartphones (and, presumably, any future phones running Palm's WebOS operating system) support up to five Wi-Fi devices while operating as a MiFi-like 3G personal hot spot. Downloading an app from the Palm store called "3G mobile hotspot" enables this feature. The best part? It's free, at least if you have a Verizon Palm Pre or Pixi. (AT&T has not yet tipped its hand about whether it will support this feature on the Palm phones that it sells.)

- ✔ **Sprint HTC Evo:** This smartphone has a *lot* going for it. First, it's the world's first 4G phone, supporting Sprint's WiMAX network. So, if you can get coverage where you are, you'll get the fastest wireless downloads available, bar none. And it includes a hot spot service like the one that's included with Palm WebOS phones (described in the preceding bullet).

There's a downside though; the hot spot plan adds $30 per month on top of your already hefty (approximately $80 to $110) per month service plan for the phone itself (which does, admittedly, include unlimited data and hefty-to-unlimited text messages and voice calls).

✔ **Go Froyo:** No, not frozen yogurt. Froyo is the codename for the still forthcoming (as we write in the summer of 2010) 2.2 version of Google's Android smartphone operating system. Pricing and availability (and a whole lot of other details) are still pending as we write, but a MiFi-like Wi-Fi hot spot is *definitely* baked right into the operating system, and by the end of 2010, many millions of phones will be running Froyo.

# Boosting Your Mobile Network at Home with a Femtocell

We mention at the beginning of the chapter that the great Achilles heel of 3G broadband is coverage (at least in the U.S.; most of the rest of the world has considerably better coverage). Apologists for the sorry state of U.S. mobile coverage will say things like, "Well, it's a big country with a lot of rural areas to cover," and they're right. But even in the denser suburbs and urban areas of the country, many users have experienced dropped calls, slow e-mails, and general pokiness. In many ways, the mobile carriers have been the victims of their own success; selling tens of millions of broadband-enabled smart-phones has pushed the volume of data that's going over mobile networks right through the roof.

And although everyone has "dead zone" areas (Pat's is the canyon behind his house, and Danny has a hill on the way home that forces him to warn people that the call *will* be lost), for many, the absolute worst place to get a good cell signal is in our homes. Radio waves pass through walls, but they lose some of their strength (that is, they *attenuate*) as they do. And weaker radio waves equal a poor signal.

Now if you're wondering what the big deal is, think about the tens of millions of "cord cutters" out there — people who've dropped their landline phones and switched solely to their mobile phones. Mobile phone operators offer huge bundles of voice minutes in their packages, with no long-distance charges and usually all sorts of incentives like rollover minutes, friends and family plans, or "favorite five" plans. If you're already paying a monthly cell-phone bill, do you really even need that home phone? A lot of people have decided they don't.

So the no-coverage-in-the-home issue is a real problem for a *lot* of people. Even if you haven't gotten around to cutting the cord, you still get calls on your mobile when you're home. Wouldn't you like to be able to answer them?

In the past, poor coverage in the home was "fixed" by expensive and difficult-to-install repeater systems. These systems consisted of a specialized antenna that you mounted somewhere high — as high as possible (think "roof of a three-story building" high) — as well as an amplifier and indoor antenna that you'd run cables throughout the home to install. Essentially these repeater systems were like a big funnel — grabbing the over-the-air signal from outside and funneling it down a cable to the antenna in your house. Danny installed one of these systems in his house in Connecticut (he lives waaaaay out in the boonies), and it worked. But it was not, shall we say, a quick and easy installation.

There's a newer solution now that makes the job of extending your mobile coverage *much* easier. It's called a *femtocell,* and essentially it's a tiny little cell-phone tower right in your house. (*Femto* is the metric prefix for 10 to the negative 15th power — and if that doesn't imply "little," we don't know what does.)

## Exploring the pros and cons of femtocells

Unlike the older generation of cellphone repeaters, femtocells don't sit in between your mobile devices and the local cell towers; instead, they completely bypass those towers (within your home) and convert your mobile signals to IP (Internet Protocol) data and send them over your home's broadband Internet connection and on to their destination. Essentially you just connect your femtocell to a wired Ethernet port of your broadband router, turn it on, and you're set. Figure 13-2 shows the AT&T 3G Microcell, produced by Cisco.

Well, there's a bit more to it than that, but first let's talk about the pros and cons of femtocells. (They're not perfect.)

On the pro side:

- ✔ **They give you true "5 bar" service throughout your home.** Femtocells don't have a huge range — by their nature, they're designed to not radiate much outside the home so that they don't interfere with actual cell towers or your neighbor's femtocell — but they provide good coverage throughout a typical home, up to about 5,000 square feet.

- ✔ **They're easy to use.** After a phone has been associated with a femtocell, it will automatically connect to it when the signal is strong enough. Just like you don't spend any time worrying about which cell tower your phone is associating with as you drive down the street, neither will you worry about connecting to your femtocell in your house. It just works.

- ✔ **They can save you minutes.** Depending upon your carrier and service plan, you may be able to make calls at home, using your femtocell, without using up the minutes in your voice plan. If you run out of minutes every month and make a lot of calls from home, you might be able to justify a femtocell on those savings alone.

**Figure 13-2:**
Femtocells plug into your home wireless router and give you your own cell tower!

And now the cons (there are always cons!):

✔ **You have to pay for them.** Some people just can't get past this point: You're paying (an upfront fee, a monthly service plan, or both) to "fix" the cellphone company's inadequate network. Most mobile carriers charge about $100 to $200 for their femtocells, often with a $5 to $10 monthly charge. (You'll typically pay more for a plan with unlimited "home" voice minutes.)

✔ **Femtocells are carrier-specific.** An AT&T femtocell works with AT&T phones, a Verizon femtocell works with Verizon phones, and so on. If you're in a mixed marriage (you and your spouse are on different cell carriers), or if you live with roommates with different carriers, you won't all be able to use the femtocell.

✔ **You have to live within a designated coverage area of your carrier to use a femtocell.** Yes, the carrier will actually check, using a GPS device built into the femtocell. For most people, this isn't a problem, but if for some reason (perhaps you moved) your home isn't in an official coverage area for your carrier, you can't use a femtocell. Period. It's a legal thing, and there's no getting around it

*Note:* You *can* take your femtocell with you — for example to your vacation home — but only if your destination is also part of your carrier's coverage zone.

✔ **Femtocells are best for voice, not data.** Several carriers offer femtocells that don't support 3G data at all. The AT&T *MicroCell* femtocell *does* support 3G data, but any data services you use count against your service plan data caps (even though your own broadband network is carrying the data — yes, we know how ridiculous this is). You're better off using your home Wi-Fi network for any data (e-mailing, Web browsing, using Facebook, and so on) you use. If your mobile phones don't support Wi-Fi, check the fine print before you jump into the femtocell world.

In the U.S., Verizon Wireless, AT&T, and Sprint all offer femtocells. As we mention earlier, the AT&T femtocell supports 3G data, and the other two don't, though we suspect they'll offer 3G femtocells in the very near future.

## Setting up a femtocell

Your carrier will provide specific instructions for configuring a femtocell, but here are the general steps:

1. Place your new femtocell near a window or, if you can't get near a window, connect the external GPS antenna (which should be supplied with the femtocell) and place it near a window. Your femtocell needs to be able to pick up a GPS signal for two purposes:

   • To confirm you're in the carrier's service area

   • To provide your exact location for E-911 purposes

2. Using an Ethernet cable, connect your femtocell to your home broadband router (which must be connected to a broadband Internet connection) and then plug it into a power outlet.

3. Sit and wait. It'll take a while for the GPS chip in the femtocell to find the satellites, fix your position, and report it back to the mobile phone company over the Internet. Typically, you see a blue or green light or some other visual indication when this process is complete. It might be two minutes, or if your GPS signal is weak, this could take as long as an hour.

4. Register your femtocell and/or mobile phones with the system and start using it. In some cases, this is automatic after the GPS has done its work. In other cases, you need to log into your cellphone provider's Web site with your account information and provide the serial number of your femtocell and the phone numbers of the phones you want to use with the femtocell.

We can't tell you whether a femtocell will be worthwhile for you, but if you're ready to throw your cellphone out the window because of poor coverage, it could be the best $100 you ever spent. Danny, by the way, replaced his repeater system with a Verizon femtocell, and he's been very happy with it. You may be too!

# Chapter 14

# Other Cool Things You Can Network

*T*he wireless age is upon us, with all sorts of new devices and capabilities that you can add to your network to save you time and enhance your lifestyle. When you have your wireless local area network in place, which we show you how to do in Parts II and III, you can do a nearly unlimited number of things. It sort of reminds us of the Dr. Seuss book *Oh, the Places You'll Go!*

In this chapter, we introduce you to some of the neater things that are available now for your wireless home network. In Chapter 19, we talk about the things that are coming soon to a network near you! If you read this chapter along with the gaming, A/V, and mobile discussions in Chapters 11, 12, and 13, respectively, you can see why we say that wireless home networking isn't just for computers anymore.

In this chapter, we give you an overview of many new products, but we can't give much specific information about how to set up these products. In general, you have to provide your service set identifier (SSID) and WPA passphrase (or WEP key, if your network doesn't support WPA). That should be 95 percent of what you need to do to set up your device for your wireless network. In this chapter and in Chapter 19, we feel that it's important to expose you to the developments happening now so that you can look around and explore different options while you wirelessly enable your home. To say that your whole house will have wireless devices in every room within the next few years is *not* an understatement — it's truly coming on fast, so hold on tight!

The wireless-enablement of consumer goods is spreading faster than a wildfire. As we write, products are coming out daily. If you're interested in seeing what else has popped up since we wrote this book, check out our book update site at www.digitaldummies.com.

# "Look, Ma, I'm on TV" — Video Monitoring over Wireless LANs

The heightened awareness for security has given rise to a more consumer-friendly grade of video monitoring gear for your wireless network — this stuff used to be the exclusive domain of security installers. You can get network-aware Wi-Fi video cameras that contain their own integrated Web servers, which eliminates the need to connect a camera directly to your computer. After installation, you can use the camera's assigned Internet Protocol (IP) address on your network to gain access to the camera, view live streaming video, and make necessary changes to camera settings.

## Finding the right wireless network camera for you

Network cameras are much more expensive than cameras you attach to your PC via a USB connection because they need to contain many of the elements of a PC to maintain that network connection. Expect to pay from $100 to more than $1,000 for network cameras; the more expensive versions offer pan-tilt-zoom capabilities and extra features such as two-way audio, digital zoom, and motion detection. (The average price for a well-equipped camera is $200.)

D-Link (www.dlink.com) is the leading vendor of wireless-based video surveillance. It has a special line networked cameras, the mydlink line, that include secure Web site access so you can access them from anywhere in the world, as well as a large number of other wireless and wired network camera products. D-Link has the best selection of wireless cameras — you can probably find the perfect camera for your needs there. Here are a few D-Link cameras that we recommend:

  ✔ A great starter camera from D-Link is the DSC-1130 Wireless N camera, which includes the mydlink service and retails for about $220. With this camera all you need to do is plug it into a power source, enter your SSID and security passphrase, and then log in to mydlink.com. You can access the camera from any Web browser, including those on 3G mobile phones. So you'll always be able be able to know what's going on.

✔ Another example is the DCS-6620G Wireless N 10x Optical Zoom Internet Camera (www.dlink.com, $819), which is on the higher end of the product line. (See Figure 14-1.) This 802.11g camera has some really nice features:

- Motorized pan-tilt-zoom so that you can look around an area and zoom in

- Two-way audio support so that you can hear people and talk to them as well

- Dual-motion MJPEG and MPEG-4 support so that you can stream video using different bandwidth levels and quality

- Extreme low-light sensitivity so that you can take pictures in dark rooms

- A frame capture rate of up to 30 fps

You can remotely monitor your camera using a Web-based interface or through the D-Link IP surveillance software. Your cameras can be accessed via the Web, with as many as ten simultaneous users viewing the live feed. Using the IP surveillance program, you can monitor and manage as many as 16 cameras, set recording schedules, configure motion-detection settings, and change settings to multiple cameras — all from one place.

**Figure 14-1:**
The D-Link
SecuriCam
DCS-6620G
wireless
network
camera.

Go to www.dlink.com/products/?pid=342 and click the Product Demo link on the bottom of the page for a live demo of the D-Link DCS-5300 camera. See what it's like to pan, tilt, and zoom!

Panasonic also has a large lineup of cameras. Its BL-C121A wireless network camera (www.panasonic.com, $199.95) allows as many as 20 simultaneous viewers to see as many as 30 frames per second (fps) of live-motion video at 640 x 480 pixels. Through a Web-based interface, you can perform remote pan and tilt functions and click to eight preset angles.

Love pets? Panasonic has been specializing in the remote pet experience with a series of products marketed as petcams. Panasonic sponsors an online video Web site for pet lovers at www.seemypetcam.com. You can upload your pet's IP wireless camera videos for others to see!

You can also get cameras from other players, such as Cisco's Linksys brand (http://home.cisco.com/en-us/wireless/linksys/), Hawking Technologies (www.hawkingtech.com), and TRENDnet (www.trendware.com). You will often find video cameras bundled into other packages; Hawking's Net-Vision HRPC1 Wireless-G Network Camera ($115) interworks with its Hawking HomeRemote Wireless Home Automation System HRPZ1 Gateway ($180), which enables you to turn lights on and off in the house remotely. Often you'll find packages of three or four cameras for a lower bundled price as well.

Have you upgraded to 802.11n? As we write, many wireless networked cameras still use 802.11g. D-Link and Linksys, however, are both offer 802.11n cameras. Over time, everyone will move to 802.11n — it just makes sense.

The wireless communication doesn't have to be all 802.11 based, although we would argue that it makes sense to use standards-based gear whenever you can. Danny likes his X10 FloodCam (www.x10.com, $99), which videotapes all activity around the house, night and day, and sends the color images to a VCR or PC. That system uses 2.4 GHz to send the signals, but it's not standardized wireless LAN traffic. We believe that over time, many of these systems will move to 802.11 or Bluetooth as chip and licensing costs continue to come down.

Security varies tremendously among video camera offerings. If security is important to you (as it should be!), you should check the technical specs of any camera before you buy. Panasonic's BL-C30A, for instance, is an older model and has only 40/64/128-bit WEP encryption to help protect your wireless network from illegal intrusion. The D-Link cameras top out at WPA as of this writing too. TrendNet's TV-IP312W Wireless 2-Way Audio Day/Night Internet Camera Server (www.trendware.com, $220), on the other hand, supports 64/128-bit WEP, WPA-PSK, and WPA2-PSK. (We talk more about WEP and WPA in Chapters 6 and 9, if you need to know more.) Look for a camera that has at least WPA2 Personal (PSK) on board — over time more cameras will have this.

## Setting up the camera

Installing a wireless network camera is incredibly simple. These network devices usually sport both an RJ-45 10Base-T wired network interface along with an 802.11b/g air interface. Installing the camera usually involves first connecting the camera to your network via the wired connection and then using the provided software to access your camera's settings. Depending on how complicated the camera is (whether it supports the ability to pan, to e-mail pictures on a regular basis, or to allow external access, for example), you may need to set any number of other settings.

To allow anyone from outside your home's LAN to view your camera feed directly (that is, not from a window pane published on your Web page), you need a static WAN IP address. Although you can probably get such an address from your broadband connection provider, it will probably be pricey. More likely, you'll use a *dynamic DNS service* (DDNS), which allows you to assign a permanent Web address to the camera. A DDNS is easier to remember than an IP address and is static. Your camera vendor should help you do this as part of the setup process. D-Link, for example, has its own free DDNS service (www. dlinkddns.com) that you can activate during your setup process. Panasonic has its free Viewnetcam.com (www.viewnetcam.com).

# Controlling Your Home over Your Wireless LAN

Another area of wireless activity is home control. If you got excited about going from the six remote controls on your TV set to one universal remote control, you ain't seen nothin' yet. (And if you still have those six remote controls, we have some options for you, too.)

The problem with controlling anything remotely is having an agreed-on protocol between the transmitter and receiver. In the infrared (IR) space, strong agreement and standardization exist among all the different manufacturers of remote controls, so the concept of universal remote control is possible for IR. (IR remotes are the standard for the majority of home audio and video equipment.) But there has not been the same rallying around a particular format in the *radio frequency* (RF) space, thus making it difficult to consolidate control devices except within the same manufacturer's line. And then you have issues of controlling nonentertainment devices, such as heating and air-conditioning and security systems. Those have different requirements just from a user interface perspective.

The advent of 802.11 technologies, ZigBee, Z-Wave, and Bluetooth — as well as touchscreen LCDs and programmable handheld devices — offers the opportunity to change this situation because, at the least, manufacturers can agree on the physical transport layer of the signal and a common operating system and platform. We're now starting to see the first moves toward collapsing control of various home functions to a few form factors and standards. We talk about these topics throughout this section.

## Controlling your home-automation system with a touch panel

Cool new handheld devices — namely, Web tablets and standalone touch-screens — are sporting IR interfaces and can become remotes for your whole home. (*Whole home* means that you can use it anywhere that your wireless net reaches for a broad range of devices anywhere in your home; check out Chapter 1 for more details about whole-home networks.)

You're probably familiar with touchscreens if you've ever used a kiosk in a mall to find a store or in a hotel to find a restaurant. Touch panels are smaller (typically 6- to 10-inch screens) and are wall mounted or simply lie on a table; you touch the screen to accomplish certain tasks.

Touch panels have become a centerpiece for expensive home control installations. They allow you to turn the air conditioning on and off, set the alarm, turn off the lights, select music, change channels on the TV — and the list goes on. These are merely user interfaces into often PC-driven functionality that can control almost anything in your house — even the coffee maker.

Here are a few touch-panel manufacturers to consider:

✔ **Crestron** (www.crestron.com) rules the upper end of touch-panel options with an entire product line for home control that includes wireless-enabled touch panels. The Crestron color touch panel systems are to die for (or at least to second-mortgage for). We would say, "The only thing these touch panels cannot do is let the dog out on cold nights," but if we said it, someone would retort, "Well, actually, they can."

Crestron's Isys i/O WiFi TPMC-8x is a modified tablet-style PC with an 8.4-inch screen. This product runs a specially modified version of Windows and communicates using 802.11b/g/a. With this device, you can control your home theater and home automation system, turn on lights, and basically control anything in an automated house. You can also listen to music files and view streaming video directly on the tablet itself!

Crestron is definitely high end: The average installation tops $50,000. But if you're installing a home theater, a wireless computing network, a slew of A/V, and home automation on top of that, you probably will talk to Crestron at some point.

✔ **Control4:** A popular, lower-cost alternative to Crestron is Control4 (www.control4.com). Control4 makes a line of home entertainment, control, and automation devices, ranging from home controllers that can centrally control all the devices in a home; home theater controllers, which centralize control of your home theater components; whole-home audio distribution systems; and ZigBee lighting and HVAC (heating, ventilation, and air conditioning) controllers. Control4's latest touchscreen panels start at about $599, which is considerably less expensive than similar systems from other vendors.

Control4 uses widely adopted standards such as Ethernet, 802.11, and ZigBee to keep its prices down while still offering the kind of space-age automation that used to be in the realm of only the truly wealthy. It's the home control system "for the rest of us" (just like our *For Dummies* book)!

To keep tabs on all your automated and remotely controlled systems, Control4 offers touchscreens such as the 10.5-inch wireless touchscreen (shown in Figure 14-2). This device uses 802.11g and that big color screen to show you the status of all sorts of devices and systems in your home, and the 802.11g Wi-Fi connection can send control commands back to your Control4 home or home theater controllers from anywhere in the house.

**Figure 14-2:** Control4's wireless touchscreen can control all sorts of devices in your home.

Do you own a smart phone or a tablet computer like an iPad? Well if you're wondering why you'd need to buy a separate touchscreen controller for your home control system, wonder no more. Major home control manufacturers like Crestron and Control4 have created *apps* (downloadable applications) for major smartphone platforms like iOS4 (Apple) and Android that provide all of the functionality found in their expensive standalone tablet-style controllers. So instead of spending hundreds (or thousands) of dollars on dedicated controllers, you download an app for free or for a nominal fee (usually just a few bucks). Just another reason to consider upgrading to a smartphone if you're been holding out.

If you're interested in home automation and linking the various aspects of your home, try *Smart Homes For Dummies,* 3rd Edition. It's the best book on the topic. (Can you tell that we wrote it?)

## Doing your wireless control less expensively

You don't need to spring for a $50,000 Crestron installation (or even a $5,000 to $10,000 Control4 installation) to get wireless control over devices in your home. That's because the advent of ZigBee and Z-Wave (discussed in Chapter 3) have brought lower, commodity prices to wireless control systems.

If you can forgo the fanciness and limit your ambitions, you can find *universal remote controls* (the kind of programmable all-in-one remotes that many folks buy for their home theater) that can move beyond the TV and DVD player and control other systems in your house without wires.

An example here is Monster Cable's tidily named Home Theater and Lighting Controller 300 featuring OmniLink (www.monstercable.com). This $400 remote provides all the high-end home theater remote control features you'd ever want (including the ability to use *macros,* a series of sequential commands that let you do a complex task with a single push of a button) and adds into the mix wireless lighting controls using the Z-Wave technology standard (a mesh wireless control network, which we discuss in Chapter 3).

Monster sells its own line of Z-Wave lighting control modules (manufactured for Monster by the giant electrical company Leviton, www.leviton.com), including both dimmers and switches. These control modules are available as plug-ins (you plug them into an outlet and then plug a lamp into them) and in-wall switches (you replace an existing switch). Monster also offers an in-wall controller that can be used with the remote control, so you can turn lights on and off or dim them throughout the home from a single wall switch.

## Maximizing your entertainment with macros

The most advanced remote controls can interface with your A/V gear through *macros.* Select Watch TV, for example, and the remote sequentially goes through all the motions to turn on the TV, turn on the home theater receiver, select the right inputs on the TV and home theater receiver, turn on the satellite receiver or cable set-top box, and do anything else that's required to watch television. You can program the remote by simply plugging it into your PC or Mac (with a USB cable) and then selecting the components you use from vast libraries of components available online from the remote's manufacturer. Answer a few questions about the configuration of your particular system (for example, do you listen to the TV through the TV's speakers or through your home theater receiver?) and you're on your way to one-remote Zen. Examples of remotes that use macros are Logitech's Harmony remotes (`www.logitech.com/harmony`).

# *Storing Your (Digital) Stuff on Your Wireless Network*

No matter what you do with your network, you're probably going to end up with a lot of digital files that need to be stored somewhere so that you can share and access them from PCs and Macs, smartphones, or even your audio and video gear. Yes, you can store files on the hard drive of your computer, but you may find that it's more convenient to store (or back up) files on some sort of a *server.* A server is simply a dedicated computing device that's always on, always attached to the network, and always available to "serve" files to the devices on your network. Storing files on a server puts them in an easily accessible central location — a location that's not one of your PCs, which may be turned off, put in a bag and brought to work, or otherwise not available.

A server in your home operates just like a server does in a work environment — it serves as a central file repository accessible from any device connected to the network. With a file server on your network, you can do things like the following:

✔ Store any type file from your computers — text files, spreadsheets, music or video files, photographs, anything at all.

✔ Back up your computers (you *do* back up regularly, don't you? You should!) automatically if you have the right software.

✔ Create a media server for serving up files to your networked audio/video equipment.

✔ Print wirelessly from any location in the house, with print server capabilities built into your server.

✔ Access your files from anywhere in the world with remote access.

In the following sections, we describe the different server options that are available as well as give you some tips for what to look for when buying a server.

## Exploring your server options

You have several options when choosing a server for your home — at varying prices and with some or all of these features. Generally you can choose from a Windows Home Server, a network attached storage (NAS) server, or a wireless router with external storage.

### Windows Home Server

Windows Home Servers are usually the most expensive option because they are, for all intents and purposes, full-fledged Windows PCs operating a special version of the Windows OS, without a monitor or keyboard — *headless* in the geek parlance. A Windows Home Server offers all the options we discuss in the earlier list, for a starting price of about $500.

If you have a network primarily made up of Windows computers and you want everything to be as easy as possible, you should seriously consider a server based upon the Windows Home Server platform. These servers offer pretty much every feature you'd want — media serving, remote access, and so on — and they're essentially a plug-and-play proposition. Buy it, take it out of the box, and plug it into your network, and it's ready to go.

You *can* build your own home server (or have a local PC builder create one for you) using a desktop PC and buying the home server software from Microsoft. (You can find the software for sale online at sites like Amazon.com and NewEgg.com.) But we think the best way to get a home server set up is to buy a dedicated home server device from a company like HP (www.hp.com) or Lenovo (www.lenovo.com).

For about $500, you can get an upgradable and expandable hardware system complete with all the networking you need, a powerful processor to run the Home Server OS, and at least 500GB of storage to get you started.

To see the current choices for a Home Server, look at the list that Microsoft maintains at www.microsoft.com/windows/products/winfamily/windowshomeserver/buy.mspx.

### Network attached storage (NAS) server

These devices are mainly focused just on the file storage and sharing part of the equation, but many include support for a number of the other features we discuss at the beginning of this section. Most NAS servers look just like a big external hard drive, but they have built-in networking capabilities and an operating system (typically a version of a UNIX operating system). NAS servers vary widely in price, depending upon features and the amount of storage included, but start at prices of about $150.

If you're interested in using a NAS device instead of a Windows Home Server, you have a huge number of choices. There are dozens, maybe hundreds, of companies selling NAS servers, and they range from simple and inexpensive (less than $150) home focused servers right up to huge multi-terabyte servers designed to support a large office. We couldn't possibly provide you with a list of all the consumer-focused NAS vendors (such a list will be out of date by the time we finish writing this chapter!), but here are a few of the leading vendors you may want to check out:

- **Buffalo Technologies:** www.buffalotech.com
- **Western Digital:** www.wdc.com
- **Drobo:** www.drobo.com
- **LaCie:** www.lacie.com
- **Synology:** www.synology.com
- **Iomega:** www.iomega.com
- **NETGEAR:** www.netgear.com

### Wireless router with external storage

A number of wireless routers can support a USB connection to an external hard drive. The features here depend entirely upon what the router itself supports, but it's easy to pick up a large external hard drive (for example, 1 terabyte) for under $100.

## Comparing features when buying a server

Before we start talking about things you should look for when buying a server for your home, here's an important thing to keep in mind: It doesn't need to be wireless. You can buy a wireless server, but in our opinion, that's not an option we'd pay more for. As long as your server is connected to your network and router via an Ethernet connection, it's accessible to all the wireless devices on the network. A wireless server can come in handy if you want to stash it somewhere out of the way, but otherwise, there's no real advantage to choosing one over a wired server.

In fact, a wireless server probably won't perform as well as a wired one, simply because wireless connections are slower both in terms of absolute throughput and also in terms of *latency* (the delay in transmitting data).

Keep the following things in mind when you're comparing servers:

✔ **Storage space:** You're probably going to need more storage space than you think! Luckily hard drives are cheap, so you'll actually have a hard time finding a server that holds less than 500GB of data. More important than the actual amount of storage space are some other storage-related factors, specifically:

- *Number of drive bays:* What you *don't* want is a storage device with a single gigantic hard drive on it. Hard drives can and do fail, usually at the most inopportune time. (That's why we do backups!) Many servers have two or more *bays* to hold hard drives. Rather than putting all of your data on one 1TB drive, you're better off putting it on two 500GB drives — or even better on two 1TB drives. (We talk about redundancy in a second.)

- *Upgradeability:* As we mention earlier, you need more space than you think. When you start backing up two or three computers, storing thousands of digital photos storing hundreds of hours of digital video (personally recorded video as well as TV and movies), and adding your music library, suddenly your backup takes a *lot* of space. So even if you start with a lot of space, you might end up needing more. If your server allows it, you can cheaply buy bigger drives and easily replace your existing ones without shelling out money for a newer, bigger server.

You can buy a server with only a small amount of storage and then upgrade it when needed — the disks will no doubt be cheaper in six months or a year than they are today. You can even find servers with *no* storage in them, so you can pick and choose the disks you want to use.

- *Storage redundancy:* The *safest* way to store data is to do so *redundantly.* In other words, having your data in more than one place, so if one drive fails your data doesn't disappear. If you choose a server with more than one drive, it will probably include some sort of data redundancy mechanism (such as redundant array of inexpensive disks, or RAID). You'll probably have several options to choose from — the more redundant you make your data, the more space it will take on your server.

✔ **Connectivity:** As we mention earlier, you can find both wireless and wired-only servers. (All the wireless servers will also include a wired Ethernet connection.) If you choose wireless, make sure that it supports the type of Wi-Fi you're using in your network (like 802.11n) and whatever security mechanism you're using (like WPA2). On the wired side of the equation, look for a server that includes a Gigabit Ethernet connection if your router supports Gigabit Ethernet — it'll make for a faster experience all around.

✔ **File system support:** Different computer operating systems use different _file systems_ — essentially the structure of data on the disk. Most home server devices support file systems for both Windows and Macintosh computers, but if you also use the Linux operating system, you'll want to make sure your server can support it.

✔ **Media server support:** Any server can store any files you may want to put on it, but not all can serve those files up as streaming media to your networked home entertainment gear (as discussed in Chapter 13). If you want to do this, make sure that your server supports it. You need to match the server's capabilities to the requirements of your A/V gear, but generally look for the following things:

- _DLNA:_ DLNA (Digital Living Network Alliance) is an industry standard for supporting media streaming. DLNA certification of both your media player/adapter and your server ensures that they'll work together, which is always nice!

- _UPnP:_ Universal Plug and Play is another industry standard for media streaming and compatibility. (In fact, DLNA is built upon this standard.)

- _iTunes server:_ If you use Apple's iTunes as your primary media software, look for a server that works as an iTunes server — you can then centralize all of your iTunes media on the server and access it from your Macs and even from wirelessly connected iPhones and iPod touch devices.

✔ **Remote access support:** Some servers provide remote access support, meaning they make your files and media available to you (and to those to whom you grant access — like the grandparents) over the Internet. You can get this access in a number of ways (including services like FTP), but the _best_ way for most users (us included) is to use a server that's integrated with a Web access service. A Web access service is a hosted and secured service offered by the manufacturer of your server or a third party. Users can log in to your server by going to a specific Web address and logging in with a username and password. This is how Windows Home Servers do it, as do a number of NAS server manufacturers.

# Having Your Very Own Wi-Fi Robot

We like to have some fun with our Wi-Fi networks. We're not just all business all the time! And what's more fun than robots and drones? Yeah, we know — not much, right?

Well, toy manufacturers have kept up with the wireless revolution and have incorporated Wi-Fi in some very cool robotic toys that are guaranteed to keep you occupied on those long, boring winter nights.

The first one we want to mention — and it's still a month away from shipping to customers as we write — is a Wi-Fi controlled drone or UAV (unmanned aerial vehicle). It's not quite the same as the ones used by the military (no missiles, for example), but it's pretty darned cool. It's from Parrot (www. parrot.com), a company best known for its Bluetooth headsets and hands-free Bluetooth kits for cars. The AR.Drone (http://ardrone.parrot.com) is a 4-bladed indoor/outdoor helicopter-ish flying device that has built-in Wi-Fi and is controlled from any Apple iPhone, iPod touch, or iPad connected to the network (see Figure 14-3). Not only does the AR.Drone include Wi-Fi, but it also has a built-in video camera (just like "real" drones) that displays on the screen of your iOS 4 device. So you can see where you're flying and then use simple touch controls on the screen to navigate. Parrot is creating games so you can have dogfights with other AR.Drones or simply take it on a surveillance mission. They promise support for other smartphone/tablet OSes in the near future (for example, Android). We're getting on the waiting list for this one.

**Figure 14-3:**
The Parrot
AR.Drone.

If your preferences run more to the earthbound, check out the WowWee Rovio (www.wowwee.com). This is a Wi-Fi and Webcam equipped wheeled robot that WowWee calls a "mobile Webcam" but we just call "cool." You can control the Rovio (and view its Webcam video) from anywhere in the world where you have a Web browser and an Internet connection — even from a mobile phone or gaming console like a PS3 or Xbox 360. The Rovio has a bright LED headlight, so you can see in the dark. You can even send it back to its charging station when its battery gets low (you can be a thousand miles away and send it back to its charging station over the Internet). We're not sure about you, but we might rather have this in the house than a dog!

# Wirelessly Connecting Your Digital Cameras

When the first Wi-Fi-connected digital cameras came on the market, we were jealous beyond belief. We hate cables (which is why we try to wirelessly connect everything we can). The problem was that only a few cameras had Wi-Fi (or any other wireless) on board, and it wasn't worth throwing away a perfectly good working camera because we were lazy about cables.

A number of digital camera vendors are finally getting around to adding Wi-Fi to their cameras, but you'd be surprised how many otherwise awesome cameras still lack the capability to connect to your network on their own.

Well now, we can be lazy and happy with a brilliant product from Eye-Fi (www.eye.fi). Eye-Fi offers an SD memory card outfitted with Wi-Fi on board — how cool is that? Simply pop the card in your camera, take pictures, and watch the pictures upload automatically as soon as you return to your home network. Worried about security? No need — the Eye-Fi supports static WEP 40/104/128, WPA-PSK, and WPA2-PSK security. (See Chapter 9 if you need some background on these abbreviations.)

To date, Eye-Fi has been the only company to offer Wi-Fi equipped memory cards for cameras, but we've seen news that other companies such as Toshiba (who is one of the major manufacturers of the memory chips used in such cards) are beginning to develop similar cards. So don't be surprised if there are some alternatives on the shelf when you start shopping for an Eye-Fi.

You can automatically load pictures to sharing and printing Web sites, including Kodak Gallery, Shutterfly, Wal-Mart, Snapfish, Photobucket, Facebook, Webshots, Picasa Web Albums, SmugMug, Flickr, Fotki, TypePad, VOX, dotPhoto, Phanfare, Sharpcast, and Gallery. The Eye-Fi Service intelligently downloads your photos from your camera, handles log-ins and passwords for the site, and resizes pictures (if your site requires it) — all over a wireless connection. Photo uploads are free and unlimited because they're using your home's Wi-Fi and Internet connections — some Eye-Fi systems even include free access to hotspots at Starbucks and other locations.

The latest Eye-Fi models add a new feature: GPS support. That's right, there's a GPS chip included in the memory card (we don't know *how* they cram so much in there!), so that you can *geotag* your photos. What's geotagging? Essentially the GPS records the location you're at when you snap a picture and includes it in the EXIF (exchangeable image file format — the data about your picture that all cameras record, things like type of camera, f-stop, aperture, and so on) data of the picture. When you upload the pictures to your computer (using programs like iPhoto and Picasa) or to online services that support geotagging, you'll be able to see on a map exactly where your pictures were taken. Most photo management programs even let you group pictures together by location automatically, so you can click on a map and see all the pictures you took at Disneyland or at your kids' school or at grandma's house.

All of Eye-Fi's current cards support 802.11n networking and are fully backward compatible with 802.11b and g networks. Here's a rundown of some of the available cards:

- ✔ The entry-level 4GB card, the Connect X2, costs about $49 retail. The great thing about these is that you don't need to buy as large a card because it can be offloaded more easily and more often.

- ✔ Do you want to mix in GPS? Choose the Geo X2 for $69 and you'll be able to Geotag your photos.

- ✔ Do you want GPS, an extra 4GB of storage (8 GB total) and the ability to upload your pictures for free at thousands of hot spots at Starbucks and major hotel chains? Choose the $99 Explore X2.

- ✔ Do you want all of the above features plus pro photographer features like RAW image support? Pick up the $149 Pro X2. X2 is just too great a product line to resist!

If you want to find out whether your digital camera is compatible with an Eye-Fi card, go to the Eye-Fi Web site, select the Camera Compatibility tab on the left side of the page, and then select Compatibility from the options that appear below the tab.

# Chapter 15

# Using a Bluetooth Network

*M*ost of the time, when people talk about wireless networks, they're talking about wireless local area networks (LANs). LANs, as the name implies, are *local,* which means that they don't cover a wide area (like a town or a city block). Wide area networks (WANs), like the Internet or a 3G wireless network from a company like Verizon or AT&T, do that bigger job. For the most part, you can think of a LAN as something that's designed to cover your entire house (and maybe surrounding areas, such as the back patio).

Another kind of wireless network is being developed and promoted by wireless equipment manufacturers. The *personal area network* (PAN) is designed to cover just a few yards of space and not a whole house (or office or factory floor or whatever). PANs are typically designed to connect personal devices (cellphones, laptop computers, handheld computers, and other devices like netbooks or iPads) and also as a technology for connecting peripheral devices (like headsets or printers) to these personal electronics. For example, you could use a wireless PAN technology to connect a mouse and a keyboard to your computer without any cables under the desk for your beagle to trip over.

 The difference between LANs and PANs isn't clear cut. Some devices may be able to establish network connections by using either LAN or PAN technologies. The bottom-line distinction between LANs and PANs is this: If something connects to a computer via a network cable, its wireless connection is usually a LAN; if it connects by a local cable (such as USB), its wireless connection is usually a PAN.

In this chapter, we discuss the most prominent wireless PAN technology: Bluetooth, which we introduce in Chapter 3. The Bluetooth technology has been in development for years and years. We first wrote about it in our first edition of *Smart Homes For Dummies* way, way back in 1999. For a while, it seemed

that Bluetooth might end up in the historical dustbin of wireless networking —
a great idea that never panned out — but these days Bluetooth seems to be
everywhere. You can't swing a stuffed cat walking down the street without
seeing someone with a Bluetooth headset jammed in his ear. With *billions* of
devices out there in the world, it's safe to say that Bluetooth has truly arrived!

# Discovering Bluetooth Basics

You probably want to get the biggest question out of the way first: What
the heck is up with that name? Well, it has nothing to do with what happens
when you chew on your pen a bit too hard during a stressful meeting. Nor
does it have anything to do with blueberry pie, blueberry toaster pastries,
or any other blue food. Bluetooth — www.bluetooth.com is the Web site
for the industry group — is named after Harald Blåtand (Bluetooth), king
of Denmark from A.D. 940 to 981, who was responsible for uniting Denmark
and Norway. (We're a little rusty on our medieval Scandinavian history, so if
we're wrong about that, blame our high school history teachers. If you're a
Dane or a Norwegian, feel free to e-mail us with the story!) The idea here is
that Bluetooth can unite things that were previously un-unitable.

The big cellphone (and other telecommunications equipment) manufacturer
Ericsson was the first company to promote the technology (back in the 1990s,
as we mention earlier), and other cellphone companies joined in with Ericsson
to come up with an industry de facto standard for the technology. The *Institute
of Electrical and Electronics Engineers* (IEEE) — the folks who created the 802.11
standards that we talk about throughout this book — have since become
involved with the technology under the auspices of a committee named 802.15.

The initial IEEE standard for PANs, 802.15.1, was adapted from the Bluetooth
specification and is fully compatible with Bluetooth 1.1, right on through to
the 1.2, 2.0 + EDR, and now 2.1 + EDR versions of the technology, as we discuss in Chapter 3. All these versions of Bluetooth are compatible with each
other, so if your new smartphone supports Bluetooth 2.1, it'll work with your
headset or other device, even if that device supports only an older version of
Bluetooth.

If you're looking for a few facts and figures about Bluetooth, you've come to
the right chapter. Here are some of the most important things to remember
about Bluetooth:

> ✔ **Bluetooth operates in the 2.4 GHz frequency spectrum.** It uses the
> same general chunk of the airwaves as do 802.11g and 802.11n. (This
> means that interference between the two technologies is indeed a possi-
> bility, though 802.11n draft 2.0 is designed to sense Bluetooth transmis-
> sions and switch to different channels so they don't interfere.)

✔ **The Bluetooth specification allows a maximum data connection speed of 3.0 Mbps.** Many Bluetooth devices connect at even slower speeds (2.1 Mbps or even as low as 723 Kbps), so Bluetooth is *not* designed for transferring large files, but rather for lower bandwidth applications like printing, audio streaming, and small file transfers (like address book contacts from phone to phone).

✔ **Bluetooth uses much lower power levels than do wireless LAN technologies (802.11).** Thus, Bluetooth devices have a much smaller effect, power-wise, than 802.11 devices. This is a huge deal for some of the small electronic devices because Bluetooth eats up a whole lot less battery life than 802.11 systems. The proposed lower power specification of Bluetooth will use even less power than the current version; it's designed to be used in wireless-enabled watches and will increase the battery life of your cellphone Bluetooth headset five times what it is today.

Because Bluetooth uses a lower power level than 802.11, it can't beam its radio waves as far as 802.11 does. Thus, the range of Bluetooth is considerably less than that of a wireless LAN. Theoretically, you can get up to 100 meters (these are called *Class 1* devices), but most Bluetooth systems use less than the maximum allowable power ratings, and you typically see ranges of 30 feet or less with most Bluetooth gear — which means that you can reach across the room (or into the next room), but not all the way across the house.

✔ **Bluetooth uses a peer-to-peer networking model.** This means that you don't have to connect devices back through a central network hub like an access point (AP). Devices can connect directly to each other using Bluetooth's wireless link. The Bluetooth networking process is highly automated; Bluetooth devices actively seek out other Bluetooth devices to see whether they can connect and share information.

✔ **Bluetooth doesn't require line of sight between any connected devices.** Bluetooth uses radio signals that can pass through walls, doors, furniture, and other objects. So you don't need to have a direct line of sight like you do with infrared systems.

✔ **Bluetooth can also connect multiple devices in a point-to-multipoint fashion.** One *master* device (often a laptop computer or a PDA) can connect with as many as seven slave devices simultaneously in this manner. (*Slave* devices are usually things such as keyboards and printers.)

The really big deal you should take away from this list is that Bluetooth is designed to be a low-power (and low-priced!) technology for portable and mobile and computing devices. Bluetooth (do they call it *Bleutooth* in France? We've always wondered!) isn't designed to replace a wireless LAN. It's designed to be cheaply built into devices to allow quick and easy connections.

Some of the PAN applications that Bluetooth has been designed to perform include:

- ✔ **Cable replacement:** Peripheral devices that use cables today — keyboards, mice, cellphone headsets, and the like — can now cut that cord and use Bluetooth links instead.

- ✔ **Synchronization:** Many people have important information (such as address books, phone number lists, and calendars) on multiple devices (such as PCs, PDAs, and cellphones), and keeping this information *synchronized* (up-to-date and identical on each device) can be a real pain. Bluetooth (when combined with synchronization software) allows these devices to wirelessly and automatically talk with each other and keep up-to-date.

- ✔ **Simple file sharing:** If you've ever been at a meeting with a group of technology geeks (we go to these meetings all the time, but then, we're geeks ourselves), you may have noticed these folks pulling out their Windows Mobile and Palm PDAs and doing all sorts of contortions with them. What they're doing is exchanging files (usually electronic business cards) via the built-in infrared (IR) system found on Palms. This system is awkward because you need to have the Palms literally inches apart with the IR sensors lined up. Bluetooth, because it uses radio waves, has a much greater range, which doesn't require direct IR alignment — and is much faster to boot.

Unfortunately, the most popular smartphone out there — the Apple iPhone — doesn't allow you to use Bluetooth for simple file transfers (something that is common for many other phones). The Bluetooth support on the iOS platform is relegated mainly to audio (headsets for phone calls and Bluetooth headphones or speakers for listening to music) and peripherals (such as keyboards).

Look for even more cool applications in the future. For example, Bluetooth could be used to connect an electronic wallet (on your cellphone) to an electronic kiosk. For example, a soda machine could be Bluetooth enabled, and if you wanted a soda, you wouldn't need to spend ten minutes trying to feed your last, raggedy dollar bill into the machine. You would just press a button on your PDA or cellphone, and it would send a buck from your electronic wallet to the machine and dispense your soda.

# Taking a Look at Bluetooth Mobile Phones

The primary place where Bluetooth technology has become almost ubiquitous is in the cellphone world. This statement probably shouldn't be a surprise because Sony Ericsson, a huge cellphone maker, was the initial proponent of the technology, and other huge cellphone companies, such as Nokia, are also proponents.

Today just about every new phone being announced (except for the cheap-o ones) includes Bluetooth technology. Sony Ericsson, Nokia, Motorola, Samsung, and Siemens, among others, are all selling Bluetooth-enabled phones. The adoption of the technology has been spectacular. A few years ago, Bluetooth was a rarity; now it's a standard.

You can do many things with Bluetooth in a cellphone, but the five most common applications are

✔ **Eliminate cables.** Many people use headsets with their cellphones. It's much easier to hear with an earpiece in your ear than it is to hold one of today's miniscule cellphones up to your ear — and much more convenient. The wire running up your torso, around your arm, and along the side of your head into your ear is a real pain, though. (Some people go to great lengths to keep from being tangled up in this wire — check out the jackets at www.scottevest.com.) A better solution is to connect your headset wirelessly — using Bluetooth, of course. Literally dozens of Bluetooth headsets are on the market, from specialized headset manufacturers such as Plantronics (www.plantronics.com), Jawbone (www.jawbone.com), and Jabra (www.jabra.com), as well as from the cellphone manufacturers themselves.

✔ **Synchronize phone books.** Lots of folks keep a phone book on their PCs or PDAs — and most people who do have been utterly frustrated by the difficulty they face when they try to get these phone books onto their cellphones. If you can do it at all, you end up buying some special cable and software, and then you still have to manually correct some of the entries. But with Bluetooth on your cellphone and PC or PDA, the process can be automatic.

✔ **Get pictures off your camera phone.** Many new cellphones are camera phones with a built-in digital camera. The cellphone companies promote this concept because they can charge customers for multimedia messaging services (MMS) and allow people to send pictures to other cellphone customers. But if your PC has Bluetooth capabilities, you can use Bluetooth to send the picture you just snapped to your PC's hard drive (or even use Bluetooth to transfer the file directly to a buddy's cellphone when he or she is within range — for free!).

✔ **Go hands-free in the car.** Face it — driving with a cellphone in your hands isn't safe. Using a headset is better, but the best choice (other than not using your phone while driving) is to use a completely hands-free system, which uses a microphone and the speakers from your car audio system. This used to take a costly installation process and meant having someone rip into the wiring and interior of your car. If you bought a new phone, you probably needed to have the old hands-free gear ripped out and a new one installed. No more — Bluetooth cars are here, and they let you use any Bluetooth-enabled cellphone to go hands-free. Just set the phone in the glove box or dashboard cubbyhole and don't touch it again. Keep your hands and eyes on the road!

If your current car isn't outfitted with Bluetooth, don't despair. Dozens of Bluetooth retrofit kits are available on the market — ranging from simple speaker/microphone devices that plug into your 12-volt power source (the lighter, in other words) to custom-installed, fully integrated systems that can even use your car's steering wheel controls.

✔ **Get your laptop on the Internet while on the road.** We think that the best way to connect your laptop to the Internet when you're out of the house is to find an 802.11 hot spot (we talk about them in Chapter 16), but sometimes you're just not near a hot spot. Well, worry no more because if you have a cellphone and laptop with Bluetooth, you can use your cellphone as a wireless modem to connect to the Internet. With most cellphone services, you can establish a low-speed, dial-up Internet connection for some basic stuff (such as getting e-mail or reading text-heavy Web pages). If your cellphone system (and plan) includes a high-speed option (one of the 3G systems we talk about in Chapter 16), you can get online at speeds rivaling (although not yet equaling) broadband connections such as DSL — all without wires!

Some cellphones have Bluetooth capabilities but have been artificially limited by the cellphone companies. For example, some Bluetooth phones have had their software configured by your cellphone company in such a way that you can't use the phone as a modem for your laptop, as described in the preceding bullet. There's no easy way to know this up front — but it's a good reason to read the reviews in sources such as CNET (www.cnet.com) before taking a leap.

Check out the section "Communicating with another Bluetooth Device: Pairing and Discovery," at the end of this chapter, for more details on making Bluetooth connections.

# Exploring Other Bluetooth Devices

Cellphones and PDAs aren't the only devices that can use Bluetooth. In fact, the value of Bluetooth would be considerably lessened if they were. It's the *network effect* — the value (to the user) of a networked device that increases exponentially as the number of networked devices increases. To use a common analogy, think about fax machines (if you can remember them — we hardly ever use ours any more). The first guy with a fax machine found it pretty useless, at least until the second person got hers. As more and more folks got faxes, the fax machine became more useful to each one of them simply because they had many more people to send faxes to (or receive them from).

Bluetooth is the same. Just connecting your PDA to your cellphone is kind of cool, in a geek-chic kinda way, but it doesn't set the world on its ear. But when you start considering wireless headsets, printers, PCs, keyboards, and even global positioning system (GPS) receivers, the value of Bluetooth becomes much clearer. In the following sections, we discuss some of these other Bluetooth devices.

## Printers

We talk about connecting printers to your wireless LAN in Chapter 10, but what if you want to access your printer from all the portable devices that don't have wireless LAN connections built into them? Or, if you don't have your printer connected to the wireless LAN, what do you do when you want to quickly print a document that's on your laptop? Well, why not use Bluetooth?

You can get Bluetooth onto your printer in two ways:

- **Buy a printer with built-in Bluetooth.** This item is relatively rare as we write, and it looks as though Wi-Fi enabled printers will replace these completely over time. An example comes from HP (www.hp.com), with its Photosmart C309gAll-in-One printer ($200 list price). In addition to connecting to laptops, PDAs, and other mobile devices using Bluetooth, this Mac- and Windows-compatible printer can connect to your PC with a standard USB cable or via a Wi-Fi connection — so all your bases are covered. So, you can connect just about any PC or portable device directly to this printer, with wires or wirelessly.

- **Buy a Bluetooth adapter for your existing printer.** Many printer manufacturers are focusing on building printers with built-in Wi-Fi, but that doesn't have to stop you. iOGEAR (www.iogear.com), for example, offers a Bluetooth printer adapter, the GBP302KIT (about $120), that plugs into the USB or parallel port and works with most inkjet printers.

## Audio systems

Another area where Bluetooth is starting to make some inroads is in the realm of audio systems. This really should come as no surprise, considering that cellphone audio (for example, hands-free and headset systems) is where the vast majority of Bluetooth action occurs.

What we're talking about here is Bluetooth devices that carry higher-quality audio signals — hi-fi (as opposed to Wi-Fi), as it were. Well, this is an exciting new area for the Bluetooth world because Bluetooth is designed for audio and supports relatively high-quality digital audio transmissions.

You may find Bluetooth audio devices in two distinct places:

- ✔ **Headphones:** Many of people now carry iPods or music-capable smartphones wherever they go. You can identify them by their ubiquitous (at least among the 80 percent or so of MP3 player owners who use iPods) white headphone cords snaking up out of their pockets and into their ears. Well it's time to cut *that* cord too. With systems like the Sony's DR-BT160AS ($129.99), you can connect to any Bluetooth audio-equipped music player without any cords. And if you're using your headphones with a smartphone, they even work as a headset so you can stop the music to answer a call without missing a beat — so to speak.

- ✔ **Speaker systems:** If you have a stereo or multichannel audio system in your house, you know the Achilles' heel of all such systems: those ugly speaker wires running from the back of your receiver or amplifier to the speakers. For home theater systems, this problem is particularly acute because you have speakers in the *back* of the room. (We wrote *Home Theater For Dummies,* and even we have trouble dealing with that speaker wire run.) Well, Bluetooth can come to the rescue. Many manufacturers make Bluetooth speaker systems that work with your Bluetooth-enabled devices. A good example is Sony's Bluetooth Transmitter & Receiver ($79 each — you'll need to buy them a pair at a time). So you can cut the cord and still enjoy your music.

In Chapter 12, we talk about wirelessly enabling your home entertainment systems. We talk more about Bluetooth speakers there, as well as a whole bunch of other wireless systems that fit into your home theater, TV, and audio systems.

## *Keyboards and meeses (that's plural for mouse!)*

Wireless keyboards and mice have been around for a while (Danny has been swearing by his Logitech wireless mouse for years and years), but they've been a bit clunky. To get them working, you have to buy a pair of radio transceivers to plug into your computer, and then you have to worry about interference between your mouse and other devices in your home. With Bluetooth, things get much easier. Danny recently upgraded to the Bluetooth version of his Logitech mouse. He also attached a Bluetooth presenter mouse that works at the same time — Bluetooth is the only way to connect more than one mouse to a single computer — so he can work out and scroll through his e-mail. (Unfortunately, you can't connect more than one keyboard to a computer, but if you have a Bluetooth keyboard it's easy enough to pick it up and take it with you.)

If your PC (or PDA, for that matter) has Bluetooth built in, you don't need to buy any special adapters or transceivers. Just put the batteries in your keyboard and mouse and start working. You probably don't even need to install any special software or drivers on your PC to make this work. For example, if you have a Mac, check out the Apple Wireless Keyboard and Mouse (www. apple.com/keyboard). It's slickly designed (of course — it's from Apple!) and goes for months on its batteries without any cords.

If your PC isn't already Bluetooth equipped, consider buying the Logitech diNovo Media Desktop Laser (www.logitech.com, about $179). This system includes both a full-function wireless keyboard — one of those cool multimedia models with a ton of extra buttons for special functions (such as audio volume and MP3 fast forward and rewind) — and a detached media pad that acts as a hand remote or numeric keyboard with a built-in calculator. It also includes a wireless optical mouse (no mouse ball to clean) with the cool four-way scrolling feature, and a Bluetooth adapter that plugs into one of your PC's USB ports. This adapter turns your PC into a Bluetooth PC. In other words, it can be used with any Bluetooth device, not just with the keyboard and mouse that come in the box with it. This kit is a great way to unwire your mouse and keyboard *and* get a Bluetooth PC, all in one fell swoop.

The diNovo Media Desktop Laser (`www.logitech.com`) is easy to set up. You just plug the receiver into a USB port on the back of your computer and install the keyboard and mouse driver software. (This isn't a Bluetooth requirement; rather, it allows you to use all the special buttons on the keyboard and the extra mouse buttons.) You must have an up-to-date version of Windows XP. (Simply use the built-in Windows XP software update program.)

## Bluetooth adapters

Most laptop and netbook computers and an increasing number of desktop computers — like most of the Apple product line — have built-in Bluetooth. However, if your PC doesn't, you need some sort of adapter, just like you need an 802.11 adapter to connect your PC to your wireless LAN. The most common way to get Bluetooth onto your PC is by using a USB adapter (or *dongle*). These compact devices (about the size of your pinkie — unless you're in the NBA, in which case, we say *half* a pinkie) plug directly into a USB port and are self-contained Bluetooth adapters. In other words, they need no external power supply or antenna. Figure 15-1 shows the D-Link DBT-120 USB Bluetooth adapter.

Because Bluetooth is a relatively low-speed connection (remember that the maximum speed is only 732 Kbps in most cases, and a maximum of 3 Mbps for the fastest USB devices), USB connections will always be fast enough for Bluetooth. You don't need to worry about having an available Ethernet, PC Card, or other high-speed connection available on your PC.

Street prices for these USB Bluetooth adapters generally run under $25, and you can find them at most computer stores (both online and the real brick-and-mortar stores down the street). Vendors include companies such as D-Link (`www.dlink.com`), Belkin (`www.belkin.com`), and ioGEAR (`www.iogear.com`).

## Connecting multiple USB devices with a hub

Because many people have more USB devices than USB ports on their computers, they often use USB *hubs,* which connect to one of the USB ports on the back of the computer and connect multiple USB devices through the hub to that port. When you're using USB devices (such as Bluetooth adapters) that require power from the USB port, you should plug them directly into the PC itself and not into a hub. If you need to use a hub, make sure that it's a *powered* hub (with its own cord running to a wall outlet or power strip). Insufficient power from an unpowered hub is perhaps the most common cause of USB problems.

If you have lots of USB devices, using a USB hub is simple. We've never seen one that even required special software to be loaded. Just plug the hub (use a standard USB cable — there should be one in the box with the hub) into one of the USB ports on the back of your PC. If it's a powered hub (which we recommend), plug the power cord into your power strip and into the back of the hub (a designated power outlet is there), and you're ready to go! It's as easy as can be. Now you can plug any USB device you have (keyboard, mouse, digital camera, printer — you name it) into the hub and away you go.

**Figure 15-1:**
The D-Link USB Bluetooth adapter is tiny; it's about the size of a small pack of gum.

# Communicating with Another Bluetooth Device: Pairing and Discovery

A key concept to understand when you're dealing with a Bluetooth device (like a cellphone or cordless headset) is pairing. *Pairing* is simply the process of two Bluetooth-enabled devices exchanging an electronic *handshake* (an electronic "greeting" where they introduce themselves and their capabilities) and then "deciding," based on their capabilities and your preferences (which you set up within the Bluetooth preferences menu on your device), how to communicate.

A typical Bluetooth cellphone has three key settings you need to configure to pair with another Bluetooth device:

- ✔ **Power:** First, you need to make sure that Bluetooth is turned on. Many phones (and other battery-powered devices) have Bluetooth turned off by default, just to lower power consumption and maximize battery life. On your phone's Bluetooth menu, make sure that you've turned on the power.

- ✔ **Discoverable:** With most Bluetooth devices (such as cellphones or PCs and Macs), you can configure your Bluetooth system to be *discoverable,* which means that the device openly identifies itself to other nearby Bluetooth devices for possible pairings. If you set your device to be discoverable, it can be found — if you turn off this feature, your phone can still make Bluetooth connections, but only to devices with which it has previously paired.

  This setting has different names on different phones. On Pat's old Motorola phone, it's Find Me; yours may be different.

  Some phones and other devices aren't discoverable *all the time.* For example, Pat's old RAZR II phone becomes discoverable for 60 seconds when you select Find Me.

- ✔ **Device name:** Most devices have a generic (and somewhat descriptive) name identifying them (like Motorola V3 RAZR). You can modify this name to whatever you want ("Pat's phone," for example) so that you recognize it when you establish a pairing.

One other important Bluetooth concept affects the ability of two Bluetooth devices to talk to each other: Bluetooth profiles. A *profile* is simply a standardized *service,* or function, of Bluetooth. There are more than two dozen profiles for Bluetooth devices, such as *HFP* (Hands Free Profile) for hands-free cellphone use, or *FTP* (File Transfer Profile) for sending files (like pictures or electronic business cards) from one device to another.

For two devices to communicate using Bluetooth, they *both* must support a common profile (or profiles). And, for two Bluetooth devices to not only communicate but also do whatever it is that you want to do (such as send a picture from your camera to your Mac), they both need to support the profile that supports that function (in this case, the FTP profile).

Making all this happen is, we're sorry to tell you, highly dependent on the particular Bluetooth devices you're using. And because many tens of thousands of Bluetooth devices are available, we can't account for every possibility here. This is one of those times where you should spend a few minutes reading the manual (sorry!) and figuring out exactly which steps your device requires. (We hate having to tell you that, but it's true.)

We don't totally leave you hanging here though. Here are some generic steps you need to take:

1. **Go to the Bluetooth setup or configuration menu of both devices and do the following:**

   a. *Turn on the Bluetooth power.*

   b. *(Optional) Customize your device name to something you recognize.*

   c. *Make the devices discoverable.*

   Typically, you set up one device to be discoverable and the other to look for discoverable devices. For example, you may press a button on a Bluetooth cordless headset to make it discoverable, and then you would invoke a menu setting on your phone to allow it to discover compatible Bluetooth devices.

   One device notifies you with an alert or onscreen menu item that it has discovered the other, and it asks whether you want to pair. For example, if you press the button on your headset, your cellphone displays a message asking whether you want to pair.

2. **Confirm that you do indeed want to make your device discoverable by pressing Yes or OK (or whatever positive option *your* device offers).**

3. **Enter the passkey and press Yes or OK.**

   Most Bluetooth devices use a *passkey* (numeric or alphanumeric code), which allows you to confirm that it's your device that's pairing and not the device belonging to the guy in the trench coat who's hiding behind a newspaper across the coffee shop. You find the passkey for most devices in their manuals (drat! — the dreaded manual pops up again). In some cases (like pairing with a PC or Mac), one device generates and displays a passkey, which you then enter into the other device.

   Your devices verify the passkey and pair. That's all you have to do in most cases — you now have a nice wireless Bluetooth connection set up, and you're ready to do whatever it is you want to do with Bluetooth (like talk on your phone hands free!).

After you've paired two devices, they *should* be paired for good. The next time you want to connect them, you should only have to go through Steps 1 and 2 (maybe even just Step 1) and skip the whole passkey thing. Bluetooth devices are supposed to mate for life (like penguins). Sometimes, however, Bluetooth is a bit funky and things don't work as you had planned. Don't be surprised if you have to repeat all these steps the next time you want to connect. A great deal of work is going on to make Bluetooth more user friendly, and making pairing easier and more consistent is the primary focus.

# Chapter 16

# Going Wireless Away from Home

*T*hroughout this fourth edition of *Wireless Home Networking For Dummies*, we focus (no big surprise here) on wireless networks in your home. But wireless networks aren't just for the house. For example, many businesses have adopted wireless networking technologies to provide network connections for workers roaming throughout offices, conference rooms, and factory floors. Just about every big university has a wireless network that enables students, faculty, and staff members to connect to the campus network (and the Internet) from just about every nook and cranny on campus. In some cases, entire cities have been "unwired," as metropolitan Wi-Fi networks have been created (by service providers or even by the cities themselves) that provide free or cheap wireless access to residents, workers, and visitors.

These networks are useful if you happen to work or teach or study at a business or school that has a wireless network. But you don't need to be in one of these locations to take advantage and get online wirelessly. You can find tens of thousands of *hot spots* (places where you can log on to publicly available Wi-Fi networks) across the United States (and the world, for that matter). In this chapter, we give you some background on public hot spots and discuss the various types of free and for-pay networks out there. We also talk about tools you can use to find a hot spot when you're out of the house.

We focus mainly on Wi-Fi hot spot networks in this chapter, designed to let you get your laptop or netbook computer online when you're away from home. In Chapter 13, we talk about broadband mobile networks (the so-called 3G and 4G networks offered by companies like AT&T, Verizon Wireless, and Sprint in the U.S. — and hundreds of similar countries elsewhere in the world). With a portable Wi-Fi router or a smartphone (like an iPhone, Blackberry, Palm, or Android phone), you can *always* be online wherever you are (except maybe in the middle of the desert or on top of a mountain).

# Discovering Public Hot Spots

The key thing to remember about hot spots — the really cool part — is that they use 802.11 (Wi-Fi) wireless networking equipment. In other words, they use the same kind of equipment you use in your wireless home network, so you can basically bring any wireless device in your home with you (as long as it's portable enough to lug around) and use it to connect to a wireless hot spot. In the majority of cases, you don't need any special software on your computer either — if you need to log in to a hot spot to pay to use it (or to enter a code that gives you permission to use the network), you simply do so using your Web browser, which will automatically take you to a *captive portal* page asking for credentials when you try to load *any* Web page.

A wide variety of people and organizations have begun to provide hot spot services, ranging from individuals who have opened up their wireless home networks for neighbors and strangers to multinational telecommunications service providers who have built nationwide or worldwide hot spot networks containing many thousands of access points. There's an in-between here, too. Perhaps the prototypical hot spot operator is the hip (or wannabe hip) urban cafe with a broadband connection and an access point (AP) in the corner. In Figure 16-1, you can see a sample configuration of APs in an airport concourse, which is a popular location for hot spots because of travelers' downtime when waiting for flights (or the everlasting gobstopper that is the TSA line — "your papers please").

Most hot spots use 802.11g networking technology, though a few have begun to upgrade to 802.11n. The key thing to keep in mind is that if you have an 802.11b, g, or n network adapter in your laptop or other device (you'll almost assuredly have one of the three!), you should be able to connect.

Of the myriad reasons that someone (or some company or organization) may open up a hot spot location, the most common we've seen include

✔ **In a spirit of community-mindedness:** Many hot spot operators strongly believe in the concept of a connected Internet community, and they want to do their part by providing a hop-on point for friends, neighbors, and even passers-by to get online. For an example of this, check out a service provider called *Fon* (www.fon.com/en), which has built a worldwide network of hot spots around this principle — if you install a Fon router in your home or business, you get free access to the 1.5 million other Fon routers throughout the world (mainly in Europe).

✔ **As a municipal amenity:** Not only individuals want to create a connected community. Many towns, cities, and villages have begun exploring the possibility of building municipality-wide Wi-Fi networks. A cost is associated with this concept, of course, but they see this cost as being less than the benefit the community will receive. For example, many towns are looking at an openly accessible downtown Wi-Fi network as a way to attract business (and businesspeople) to downtown areas that have suffered because of businesses moving to the suburbs.

✔ **As a way to attract customers:** Many cafes and other public gathering spots have installed free-to-use hot spots as a means of getting customers to come in the door and to stay longer. These businesses don't charge for the hot spot usage, but they figure you will buy more double espressos if you can sit in a comfy chair and surf the Web while you're drinking your coffee — in many cases, the business provides you with free access after you buy something.

✔ **As a business in and of itself:** Most of the larger hot spot providers have made public wireless LAN access their core business. They see that hot spot access is a great tool for traveling businesspeople, mobile workers (such as sales folks and field techs), and the like. They've built their businesses based on the assumption that these people (or their companies) will pay for Wi-Fi access mainly because of the benefits that a broadband connection offers them compared with the dial-up modem connections they've been traditionally forced to use while on the road.

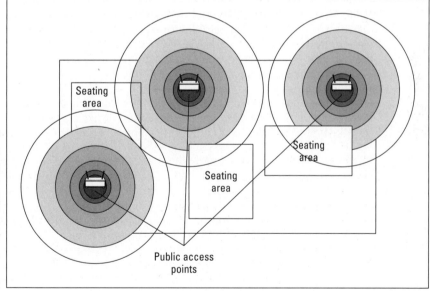

**Figure 16-1:**
An airport concourse is a perfect location for a hot spot, using several access points.

Seating area

Seating area

Seating area

Public access points

Another group of hot spot operators exists that we like to call the _unwilling_ (or _unwitting!_) hot spot operators. These are often regular Joes who have built wireless home networks but haven't activated any of the security measures we discuss in Chapter 9. Their access points have been left wide open, and their neighbors (or people sitting on the park bench across the street) are taking advantage of this open access point to do some free Web surfing. Businesses, too, fall in this category: You would be shocked at how many businesses have unsecured access points — in many cases, their IT people don't even know about it. It's all too common for a department to install its own access point (a *rogue access point*) without telling the IT staff that they've done so.

# Exploring Different Types of Hot Spots

We tend to divide hot spot operators into two categories: free networks, or *freenets,* which let anyone associate with the hot spot and get access without paying, and *for-pay* hot spots, which require users to set up an account and pay per use or a monthly (or yearly) fee for access. In the following sections, we talk a bit about these two types of operators, as well as a third type of operator who could fit into either category — the municipal/metro hot spot (or hot zone) operator.

## Freenets and open access points

Most open access points are just that: individual access points that have been purposely (or mistakenly) left open for others to use. Because this is essentially an ad hoc network created by individuals, without any particular organization behind them, these open hot spots can be hard to find. (**Note:** This is different from an ad hoc network that doesn't use an access point; refer to Chapter 7.) In some areas, the owners of these hot spots are part of an organized group, which makes these hot spots easier to find. But in other locations, you need to do some Web research or use some special programs on your laptop or handheld computer to find an open access point.

The more organized groups of open access points — often called *freenets* — can be found in many larger cities. You can find a list of freenets at www. freenetworks.org. One of the biggest of these freenets is NYCwireless (www.nycwireless.net), a freenet serving Manhattan, Brooklyn, and other areas of the metro New York City region. Similar informal and grassroots networks exist in other big cities.

A growing number of businesses are offering free hot spot services as well. These range from entire shopping malls or even city blocks offering the service as an amenity to attract customers to restaurants and cafes which simply have an access point turned on out of neighborliness. A growing number of chain restaurants (such as Panera Bread) now offer free Wi-Fi hot spots in all their locations.

You'll have much more luck finding freenets and free public access points in urban areas. The nature of 802.11 technologies is such that most off-the-shelf access points reach only about 200 feet with any kind of throughput. So, when you get out of the city and into the suburbs and rural areas, chances are good that an access point in someone's house won't reach any place you're going to be — unless that house is right next door to a park or other public space. There's just a density issue to overcome. In a city, where numerous access points may be on a single block, you have much better luck getting online.

## For-pay services

Although we think that freenets are an awesome concept, if you have an essential business document to e-mail or a PowerPoint presentation that you absolutely have to download from the company server before you get to your meeting, you may not want to rely solely on the generosity of strangers. You may even be willing to pay to get a good, reliable, secure connection to the Internet for these business (or important personal) purposes.

Trust us: Someone out there is thinking about how he can help you with that need. In fact, a bunch of companies are focusing on exactly that business. It's the nature of capitalism, right? The concluding sections of this chapter talk about a few of these companies, but for now, we talk just in generalities. Commercial hot spot providers are mainly focused on the business market, providing access to mobile workers and road-warrior types. Many of these providers also offer relatively inexpensive plans (by using either prepaid calling cards or pay-by-the-use models) that you may use for nonbusiness connectivity (at least if you're like us, and you can't go an hour without checking your mail or reading DBR — www.dukebasketballreport.com — even when you're on vacation).

Unless you're living in a city or town right near a hot spot provider, you probably don't pick up a hot spot as your primary ISP, although in some places (often, smaller towns), ISPs are using Wi-Fi as the primary pipe to their customers' homes. You can expect to find for-pay hot spot access in lots of areas outside the home. The most common include

- Hotel lobbies and rooms
- Coffee shops and Internet cafes
- Airport gates and lounges
- Office building lobbies
- Train stations
- Meeting facilities
- Everywhere else!

Basically, anywhere that folks armed with a laptop or a handheld computer may find themselves is a potential for a hot spot operator to build a business.

## Free Wi-Fi . . . kinda

A number of businesses have Wi-Fi networks that fall somewhere in between the "free" networks and "pay" networks we discuss in this chapter. Typically these "kinda free" networks are free for you to use if you meet some sort of condition — like having a specific kind of wireless device (for example, an iPhone in any Starbucks with an AT&T provided hot spot, or a Barnes & Noble Nook e-reader in any B&N bookstore), or if you're a customer. (For example, Pat's favorite coffee shop, Peets, will print out a ticket with a passcode good for a few hours of free Wi-Fi when you buy your espresso — mmm, espresso!) In these cases, if you don't meet the specific conditions, you can always just buy your Wi-Fi access (typically from one of the major hotspot providers like AT&T, T-Mobile, or Boingo). We talk more about buying Wi-Fi access in the section "For-pay services."

We've also got some good news on this front: Many of these businesses are loosening their restrictions and making actual-free-as-in-you-don't-have-to-buy-something Wi-Fi available. The biggest example here is Starbucks, who, in July 2010, changed their previous for-fee Wi-Fi service into a *free* Wi-Fi service in *all* of their (many, many thousands) of stores. We guess they figure if you come in for the free Wi-Fi, you're probably going to buy a drink anyway. And if you spend as much at Starbucks as Pat (and his kindergartener) do, you really do *deserve* free Wi-Fi anyway.

 Depending upon what airline you regularly fly, you may even be able to plug into a Wi-Fi network on an airplane. In the mid-00s, there was a lot of talk about in-flight Wi-Fi, and it went absolutely nowhere. However, in 2008, a company called Aircell (www.aircell.com) got the ball rolling again, and it has partnered with just about all of the major airlines. As we write, their AirGo service has been installed on just shy of 1,000 airplanes. So while you may have to turn off your cellphone while you fly, you don't need to be away from Facebook, if you don't want to.

A continuing issue that has been holding back the hot spot industry so far — keeping it a huge future trend rather than a use-it-anywhere-today reality — has been the issue of roaming. As of this writing, no single hot spot operator has anything close to ubiquitous coverage, though a few companies (such as Boingo) are making deals and getting closer. Instead, dozens of different hot spot operators, of different sizes, compete with each other. As a user, perhaps a salesperson who's traveling across town to several different clients in one day, you may run into hot spots from three or four providers — and need accounts from each of those providers.

This situation is much different than the cellphone industry, in which you can pretty much take your phone anywhere and make calls. The cellphone providers have elaborate roaming arrangements in place that allow them to bill each other (and in the end, bill you, the user) for these calls. Hot spot service providers haven't reached this point.

If you're looking to join a fee-based hot spot network, here are some of your main choices:

- **Boingo Wireless aggregates hot spots.** Boingo (founded by Sky Dayton, who also founded the huge ISP EarthLink), doesn't operate any of its own hot spots but instead has partnered with a huge range of other hot spot operators, from little mom-and-pop hot spot operators to big operations, such as AT&T. Boingo provides all the billing and account management for users. Thus, a Boingo customer can go to any Boingo partner's hot spot, log on, and get online. Boingo is unique in this group not only because it doesn't "own" the hot spots, but also because it has its own special software designed to manage your account and to help you find hot spots. You can find out more about Boingo at www.boingo.com.

- **Cellphone companies have become the biggest players in the hot spot business.** T-Mobile, AT&T, and Verizon Wireless run networks consisting of thousands of hot spots. In fact, wireless carriers like AT&T are building even more Wi-Fi hotspots to supplement their cellular networks. All of those iPhones use a lot of data, and it costs the cellular carriers a *lot* less to provide that data by Wi-Fi than it does on their expensive 3G cellular towers. Typically you'll get some level of "free" access with these providers if you purchase your home Internet or your wireless services from them; otherwise you'll pay a daily, monthly, or annual rate, as you prefer. (The longer term you sign up for, the less you pay on a per-day basis.) You can find out more about these services at http://hotspot.t-mobile.com, www22.verizon.com/Residential/WiFi and www.att.com/gen/general?pid=5949.

# Tools for Finding Hot Spots

When you're on the road looking for a freenet, a community hot spot, or a commercial provider, here are a few ways that you can get your laptop or handheld computer to find available networks:

- **Do your homework.** If you know exactly where you're going to be, you can do some online sleuthing, find available networks, and write down the SSIDs or WPA passphrases or WEP keys (if required) before you get there. (We talk about these items in more detail in Chapter 9.) Most hot spots don't use WPA or WEP (it's too hard for their customers to figure out), but you can find the SSID on the Web site of the hot spot provider you're planning to use. Just look in the support or how-to-connect section.

  The folks at Wi-Fi Planet (one of our favorite sources of industry news) run the Web site Wi-FiHotSpotList.com (www.wi-fihotspotlist.com), which lets you search through its huge worldwide database of hot spots. You can search by city, state, or country. Wi-FiHotSpotList.com includes both free and for-pay hot spots, so it's a comprehensive list.

Another great site is JiWire (www.jiwire.com). This site includes a comprehensive listing of free and for-pay hot spots, a great Wi-Fi news site (Wi-Fi Net News), and even special software you can download to help you locate hot spots without being online. (Just enter the address and you can search a locally stored database on your PC.)

✔ **Look for a "Wi-Fi access" sign.** Providers that push open hot spots usually post some prominent signs and otherwise advertise this service. Most are providing you with Wi-Fi access as a means of getting you in the door as a paying customer, so they find a way to let you know what they're up to.

✔ **Just look in your list of available networks.** Windows XP through 7 and all versions of OS X will search out available APs and present them in a nice pull-down list for you to pick and choose from. In most cases, this list doesn't provide details about the access points, but you can use trial-and-error to see whether you can get online.

✔ **Use a network sniffer program.** These programs work with your network adapter to ferret out the access points near you and provide a bit of information about them. The most famous Wi-Fi network sniffer, NetStumbler, has been neglected and doesn't support anything beyond Windows XP, but a new program on the market, inSSIDer (www.metageek.net/products/inssider), does. You can find a good list of network sniffer programs for any operating system at http://wiki.personaltelco.net/WirelessSniffer.

*Note:* In most cases, *network sniffer programs* are used to record and decode network packets — something the highly paid network analysts at your company may use. In this case, we're referring to programs that are designed solely for wireless LANs and that sniff out radio waves and identify available networks.

Network sniffer programs are also a good way to help you evaluate the security of your own network. In fact, they're the main reason why the developers of Network Stumbler created the program. After you implement some of the security steps we discuss in Chapter 9, you can fire up your favorite sniffer program and see whether you've been successful.

Some of the hot spots you find by using these tools, or some of the online Web pages that collect the reports of people using these tools, are indeed open, albeit unintentionally. We don't get involved in a discussion of the morality or ethics of using these access points to get online. We would say, however, that some people think that locating and using an open access point is a bad thing, akin to stealing. So, if you're going to hop on someone's access point and you don't know for sure that you're meant to do that, you're on your own.

# Staying Secure in a Hot Spot Environment

As we mention earlier in the chapter, most Wi-Fi hot spots, whether they're free or for pay, utilize no network security and encryption. (This is simply because it's easier for users to get online without trying to figure out WPA passphrases and the like.) There are some exceptions, but the vast majority of hot spots are completely without encryption.

What this means to you, as a user of a hot spot, is that everything that you send and receive from your laptop is "in the clear." Anyone else in Wi-Fi range could intercept your transmissions and read them. If that doesn't give you pause, it should!

The lack of hot spot encryption also could lead to a situation where you unwittingly log on to a "fake" hot spot with a similar SSID to the one you're trying to log on to. In this *evil twin* attack, some bad person sets up an access point with an SSID such as Starbucks right near the Starbucks where you think you're logging in to an AT&T hot spot. You log on and they capture everything you do online (for example, online banking and Webmail passwords). Not a good situation.

Fortunately, you can do a few things to secure yourself in a hot spot environment: Use a VPN and practice safe browsing, as described in the following sections.

## Using a VPN

The first (and best) way to stay secure is to use a Virtual Private Network (or VPN). Using a VPN in a hot spot gives you three distinct benefits:

- ✔ Provides **security** even without airlink encryption (WPA or WEP) by encrypting *all* your inbound and outbound traffic. Even though someone could freely "read" and copy all your Wi-Fi signals, those signals would be protected by the VPN's encryption and would be nothing but gibberish to the person doing the reading and copying.

- ✔ Provides **privacy and anonymity** online (even beyond the bounds of the hot spot) by making your public "face" on the Internet an IP address in your VPN provider's network rather than your own IP address. This means that any online tracking (both the benign and the malign kinds) that relies on your IP address would never be able to associate *you* with your actual IP address. This benefit could also apply at home or anywhere you go online.

✔ Offers **better access** to the Internet in locations where certain Web sites or Internet applications (such as VoIP, discussed in Chapter 13) are imposed by the government or other organizations. For example, many western travelers in China find that they can't access Web sites that they normally view. (For example, some parts of Wikipedia are blocked.) A VPN lets you tunnel through national firewalls and do what you want to do on the Internet without being blocked.

Many corporations provide VPN services for their remote (work at home) and mobile workers. If yours does, make sure you use it in hot spots. If you don't have access to a corporate VPN, consider subscribing to a VPN service such as WiTopia's Personal VPN (www.witopia.net) or HotSpotVPN (www.hotspotvpn.com). These are *hosted* VPN services, which provide you with a secure and reliable VPN solution over the Internet for a monthly or annual fee. For more information about WiTopia, check out the sidebar titled "Securing your Wi-Fi with WiTopia."

## Practicing safe browsing

If you can't (or don't want to) bother with a VPN service in unsecured hot spots, you should practice safe browsing. That means you should

✔ **Pay close attention to the SSID you're connecting to and make sure it is the one you mean to connect to.** Don't connect to a free public Wi-Fi network unless that's actually the SSID advertised for the hot spot you're in!

✔ **Use secured/encrypted connections whenever possible.** That means, for example, connecting to secure Web pages and checking your browser to make sure you have actually done so whenever you're doing something sensitive online (such as online banking or even e-mail). Make sure that, whenever possible, you are connected to a Web site with an *https* rather than *http* prefix to the URL. When you're on the secured site, click the lock icon in your browser. (It's typically up in the address bar of your browser, or in the bottom-right corner on the status bar, depending on which browser you're using.) Check the certificate that pops up and make sure the name of the business in the certificate is the one you think you're connected to.

✔ **If your ISP supports it, configure your e-mail client to use a secure login.** This ensures that when you download e-mail you'll be using an encrypted connection. How you set this up depends on both your e-mail client and your ISP's configuration, so search your ISP's Web site support section for "Secure IMAP" or "Secure POP."

# Securing your Wi-Fi with WiTopia

Our favorite hosted VPN service comes from the folks at WiTopia (www.witopia.net), with their Personal VPN service. For $39.99 a year, WiTopia secures your Wi-Fi traffic by routing it through an encrypted *VPN tunnel*, which keeps your data from prying eyes all the way from your Mac or PC (or iPhone, more on this in a moment) to WiTopia's secure server (from which it then makes its way onto the wild world of the Internet).

You can get two types of VPNs from WiTopia:

✔ **An SSL VPN,** which uses the same technology (secure sockets layer) that secure Web pages use to encrypt all your data traffic. This is fastest, but it requires a software client and doesn't work with every device (see WiTopia's Web site for details).

✔ **A PPTP VPN,** which uses the same technology used by many big corporations in their VPNs. (PPTP stands for Point-to-Point Tunneling Protocol.) This is slower and may be blocked in some countries (like China) but doesn't require you to install software and can be used on more devices. (You can even use it to secure your iPhone or iPad's connections!)

✔ Or, you can buy **a combination service that offers both options.** You'd choose this option if you wanted to maximize your options (using SSL whenever possible, but keeping the option of PPTP available when needed).

The SSL VPN has been WiTopia's traditional product, built around an open source software effort called (appropriately) OpenVPN (www.openvpn.net). The WiTopia folks added PPTP VPN support in 2007 as a way of adding support for even more clients, including the Apple iPhone. Mac and Windows users can download the OpenVPN software from WiTopia's Web site; for PPTP VPNs, users simply take advantage of the PPTP VPN client software built into most operating systems (including Windows XP and beyond, Mac OS X, and Apple's version of OS X for the iPhone, iPad, and iPod touch).

WiTopia charges an annual fee of $59.99 for its SSL product, $39.99 for PPTP, and $69.99 for the combined product. Whatever you choose, it's a good deal and a great way to secure your network.

If you use Google's Gmail service (http://mail.google.com), go into your Gmail Settings page, look under the General tab, and make sure that Browser Connection is set to Always Use https.

No matter what you do for security in a hot spot, always be aware that you are in a *public* place using unsecured airwaves. People can eavesdrop on your Wi-Fi signal, and they can probably also "shoulder surf" and just read your screen. Keep that in mind!

# Dealing with Hot Spots on Mobile Devices

A number of mobile devices — by that we mean smartphones and PDAs — are now equipped with built-in Wi-Fi capabilities. You can also find Wi-Fi built into handheld gaming devices (such as the Nintendo DS) and in music/video players such as Apple's iPod Touch and Microsoft's Zune. Due to the portable nature of these devices, you'll find that you're *more* likely to have them tucked away in your pocketbook (or "man purse" . . . oops, we mean trendy messenger bag) when hot spot access is available.

Getting online with one of these devices is easy when there's an open hot spot available to you. In fact, most of them will automatically associate with the hot spot and get you online. (***Note:*** How this works is a device-by-device process, so read the manual if you don't know how to connect to a Wi-Fi network with your particular portable device.)

Where this process gets to be a bit difficult is when you're in a location that requires you to register to get online (either as a way of making a payment or just to register with a free hot spot for access). Typically, hot spots that require registration do so in one of two ways:

- ✔ **Using a captive portal:** A *captive portal* is a system that automatically directs you to a registration Web page before allowing you unfettered access to the Internet over a hot spot connection. This process works fine *if* your mobile device has a built-in Web browser but is stopped dead in its tracks if you're using a device without a Web browser (such as a Wi-Fi Skype phone).

  Not all mobile device Web browsers support captive portal systems, usually due to a lack of JavaScript functionality in the browser. Newer operating systems like iOS and Android *do,* however.

- ✔ **Using client software:** A smaller number of hot spots require (or offer as an option) a software client that handles user authentication and authorization. With a client installed on your device, you can bypass the requirement to load a Web page and get yourself on the network without the hassle. For example, Boingo offers client software for iOS (iPod touch, iPhone, and iPad), Android, Windows Mobile, and Nokia Series 60 smartphones.

So the bottom line here is that you need a Web browser, a special bit of client software, or an open hot spot to get online with your mobile device. We wish we had a better answer, but, in fact, this is a major issue in the hot spot industry today.

# Part V
# The Part of Tens

By Rich Tennant

"We should cast a circle, invoke the elements, and direct the energy. If that doesn't work, we'll read the manual."

# In this part . . .

Part V is the one you've been waiting for, right? We have four top-ten lists here that we hope you will find interesting as well as helpful: ten frequently asked questions about wireless home networking; ten ways to improve the performance of your wireless home network; ten way-cool devices that you will (eventually) connect to your wireless home network; and ten sources for more info in case you can never get enough about wireless.

# Chapter 17

# Ten FAQs about Wireless Home Networks

*W*ireless networks are increasingly easy to set up, configure, and con- nect to. But they're far from foolproof and dead simple. Despite some great efforts by vendors and industry organizations to simplify the wireless buying, installing, and using experience, things can get a bit confusing, even to those in the know.

In this chapter, we look at ten issues we hear the most often when friends and family ask us for help with getting started in the wireless LAN world. We talked to our helpful friends at several of the most popular vendors of wireless net- working equipment and asked them what *they* hear (or what their customer service reps, sales partners, and others close to real-life users hear).

If you don't see in this chapter the particular question you're asking, we recommend that you at least skim this chapter anyway. You never know: You may find your answer lurking where you least expect it, or you may come across a tidbit of information that may come in handy later. And, throughout this chapter, we also steer you to the places in the book where we further discuss various topics — which may in turn lead you to your answer (or to other tidbits of information that come in handy later). What we're saying is that reading this chapter can only help you. Also check out Chapter 18, where we give you some troubleshooting tips.

We firmly believe in the power of the Web and of using vendor Web sites for all they're worth. Support is a critical part of this process. When you're deciding on a particular piece of equipment for your home network, take a look at the support area on the vendor site for that device. Look at the frequently asked questions (FAQs) for the device; you may find some of those hidden gotchas that you wish you had known about *before* buying the gear.

# Which Standard Is Right for Me?

As we discuss in Chapters 2 and 4 (among other places), Wi-Fi wireless network standards have gone through multiple iterations: 802.11b, 802.11a, 802.11g, and, now, 802.11n. When you shop for wireless networking equipment, you'll find that there's still a pretty even mix of 802.11g and newer 802.11n gear available in stores and online. You'll also find that although 802.11g gear is cheaper than 802.11n equipment, the price difference is not all that great. Because this price difference is so low (as low as $20 separating an 802.11g wireless router from an 802.11n version), we absolutely recommend that you choose equipment that's compatible with (and Wi-Fi certified for) 802.11n. Even if everything else that you own now — all your laptop computers, smartphones, game consoles, and so on — support only 802.11g, we recommend that you invest in the future with an 802.11n wireless router. Pretty much every new bit of wireless-equipped gear being released these days supports 802.11n, so that 802.11n wireless router will come in handy the first time you buy something new.

The bottom line is that 802.11n is not only a safe recommendation, but also a good one. Although it's far from perfect (the state of the art *always* moves forward), 802.11n provides a combination of range, compatibility, and speed that makes it good enough for most people. You aren't going to find more speed or range than 802.11n systems offer.

# Are Dual-Band Routers Worth The Extra Money?

As we discuss in Chapter 2, the 802.11n standard supports Wi-Fi connections using both of the frequency bands available to Wi-Fi systems — 2.4 GHz and 5 GHz. Previous Wi-Fi standards (802.11a, b, and g) supported only one or the other band (mainly 2.4 GHz).

But the fact that the standard supports both bands doesn't mean all 802.11n equipment does. In fact a lot of lower-priced 802.11n gear — both wireless routers and network adapters — uses only the 2.4 GHz band.

From the perspective of band capabilities, there are three types of wireless routers or adapters:

- ✔ **Single band:** This equipment works only on the 2.4 GHz band.

- ✔ **Dual band:** This equipment works on *either* the 2.4 or the 5 GHz band, but not both at the same time.

- ✔ **Simultaneous dual band:** Applicable only to routers/access points (because they "talk" to multiple devices at once), this equipment can operate on both frequency bands at the same time.

When you're shopping for a new wireless router, you'll find that the price increases as you go in this order — single band equipment is just a bit more than 802.11g, dual band is about twice the price of 802.11g, and simultaneous dual band is significantly more expensive. As we write in the summer of 2010, simultaneous dual-band routers start at around $150 — more than double the price of single band routers.

Which to choose? If you have the money, simultaneous dual band is your best bet and the most future-proofed alternative. If you're more budget-minded, think about the following points and figure out how far your budget will stretch:

- ✔ Single band routers are the cheapest, and they'll work well with any Wi-Fi equipment that you already own. There are two downsides:

  - You won't get the maximum 802.11n performance when you're mixing 802.11b or g gear using the same channel as your 802.11n gear. It's not a *huge* deal, but if you're doing a lot video transfers and the like, it's nice not to mix standards.

  - The 2.4 GHz band is crowded and therefore more prone to interference from your neighbor's network and other devices like microwaves and cordless phones.

- ✔ Dual-band (non-simultaneous) routers are useful if you have an *all* 802.11n network and you'd like to use the 5 GHz band. If, however, you're going to bring some non-802.11n or non–dual-band devices into your network (like a gaming console or most smartphones), you'll have to use the 2.4 GHz band instead. In other words, you'll gain nothing from one of these routers unless *all* of your equipment supports the 5 GHz band.

- ✔ Simultaneous dual-band routers offer the best of both worlds: you can put your 802.11n gear on the 5 GHz band at the fastest speeds and still support all of your 2.4 GHz gear at the same time. But you have to pay for the privilege.

We have simultaneous dual-band routers in our homes. But then again, we have dozens of wireless devices. If you're like us — or think you might be someday soon — spend the extra money on the simultaneous dual band. Otherwise, an inexpensive single band router will do the trick.

# I Can Connect to the Internet with an Ethernet Cable But Not with My Wireless LAN. What Am I Doing Wrong?

You're almost there. The fact that everything works for one configuration but not for another rules out many problems. As long as your AP and router are the same device (which is most common), you know that the AP can talk to your Internet gateway (whether it's your cable modem, digital subscriber line [DSL] modem, or dial-up routers, for example). You know that because, when you're connected via Ethernet, there's no problem. The problem is then relegated to being between the AP and the client on the PC.

Most of the time, this is a configuration issue dealing with your service set identifier (SSID) and your security configurations with Wi-Fi Protected Access (WPA2) or Wired Equivalent Privacy (WEP). Your SSID denotes your service area ID for your LAN, and your WEP controls your encryption keys for your data packets. Without both, you can't decode the signals traveling through the air.

Bring up your wireless configuration program, as we discuss in Chapter 7, and verify again that your SSID is set correctly and your WPA2 passphrase or WEP key is correct. Most configuration programs will find all the wireless transmitters in your area. If you don't see yours, you've set up your AP in stealth mode so it doesn't broadcast its name. If that's the case, you can try typing the word **any** into the SSID to see whether it finds the AP, or you can go back to your AP configuration using a wired connection and copy the SSID from the AP's configuration screen. Keep in mind that SSIDs are case sensitive.

If neither of those issues is the problem, borrow a friend's laptop with a compatible wireless connection to see whether his or her card can find and sign on to your LAN when empowered with the right SSID and WPA2 or WEP code. If it can, you know that your client card may have gone bad.

If a card (or any electronics, generally speaking) is going to go bad, it's most likely to have technical problems within the first 30 days.

If your friend's PC cannot log on, the problem may be with your AP. At this point, we have to say "Check the vendor's Web site for specific problem-solving ideas and call its tech-support number for further help."

# How Do I Get My Video Games to Work on My Wireless LAN?

This question has an easy answer and a not-so-easy answer. The easy answer is that you can get your Xbox/Xbox 360, PlayStation 2/3, or Wii onto your wireless LAN using its built-in Wi-Fi or by linking the Ethernet port on your gaming device (if necessary, by purchasing a network adapter kit to add an Ethernet port on your system) with a wireless bridge — which gets your gaming gear onto your wireless network in an easy fashion. You just need to be sure to set your bridge to the same SSID and WEP key or WPA passphrase as your LAN.

That's the easy part, and you should now be able to access the Internet from your box.

The tough part is allowing the Internet to access your gaming system. This requirement applies to certain games, two-way voice systems, and some aspects of multiplayer gaming. You may need to open certain ports in your router to enable those packets bound for your gaming system to get there. This process is called *port forwarding* (or something like that — vendors love to name things differently among themselves). Port forwarding basically says to the router that it should block all packets from accessing your system except those with certain characteristics that you identify. (These types of data packets can be let through to your gaming server.) We talk a great deal about this topic in Chapter 11, in the section about dealing with port forwarding, so be sure to read up on that before tinkering with your router configuration.

If this process is too complex to pull off with your present router, consider just setting up a demilitarized zone (DMZ) for your gaming application, where your gaming console or PC sits fairly open to the Internet. (We discuss setting up a DMZ in Chapter 11.) This setup isn't a preferred one, however, for security reasons, and we recommend that you try to get port forwarding to work.

Our esteemed tech editor has a great suggestion if you're having issues with port forwarding: a Web site called `http://portforward.com`. Check it out!

# My Videoconferencing Application Doesn't Work. What Do I Do?

In some ways, videoconferencing is its own animal in its own world. Videoconferencing has its own set of standards that it follows; typically has specialized hardware and software; and, until recently, has required special telephone lines to work.

The success of the Internet and its related protocols has opened up video-conferencing to the mass market with IP standards-based Web cameras and other software-based systems (like Skype) becoming popular.

Still, if you've installed a router with the appropriate protection from the Internet bad guys, videoconferencing can be problematic for all the same reasons as in gaming, which we mention in the preceding section. You need to have packets coming into your application just as much as you're sending packets out to someone else.

Wait a minute. You may be thinking "Data packets come into my machine all the time (like when I download Web pages), so what are you saying?" Well, those packets are requested, and the router in your AP (or your separate router, if that's how your network is set up) knows that they're coming and lets them through. Videoconferencing packets are often unrequested, which makes the whole getting-through-the-router thing a bit tougher.

As such, the answer is the same as with gaming. You need to open ports in your router (called port forwarding) or set up your video application in a DMZ. Again, Chapter 11 can be a world of help here.

# How Do I Secure My Network from Hackers?

Nothing is totally secure from anything. The adage "Where there's a will, there's a way" tends to govern most discussions about someone hacking into your LAN. We tend to fall back on this one instead: Unless you have some major, superse-cret hidden trove of something on your LAN that many people would simply kill to have access to, the chances of a hacker spending a great deal of time to get on your LAN is minimal. This statement means that as long as you do the basic security enhancements we recommend in Chapter 9, you should be covered. This doesn't mean you're safe from maliciousness. Even if hackers care nothing for the contents of your computer, they care a lot about using the processing power of that computer for their own ends. Nasty software called viruses, or Trojans, can get to your computer in many ways. These programs give hackers control of your computer unbeknownst to you so they do other more malicious things such as sending more spam e-mail or infecting more machines.

You can secure the following parts of your network by taking the following actions:

- ✔ **Your Internet connection:** You should turn on, at minimum, whatever firewall protection your router offers. If you can, choose a router that has *stateful packet inspection* (SPI). You should also use antivirus soft-ware and seriously consider using personal firewall software on your

PCs. Using a firewall in both your router and on your PC is defense in depth: After the bad guys get by your router firewall's Maginot line, you have extra guns to protect your PCs. (For a little historical perspective on defense strategies, read up on Maginot and his fortification.)

✔ **Your airwaves:** Because wireless LAN signals can travel right through your walls and out the door, you should strongly consider turning on WPA2 (and taking other measures, which we discuss in Chapter 9) to keep the next-door neighbors from snooping on your network.

# What Is Firmware, and Why Might I Need to Upgrade It?

Any consumer electronics device is governed by software seated in onboard chip memory storage. When you turn on the device, it checks this memory to find out what to do and loads the software in that area. This software turns the device on and basically tells it how to operate.

This *firmware* can be updated through a process that's specific to each manufacturer. Often, you see options in your software configuration program for checking for firmware upgrades.

Some folks advocate never, ever touching your firmware if you don't need to. Indeed, reprogramming your firmware can upset much of the logical innards of the device you struggled so hard to configure properly in the first place. In fact, you may see advice on a vendor site, such as this statement from the D-Link site: "Do not upgrade firmware unless you are having specific problems." In other words: If it ain't broke, don't fix it. Many times, a firmware upgrade can cause you to lose all customized settings you've configured on your router. Although not all vendor firmware upgrades reset your settings to their defaults, many do. Also, it's always best to do a firmware upgrade with a *wired* connection to the router — if you lose the wireless signal during the upgrade, you could be forced to totally reset your router — the router might even become inoperable. Be careful!

Despite those warnings, we say "Never say never." Most AP and router vendors operate under a process of continuous improvement, by adding new features and fixing bugs regularly. One key way that you can keep current with these standards is by upgrading your firmware. Over time, your wireless network will fall out of sync with the latest bug fixes and improvements, and you'll have to upgrade at some point. When you do so, follow all the manufacturer's warnings.

In Chapter 9, we discuss Wi-Fi Protected Access 2 (WPA-2). Many older APs and network adapters will be able to use WPA-2, but only after their firmware has been upgraded.

# Is NAT the Same as a Firewall?

If you find networking confusing, you're not alone. (If it were easy, we would have no market for our books!) One area of confusion is Network Address Translation (NAT). No, NAT isn't the same as a firewall. It's important to understand the difference to make sure that you set up your network correctly. Firewalls provide a greater level of security than NAT routers and, thanks to dropping hardware costs, are generally available in all routers these days. The quality of the firewall built into your AP is not necessarily related to the price of the AP. We recommend checking the reviews of any hardware you're looking to purchase from sites such as www.cnet.com.

Often, you hear the term *firewall* used to describe a router's ability to protect LAN IP addresses from Internet snoopers. But a true firewall goes deeper than that, by using SPI. SPI allows the firewall to look at each IP address and domain requesting access to the network; the administrator can specify certain IP addresses or domain names that are allowed to be let in while blocking any other attempt to access the LAN. (Sometimes you hear this called *filtering*.)

Firewalls can also add another layer of protection through a Virtual Private Network (VPN). It enables remote access to the private network through the use of secure logins and authentication. Finally, firewalls can help protect your family from unsavory content by enabling you to block content from certain sites.

Firewalls go well beyond NAT, and we highly recommend that you have a firewall in your home network. Check out Chapter 9 for more information on firewalls.

# How Can I Find Out My IP Address?

First off, you have two IP addresses: a public IP address and a private IP address. In some instances, you need to know one or the other or both addresses.

Your *private* IP address is your IP address on your LAN so that your router knows where to send traffic in and among LAN devices. If you have a LAN printer, that device has its own IP address, as does any network device on your LAN.

The address these devices have, however, is rarely the public IP address (the address is the "Internet phone number" of your network), mostly because public IP addresses are becoming scarce. Your Internet gateway has a *public* IP address for your home. If you want to access from a public location a specific device on your home network, you typically have to enable port forwarding in your router and then add that port number on the end of your public IP address when you try to make a connection. For example, if you had a Web server on your network, you would type the address **68.129.5.29:80** into your browser when you tried to access it remotely — 80 is the port used for HTTP servers.

You can usually find out your wide area network (public IP address) and LAN (private IP address) from within your router configuration software or Web page, such as `http://192.168.1.1`. You may see a status screen; this common place shows your present IP addresses and other key information about your present Internet connection.

If you have Windows Vista or Windows 7, you can find your private IP by following these steps:

1. **Click the Windows Start button and then choose Control Panel⇨ Network and Sharing Center.**

   You need to have Administrator access to be able to get to the Network and Sharing Center.

2. **In the Network and Sharing Center, click Wireless Network Connection (*Network Name*).**

   *Network Name* is the SSID of your wireless network.

3. **On the screen that appears, click the Details button.**

   This screen gives you your IP address (along with a lot of other information!).

This IP address is your *internal,* or *private,* IP address, not the public address that people on the Internet use to connect to your network. If you try to give this address to someone (perhaps so that they can connect to your computer to do videoconferencing or to connect to a game server you're hosting), it doesn't work. You need the public IP address that you find in the configuration program for your access point or router. A number of Web sites are available to help you determine your *external,* or public, IP address (for example, `www.whatismyip.com`).

# If Everything Stops Working, What Can I Do?

The long length of time it can take to get help from tech support these days leads a lot of people to read the manual, check out the Web site, and work hard to debug their situations. But what happens if you've tried everything and it's still a dead connection — and tech support agrees with you?

In these instances, your last resort is to reset the system back to its factory defaults and start over. Typically you reset your router by pressing a small, recessed button on the back or bottom of the router. (Check your router's manual — you may have to do this step for a particular length of time, or with another step such as unplugging and replugging the power cord on your router.) If you do this, be sure to upgrade your firmware while you're at it because it resets your variables anyway. Who knows? The more recent firmware update may resolve some issues that could be causing the problems.

Resetting your device is considered a drastic action and should be taken only after you've tried everything else. Make sure that you at least get a tech-support person on the phone to confirm that you *have* tried everything and that a reset makes sense.

# Chapter 18

# Ten Ways to Troubleshoot Wireless LAN Performance

*A*lthough troubleshooting any piece of network equipment can be frustrating, troubleshooting wireless equipment is a little more so because there's so much that you just can't check. After all, radio waves are invisible. That's the rub with improving the throughput (performance) of your wireless home network, but we're here to help. And don't get hung up on the term *throughput* (the effective speed of your network); when you take into account retransmissions attributable to errors, you find that the amount of data moving across your network is *lower* than the *nominal* speed of your network. For example, your PC may tell you that you're connected at 54 Mbps, but because of retransmissions and other factors, you may be sending and receiving data at about half that speed.

The trick to successfully troubleshooting anything is to be logical and systematic. First, be logical. Think about the most likely issues (no matter how improbable) and work from there. Second, be systematic. Networks are complicated things, which mandate a focus on sequential troubleshooting on your part. Patience is a virtue when it comes to network debugging.

Perhaps hardest of all is making sense of performance issues — the subject of this chapter. First, you can't get great performance reporting from consumer-level access points, or APs. (The much more expensive ones sold to businesses are better at that.) Even so, debugging performance based on performance data in arrears is tough. Fixing performance issues is a trial-and-error, real-time process. At least most wireless client devices have some sort of signal-strength meter, which is one of the best sources of information you can get to help you understand what's happening.

Signal-strength meters (which are usually part of the software included with your wireless gear) are the best way to get a quick read on your network. These signal-strength meters are used by the pros, says Tim Shaughnessy at NETGEAR: "I would highlight it as a tool." We agree.

It's a good idea to work with a friend or family member. Your friend can be in a poor reception "hole" with a notebook computer and the wireless utility showing the signal strength. You can try moving or configuring the access point to see what works. Just be patient — the signal meter may take a few seconds to react to changes. (Count to ten after each change, it's what we do to make sure we are not rushing the process.)

Because not all performance issues can be tracked down (at least not easily), in this chapter we introduce you to the most common ways to improve the performance of your wireless home network. We know that these are tried-and-true tips because we've tried them ourselves. We're pretty good at debugging this stuff by now. We just can't seem to figure out when it's not plugged in! (Well, Pat can't. Read the "Check the obvious" section to see what we mean.)

## Check the Obvious

Sometimes, what's causing you trouble is something that's simple to fix. For example, one of us (and we won't say who — *Pat*) was surprised that his access point just stopped working one day. The culprit was his beagle, Opie, who had pulled the plug out of the wall. As obvious as this sounds, it took the unnamed person *(Pat)* an hour to figure it out. Now, if someone told you, "Hey, the AP just stopped working," you would probably say "Is it plugged in?" The moral: Think of the obvious and check it first.

Here are a few more "obvious" things to check:

- ✔ **Problem:** The power goes out and then comes back on. Different equipment takes different lengths of time to reset and restart, which causes the loss of connectivity and logical configurations on your network.

  **Solution:** Sometimes, you need to turn off all your devices. Leave them all off for a minute or two, and then turn them all back on, working your way from the Internet connection to your computer — from the wide area network (WAN) connection (your broadband modem, for example) back to your machine. This process allows each device to start up with everything upstream properly in place and turned on.

✔ **Problem:** Your access point is working fine, with great throughput and a strong signal footprint, until one day it all just drops off substantially. No hardware problem. No new interferers installed at home. No new obstructions. No changes of software. Nothing. The cause: Your next-door neighbor got an access point and is using his on the same channel as yours.

**Solution:** This problem is hard to debug in the first place. How the heck do you find out who is causing invisible interference — by going door to door? "Uh, pardon me; I'm going door to door to try to debug interferers on my access point. Are you suddenly emitting any extraneous radio waves? No, I'm not wearing an aluminum foil hat. Why?" Often, when debugging performance issues, you need to try many of the one-step solutions, to see whether they have an effect. If you can find the solution, you have a great deal of insight into what the problem was. For example, you might use your AP's configuration software (or go to its Web page) and change channels and find that solves the problem; maybe the problem was that a neighbor just installed a new access point and it is causing interference by operating on your chosen channel. (See the section "Change Channels," later in this chapter, for more on this possible solution.)

The wireless utility for the adapter may have a tab, called a *site survey* or *station list,* that lists the APs in range. The tab may show your neighbor's access point and the channel it's on.

APs that follow the 802.11n standard dynamically switch channels when there's too much interference. The 802.11n equipment we have seen doesn't even give you an option to choose a channel because of this dynamic switching capability. Keep in mind that the higher speed of these APs is achieved by combining channels so they can send and receive data on more than one channel at a time and can use more than one antenna to send and receive data. To take full advantage of the dynamic nature of 802.11n, you need an 802.11n AP or router as well as an 802.11n network adapter in your computer.

Before you chase a performance issue, make sure that you *have* one. The advertised rates for throughput for the various wireless standards are misleading. What starts out at 54 Mbps for 802.11g is really more like a maximum of 36 Mbps in practice (and less as distance increases). For 802.11n, it's more like 125 Mbps at best, rather than the 300 Mbps you hear bandied about. You *occasionally* see high levels (like when you're within a few yards of the access point), but that's rare. The moral: If you think that you should be getting 300 Mbps but you're getting only 100 Mbps, consider yourself lucky — very lucky.

# Move the Access Point

A wireless signal degrades with distance. You may find that the place you originally placed your access point, or AP, doesn't really fit with your subsequent real-world use of your wireless local area network. A move may be in order.

After your AP is up and working, you'll probably forget about it — people often do. APs can often be moved around and even shuffled aside by subsequent gear or by overenthusiastic house cleaning. Because the access connection is still up (that is to say, working), sometimes people don't notice that the AP's performance degrades when you hide it more or move it around.

Make sure that other gear isn't blocking your AP, that it isn't flush against a wall (which can cause interference), that its vertical orientation isn't too close to the ground (more interference), and that it isn't in the line of sight of radio wave interference (such as from microwaves and cordless phones). Even a few inches can make a difference. The best location is in the center of your desired coverage area (remember to think in three dimensions!) and on top of a desk or bookcase. For more about setting up APs, check out Chapter 6.

# Move the Antenna

Remember the days before everyone had cable or satellite TV? There was a reason why people would fiddle with the rabbit ears on a TV set — they were trying to get the antenna into the ideal position to receive signals. Whether the antenna is on the client or on the access point, the same concept applies: Moving the antenna can yield results. Because different antennas have different signal coverage areas, reorienting them in different declinations (or angles relative to the horizon) changes their coverage patterns. A strong signal translates to better throughput and performance.

Look at it this way: The antenna creates a certain footprint of its signal. If you're networking a multistory home and you're not getting a great signal upstairs, try shifting your antenna to a 45 degree angle, to increase a more vertical signal — that is, to send more signal to the upstairs and downstairs and less horizontally.

Because 802.11n wireless routers use special *MIMO* antennas, the antennas on these devices are often built into the router and can't be individually adjusted. In this case, you can try to move the orientation and positioning of the router itself because there's no antenna to move.

# Change Channels

Each access point broadcasts its signals over segments of the wireless frequency spectrum called *channels.* The 802.11g standard (the most common system at the time we wrote this chapter) defines 11 channels in the United States that overlap considerably, leaving only 3 channels that don't overlap with each other. The IEEE 802.11a standard specifies 12 (although most current products support only 8) nonoverlapping channels. The 802.11n standard uses the same 11 channels as 802.11g at 2.4 GHz and — if your device is *dual band* and supports it — the 12 channels of 802.11a at 5 GHz in the United States. With 802.11n, your router may actually use two of these channels at once to give you more throughput.

802.11n is designed to work with all the previous standards. The dynamic switching of channels on either frequency available to it means you have a lot less to configure during setup. Some single band APs still give you the option to choose channels at the beginning, but they don't necessarily have to stay on that channel as they work.

This situation affects your ability to have multiple access points in the same area, whether they're your own or your neighbors'. Because channels can overlap, you can have the resulting interference. For 802.11g access points that are within range of each other, set them to different channels, five apart from each other (such as 1, 6, and 11), to avoid inter-access point interference. We discuss the channel assignments for wireless LANs further in Chapter 6.

# Check for Dual-Band Interference

Despite the industry's mad rush to wirelessly enable every networkable device it makes, a whole lot hasn't been worked through yet, particularly interoperability. We're not talking about whether one vendor's 802.11n PC Card works with another vendor's 802.11n wireless router — the Wi-Fi interoperability tests usually make sure that's not a problem (unless one of your products isn't Wi-Fi certified). Instead, we're talking about having Bluetooth (see Chapter 15 for more on this technology) working in the same area as 802.11b, g, and n, or having older 802.11a APs and 802.11b, g, and n APs operating in the same area. In some instances, like the former example, Bluetooth and 802.11b, g, and (single band) n operate in the same frequency range, and therefore have some potential for interference. (*Interference* is when another radio transmission affects the one you're using, like a cordless phone interfering with your Wi-Fi.) Dual-band 802.11n systems can also work in the 5 GHz channels, which greatly reduces the chances of interference.

Another issue — one that's not, strictly speaking, interference — is the use of multiple Wi-Fi standards on a single channel. In other words, the effect on your network's speed and throughput when you mix 802.11b, g and n systems on a single channel.

We've told you that all versions of Wi-Fi (with the exception of the rarely-seen 802.11a) are *backward compatible* with older versions. In other words, you can use 802.11b equipment on an 802.11g network, and you can use both 802.11b and 802.11g on an 802.11n network (as long as it's operating in the 2.4 GHz frequency range). There's a downside to that compatibility, however, and that's the fact that *mixed* networks (with slower 802.11b or g clients in them) will be slower for *all* devices on the network. This is *not* a major issue for most folks, but if having the maximum speed on your 802.11n devices is very important to you (perhaps you're sending high-definition video to your home entertainment system wirelessly), it could be a problem.

If you run into network performance issues because of a mixed network, there's a very simple (but not cheap) fix: Buy a *simultaneous dual-band* wireless router (discussed in Chapter 17) and run all of your 802.11b and g devices on the 2.4 GHz band, and all of your 802.11n gear on the 5 GHz band.

# Check for New Obstacles

Wireless technologies are susceptible to physical obstacles. In Chapter 4, Table 4-1 tells you the relative attenuation of your wireless signals (radio frequency, or RF) as they move through your house. One person in our neighborhood noticed a gradual degradation of his wireless signal outside his house, where he regularly sits and surfs the Net (by his pool). The culprit turned out to be a growing pile of newspapers for recycling. Wireless signals don't like such masses of paper.

Move around your house and think about it from the eyes of Superman, using his X-ray vision to see your access point. If you have a bad signal, think about what's in the way. If the obstacles are permanent, think about using a HomePlug or other powerline networking wireless access point (which we discuss in Chapter 3) to go around the obstacle by putting an access point on either side of the obstacle.

Another way to get around problems with obstacles is to switch technologies. In some instances, 802.11n products could provide better throughput and reach than your old 802.11g when it comes to obstacles. Many 802.11n products use special radio transmission techniques that help focus the signal into the areas containing your wireless client devices, as well as sending multiple signals at once (over different paths) using 802.11n's MIMO technology. These aimed, multiple signals can help you overcome environments that just don't work with regular Wi-Fi gear. If you're in a dense environment with lots of clutter and you're using 802.11g, switching to 802.11n may provide some relief.

# Install Another Antenna

In Chapter 5, we point out that a detachable antenna is a great idea because you may want to add an antenna to achieve a different level of coverage in your home. Different antennas yield different signal footprints. If your access point is located at one end of the house, putting an omnidirectional antenna on that access point is a waste because more than half the signal may prove to be unusable. A directional antenna better serves your home.

Antennas are inexpensive relative to their benefits and can more easily help you accommodate signal optimization because you can leave the access point in the same place and just move the antenna around until you get the best signal. In a home, there's not a huge distance limitation on how far away the antenna can be from the access point.

802.11n systems, with their special MIMO transmission technologies, are typically designed to use only the antenna that came with the system. You can't just slap any old antenna onto an 802.11n AP or router. For the most part, this isn't a problem, simply because 802.11n has significantly better range than older systems such as 802.11g.

## Should I use a signal booster?

Signal boosters used to be offered when 802.11g came out a few years ago. The concept was that if you have a big house (or lots of interference), you can add a *signal booster,* which essentially turns up the volume on your wireless home network transmitter. Unfortunately, it does nothing for the wireless card in your computer, and that was the great failing in this product. Your base station would be stronger, but your workstation's signal would be the same. So, you could see your base station better but couldn't communicate with it any better because your wireless card was at the same signal strength.

Signal boosters have pretty much been discontinued, and even though you can still get them, we strongly recommend staying away from them because you have many other options that are more versatile and compatible with what you already have and that keep you up-to-date with the newest technologies.

Today's 802.11n products have excellent range — increased range is one of the major benefits of the *MIMO* (Multiple Input, Multiple Output) antenna systems used by 802.11n. With 802.11n, you don't need a signal booster in most cases, and the specialized MIMO antennas don't work with signal boosters anyway. The only situation where we might recommend a signal booster would be if you had an 801.11g AP that you were using outdoors or in some other very large area (maybe you live in a converted convention center?). Otherwise, don't bother with one; move up to 802.11n, and if you still don't have enough reach, consider installing a Wi-Fi repeater or using a wired or powerline connection to install a second AP in the areas that don't get a good signal in your house. We discuss adding additional APs and repeaters in the sections "Add an Access Point" and "Add a Repeater or Bridge," elsewhere in this chapter.

# Add an Access Point

Adding another access point (or two) can greatly increase your signal coverage, as shown in Figure 18-1. The great thing about wireless is that it's fairly portable — you can literally plug it in anywhere. The main issues are getting power to it and getting an Ethernet connection (which carries the data) to it.

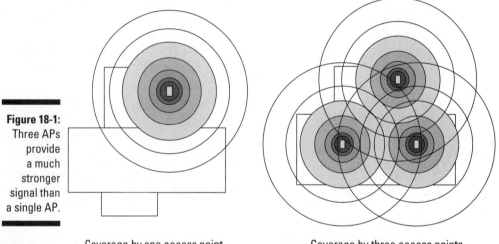

**Figure 18-1:**
Three APs
provide
a much
stronger
signal than
a single AP.

Coverage by one access point –
Signal fades with distance

Coverage by three access points –
Strong combined signals

The first item is usually not a problem because many electrical codes require, in a residence, that power outlets be placed every eight feet. The second issue (getting the Ethernet connection to your AP) used to be a matter of running all sorts of wiring around the house. Depending on the actual throughput you're looking to provide, however, you may be able to set up another AP by using the HomePlug, DS2, or even wireless repeater functionality that we mention in Chapter 3 and elsewhere in this chapter. We don't repeat those options here, but know that you have those options when you're moving away from your office or other place where many of your network connections are concentrated.

After you get the connectivity and power to the place you want, what do you need to consider when you're installing a *second* AP? Choose the right channel: If you have auto channel selection in your AP, you don't need to worry because your AP's smarts handle it for you. If you're setting the channel manually, don't choose the same one that your other AP is set to.

Carefully choose which channels you use for each of your access points. Make sure that you have proper spacing of your channels if you have 802.11g access points (which have overlapping bands). Read the section "Change Channels," earlier in this chapter, for more information on channels.

# Add a Repeater or Bridge

Wireless repeaters are an alternative way to extend the range of an existing wireless network instead of adding more APs. In Chapter 2, we talk about the role of bridges and repeaters in a wireless network. The topic of bridges can be complex, and we don't want to rehash it here — be sure to read Chapter 2 for all that juicy detail.

If you want to expand you network, you can install a wireless repeater or use WDS:

- ✓ A **wireless repeater** doesn't require any special configuration of your main wireless router. You just set it up with the SSID and encryption credentials of your main network and let it do its thing.

  If you want to expand your network by installing a wireless repeater, look for a product like Hawking Technology's HW2R1 Hi-Gain Wireless N Dual Band Repeater (which you can buy for about $155 to $180 online; you'll find the details at `www.hawkingtech.com/products/productlist.php?CatID=32&FamID=105&ProdID=400`). This device connects to *any* 802.11b, g, or n wireless router using special *high-gain* (in other words, super-sensitive) antennas, and then rebroadcasts that router's signals locally. It's not a cheap solution, but when you need the coverage, it'll provide it.

- ✓ **WDS** (Wireless Distribution Service) is a standards-based approach at bridging between two wireless networks (the *main* and *remote*) in such a way that the remote network access point will receive and then retransmit signals from the main station. A WDS system requires configuration of both the repeater (WDS remote) and your main wireless router (the WDS main), using the provided software or Web configuration tools.

  A repeater in a WDS system is cheaper than a standalone repeater like the Hawking we mention earlier. In fact, it's just a regular access point or wireless router that has the right software built into it.

Installing repeaters, whether standalone or using WDS, is not without its downsides. Some testing labs have cited issues with throughput at the main AP because of interference from the new repeating AP (which is broadcasting on the same channel). And because the repeater must receive and retransmit each frame (or burst of data) on the same RF channel, it effectively doubles the number of frames that are sent. This effectively cuts throughput in half. So repeaters are something you should deal with only if you really need to. Fortunately, unless your home is *gigantic,* the long range of modern 802.11n wireless routers makes the need for repeaters quite rare.

When you're using the WDS to extend your network, we recommend that you use products from the same manufacturer at both ends of the bridge, to minimize any issues between vendors. Most companies support this functionality only between their own products and not across multiple vendors' products.

# Check Your Cordless Phone Frequencies

The wireless frequencies at 2.4 GHz and 5.2 GHz are unlicensed (as we define in Part I of this book), which means that you, as the buyer of an AP and operator of a wireless broadcasting capability, don't need to get permission from the FCC to use these frequencies as long as you stay within certain power and usage limitations as set by federal guidelines. It also means that you don't have to pay any money to use the airwaves — because no license is required, it doesn't cost anything.

Many consumer manufacturers have taken advantage of free radio spectrums and created various products for these unlicensed frequencies, such as cordless phones, wireless A/V connection systems, RF remote controls, and wireless cameras.

A home outfitted with a variety of Radio Shack and X10.com gadgets may have a fair amount of radio clutter on these frequencies, which can cut into your network's performance. These sources of RF energy occasionally block users and access points from accessing their shared air medium.

As home wireless LAN use grows, people report more interference with home *X10 networks,* which use various wireless transmitters and signaling over electrical lines to communicate among their connected devices. If you have an X10 network for your home automation and it starts acting weird (such as the lights go on and off and you think your house is haunted), your LAN might be the source of the problem. A strong wireless LAN in your house can be fatal to an X10 network.

At some point, you have to get better control over these interferers, and you don't have many options. First, you can change channels, like we mention earlier in this chapter. Cordless phones, for example, use channels just like your local area network does; you can change them so that they don't cross paths (wirelessly speaking) with your data heading toward the Internet.

Second, you can change phones. The newest cordless phone system, DECT, uses an entirely different set of frequencies that won't interfere on either the 2.4 GHz or 5 GHz bands. *Note:* An old-fashioned 900 MHz phone doesn't interfere with either one, but finding one these days is a miracle.

You may find that your scratchy cordless phone improves substantially in quality and your LAN performance improves too. Look for other devices that can move to other frequencies or move to your 802.11 network. As we discuss in Chapter 19, all sorts of devices are coming down the road that will work *over* your 802.11 network and not compete with it. Ultimately, you need to keep the airwaves relatively clear to optimize all your performance issues.

# Chapter 19

# Ten Devices to Connect to Your Wireless Network in the Future

*W*e tell you throughout this book to think about the big picture — to think about networking more than just your home computers. There's hardly anything you can't hook up to your home network: Peripheral devices (such as a printer), gaming gear, audiovisual equipment, cameras, servers, and even robots are all fair game (all discussed in earlier chapters).

Clearly, the boom is on among the consumer goods manufacturers to wirelessly network enable everything with wireless processing chips. You get the convenience (and cool factor) of monitoring the health of your gadgets, and vendors want to sell you add-on services to take advantage of that wireless chip. This transformation is happening to everything: clocks, sewing machines, automobiles, toaster ovens — even shoes. If a device can be added to your wireless home network, value-added services can be sold to those who want to track their kids, listen to home-stored music in the car, and know when Fido is in the neighbor's garbage cans again.

In this chapter, we expose you to some things that you could bring to your wireless home network soon. Many of these products already exist. Expect in the coming years that they will infiltrate your home, your car, your whole life. Like the Borg says on *Star Trek,* "Prepare to be assimilated."

---

## Apps on the rise

The phenomenal success of 3G smartphones like Android phones and the iPhone are changing the way wireless applications will be delivered in the future. Just a few years ago, putting a wireless application or service in your living room or your car or on your bike required a specific bit of wireless hardware that did whatever it was that application did and communicated with your wireless network. Now, however, when many tens of millions of people have smartphones that are equipped with 3G

and Wi-Fi, more developers are delivering solutions for your daily needs through apps for smartphones rather than devices. This is a trend that's not going away, especially since smartphones can connect to other devices via Wi-Fi or Bluetooth. Today you might replace a GPS navigation system or a digital camera with a smartphone; tomorrow it might be any one of the wireless applications we discuss in this chapter.

---

# *Your Bike*

You don't have to spend every July filling your DVR with hours and hours of *Le Tour De France* to know that bikes are a big deal. Bikes aren't just fun for the kids or for the weekend rider wearing tight pants and colorful jerseys — they're also serious transportation. So why should cars get all the wireless fun? Well, they shouldn't!

You're probably not going to want to be doing too much phone calling or video watching while you're commuting to work in the bike lane next to all of those 3-ton SUVs, but that doesn't mean you might not want some information, navigation, and entertainment help. But you obviously don't have room on a bike for too much gear, nor do you want to attach anything to your bike that might be easily stolen. Luckily, we have smartphones coming to the rescue.

The first example — one you can buy today — is the New Potato Technology LiveRider ($99, www.newpotatotech.com/LiveRider/liverider.html). The LiveRider is a combination of a wireless sensor, a wireless receiver, and a mounting device that turns any iPhone or iPod touch into a full-fledged bike computer. To get started, just mount the 2.4 GHz wireless sensor over your rear wheel and attach the combined receiver/mount to your handlebars. Then go to the iTunes Store and download the free LiveRider app, put your iPhone/iPod touch into the mount, and start riding!

If you've got an iPod Touch, you won't be able to take advantage of the navigation features, but you'll still have a pretty cool bike computer!

The LiveRider app records your current and maximum speed, inclination, pedaling rate and (if your iPhone has GPS — which all but the original have) your location. You can use the LiveRider as a navigation system or a training aid, or simply to log your miles to brag about to your friends on Facebook. You can even create "ghost rides" of your fastest times on a particular route and then display those rides on your route map when you try to beat the time (like trying to beat the "ghosts" in Mario Kart Wii!). Awesome stuff.

LiveRider might not be the only such wireless bike solution out there. Apple has filed a patent for a "smart bike accessory." If that sounds like an odd thing for Apple to be working on, remember that it has created, in conjunction with Nike, the Nike+ wireless training system for the iPod. The Nike+ uses wireless sensors built into Nike shoes to record your running movements to your iPod so you can track how far you've gone, how fast, and how many calories you've burned.

Exactly what Apple's planning on doing isn't entirely clear, but the consensus opinion is that it will combine a number of wireless sensors for things like speed, GPS position, acceleration, and heart rate to provide a similar training application for biking. We have our bike pants at the ready for a chance to try this out!

# *Your Car*

In Chapter 15, we discuss how cars are sporting Bluetooth interfaces to enable devices to interact with the car's entertainment and communications systems. In Chapter 13, we talk about the ways you can buy or build an 802.11-based Wi-Fi hot spot in your car, so that all of your devices (smartphones, iPads, and so on) can get online (for your passengers' use) while you're driving.

Now car manufacturers are catching on and beginning to develop their own "connected car" packages that go beyond just hands-free Bluetooth phone access and provide a whole suite of wireless connectivity applications. Imagine a car that connects to the Internet using high-speed 3G connectivity and provides entertainment services, traffic updates, always-up-to-date navigation services, car maintenance diagnostics, and more. It's coming. If you've seen the ads for Ford's SYNC system (developed by Microsoft, www.fordvehicles. com/technology/sync), you know how close we already are.

A wireless connection in the car enables you to talk to your car via the Internet no matter where you are. Now, before you accuse us of having gone loony for talking to our cars, think about whether your lights are still on. Wouldn't it be great to check from your 40th-floor apartment rather than head all the way down to the parking garage? Just grab your computer or smartphone, surf to your car's Web server, and check whether you left the lights on again. Or perhaps you're filling out a new insurance form and forgot to check the mileage on your car. Click over to the dashboard page and see what it says.

## OnStar calling

Although what they're doing isn't as fancy as the LTE Connected Car, car manufacturers are already providing connectivity to your car. Perhaps the most well-known service is OnStar (www.onstar.com), offered on a number of GM and other vehicles. OnStar offers emergency car services, such as the ones from the American Automobile Association (AAA), with GPS and two-way cellular communications thrown in. You can not only make cellphone calls with the system, but also get GM to unlock your car doors, call 911 when the vehicle senses a crash, or track down your car if it has been stolen. It's a factory-installed-only option, so you can't get it if it wasn't in your car when you bought it. You have to pay monthly service fees that start at $18.95 per month, or $199.00 per year for the basic plan, with extra fees for things like turn-by-turn directions. You can add turn-by-turn instructions for another $10.00 per month.

Other car manufacturers are following suit. BMW offers the similar BMW Assist, for example. We expect all car manufacturers to offer something similar within a few years — it makes too much sense. Check out some of the short movies on how OnStar has gotten people out of sticky situations at www.onstar.com/web/portal/realstories.

You can also, on request, check out your car's exact location based on GPS readings. (GPS is a location-finding system that effectively can tell you where something is, based on its ability to triangulate signals from three or more satellites that orbit the Earth. GPS can usually spot its target within 10–100 meters of the actual location.) You can, again at your request, even allow your dealer to check your car's service status via the Internet. You can also switch on the lights or the auxiliary heating, for example, call up numbers in the car telephone or addresses in the navigation system, and unlock and lock the car — all from the wireless comfort of your couch (using some of those neat touch-panel remote controls that we talk about in Chapter 14). Just grab your wireless Web tablet, surf, and select. Pretty cool. The opportunities to wirelessly connect to your automobile are truly endless.

The coolest example of what's to come in the car is the LTE Connected Car project (www.ngconnect.org/ecosystem/connected-car.htm), a joint venture by dozens of companies including Toyota and Alcatel-Lucent (one of the largest wireless telecommunications companies in the world — which makes perfect sense when you realize the "LTE" in the project name refers to the next-generation 4G mobile broadband service).

The LTE Connected Car is built around a 3G wireless connection combined with in-car Wi-Fi and multiple touchscreens throughout the car (four in the Toyota Prius that the project has outfitted as its demonstrator). The system ties together a number of sensors throughout the car (vehicle speed sensors, GPS, maintenance sensors, and so on) through a central car computer to provide:

✔ On-demand entertainment from online music and video services

✔ Real-time traffic and navigation services with enhanced content based upon where you are and what you're doing

✔ Wi-Fi access to the Internet to all your personal devices

✔ Access to Internet and social networking content through the touch-screens — so your kids can update their Twitter accounts about how much fun they're having on your road trip

✔ Multiplayer gaming within the car, except for the driver (we hope!)

✔ Integration with networked home control systems so your car can monitor what's happening in your house and change settings for things like lights and heating before you get home

✔ Monitoring and display of vehicle and road conditions — the system can even share road conditions with other vehicles and car conditions with your mechanic

# *Your Home Appliances*

Most attempts to converge the Internet and home appliances have been pro-totypes and concept products — a few products are on the market, but we would be less than honest if we said that the quantities being sold were any-thing but mass market yet. LGE (www.lge.com) was the first in the world to introduce the Internet refrigerator — a Home Network product with Internet access capability — way back in June 2000. (See Figure 19-1.) LGE soon intro-duced other Internet-based information appliance products in the washing machine, air conditioner, and microwave areas. The Internet refrigerator is outfitted with a 15-inch detachable LCD touchscreen that serves as a TV mon-itor, computer screen, stereo, and digital camera all in one. You can call your refrigerator from your cellphone, PDA, or any Internet-enabled device.

LGE also has an Internet air conditioner that allows you to download pro-grams into the device so that you can have preprogrammed cooling times, just like with your heating system setbacks. Talk to your digital home theater to preprogram something stored on your audio server to be playing when you get home. It's all interrelated, by sharing a network in common. Wireless plays a part by enabling these devices to talk to one another in the home.

Sadly, due to this high cost and other reasons, these connected home appli-ances haven't really taken off. The market demand has not been there for the all-in-one products — people still seem tied to their TVs and PC screens as separate from the appliances. Indeed, the latest moves by the consumer electronics and appliances industry seems more focused on making TVs more functional.

# The wireless orb knows all

Ambient Devices (www.ambientdevices.com) offers wireless products that make tangible interfaces to digital information. This sounds broad, but so are its product offerings. It offers glowing orbs that change colors based on stock prices; umbrellas whose handles glow when it's going to rain; weather displays that tell you, at a glance, what the weather is going to be for the next 7 days; even an "Energy Joule" that tells you the current price of electricity and your consumption at a specific outlet. The key to the devices' ability to do this is the company's wireless network. All products tune into the wireless Ambient Information Network to receive broadcasted data. Our favorite product is the Ambient Orb, the colorful globe that we've programmed to tell us when we've sold more books on Amazon.com!

**Figure 19-1:**
The first LGE Internet refrigerator was wirelessly enabled.

More wireless changes are coming too. With recent developments in radio frequency identification (RFID), near field communications (NFC), and other low-power and low-priced technologies, you may indeed get to the point where your kitchen monitors all its appliances (and what's in them — "We need more milk").

# *Your Entertainment System*

In Chapter 12, we talk about ways you can connect your entertainment systems (your home theater, TV, and audio equipment) to your wireless network. Today, that primarily means getting content from your PC and/or the Internet into those devices using *media adapters* that connect to your wireless network on one end and to your TV or audio gear on the other end.

In the not-so-distant future, however, you'll be able to skip the extra gear because wireless will be built right into your audio/visual gear. In fact, a number of manufacturers are already including wireless in their equipment, mainly in more expensive gear. Read on for some examples of how this will happen in all sorts of A/V equipment in the near future.

## *Wi-Fi networking will be built into receivers, Blu-ray disc players, and TVs*

For the past several years, network-equipped A/V gear has become more and more common, as first televisions and then home theater receivers and finally Blu-ray disc players began to sprout Ethernet (RJ-45) jacks on their backs. Today, it's hard to find a Blu-ray disc player *without* network capabilities, but TVs and receivers with networking are still relatively rare.

Wireless? Well that's still a *future* capability for most manufacturers, but it's coming soon.

Why would you network your A/V gear? Well, as discussed in Chapter 12, there are a few reasons:

- **Access to BD-Live content:** This is the most common application for networked A/V gear (specifically Blu-ray disc players). BD-Live is essentially Internet-provided "extras" for your Blu-ray disc movie providing enhanced online content such as movie trailers, additional movie content (like commentary from the director), message boards, and more. BD-Live content is tied to the disc you're playing on your Blu-ray disc player, so you don't just fire up your player and go online — you actually access this Internet content from within the disc's menu.

- **Other Internet content:** Several online content providers — most notably Netflix (www.netflix.com) — offer subscription-based on-demand audio or video content that you can listen to or view on your home theater. This capability is being built into both TVs and Blu-ray disc players.

✔ **Widgets:** Widgets are small, standalone applications like the modules you find on your my Yahoo! or iGoogle Web page that can display news, weather, stock prices, or snippets of Web content on your TV. This capability is being built into both Blu-ray disc players and TVs.

✔ **Your in-home content:** Networked TVs and home theater receivers are including DLNA capabilities that let you directly access music, photos, and video content stored on your PCs or on a home server. Essentially this puts the media adapter/media player we talk about in Chapter 12 right in the TV or receiver.

Of course none of this does any good if you can't get your A/V equipment onto the network. And most people don't happen to have a couple of Ethernet ports on the wall behind their home theater gear (though if you're building a new house, it's a great idea to do so!).

Wireless is the technology that's going to bring this content to the home theater. 802.11n, which we cover in detail in Chapter 2, was designed specifically to support multimedia networking among all the devices in the home. Today, a growing number of Blu-ray disc players come with built-in Wi-Fi. In the TV market, built-in Wi-Fi is rare, but manufacturers like Toshiba, LG, and Samsung offer USB Wi-Fi adapters that connect to the TV via a USB port and cost about $80. Wi-Fi is still quite rare inside receivers, but network capabilities are not, so we expect that Wi-Fi will become widely available in the near future.

Our prediction? Within a few years of the time we're writing this, every TV and Blu-ray disc player, and most home theater receivers, will come with built-in Wi-Fi. During the few months we've been writing this edition of the book, we've seen dozens of announcements of Wi-Fi-equipped gear from just about every major manufacturer.

## Combining your iPhone and Blu-ray player

When you have your Blu-ray disc player connected to your wireless network, why stick with that old fashioned remote control? Well, you don't have to with PocketBlu (www.pocketblu.com). This free app works on your iOS device (iPhone, iPod touch, and iPad) and turns it into a touchscreen remote control. You can operate any of your Blu-ray disc player's features and even access additional content right from your iPhone (like movie trailers). All you need is the free app and a movie that includes PocketBlu support as part of its BD-Live content. Right now, only a handful of movies support PocketBlu, but that number is sure to grow. The cool thing about PocketBlu is that it works with *any* BD-Live capable player, no matter who made it.

Similarly, Sony has created an app for its Blu-ray disc players, BD Remote, that provides similar functionality.

## *Cables? Who needs them?*

Another and quite different wireless change looming on the horizon is wireless cabling. You may not care much about wireless cabling until you put that 50-inch LCD on the wall and realize that there's an HDMI cable coming down the wall — serious spousal issues on *that* one!

Wireless HDMI comes to the rescue. Wireless HDMI is exactly what it sounds like: a wireless high-definition multimedia interface that links your HDMI port on your TV to your HDMI output on your satellite box, A/V receiver, PS3, or whatever. Wireless HDMI isn't a standard per se, but many early implementations are coming to market using ultra wideband (UWB) under the WiMedia standard. Early wireless HDMI chipsets can use the WiMedia UWB standard to deliver more than 300 Mbps of sustained throughput for in-room coverage. The theoretical maximum throughput of UWB is 480 Mbps. At this rate, Wireless HDMI will have to compress the HD signal.

A group of consumer electronics kingpins got together in 2005 to form the WirelessHD Consortium aimed at developing a noncompressed wireless standard for high-definition audio/video transmission. Instead of UWB, the WiHD standard uses the 60 GHz band to offer HD content without the need for compression. Instead of providing up to 300 Mbps using UWB, WiHD reportedly will transmit at 5 Gbps.

Wireless HDMI technologies will be available to consumers first. The first WirelessHD products hit the market in 2008. Gefen, for instance, has its GefenTV Wireless for HDMI 60 GHz ( www.gefen.com/kvm/dproduct. jsp?prod_id=8255, $999), offering transmission of high-definition video. (If you're a video geek, you may be interested to know that the system supports up to 1080p at 30 fps, or 1080i at 60 fps, at distances up to 33 feet.) This system offers full support for HDMI 1.3 (we're talking video geek stuff here, so bear with us), which means any HD source component (such as a Blu-ray disc player or A/V receiver) can plug into the transmitter, and the receiver can plug into the HDMI connector on the back of your TV. What this Gefen device doesn't yet support, however, is HDMI 1.4, the 3D version of HDMI. We're sure that feature's on the way however.

You can keep up with the latest in WirelessHD products on the WirelessHD consortium's Web site at www.wirelesshd.org/consumers/ product-listing/.

Other major brands are getting into the wireless HDMI business as well, and we're expecting the current high prices to drop considerably over the next few years as we move along the chip volume production curve and as competing WiHD products come to market.

The wireless cable experience is not limited to HDMI though. We expect to see short-distance, high-capacity wireless technologies turn the mess of wires behind your stereo gear into a totally wireless network with logical configurations done on your browser or through your TV set. Want to connect your DVD player to your receiver? No problem; just configure the wireless ports on both machines to see each other, and you're done. We're excited about this development, which we hope will happen in the next three to five years.

# Your Musical Instruments

Band gear has been wireless for some time. You can get wireless mics, guitars, and other musical instruments. But what's new is the bevy of musical gear that has been a big hit in the gaming market over the past couple of years. These devices are designed for hopping on your wireless LAN and making your life fun. We're talking wireless band mayhem!

*Guitar Hero* (www.guitarhero.com, $90), the runaway success from Activision, jump-started this trend in our minds. A simple wireless guitar with buttons instead of strings allows even the most unmusically minded player to play with the best bands on Earth.

*Rock Band* (www.rockband.com, $170) takes the idea a step higher by taking the four key instruments you need to make a band (guitar, bass, drums, and vocals) and building them into a highly playable (and addictive) game. Each person plays their respective role in the game, using their wireless instruments, and everyone drums, strums, bangs, and yells their way into rock history. You can find Rockband for Wii, PS3, and Xbox 360, and there are even versions for the iPhone and other mobile devices. Rock Band has versions of the games specifically built around a popular band's music, like The Beatles and Green Day (so you pretend you're Paul McCartney or Billy Joe Armstrong). It's only a matter of time before you can virtually play with other players all over the globe via the Internet.

A wireless home backbone enables fast access to online music scores, such as those from www.score-on-line.com.

Other musical instruments are also growing more complex and wireless. With ConcertMaster, from Baldwin Piano (www.gibson.com/en-us/Divisions/Baldwin), your wireless home LAN can plug into your ConcertMaster Mark II–equipped Baldwin, Chickering, or Wurlitzer piano and play almost any musical piece you can imagine. You can plan an entire evening of music, from any combination of sources, to play in any order — all via a wireless RF remote control or even by using an app on your iPhone, iPod touch, or iPad.

The internal ConcertMaster Library comes preloaded with 20 hours of performances in five musical categories, or you can create as many as 99 custom library categories to store your music. With as many as 99 songs in each category, you can conceivably have nearly 50,000 songs onboard and ready to play. Use your wireless access to your home's Internet connection to download the latest operating system software from Baldwin's servers. The system can accept any wireless MIDI interface. Encore!

You can record on this system too. A one-touch Quick-Record button lets you instantly save piano performances, such as your child's piano recital. You can also use songs that you record and store on a CD or USB flash drive with your PC to use in editing, sequencing, and score notation programs.

Gibson (the maker of the famous Les Paul guitar and owner of Baldwin Pianos) has also announced — but not yet delivered — a "digital" guitar with wireless on-board. Wireless is not new in the world of electric guitars, as guitars have had wireless connections to their amplifiers for years (all the better for those running-start knee slides across the stage during your shredding solo!), but the Gibson Dark Fire (www2.gibson.com/Products/Electric-Guitars/Les-Paul/Gibson-USA/DarkFire.aspx) will soon go a step further by including Bluetooth.

The Dark Fire is a $3,500 Les Paul model with just about every bell and whistle you could possibly imagine. Of particular interest to Pat, who not only can't play but can barely tune his guitar, is the Robot Tuner that does the tuning for you automatically. The Dark Fire is already on sale, but what's not available yet is a Bluetooth module that allows your guitar to connect directly to your desktop or laptop computer. Combine that with music composition or recording software and you have the makings of an awesome home studio.

# Your Pets

GPS-based tracking services can be used for pets, too! Just about everyone can identify with having lost a pet at some point. The GPS device can be collar-based or a subdermal implant. This device can serve as your pet's electronic ID tag; it also can serve as the basis for real-time feedback to the pet or its owner, and perhaps provide automatic notification if your dog goes out of the yard, for example.

Globalpetfinder.com is a typical example of a GPS-enabled system (www.globalpetfinder.com, $349). With this system, you create one or more circular virtual fences defined by a GPS location. Your home's address, for example, is translated by its online site into a GPS coordinate, and you can create a fence that might be 100 feet in radius. If your pet wanders outside this fence, the service alerts you and sends the continuously updated location of your pet to the two-way wireless device of your choice — cellphone, PDA, or computer, for example. You can find your pet by dialing the collar's phone number, and it replies with the present location. If you're using a PDA with a graphical interface, such as a Treo or Blackberry, you can see the location on a street map. You have to pay a monthly subscription fee for the service — to cover the cell costs — which ranges from $18 to $20 per month. If your dog runs away often, go for the Escape Artist Peace of Mind plan!

Wi-Fi technologies are making their way into the pet-tracking arena as well. Several companies are testing prototypes of wireless clients that would log on to neighborhood Wi-Fi APs and send messages about their positions back to their owners. Although the coverage certainly isn't as broad as cellular service, it certainly would be much less expensive. So your LAN may soon be part of a neighborhood wireless network infrastructure that provides a neighborhood area network (NAN), one of whose benefits is such continual tracking capability for pets.

## Checking out new wireless gadgets

The merging of wireless and other consumer goods is a major economic trend. You can expect that you will have many more options in the future to improve your life (or ruin it) using Wi-Fi devices. Here are three great places to keep track of the latest and greatest in new wireless products:

✔ **Gizmodo** (www.gizmodo.com): Gizmodo tracks all the leading-edge gadgets of any type. This site is fun to visit, just to see what someone has dreamed up. As we write this chapter, there's a neat story about new light bulbs that double as wireless speakers in your home; they install in your recessed lighting fixtures in the ceiling — check them out at www.lightspeaker.net. For your wire-

less fancy, all sorts of articles on new wireless wares appear each week; just be prepared — many are available only in Asia. Rats!

✔ **Engadget** (www.engadget.com): Engadget was founded by one of the major editors from Gizmodo. It largely mimics Gizmodo but with meatier posts and reader comments for many articles.

✔ **EHomeUpgrade** (www.ehomeupgrade.com): EHomeUpgrade covers a broader spectrum of software, services, and even industry trends, but hardcore wireless is a mainstay of its fare as well.

You can't go wrong checking these sites regularly to see what's new to put in your home!

# Your Robots

Current technology dictates that robots are reliant on special algorithms and hidden technologies to help them navigate. For example, the Roomba robotic vacuum cleaner, from iRobot (www.irobot.com, $119–$499), relies on internal programming and virtual walls to contain its coverage area. The Friendly Robotics Robomow robotic lawnmower relies on hidden wiring under the ground (www.robomow.com, $999 to $1,999).

iRobot also has been busy shaking up the home with robots for floor washing (Scooba, $299–$499), shop sweeping (Dirt Dog, $129), pool cleaning (Verro, $799–$1,099), and gutter cleaning (Looj, $99–$169). They even have a robot (ConnectR, $499) for remote visitation: You can remotely control ConnectR to roam your house and send back audio and video. Who needs a dog anymore?

As your home becomes even more wirelessly connected, devices can start to triangulate their positions based on home-based homing beacons of sorts that help them sense their position at any time. The presence of a wireless home network will drive new innovation into these devices. Most manufacturers are busy designing 802.11 and other wireless technologies into the next versions of their products.

The following list highlights some other product ideas that manufacturers are working on now. We can't yet offer price points or tell you when these products will hit the market, but expect them to come soon:

- **Robotic garbage taker-outers:** Robotic firms are designing units that take the trash out for you, on schedule, no matter what the weather — simple as that.

- **Robotic mail collectors:** A robotic mail collector goes and gets the mail for you. Neither snow, nor rain, nor gloom of night, nor winds of change, nor a nation challenged can stay them from the swift completion of their appointed rounds. New wirelessly outfitted mailboxes tell you (and the robots) when your mail has arrived.

- **Robotic snow blowers:** Manufacturers are working to perfect robotic snow blowers that continually clear your driveway and sidewalks while snow falls.

- **Robotic golf ball retrievers:** These bots retrieve golf balls. Initially designed for driving range use, they're being modified for the home market.

✔ **Robotic guard dogs:** Robots that can roam areas and send back audio and video feeds are coming to the market. These new versions of man's best friend can sniff out fires or lethal gases, take photos of burglars, and send intruder alerts to homeowners' cellphones. Some have embedded artificial intelligence (AI) to act autonomously and independently. Check out the dragonlike Sanyo Banryu or its R2D2-like successor TMSUK's Mujiro Rigurio, the Mitsubishi Wakamaru, Takenaka Engineering's Mihari Wan, and others emerging even as we write this book.

✔ **Robotic gutter cleaners:** A range of spiderlike robots is available that can maneuver on inclines, such as roofs, and feature robotic sensors and arms that can clean areas.

✔ **Robotic cooks:** Put the ingredients in, select a mode, and wait for your dinner to be cooked — it's better than a TV dinner, for sure.

✔ **Robotic pooper scoopers:** The units we've discovered roam your yard in search of something to clean up and then deposit the findings in a place you determine.

The world is still getting used to robots and their limitations. More than one company has canceled its robotic development programs until the market is more rational about its expectations. Early household robots were panned in the market because people expected them to act like people — to cook them dinner and scratch their backs on demand. The market success of the iRobot purpose-built robots has shown that buyers want robots that do something and do it well.

Still, the quest for the all-purpose android remains strong. For this reason, you're more likely to see humanoid robots demonstrating stuff such as skipping rope at special events rather than cooking dinner in your kitchen. Products such as Honda's ASIMO (Advanced Step in Innovative Mobility, `http://world.honda.com/ASIMO`) are remarkable for the basic things they can do, such as shake hands and bow, but the taskmasters we mention in the preceding list can help you with day-to-day chores.

# *Your Apparel*

Wireless is making its way into your clothing. Researchers are already experimenting with *wearables* — the merging of 802.11 and Bluetooth directly into clothing so that it can have networking capabilities. Want to synch your smartphone? No problem: Just stick it in your pocket. All sorts of companies are working on waterproof and washer-proof devices for wirelessly connecting to your wireless home network. We mention earlier in the chapter the Nike+ running shoes, developed in conjunction with Apple, that sense your workout movements and wirelessly transmit them to your iPod or iPhone to record and monitor your workout. Like to ski? Recon Instruments (`www.reconinstruments.com/company.htm`) is launching ski goggles with

GPS, communications capabilities, and a heads-up display that will overlay this information on the lens of the goggles. Want to go whole hog and give yourself a continual electrocardiogram (ECG)? Check out the Biodevices Vital Jacket (`www.biodevices.pt`), which can record what your heart is up to for up to five days and transmit it via Bluetooth to a PC.

## Understanding the technology behind wearables

Wireless technology will also infiltrate your clothing through radio frequency identification tags, or RFIDs, which are very small, lightweight, electronic, read-write storage devices (microchips) half the size of a grain of sand. They listen for radio queries and, when pinged, respond by transmitting their ID codes. Most RFID tags have no batteries because they use the power from the initial radio signal to transmit their responses; thus, they never wear out. Data is accessible in real time through handheld or fixed-position readers, using RF signals to transfer data to and from tags. RFID applications are infinite, but when embedded in clothing, RFIDs offer applications such as tracking people (such as kids at school) or sorting clothing from the dryer (no more problems matching socks or identifying clothes for each child's pile).

A technology of great impact in our lifetime is GPS, which is increasingly being built into cars, cellphones, devices, and clothing. GPS equipment and chips are so cheap that you can find them everywhere. They're used in amusement parks to help keep track of your kids. There are already prototypes of GPS-enabled shoes. (The initial application has been to protect prostitutes.)

Most GPS-driven applications have software that enables you to interpret the GPS results. You can grab a Web tablet at home while on your couch, wirelessly surf to the tracking Web site, and determine where Fido (or Fred) is located. Want to see whether your spouse's car is heading home from work yet? Grab your PDA as you walk down the street, log on to a nearby hot spot, and check it out. Many applications are also being ported to cellphones, so you can use those wireless devices to find out what's going on.

GPS-based devices — primarily in a watch or lanyard-hung form factor — are available that can track people, as discussed next.

## Wearing personal tracking devices

Many perimeter-oriented child-safety devices emit an alarm if your child wanders outside an adjustable safety zone (such as wanders away from you in the mall). For instance, the GigaAir Child Tracking system ($190) is a two-piece, battery-powered system that consists of a clip-on unit worn by the child and a second pager-size unit carried by the parent or guardian. The safety perimeter is set by the parent and can be as little as 10 feet and as much as 75 feet. The alarm tone also acts as a homing device to help a parent and child find each other after it has gone off — important for those subway rush hours in New York City. Many other person-locator products are on the market, such as a more removal-resistant unit from ionKids (www.ion-kids.com, starting at $240) and the LOK8U tracker (www.lok8u.com/us, $190).

Note that there's a difference between a tracking device and a locator device. Tracking devices will tell where someone has been, but only after the device returns to you. A popular example is the GPS Trackstick (www.trackstick.com). A locator device, on the other hand, will remotely tell you where it is at any particular time. GPS-enabled phones and services are examples of these. Don't buy one expecting the other!

Various possible monthly fees are associated with personal tracking and location devices. Some don't have any fees; they involve short-range, closed-system wireless signals. Some charge a monthly fee, just like a cellphone plan. Some charge per-use fees, like per-locate attempts. Be sure to check the fine print when you're buying any sort of wireless location device to make sure you don't have lots of extra fees that go along with it. (That's why we like 802.11-based products. They're cheap and often don't have these fees. But then again, they don't have the range that some of these other systems do.)

Applied Digital Solutions (www.digitalangel.com) is on the leading edge. The company has developed the VeriChip, which can be implanted under the skin of people in high-risk (think kidnapping) areas overseas. This chip is an implantable, 12mm x 2.1mm radio frequency device, about the size of the point of a ballpoint pen. The chip contains a unique verification number.

---

## Having wireless fun with geocaching

*Geocaching* is an entertaining adventure game based around the GPS technology. It's basically a wireless treasure hunt. The idea is to have individuals and organizations set up caches all over the world; the GPS locations are then posted on the Internet, and GPS users seek the caches. When they're found, some sort of reward may be there; the only rule is that if you take something from the cache, you need to leave something behind for others to find later. Check out what caches are near you: www.geocaching.com.

Want to find out more about GPS? Visit a couple of fun GPS tracking (pun intended!) sites, such as www.gps-practice-and-fun.com and www.gpsinformation.net.

## Going wireless with jewelry and accessories

Although watches are a great form factor for lots of wireless connectivity opportunities, they have been hampered by either wired interface requirements (like a USB connection) or an infrared (IR) connection, which requires line of sight to your PC. Expect these same devices to quickly take on Bluetooth and 802.11 interfaces so that continual updating — as with the Microsoft Smart Personal Objects Technology (SPOT) model (http://direct.msn.com) — can occur.

Creating wireless connectivity via jewelry bears its own set of issues because of the size and weight requirements of the host jewelry for any wireless system. The smaller the jewelry, the less power the wireless transmitter has to do its job. The less power, the shorter the range and the more limited the bandwidth and application of the device.

Cellular Jewelry (www.cellularjewelry.com) offers bracelets, watches, pens, and other devices that flash when you receive a phone call. Tired of missing calls when that phone is in your purse or jacket pocket? These devices — which work well only with GSM phones, not CDMA ones — alert you in a visual fashion, and in a fashionable way too!

Wearables are going wireless — MP3 sunglasses, Wi-Finder purses, GPS belts — you name it, someone has thought of it! Check out the Engadget wearables blog at http://wearables.engadget.com.

# Everything in Your Home

Did we leave anything out? Well, yes, in fact we have. That's because *everything* in your home that uses electricity can potentially be wirelessly enabled to a *home control and automation network*. In Chapter 3, we talk a little bit about ZigBee and Z-Wave, two wireless technologies that have hit the market and are designed around very low-cost and low-power chips that can be embedded in any electrically powered device in the home. Other low-price and low-power wireless technologies, such as Wibree, are also in the works and can expand your home's wireless control network.

## Where to ZigBee and Z-Wave

Low power means short distance. It also means small. You can use technologies such as ZigBee and Z-Wave to do things such as allow lamps to be controlled by your PC and to tell you whether your doors are locked.

Energy management is a huge potential application for these technologies. Consider the following implementations of lower power chips:

- ✔ Allowing electric and gas meters to talk to your household energy hogs and tell them when it's less expensive to do their chores (such as run the laundry). Your meter can also talk to the home's wireless network to communicate usage back to the central station (so no one has to come by your house to check the meter).

- ✔ Installing programmable controllable thermostats (PCT) designed to improve energy efficiency and electric service consumption. Using their wireless connections, they can reach out to sensors in the house to drive more efficient use of energy zones and time-of-day setbacks.

- ✔ Using sensor-outfitted outlets for each appliance to monitor them for energy usage and to report back to central in-home energy control programs — programs you can monitor on your television or PC.

Z-Wave, and to a lesser extent ZigBee, are also focused on home automation. Because they're wireless, these technologies allow you to install, upgrade, and network your home control system without wires. You can configure and run multiple systems from a single remote control. You can also receive automatic notification if there's something unusual happening in the house (like your oven is on at 2:00 a.m.).

As your wireless backbone becomes pervasive in the home, expect lots of ZigBee and Z-Wave products to form the last few feet of these connections because their lower cost pushes them into smaller places around the house. This is truly the next wave of wireless expansion in your house.

Because they use *mesh networking* technologies, where signals can bounce from device to device throughout the home (like a frog crossing a pond on top of lily pads), the more ZigBee or Z-Wave devices you have in your home, the better the network works. (A frog can hop across a pond covered with lily pads a lot more easily than it can get across a pond with the pads spread far apart.) If your power utility puts ZigBee or Z-Wave in your home for energy-savings purposes, you can take advantage of these devices when you add your own home control and automation devices. Remember, with mesh networking systems, the more you have, the better they work!

# Introducing Bluetooth 4.0

A new, even lower-powered (think watch batteries, not AC power) technology is arriving that can embed wireless control and networking in *anything:* Bluetooth Low Energy Technology (Bluetooth 4.0, formerly called Wibree). Think of 4.0 as a low-power option for Bluetooth, which uses the same antenna and 2.4 GHz frequency band as Bluetooth.

Bluetooth technology (which we discuss in Chapter 15) is well suited for streaming and data-intensive applications such as file transfer, and Bluetooth 4.0 is designed for applications where ultra-low-power consumption, small size, and low cost are needed. So Bluetooth 4.0 in many cases picks up where traditional Bluetooth leaves off.

Whereas your cellphone might talk to your car via Bluetooth 3.0, your car keys might have Bluetooth 4.0 inside them. That way, when you lose your keys, you can search the house for them by querying Bluetooth 4.0 gateways to see whether anyone detects them.

Bluetooth 4.0 (and all variants of Bluetooth) is used to create wireless personal area networks (WPANs) with a star topology, and thus is truly designed for PAN. ZigBee, driven by its focus on wireless monitoring, lighting control, energy conservation, and so on, is a mesh technology in which one fixed device communicates wirelessly with another. So you might see all of these in your home.

How might you use Bluetooth 4.0?

- ✔ **Sports and wellness:** Sports watches that connect to sensors located on the body, shoes, and other fitness gear can gather data on heart rate, distance, speed, and acceleration and send the information to a mobile phone.

- ✔ **Healthcare:** Bluetooth 4.0-driven sensors can be built into standalone health-monitoring devices that can send vital health-related information (blood pressure, glucose level) to devices (such as mobile phones and personal computers), which can process this information and send alerts to the mobile phones of patients and caretakers.

- ✔ **Office and mobile accessories:** You can use Bluetooth 4.0 small size and ability to extend battery life in office and mobile accessories. These can also use Bluetooth 4.0 to avoid dongles for connectivity, which add an extra component and raise the overall cost.

- ✔ **Entertainment:** Remote controls, gaming accessories, and other entertainment devices can use Bluetooth 4.0's sensor technologies to interact with one another.

✔ **Watches:** Watches and wrist-top devices can use Bluetooth 4.0 to connect them to mobile phones and accessories. Now you can use your watch to control that inbound call or to send a quick alert via text messaging.

You'll see a lot of Bluetooth 4.0 low energy and traditional Bluetooth dual-mode implementations, where low energy Bluetooth functionality is integrated with traditional Bluetooth for a minor incremental cost by utilizing key Bluetooth components. Examples of devices that would benefit from this dual-mode implementation are mobile phones and personal computers.

# Chapter 20

# Ten Sources for More Information

*W*e've tried hard in this book to capture all that's happening with wireless networks in the home. However, we can't cover everything in one book, and so, in fairness to other publications, we're leaving some things for them to talk about on their Web sites and in their print publications. (Nice of us, isn't it?)

We want to keep you informed of the latest changes to what's in this book, so we encourage you to check out the *Wireless Home Networking For Dummies* site, at www.digitaldummies.com, where you can find updates and new information.

This chapter lists the publications that we read regularly (and therefore recommend unabashedly) and that you should get your hands on as part of your wireless home networking project. Many of these sources provide up-to-date performance information, which can be critical when making a decision about which equipment to buy and what standards to pursue.

The Web sites mentioned also have a ton of information online, but you may have to try different search keywords to find what you're looking for. Some publications like to use the term *Wi-Fi*, for example, and others use *802.11*. If you don't get hits on certain terms when you're searching around, try other ones that you know. It's rare to come up empty on a search about wireless networking these days. All sites listed here are free — even the magazines we list can be read (mostly or entirely) for free online.

# CNET.com

CNET.com (www.cnet.com) is a simple-to-use, free Web site where you can do apples-to-apples comparisons of wireless equipment. You can count on finding video reviews, pictures of what you're buying, editor ratings of the equipment, user ratings of the gear, reviews of most devices, and a listing of the places on the Web where you can buy it all — along with true pricing. What's great about CNET is that it covers the wireless networking aspect of Wi-Fi as well as the consumer goods portion of Wi-Fi (such as home theater, A/V gear, and phones). It's your one-stop resource for evaluating your future home wireless purchases.

Get started at CNET in its Wi-Fi Networking section, which at the time this book was written was at

```
http://reviews.cnet.com/networking-wifi/?tag=co
```

There, you find feature specs, reviews, and price comparisons of leading wireless gear. (CNET even certifies listed vendors, so you know that they pass at least one test of online legitimacy.) What we especially like is the ability to do a side-by-side comparison so that we can see which product has which features. By clicking the boxes next to each name, you can select that gear for comparison shopping. You can also filter the results by price, features, support, and other factors at the bottom of the page. Then just click Compare to receive a results page.

At http://wireless.cnet.com, the CNET editors provide feature stories focused on wireless use in practical applications — including the editors' tech tips for things like troubleshooting a network or extending its range. Overall, we visit this solid site often before buying anything.

## Using RSS to keep up with wireless news

CNET, like most other sites, supports RSS feeds. If you don't know about RSS, here it is in a nutshell: Most news and information sites offer RSS feeds to tell you what's happening on their Web sites. An *RSS feed* is an electronic feed that contains basic information about a particular item, like the headline, posting date, and summary paragraph about each news item on the site. You use a program called an RSS reader, such as Google Reader (http:// reader.google.com), NewsGator Online (www.newsgator.com) or any of dozens of other free RSS readers, to reach out and access these feeds regularly. You find RSS readers that load into your e-mail program, browser, and instant messaging program, for example. All these readers allow you to scan the headlines and click the ones you want to read. You could set up an RSS reader to access the RSS feeds of each of these sites in this chapter to stay current on everything wireless. We highly recommend RSS.

# Amazon.com, Shopping.com, Pricegrabber.com, and More

What? Learn about wireless on a shopping site? Ah, but you can glean a broad range of information from shopping sites that will help you in your purchase and evaluation of wireless technologies. Amazon.com shows you multiple pictures of items — usually the front and back — that you can use to see what sort of LEDs, LCDs, and ports you're getting. Many products include downloadable owner's manuals in the PDF format (*portable document format* files you can read in Adobe Acrobat and other programs). The user reviews are always helpful — we usually read the negative reviews to try to find the pitfalls and do more research on those using Google.

Amazon.com, Shopping.com, and Pricegrabber.com are great for telling you what other people are interested in and what's popular — although what everyone else is buying isn't always a good indicator of quality. All three sites can help you find out where you can buy the products and who has the cheapest pricing, although Amazon.com is more focused on selling on Amazon first and foremost. Shopping.com and Pricegrabber.com are more intent on linking you to other vendors and are a good resource as you start comparison shopping.

# Wi-Fi Planet, Wifi-Forum, and More

Wi-Fi Planet (www.wi-fiplanet.com) is a great resource for keeping up with industry news and getting reviews of access points, client devices, security tools, and software. Look for the tutorial section, where you can find articles such as "TiVo and Wi-Fi — Imperfect Together" and "Used Routers Can Create Whole New Problems."

One of the more interactive parts of Wi-Fi Planet is its forum, where you can ask questions to the collective readership and get answers. (You can ask a question, and the system e-mails you with any responses — very nice.) The forum has General, Security, Troubleshooting, Interoperability, Standards, Hardware, Applications, VoIP, and WiMAX sections. The discussions are tolerant of beginners, but can get quite sophisticated in their responses. All in all, it's a great site for information. (Wi-Fi Planet also has RSS feeds!)

Another forum that tends to get a lot of traffic is the WiFi-Forum (www.wifi-forum.com), which runs out of London and has a more international clientele.

The Wi-Fi Net News site (www.wifinetnews.com) is a great site for finding out what's going on in the wireless world. You have no doubt heard about *Weblogs,* or *blogs*: They're link-running, rambling commentaries that people keep online about topics near and dear to their hearts. Wi-Fi Net News is probably the preeminent blog covering the Wi-Fi Industry.

There's a bit of a focus on the business side of Wi-Fi here, so unless you want to track the wireless industry, though, you probably wouldn't want to check this site daily, but it's a great resource for when you want to see what the latest news is about a particular vendor or technology. We follow this site every day for interesting news and product or service developments.

The man behind Wi-Fi Net News, Glenn Fleishman also writes about technology for the New York Times and for Pat's favorite Macintosh site, TidBITS (http://db.tidbits.com). He knows his stuff!

Check out these other blogs about wireless topics: FierceWireless (www.fiercewireless.com) and DailyWireless (www.dailywireless.org). By the way, all these blogs offer RSS feeds!

# *PC Magazine and PC World*

The venerable *PC Magazine* (www.pcmag.com) is the go-to publication for PC users. This magazine regularly and religiously tracks all aspects of wireless, from individual product reviews to sweeping buyer's guides across different wireless segments to updates on key operating system and supporting software changes. If you have a PC, you should read this magazine. And if you're interested in wireless networking, you should focus in on the wireless networking reviews section at www.pcmag.com/category2/0,2806,4236,00.asp.

We really like the reviews sections of the publication, which offer you immediate insight on new product announcements and give you hands-on, quick reviews of the latest developments on the market. This site is great for the products you've heard were coming but were waiting to be ready. *PC Magazine* is usually one of the first to review these products.

Like many famous magazines, PC Magazine is no longer published in print (paper) form. You can read the magazine online or subscribe to the digital edition (for about $1 per month).

*PCWorld* (www.pcworld.com) is likewise a great resource. We'd be hard-pressed to say whether it's better than *PC Magazine* — the reviews, articles, and overall networking coverage are definitely as good in either magazine. If you're using Macs on your wireless network, you should also check out PCWorld's sister publication, MacWorld (www.macworld.com).

# Electronic House Magazine

*Electronic House* (www.electronichouse.com) is one of our favorite publications because you can read lots of easy-to-understand articles about all aspects of an electronic home, including articles on wireless networking and all the consumer appliances and other non-PC devices that are going wireless. It's written for the consumer who enjoys technology.

*Electronic House* magazine includes articles on wireless home networking, wireless home control, and subsystems such as residential lighting, security, home theater, energy management, and telecommunications. It also regularly looks at new and emerging technologies using wireless capabilities, such as wireless refrigerators and wireless touchpanels, to control your home.

The magazine costs $19.95 per year for 10 issues. Back issues are $5.95 each or six issues for $30 (plus shipping), so you can catch up on what you've missed. (We always love doing that.) You definitely want to subscribe to this one! Plus a print subscription comes with a free subscription to the digital edition — so you can read the magazine on your PC or Mac.

Electronic House's Web site is also packed with great articles and ideas, and it's a fabulous site for finding out how other people have adapted wireless devices into their home. A bevy of slideshows demonstrate all sorts of homes that have been remade into themed spaces — we love the Star Trek slideshows about homeowners who have remodeled their homes to look like the *Enterprise*! No visible wires there!

You can sign up for newsletters that will tell you about the latest articles on their site — we always find ourselves clicking through on some topic. Check them out at www.electronichouse.com/eh/newsletters.

# Practically Networked

Practically Networked (www.practicallynetworked.com) is a free site run by the folks at Internet.com. (They're the same folks who now own Wi-Fi Planet.) It has basic tutorials on networking topics, background information on key technologies, and a troubleshooting guide. The site can contain some dated information (such as the troubleshooting guide), but it does have monitored discussion groups, where you can get some good feedback, and the reviews section gives you a listing of products with a fairly comprehensive buyer's-guide-style listing of features.

# ExtremeTech.com

Ziff Davis Media has a great site (`www.extremetech.com`) with special sections focused on networking and wireless issues. There's heavy traffic at the discussion groups, and people seem willing to provide quick and knowledgeable answers. (You can find some seriously educated geeks in these groups.) Check out the links to wireless articles and reviews by ExtremeTech staff.

The site can be difficult to navigate because the layout is a little confusing. We recommend that you start out in the Networking and Security area (`www.extremetech.com/category2/0,2843,2279422,00.asp`), where wireless topics are covered in fair detail. And, if you're having a problem that you just can't seem to crack, check out the discussion groups on this site.

# Network World

*Network World* (`www.networkworld.com`) is the leading magazine for networking professionals, and although the site is geared primarily for businesses, it has lots of content about wireless because so much of the technology first appeared in commercial venues. The site has detailed buyer's guides that show the features and functionality of wireless LAN products — and almost all this information is applicable for your home. Importantly, you can also search the site for more content on Wi-Fi and 802.11 as well as on Bluetooth and WiMAX. The publication has a large reporting staff and stays on top of everything networking-related.

# Wikipedia

For having content maintained by the masses on the Internet, Wikipedia (`www.wikipedia.org`) isn't all that bad. Anyone can update information on Wikipedia, and there have been lots of publicly discussed instances where vendors wrote bad things about other vendors on the site. But as a whole, it's pretty good. Its wireless coverage includes topics such as the following:

- ✔ Wi-Fi (`http://en.wikipedia.org/wiki/Wi-Fi`)
- ✔ Wireless access points (`http://en.wikipedia.org/wiki/Access_Point`)
- ✔ IEEE 802.11n (`http://en.wikipedia.org/wiki/802.11n`)

It's a great tool to get a high-level idea of any topic, with substantial avenues offsite for more detailed information. What we like most about Wikipedia is that we usually find neat links to other related topics in the External Links section of each page — links we probably would not find elsewhere.

# Other Cool Sites

We can't list here all the sites we regularly visit, but lots of good information is out there. This section lists some other sites worth looking at.

## Tech and wireless news sites

The following sites provide daily news coverage focused on the technology industry in general, or on wireless technologies in particular. We make them part of our everyday Web surfing routine — you may want to as well!

- **FierceWireless:** www.fiercewireless.com
- **SearchMobileComputing.com:** http://searchmobilecomputing.techtarget.com
- **TechWeb:** www.techweb.com
- **ZDNet:** www.zdnet.com

## Industry organizations

The creation and maintenance of standards has driven wireless to very low price points and great interoperability. Here are some organizations pushing for change in wireless — each site has info about wireless and networks:

- **Bluetooth SIG:** www.bluetooth.com
- **FreeNetworks.org:** www.freenetworks.org
- **IEEE 802 home page:** www.ieee802.org
- **Wi-Fi Alliance:** www.wi-fi.org

  The Wi-Fi Alliance site has some good consumer-focused tutorials in their Discover and Learn section, as well as a hot spot finder and lists of Wi-Fi certified equipment. Good stuff.

- **WiMAX Forum:** www.wimaxforum.org

## Roaming services and Wi-Finder organizations

As we mention in Chapter 16, many potential services are available that you can use to log on when you're on the road. Most of these have sections of their sites devoted to helping you find out where you can log on near you. Here are some frequently mentioned services and initiatives:

- **Boingo Wireless:** www.boingo.com

- **iPass:** www.ipass.com

- **JiWire:** www.jiwire.com

- **Wi-Fi HotSpot List:** www.wi-fihotspotlist.com

## Manufacturers

Some of these firms are more oriented toward business products, but many of them have great educational FAQs (frequently asked questions) and information that are helpful for people trying to read everything they can (which we support!):

- **Actiontec:** www.actiontec.com

- **Apple:** www.apple.com/wifi

- **Belkin:** www.belkin.com

- **Buffalo Technology:** www.buffalotech.com

- **Cisco (and Cisco's Linksys brand):** http://home.cisco.com/en-us/wireless/

- **D-Link:** www.d-link.com

- **Hawking Technologies**: www.hawkingtech.com

- **Hewlett-Packard:** www.hp.com

- **Intel:** www.intel.com

- **Macsense:** www.macsense.com

- **NETGEAR:** www.netgear.com

- **Sierra Wireless:** www.sierrawireless.com

- **SMC Networks:** www.smc.com

# Index

### • B •

## Apple & Macs

iPad For Dummies
978-0-470-58027-1

iPhone For Dummies,
4th Edition
978-0-470-87870-5

MacBook For Dummies, 3rd
Edition
978-0-470-76918-8

Mac OS X Snow Leopard For
Dummies
978-0-470-43543-4

## Business

Bookkeeping For Dummies
978-0-7645-9848-7

Job Interviews
For Dummies,
3rd Edition
978-0-470-17748-8

Resumes For Dummies,
5th Edition
978-0-470-08037-5

Starting an
Online Business
For Dummies,
5th Edition
978-0-470-60210-2

Stock Investing
For Dummies,
3rd Edition
978-0-470-40114-9

Successful
Time Management
For Dummies
978-0-470-29034-7

## Computer Hardware

BlackBerry
For Dummies,
4th Edition
978-0-470-60700-8

Computers For Seniors
For Dummies,
2nd Edition
978-0-470-53483-0

PCs For Dummies,
Windows
7 Edition
978-0-470-46542-4

Laptops For Dummies,
4th Edition
978-0-470-57829-2

## Cooking & Entertaining

Cooking Basics
For Dummies,
3rd Edition
978-0-7645-7206-7

Wine For Dummies,
4th Edition
978-0-470-04579-4

## Diet & Nutrition

Dieting For Dummies,
2nd Edition
978-0-7645-4149-0

Nutrition For Dummies,
4th Edition
978-0-471-79868-2

Weight Training
For Dummies,
3rd Edition
978-0-471-76845-6

## Digital Photography

Digital SLR Cameras &
Photography For Dummies,
3rd Edition
978-0-470-46606-3

Photoshop Elements 8
For Dummies
978-0-470-52967-6

## Gardening

Gardening Basics
For Dummies
978-0-470-03749-2

Organic Gardening
For Dummies,
2nd Edition
978-0-470-43067-5

## Green/Sustainable

Raising Chickens
For Dummies
978-0-470-46544-8

Green Cleaning
For Dummies
978-0-470-39106-8

## Health

Diabetes For Dummies,
3rd Edition
978-0-470-27086-8

Food Allergies
For Dummies
978-0-470-09584-3

Living Gluten-Free
For Dummies,
2nd Edition
978-0-470-58589-4

## Hobbies/General

Chess For Dummies,
2nd Edition
978-0-7645-8404-6

Drawing
Cartoons & Comics
For Dummies
978-0-470-42683-8

Knitting For Dummies,
2nd Edition
978-0-470-28747-7

Organizing
For Dummies
978-0-7645-5300-4

Su Doku For Dummies
978-0-470-01892-7

## Home Improvement

Home Maintenance
For Dummies,
2nd Edition
978-0-470-43063-7

Home Theater
For Dummies,
3rd Edition
978-0-470-41189-6

Living the
Country Lifestyle
All-in-One
For Dummies
978-0-470-43061-3

Solar Power Your Home
For Dummies,
2nd Edition
978-0-470-59678-4

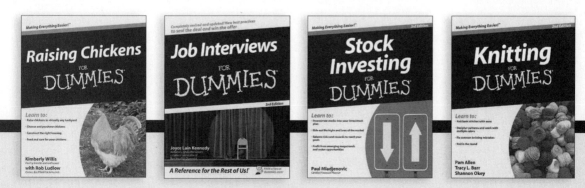

Available wherever books are sold. For more information or to order direct: U.S. customers visit www.dummies.com or call 1-877-762-2974.
U.K. customers visit www.wileyeurope.com or call (0) 1243 843291. Canadian customers visit www.wiley.ca or call 1-800-567-4797.

## Internet

Blogging For Dummies,
3rd Edition
978-0-470-61996-4

eBay For Dummies,
6th Edition
978-0-470-49741-8

Facebook For Dummies,
3rd Edition
978-0-470-87804-0

Web Marketing
For Dummies,
2nd Edition
978-0-470-37181-7

WordPress
For Dummies,
3rd Edition
978-0-470-59274-8

## Language & Foreign Language

French For Dummies
978-0-7645-5193-2

Italian Phrases
For Dummies
978-0-7645-7203-6

Spanish For Dummies,
2nd Edition
978-0-470-87855-2

Spanish
For Dummies,
Audio Set
978-0-470-09585-0

## Math & Science

Algebra I
For Dummies,
2nd Edition
978-0-470-55964-2

Biology For Dummies,
2nd Edition
978-0-470-59875-7

Calculus For Dummies
978-0-7645-2498-1

Chemistry For Dummies
978-0-7645-5430-8

## Microsoft Office

Excel 2010 For Dummies
978-0-470-48953-6

Office 2010 All-in-One
For Dummies
978-0-470-49748-7

Office 2010 For Dummies,
Book + DVD Bundle
978-0-470-62698-6

Word 2010 For Dummies
978-0-470-48772-3

## Music

Guitar For Dummies,
2nd Edition
978-0-7645-9904-0

iPod & iTunes For
Dummies, 8th Edition
978-0-470-87871-2

Piano Exercises
For Dummies
978-0-470-38765-8

## Parenting & Education

Parenting For Dummies,
2nd Edition
978-0-7645-5418-6

Type 1 Diabetes
For Dummies
978-0-470-17811-9

## Pets

Cats For Dummies,
2nd Edition
978-0-7645-5275-5

Dog Training For Dummies,
3rd Edition
978-0-470-60029-0

Puppies For Dummies,
2nd Edition
978-0-470-03717-1

## Religion & Inspiration

The Bible For Dummies
978-0-7645-5296-0

Catholicism For Dummies
978-0-7645-5391-2

Women in the Bible
For Dummies
978-0-7645-8475-6

## Self-Help & Relationship

Anger Management
For Dummies
978-0-470-03715-7

Overcoming Anxiety
For Dummies,
2nd Edition
978-0-470-57441-6

## Sports

Baseball
For Dummies,
3rd Edition
978-0-7645-7537-2

Basketball
For Dummies,
2nd Edition
978-0-7645-5248-9

Golf For Dummies,
3rd Edition
978-0-471-76871-5

## Web Development

Web Design
All-in-One
For Dummies
978-0-470-41796-6

Web Sites
Do-It-Yourself
For Dummies,
2nd Edition
978-0-470-56520-9

## Windows 7

Windows 7
For Dummies
978-0-470-49743-2

Windows 7
For Dummies,
Book + DVD Bundle
978-0-470-52398-8

Windows 7 All-in-One
For Dummies
978-0-470-48763-1

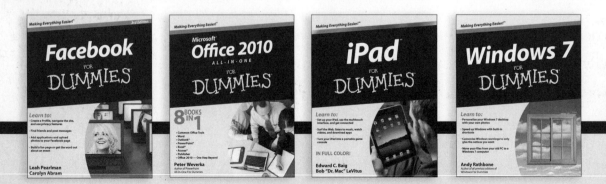

Available wherever books are sold. For more information or to order direct: U.S. customers visit www.dummies.com or call 1-877-762-297
U.K. customers visit www.wileyeurope.com or call (0) 1243 843291. Canadian customers visit www.wiley.ca or call 1-800-567-4797.